D0225963

The New Global Rulers

The New Global Rulers

*The Privatization of Regulation
in the World Economy*

■ ■ ■ ■ ■ ■

Tim Büthe and Walter Mattli

PRINCETON UNIVERSITY PRESS ■ PRINCETON AND OXFORD

HF 1411
.B88
2011

0679940574

Copyright © 2011 by Tim Büthe and Walter Mattli
Requests for permission to reproduce material from this work
should be sent to Permissions, Princeton University Press

Published by Princeton University Press, 41 William Street,
Princeton, New Jersey 08540
In the United Kingdom: Princeton University Press,
6 Oxford Street, Woodstock, Oxfordshire OX20 1TW
press.princeton.edu

All Rights Reserved

Library of Congress Cataloging-in-Publication Data
Büthe, Tim.
The new global rulers : the privatization of regulation in the world economy /
Tim Büthe and Walter Mattli.
p. cm.
Includes bibliographical references and index.
ISBN 978-0-691-14479-5 (hardback : alk. paper)
1. Commercial policy—International cooperation.
2. Foreign trade regulation. 3. International finance.
4. Standardization—International cooperation.
I. Mattli, Walter. II. Title.
HF1411.B88 2011
382'.3—dc22   2010049896

British Library Cataloging-in-Publication Data is available

This book has been composed in Sabon Typeface

Printed on acid-free paper. ∞

Printed in the United States of America

1   3   5   7   9   10   8   6   4   2

TO OUR PARENTS IN GRATITUDE

■ ■ ■ *Contents* ■ ■ ■

■ ■ ■ *Illustrations and Tables* ■ ■ ■

ILLUSTRATIONS

TABLES

Acronyms

ACCA	Association of Chartered Certified Accountants (UK)
AENOR	Asociación Española de Normalización y Certificación (Spanish Association for Standardization and Certification; Spanish ISO member body)
ANSI	American National Standards Institute (U.S. ISO member body)
API	American Petroleum Institute
ASB	Accounting Standards Board (UK, 1990–)
ASC	Accounting Standards Committee (UK, 1970–1990)
ASME	American Society of Mechanical Engineers
ASTM	American Society for Testing and Materials (now "ASTM International")
BSI	British Standards Institution (UK ISO member body)
CEN	European Committee for Standardization
CENELEC	European Committee for Electrotechnical Standardization
CAO	Chief Accounting Officer
CEO	Chief Executive Officer
CFO	Chief Financial Officer
CSR	Corporate Social Responsibility (standards)
DIN	Deutsches Institut für Normung e.V. (German Institute for Standardization, German ISO member body)
EFRAG	European Financial Reporting Advisory Group
EU	European Union
FASB	Financial Accounting Standards Board (U.S. domestic accounting standards body)
FEI	Financial Executives Institute (now "FEI International")
FSC	Forest Stewardship Council
GAAP	Generally Accepted Accounting Principles
GATT	General Agreement on Tariffs and Trade
ICT	Information and Communication Technology
IAS	International Accounting Standards (standards originally developed by the IASC)
IASB	International Accounting Standards Board (2001–)
IASC	International Accounting Standards Committee (1973–2000)

ICAEW	Institute of Chartered Accountants in England and Wales
ICAS	Institute of Chartered Accountants of Scotland
IEC	International Electrotechnical Commission
IEEE	Institute of Electrical and Electronics Engineers
IFAC	International Federation of Accountants
IFRS	International Financial Reporting Standards (standards developed by the IASB)
IGO	International Governmental Organization
ILO	International Labor Organization
IMF	International Monetary Fund
IOSCO	International Organization of Securities Commissions
ISO	International Organization for Standardization
ITU	International Telecommunications Union
N	number of observations (survey participants who answered a given question)
NTBs	nontariff barriers (to trade)
OECD	Organization of Economic Cooperation and Development
R&D	Research and Development
SEC	Securities and Exchange Commission (of the United States)
SIS	Swedish Standards Institute (Swedish ISO member)
SDO	Standards Developing Organization
TBT	Technical Barriers to Trade
WTO	World Trade Organization
UN	United Nations

▪▪▪ *Acknowledgments* ▪▪▪

THIS BOOK IS THE PRODUCT of a multiyear collaboration. Over the course of this time, we have individually and jointly incurred many debts that we are delighted to acknowledge. We have been fortunate to receive financial support for this project from the Department of Political Science and the Business School at Columbia University, the American Institute for Contemporary German Studies, the Department of Political Science, the Graduate School of Arts and Sciences, and the Center for International Studies at Duke University, the British Academy, St. John's College, the Department of Politics and International Relations as well as the Centre for International Studies at Oxford University, and especially the Research Development Fund at Oxford University. We are also grateful for research leaves and fellowships that enabled this work: Tim Büthe was a James B. Conant Fellow at the Center for European Studies at Harvard University, a Political Science Fellow at Stanford University, and a Robert Wood Johnson Foundation Scholar in Health Policy Research at the University of California, Berkeley and UCSF. Walter Mattli was a Fellow at the Wissenschaftskolleg (Institute for Advanced Study) Berlin, the Italian Academy at Columbia University, and the Center for International Studies at Princeton University, as well as the J. P. Morgan Prize Fellow at the American Academy in Berlin, and a British Academy Research Fellow.

For very helpful suggestions, advice, and constructive criticisms at various stages of this research, we express our gratitude to Mark Axelrod, Hartmut Berghoff, Sarah Büthe, Steven Brams, David Coen, Benjamin Cohen, Cary Coglianese, Christina Davis, Daniel Drezner, Henrik Enderlein, Henry Farrell, James Fearon, Erik Gartzke, Alexander George, Hein Goemans, Lucy Goodhart, John Graham, Joseph Grieco, Otto Grüter, Peter Hall, Henry Farrell, Virginia Haufler, Eric Helleiner, Ray Hill, Sunshine Hillygus, Ian Hurd, Atsushi Ishida, Miles Kahler, Ira Katznelson, William Keech, Robert Keohane, Bendict Kingsbury, Helga Köttelwesch-Büthe, Nico Krisch, Stephen Krasner, David Lake, Patrick Leblond, David Lazer, David Levi-Faur, Charles Lipson, Robert Malkin, Viktor Mayer-Schönberger, John Meyer, Johannes Moenius, Paul Pierson, Elliot Posner, Tonya Putnam, Thomas Plümper, Rachel Rubinstein, David Rueda,

Gregory Shaffer, Beth Simmons, David Singer, Duncan Snidal, David Soskice, Richard Steinberg, Richard Steward, Hendrik Spruyt, Kathleen Thelen, Joel Trachtman, John Transue, Michael Tomz, Daniel Verdier, David Vogel, Jonathan Wand, and Gregory Wawro, as well as Ranjit Lall for his exceptionally careful reading and excellent comments on the penultimate draft of the manuscript. We also received helpful comments from participants of presentations at Cornell University, Duke University, Emory University, the Fletcher School of Law and Diplomacy, George Washington University, Harvard University, Oxford University, Peking University, Princeton University, Stanford University, UCLA, Université de Montréal Business School, the University of Pittsburgh, the University of Tokyo, the University of Waterloo, WZB Berlin, and Yale University, as well as the annual meetings of the American Political Science Association, the International Political Economy Society, and the International Studies Association.

A multinational group of talented research assistants have helped us at various stages of our research. For their assistance we thank Gloria Ayee, Ana Barton, Viktor Chistyakov, Josh Cutler, Mark Dubois, Marek Hanusch, Nathaniel Harris, Anders Hellström, Tammy Hwang, Muyan Jin, Peter Khalil, Ashley Kustu, Jordan Kyle, Eugen Lamprecht, Danielle Lupton, Stephen MacArthur, Kate MacDonald, Leif Overvold, Seema Parkash, Leonid Peisakhin, Jan Pierskalla, Rahul Prabhakar, Rosa Maria Pujol, Lauren Rodriguez, Susanne Schneider, Gabriel Swank, Julia Torti, Peter Vassilas as well as Ben Johnston and other IT support staff at Columbia and Duke universities who helped with the administration of our two multi-country business surveys, as well as Dr. Gernot Nerb and his colleagues at the IFO Institute for Economic Research, Munich, from whom we learned much about the conduct of business survey.

We also thank current and former executives and staff members at the IASB, ISO, IEC, CEN, CENELEC, and standard-setting bodies and regulatory agencies in both Europe and the United States, as well as numerous business firms for sharing valuable background information and their views on, and experiences with, global private governance through interviews.

On a more personal level, Tim Büthe thanks Sarah and in the final month of this project also Nina for their loving support and for their patience when work on this book took me away from them time and again, and Walter Mattli is deeply indebted to Conchita and Karl for their good cheer and unfailing support over so many years.

Last but not least, we are very grateful to Chuck Myers at Princeton University Press for his interest in and support of this project, as well as his thoughtful and detailed comments on the book manuscript, and we thank Heath Renfroe and Mark Bellis of PUP for their help during the publication process.

CHAPTER ONE

The Rise of Private Regulation
in the World Economy

O N 28 AUGUST 2008, the world financial community awoke to stunning headline news: the Securities and Exchange Commission (SEC), the powerful U.S. financial market regulator, had put forth a timetable for switching to International Financial Reporting Standards (IFRS), produced by the International Accounting Standards Board—a private-sector regulator based in London. SEC-regulated U.S. corporations were to be required to use IFRS, possibly as soon as 2014.[1] Only a decade earlier, the suggestion that the United States might adopt IFRS "would have been laughable,"[2] as many experts expected U.S. standards to become the de facto global standards.

The SEC's decision to defer to an international private standard-setter is part of a broader and highly significant shift toward global private governance of product and financial markets. What is at stake? Financial reporting standards specify how to calculate assets, liabilities, profits, and losses—and which particular types of transactions and events to disclose—in a firm's financial statements to create accurate and easily comparable measures of its financial position. The importance of these standards, however, runs much deeper. Through the incentives they create, financial reporting standards shape research and development, executive compensation, and corporate governance; they affect all sectors of the economy and are central to the stability of a country's financial system.

---

[1] See, for example, Hughes, "US Set to Adopt IFRS Rule" (2008). The SEC's proposed "Roadmap to IFRS Adoption" of August 2008 has been elaborated and extended by the February 2010 "Work Plan." The plan envisages that, after review and confirmation in 2011, it would become mandatory for all U.S. companies whose shares are traded on a U.S. stock exchange to prepare their regular financial statements on the basis of IFRS. This requirement is to be phased in over several years (see chapter 4 for details).

[2] House, "Global Standards Here to Stay" (2005), 72.

IFRS, however, differ in some important respects from U.S. Generally Accepted Accounting Principles (GAAP), the financial reporting standards so far required by the SEC.[3] Having evolved in a very litigious business environment, U.S. GAAP are highly detailed and address a vast range of specific situations, protecting companies and auditors against lawsuits. IFRS, by contrast, have traditionally been principles-based. They lay out key objectives of sound reporting and offer general guidance instead of detailed rules.

The implications of a switch from U.S. GAAP to IFRS are therefore momentous: twenty-five thousand pages of complex U.S. accounting rules will become obsolete, replaced by some twenty-five hundred pages of IFRS. Accounting textbooks and business school curricula will have to be rewritten, and tens of thousands of accountants retrained. Companies will need to spend millions of dollars to overhaul their financial information systems; many will need to redesign lending agreements, executive compensation, profit sharing, and employee incentive programs.[4] And investors as well as financial analysts will need to learn how to interpret the new figures on assets, liabilities, cash flow, and earnings. The implications run deeper still. As explained by Robert Herz, chairman of the organization producing U.S. GAAP—the Financial Accounting Standards Board (FASB): "Liv[ing] in a world of principles-based standards involves [far-reaching] changes—institutional changes, cultural changes, legal and regulatory changes."[5] In sum, the proposed shift of rule-making authority from the domestic to the international level will affect numerous and diverse actors, and bring deep changes to the American financial market.

The United States is not the only country to switch to international standards, of course. As figure 1.1 shows, the number of jurisdictions where stock market regulators permit or even require the use of IFRS has exploded since 2001—despite the substantial costs of the switch for many countries' firms, investors, and regulators.[6] In the member states of the

---

[3] See, for example, Cunningham, "The SEC's Global Accounting Vision: A Realistic Appraisal" (2008); Deloitte, "IFRS and US GAAP" (2008); Nobes and Parker, eds., *Comparative International Accounting* (2008), 74ff, 184f; Smith, "Convergence Is 'Some Way Off'" (2007). Cf. Harris, *International Accounting Standards versus US-GAAP Reporting* (1995).

[4] Rezaee et al. warn that these costs may exceed the costs of compliance with the Sarbanes-Oxley legislation, "Convergence in Accounting Standards" (2010), 145.

[5] Robert Herz, as quoted in Dzinkowski, "Convergence or Conversion?" (2008), 115.

[6] Until 2001, international financial reporting standards were known as International Accounting Standards (IAS). Jurisdictions with domestic stock markets, only. Financial reporting

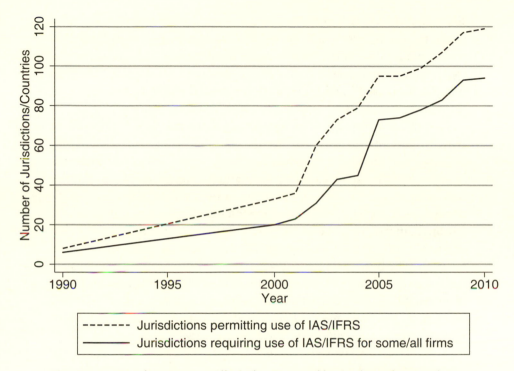

Figure 1.1 Use of IAS/IFRS as Allowed or Required by Stock Market Regulators

• • • • • •

Number of jurisdictions permitting use includes number requiring use. Sources: IASC, *Survey of the Use and Application of International Accounting Standards* (1988); Cairns, *International Accounting Standards Survey 2000* (2001); Nobes, *GAAP 2000: A Survey of National Accounting Rules* (2001); Deloitte Touche Tohmatsu, "Use of IAS for Reporting by Domestic Companies, by Country" (2002), "Use of IFRS for Reporting by Domestic Listed Companies, by Country" (2004), *IAS in Your Pocket* (2001, 2002), and *IFRS in Your Pocket* (2003, 2005–10).

rules are reported by "jurisdiction" because a few states contain more than one jurisdiction (e.g., Abu Dhabi and Dubai in the United Arab Emirates) and a few jurisdictions, such as Taiwan, are not universally recognized as states. Deloitte considers a jurisdiction to be permitting/requiring international standards when they either accept IFRS-based accounts without reconciliation or when the standards "adopted" as national standards are virtually all "word-for-word" equivalent to the international standards. Most of the countries requiring IAS/IFRS prior to 2000 were "developing or newly industrialised countries [that] do not have the resources to develop their own requirements" (Cairns, "Aid for the Developing World" (1990), 82).

European Union (EU) and about sixty other countries across all continents, the use of IFRS is already mandatory for companies with publicly traded financial securities (stocks and bonds).[7] And the trend is continuing: government regulators of several additional countries, including Japan, Canada, Brazil and India, have committed themselves to requiring IFRS in the near future.[8]

The global convergence of accounting standards is driven, in large part, by the international integration of financial markets and the increasingly multinational structure of corporations. These developments have not only led to economic growth and greater profits for many, but have also raised the costs of continued cross-national divergence of financial reporting standards for companies and investors. Indeed, cross-national differences in these rules are said to have exacerbated the global financial crisis of 2008–9—and the Asian Financial Crisis of 1997–98 before it. The belief that harmonization would bring substantial benefits has prompted firms and governments to push for a single common set of international financial reporting standards. Harmonization promises to increase the cross-national comparability of corporate information, improve the transparency of financial statements for shareholders, investors, and creditors, as well as achieve greater efficiency and stability in global capital markets.

Switching to IFRS, however, also brings costs, and these costs vary across countries. For countries with marginal capital markets and no proper accounting tradition, the costs are relatively minor.[9] However, they can be considerable for countries or regions with large and sophisticated capital markets as well as long-standing domestic accounting traditions, such as the United States and many European countries. These costs will be larger the greater the difference between IFRS and long-established domestic rules and practices. Americans and Europeans therefore have particularly strong incentives to seek to influence the process of global rule-making in accounting. International standards that end up being identical or very similar to a country's domestic standards will minimize that country's costs of switching to "international" rules. And in highly

---

[7] Deloitte, "Use of IFRS by Jurisdiction" (2010).

[8] See Deloitte, "Accounting Standards Updates by Jurisdiction" (2010).

[9] The adoption of IFRS by developing countries is discussed for instance in Zeghal and Mhedhbi, "The Analysis of Factors Affecting the Adoption of International Accounting Standards by Developing Countries" (2006).

competitive international markets, differential switching costs may jeopardize even the survival of disadvantaged firms. In sum, the international harmonization of financial standards promises substantial benefits but also will bring significant costs for some and hence distributional conflicts.[10] Given the enormous stakes involved, the battle over global rules is likely to be intensely fought, especially between the United States and Europe.

The shift of financial rule-making to the IASB is part of a striking and much wider—yet little understood—trend that is the focus of this book: the delegation of regulatory authority from governments to a single international private-sector body that, for its area of expertise, is viewed by both public and private actors as the obvious forum for global regulation. In that particular issue area, such a private body is what we call the focal institution for global rule-making. This simultaneous privatization and internationalization of governance is driven, in part, by governments' lack of requisite technical expertise, financial resources, or flexibility to deal expeditiously with ever more complex and urgent regulatory tasks. Firms and other private actors also often push for private governance, which they see as leading to more cost-effective rules more efficiently than government regulation.[11]

Besides the IASB, two such private regulators stand out: the International Organization for Standardization (ISO) and the International Electrotechnical Commission (IEC). These organizations, in which states and governments as such cannot be members, are best described as centrally coordinated global networks comprising hundreds of technical committees from all over the world and involving tens to thousands of experts representing industries and other groups in developing and regularly maintaining technical standards. ISO and IEC jointly account for about 85 percent of all international product standards.

Product standards are technical specifications of design and performance characteristics of manufactured goods.[12] Cross-national differences

---

[10] International standardization thus has characteristics of what game theorists call a coordination game with distributional conflict. See chapter 3, n1.

[11] See, e.g., Abbott and Snidal, "The Governance Triangle" (2009); Eichengreen, *Toward a New International Financial Architecture* (1999), esp. 35; Haufler, *The Public Role of the Private Sector* (2001); Vogel, "Private Global Business Regulation" (2008).

[12] More specifically, product standards cover properties such as interoperability, interconnectability, levels of safety, conformity, materials, systems of classification, methods of testing, the operation of systems, and quality assurance.

in these standards matter little when product markets are predominantly domestic. The global integration of product markets, however, has greatly and lastingly increased international interdependence and thus created strong incentives to coordinate on common technical solutions. International standards offer such a solution. ISO and IEC product standards, in particular, play a critical role in facilitating international trade and boosting economic growth. Their numbers have been growing steadily over the last twenty-five years while the production of national standards has dwindled—as illustrated by the declining number of new German (DIN) standards shown in figure 1.2.

Little known until the mid-1980s, ISO and IEC have become prominent, in part because of the Agreement on Technical Barriers to Trade, negotiated during the Uruguay Round trade negotiations from 1987 to 1994. This agreement obliges all member states of the World Trade Organization (WTO) to use international standards as the technical basis of domestic laws and regulations *unless* international standards are "ineffective or inappropriate" for achieving the specified public policy objectives.[13] Regulations that use international standards are rebuttably presumed to be consistent with the country's WTO obligations, whereas the use of a standard that differs from the pertinent international standard may be challenged through the WTO dispute settlement mechanism as an unnecessary nontariff barrier to trade and thus a violation of international trade law.

The commitment by governments to use international rather than domestic standards has enormous economic significance. Governments adopt hundreds of new or revised regulatory measures each year, in which product standards are embedded or referenced.[14] And government regulations are just the tip of the iceberg, since consumer demand and concerns about legal liability create strong incentives for firms to comply with a wealth of product standards that are not legally mandated but define best practice.

The shift from domestic regulation to global private rule-making brings substantial gains, particularly to multinational and internationally competitive firms, for which it opens up commercial opportunities previ-

---

[13] TBT-Agreement, Article 2.4.

[14] A small, though increasing, share of these new or revised national regulations is due to international regulatory harmonization, see Kawamoto et al., "Product Standards, Conformity Assessment and Regulatory Reform" (1997), 281; WTO, *Fourteenth Annual Review of the Implementation and Operation of the TBT-Agreement* (2009), 3–4.

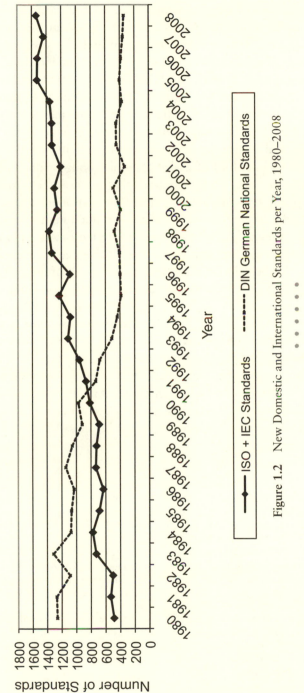

Figure 1.2   New Domestic and International Standards per Year, 1980–2008

Sources: Annual reports and private communications from DIN, DKE, IEC, and ISO.

ously foreclosed by cross-national differences in standards and related measures. The share of U.S. exports affected by foreign product standards, for instance, had risen from 10 percent in 1970 to 65 percent in 1993, and by the time the WTO's TBT-Agreement came into force, cross-national differences in product standards were estimated to result in a loss of $20–$40 billion per year in U.S. exports alone.[15] United States imports and consumers were also affected. For some manufacturing industries, U.S. nontariff barriers in the late 1980s created losses due to increased costs and reduced trade equivalent to a tariff of 49 percent.[16] Even today, about one third of global trade in goods—valued at $15.8 trillion for 2008—is affected by standards that often differ across countries, and the boost in trade from a complete international harmonization of product standards would be equivalent to a reduction in tariffs by several percentage points.[17] A shift to common international standards thus benefits internationally competitive firms by increasing their export opportunities. It also benefits consumers who, as a result of increased trade and competition, have access to a broader range of goods and services and can buy them more cheaply.

At the same time, the shift to global private-sector regulation also entails costs. To comply with international product standards, for example, firms may have to redesign their products, retool their production methods, or pay licensing fees to other firms whose proprietary technology may be needed to implement the international standard efficiently. These costs can be massive, to the point where some feel forced to discontinue production of certain goods or even go out of business.[18]

---

[15] Kawamoto et al., "Product Standards, Conformity Assessment and Regulatory Reform" (1997), 280; Mallett, "Why Standards Matter" (1998–99); NRC, *Standards, Conformity Assessment, and Trade* (1995).

[16] Melo and Tarr as quoted in OECD, *An Assessment of the Costs for International Trade in Meeting Regulatory Requirements* (2000), 9.

[17] Kawamoto et al., "Product Standards, Conformity Assessment and Regulatory Reform" (1997), 283; Moenius, "Information versus Product Adaptation: The Role of Standards in Trade" (2004); WTO, *World Trade Report* (2009), 4–5. It remains difficult to calculate the trade effects of standards precisely, due to data limitations, as noted by the WTO, *World Trade Report* (2005), 58ff.

[18] International product standardization thus also often resembles a coordination game with distributional conflict. The overall gains, as well as the conflicts over the distribution of costs in international standard-setting have been recognized and illustrated in recent economic analyses by the WTO, the World Bank, UNCTAD, the OECD and others. We discuss them in more detail in chapter 6.

In sum, while the convergence on a single set of international standards may bring overall gains for all countries, those gains may differ greatly across countries and especially across firms. Firms therefore have a strong incentive to seek to influence the process of international rule-making to minimize their switching costs. For those who succeed in pushing their domestic standards for adoption as international standards, switching costs will be minimal. The stakes thus are high in global private regulation, and severe conflicts of interest are likely, as noted in a remarkably frank statement by Gerald Ritterbusch, director of standards and regulations at the U.S. firm Caterpillar, during a Congressional hearing:

> How do standards impact our ability to compete internationally? . . . When we have domestic standards that are different from international standards, everybody loses. We lose domestically because we must build a product that is different from products we sell internationally. That raises . . . [our production] costs, hurt[ing] American consumers . . . [and] caus[ing for us] unfavourable opportunities in foreign markets. What is needed is that [our] domestic standards experts aggressively participate in international standards developments to get domestic standards accepted . . . The first to [propose a standard for adoption at the international level] . . . will most likely succeed. Thus it is necessary . . . [to] get to the international arena ahead of standards experts from other countries.[19]

A distinctive feature of global regulators such as ISO, IEC, and IASB is not only that they are private but also that they are what we call focal regulatory institutions—uncontested in their respective areas. Their prominent position in the regulation of global markets raises pressing empirical and analytical questions:

- Who exactly writes the rules in these private organizations?
- Who wins and who loses—and why—when standard-setting takes place in these private international organizations? What,

---

[19] U.S. House of Representatives, Committee on Science (Hearing) *Standards-Setting and United States Competitiveness* (2001), 24, 94. Ritterbusch served for 30 years on various technical committees of the Society of Automotive Engineers and also held the chairmanship of the ISO technical committee on earthmoving machinery.

in other words, is the nature of politics in private-sector rule-making?

- What defines power in these organizations, and how does it operate?
- Do all of those who have a commercial, financial, or socio-political stake in the content of these rules have a voice in the process?

Specific, empirical answers to these questions are hard to come by, in large part because these global regulators are private. Financed mostly by voluntary contributions from private-sector stakeholders, they are not subject to public oversight, and the writing of specific rules is in the hands of groups of experts who are not required to keep records of their proceedings. It is therefore difficult to obtain *systematic* information about these regulatory processes. Yet, global private regulation has in recent years become vastly more important and is now a phenomenon of considerable social and economic consequence—it matters to understand it. This makes the lack of reliable information all the more problematic, since comprehensive data are a crucial prerequisite for both assessing and improving the performance and processes of global private regulators.

In this book, we provide not only a framework for the analysis of private regulation but also detailed empirical answers to the above questions. We are able to test competing theoretical propositions about global regulation thanks to eight years of collecting extensive information on private rule-making in central areas of the global economy. As part of this research, we have conducted two comprehensive multi-country, multi-industry business surveys—one about international financial reporting standards and IASB standardization, the other about international product standards and ISO/IEC standardization. The surveys covered a broad range of issues, including firms' use of standards, familiarity and satisfaction with various standards, cost of switching to international standards, methods of seeking influence in private rule-making, assessments of such methods, reasons for getting involved or staying out, and general trends. We supplement the analysis of the survey data with insights gained from a large number of interviews with senior and mid-level managers, current and former IASB and ISO/IEC staff, and government regulators. Together, these data allow us to provide the first systematic analysis of key private institutions for the regulation of global markets.

The Argument in Brief

International standardization is sometimes described as an apolitical, scientific process of developing or identifying the technically optimal solution to a regulatory or technical challenge. In this view, consensus and thus rule-making is easy because "scientific technological knowledge is everywhere the same."[20] Much of the language used by private-sector regulators to describe their operations reinforces this view of standardization. The ISO, for example, characterizes its standards as "based on international consensus among the experts in the field . . . [and reflecting] the state of the art" of science and technology.[21] Similarly, the IASB notes that nationality and other political considerations play no part in the appointment and decisions of its expert rule-makers. They are chosen because they have "the best available combination of technical skills and background experience of relevant international business and market conditions in order to contribute to the development of high quality global accounting standards."[22]

We argue that such views are naïve. Standards do not embody some objective truth or undisputed scientific wisdom professed by experts. And global regulatory processes are not apolitical, for two reasons. First, expertise is not a single correct set of beliefs about what works or does not. A German accountant, or *Wirtschaftsprüfer*, who underwent eight years of studies, training, and examinations, is every bit as expert as an American Certified Public Accountant (CPA). Nevertheless, these experts are likely to disagree vigorously on how best to approach a wide range of financial reporting challenges, because any accounting tradition or school is deeply rooted in the business and legal cultures of a given country. As an official of the Accounting Standards Board of Japan (ASBJ) puts it: "There is no right or wrong answer. . . . It's like religion—Christianity or Buddhism."[23] Global standardization is rarely about reaching a compromise among different regulatory models and approaches (a fusion between Christianity and Buddhism would be impossible to engineer) but instead about battles for preeminence of one approach or solution over

---

[20] Loya and Boli, "Standardization in the World Polity" (1999), 188.

[21] ISO, "Discover ISO: The ISO Brand" (2009).

[22] IASCF, *Revised Constitution* (2009), 12.

[23] Quoted in Jopson and Pilling, "Accounting Rivals Face a Struggle to Stay in Tune" (2005).

another. The language accompanying these processes is technical; the essence of global rule-making, however, is political. Such rule-making typically has important distributional implications, generating winners and losers. To lose may mean higher production costs, steeper costs of switching to international standards, lower international competitiveness, loss of export markets, and even risk of corporate demise. As discussed in greater detail in chapters 4 and 6, and nicely put by James Barcia, U.S. congressman and member of the Subcommittee on Environment, Technology and Standards: "New [international] standards can be the source of enormous wealth or the death of corporate empires. With so much at stake, standards arouse violent passions."[24] In short, global private regulation should be understood and analyzed as an intensely political process, even if the politics may be hidden beneath a veneer of technical rhetoric.

Second, IASB, IEC, and ISO are not operationally self-sufficient, and their officials do not work in isolation. They heavily rely on private-sector standards bodies at the national level for logistical and technical support (as discussed in detail in chapters 4 and 6).[25] The domestic bodies thus are part and parcel of the global institutional structure of standardization; in a sense, they form the institutional backbone of the global regulators. Domestic standards bodies, however, are not disinterested aides to the international bodies. They seek to promote and defend at the international level the regulatory preferences of their domestic stakeholders to minimize domestic switching costs. At the same time, domestic standards bodies and systems vary widely in resources and organizational structures and are, therefore, likely to exert differing degrees of influence on global regulatory processes.

These two points—the political nature of standardization and the importance of domestic standards bodies in global processes—lay the basis for our argument, which can be summarized as follows: technical expertise and financial resources are necessary but not sufficient conditions for successful involvement in global private-sector standardization. It is timely information and effective representation of domestic interest that

---

[24] U.S. House of Representatives, Committee on Science (Hearing), *Standards-Setting and United States Competitiveness* (2001), 19.

[25] The modalities of support vary between IASB and ISO/IEC as discussed in chapters 4 and 6, but the centrality of domestic standards bodies in global private regulation is a constant theme.

confer the critical advantage in these regulatory processes, determining who wins or loses. Such representation occurs not through states, as in traditional intergovernmental organizations, but through domestic private-sector standard-setters. Their ability to speak with a single voice and effectively promote domestic preferences, however, varies—mostly for historical reasons.

The foundations of most domestic institutional structures of standardization were laid many decades ago and have changed little over time. Some countries have a single domestic institution for standard-setting or a clear organizational hierarchy, while in other countries, rule-making authority is fragmented among multiple competing standard-setters. Contestation is common in the latter system but largely absent in the former. Both systems have served their respective domestic economies well by generally producing (in very different ways) high-quality standards over time. However, they differ in how well they serve the interests of domestic stakeholders now that the main focus and locus of standardization has shifted to the global level.

Who then wins or loses and why? We argue that firms operating in a hierarchical and coordinated domestic system are likely to win because their system fits more naturally with the global structure, where a single regulator is the clear focal point. Such a domestic system enables a country's stakeholders to speak with a single voice and in a timely fashion on the global stage. We call this a case of high "institutional complementarity" between the domestic and global levels. High institutional complementarity implies that the interaction between domestic and global institutions is smooth and easy, yielding decisive strategic benefits to the firm in terms of effective interest representation in global rule-making and timely information. By contrast, firms in a fragmented domestic system, characterized by contestation among rival standard-setters, are at a distinct disadvantage. Their system renders both effective national interest representation and domestic diffusion of information about new global standards projects more difficult and thus fits relatively poorly with an institutional structure at the global level consisting of a single focal regulatory body for a given issue area. This we call a case of low institutional complementarity between the domestic and global levels. Generally, we argue that influence in global private governance is significantly a function of how complementary a country's domestic institutions are with the prevailing institutional structure at the international level.

ORGANIZATION OF THE BOOK

Part I presents the analytical framework. To situate our analysis in the larger literature on globalization and regulation, we develop in chapter 2 a typology of global regulation, which differentiates the institutional setting for rule-making, which is either public or private, from the global selection process, which is either market-based or nonmarket-based. We therefore distinguish four types of global regulatory governance: the first type, which we label "public (governmental) nonmarket standard-setting," involves collaboration through traditional intergovernmental organizations (IGOs) or transgovernmental cooperation among domestic regulators. It has a long tradition and has been the focus of most of the political science literature on global regulation. Another type is market-based private regulation. It entails rule-making by firms or other bodies competing, individually or in groups, to establish their preferred technologies or practices as the de facto standard through market dominance or other strategies. This type of global regulation has also attracted substantial analytical attention, especially from economists. A third type of global regulation—private yet nonmarket-based—is the focus of our book. Largely overlooked in the literature, regulation by focal private bodies, such as IASB or ISO/IEC, is the predominant type for major parts of the international political economy today. Finally, a fourth type of regulation results from market-like international competition between public regulatory agencies. The discussion of our typology is followed in chapter 3 by the presentation of our theoretical argument, summarized above.

Part II deals with private regulation in global financial markets. In chapter 4, we first provide a brief account of how the IASB became the focal institution for setting financial reporting standards at the international level, then analyze the institutional structures of IASB and corresponding institutions at the domestic level in the United States and the three largest European countries: Germany, France, and the United Kingdom (as well as pertinent EU-level regional institutions). The United States has a single private organization that is uncontested as the institutional setting for developing financial reporting standards at the domestic level, and consequently provides an efficient and effective mechanism for aggregating preferences. Accounting standard-setting in Europe, by contrast, is characterized by institutional fragmentation and competition for authority among multiple institutional centers, both at the domestic and the European levels. Our general analytical approach suggests that the resulting differences in institutional complementarity put U.S. firms in an advantageous position vis-à-vis European firms when standard-setting shifts to the international level.

Chapter 5 presents the main empirical analysis of global financial reporting standard-setting. Our international business survey, conducted among hundreds of CFOs and other senior financial managers of companies listed on the main stock exchanges in France, Germany, the United Kingdom, and the United States allows us to test the hypotheses derived from our analytical framework, along with alternative explanations. As predicted by the framework, we find that U.S. firms are substantially more successful than European firms when they try to influence international financial reporting standards. Responses to a battery of questions about different methods of influencing IASB standard-setting show that the greater success of American firms is indeed due to the greater fit or complementarity between IASB and U.S. domestic institutions. The statistical analyses of survey findings are supplemented by information gathered through open-ended survey questions and interviews with corporate finance experts, accounting experts in government and academia, as well as private regulators at the domestic and international level. Qualitative information from these questions and interviews provides additional support for our argument.

Part III examines private regulation in global product markets. Chapter 6 begins by providing a brief account of how ISO and IEC became, for most industries, the focal institutions for setting international product standards. We then briefly review the global institutional structure and decision-making procedures before describing the domestic structures in the United States and Europe. Rule-making for product markets constitutes a particularly interesting counterpart to private rule-making for financial markets, because the differences in product standard-setting institutions at the domestic and regional levels are the exact opposite of what we observe in accounting standard-setting. The institutional structure for setting product standards in the United States is characterized by institutional fragmentation and contestation among competing standard-setters. In Europe, by contrast, the domestic standard-setting institutions are characterized by a high degree of coordination and organizational hierarchy. We then analyze the differential complementarities between the domestic and the international institutions for the United States and the Europeans, respectively, and explain why it is more likely for Europeans than Americans to shape the content of product standards in ISO and IEC.

In chapter 7, we turn to various tests of the hypotheses developed in chapter 6 and present the findings from the international business survey that we conducted in the United States and Europe among more than a thousand senior and mid-level managers with responsibility for technical standards in research and development, production, or marketing in five main economic sectors. We find compelling evidence that high complementarity between standard-setting institutions at the domestic level and the institutional structure of standardization at the international level favors European over American interests in ISO and IEC. By contrast, the relatively poor fit between U.S. domestic institutions and the international structure puts American firms at a disadvantage.

In chapter 8, we extend our discussion of the concept of institutional complementarity and examine the implications of complementarity for our theoretical understanding of the relationship between power and institutions. We also highlight contributions of our research to several current debates among scholars of political science, sociology, law, economics, and business administration about issues such as the changing nature of regulatory politics and nontariff barriers to trade. In the conclusion, we examine the implications of our research for our understanding of global governance and for current policy debates, which often still underappreciate the political nature of seemingly technical activities such as standard-setting, and the implications for corporate strategy.

Private regulation and the interaction between domestic and international institutions are important elements of global governance. They warrant greater analytical attention from economists, political scientists, legal, and business scholars. Global private regulation is also a very timely issue for practitioners, as evidenced by now frequent reports about controversies over IFRS and ISO standards in the financial and business press. And these standards are substantively increasingly important for practitioners: product standards often are crucial for commercial success in global markets. Accounting standards affect share prices as well as risk assessments and hence the cost of insurance. Finally, global private rule-making is an important complement to, or even substitute for, formal legal collaboration through international treaties among governments. In short, global private governance is tremendously important for practitioners in many fields. Much of the process of private rule-making, however, remains shrouded in secrecy. This book aims to end the secrecy, opening the black box of private rule-making to scrutiny for a broad and varied audience. To do so, we have avoided jargon and technical minutiae—sometimes by moving more detailed discussions into appendices.

BOX 1.1

The Modern Meaning of Regulation and Standards
A Definitional Clarification

The term regulation is commonly used to describe technical rules issued by government departments and agencies. Such regulations provide clarity and guidance in their respective areas of responsibility. In the United States, for example, the Food and Drug Administration (FDA) has a legislative mandate to keep unsafe food off the market; FDA regulations define that task with respect to specific products. Although regulations are distinct from statutory law because they are not the work of the legislature, their legal effect is direct and binding.

The role played by regulations in the U.S. context is similar to the role of standards under the EU's so-called "New Approach" to regulatory harmonization, introduced in the mid-1980s, which involves the delegation of regulatory functions to private-sector standardization bodies. Under the "New Approach," EU legislation is limited to laying down in directives mandatory so-called essential requirements for health, safety, environmental, and consumer protection. These directives cover entire sectors rather than single products. The elaboration of the technical specifications that satisfy the essential requirements is delegated to two major European standardization bodies. The national authorities are obliged to recognize that products manufactured according to the standards of these private organizations are presumed to conform to the essential requirements specified in directives (EU law); they must thus allow these products to circulate freely in the EU market.

In theory, European standards are voluntary. That is, producers who come up with alternative technical solutions that meet the level of product safety or safeguards for consumer health, specified in the directives, cannot be excluded from the market. However, these producers carry the burden of proving that their standards do indeed safeguard health and safety at the required levels. In practice, then, the effect of standards is direct and binding since the cost and difficulty of proving equivalence are enormous. Similarly, many of the standards discussed in this book, including ISO, IEC, and IASB standards, are binding if not by law then by practical necessity or market pressure. We thus use the terms global *regulation, rules,* and *standards* interchangeably in this book and define them as rules established by expert bodies prescribing de jure or de facto the quality or performance of a given practice, procedure, or product.

CHAPTER TWO

Private Nonmarket Rule-Making in Context

A TYPOLOGY OF GLOBAL REGULATION

How are rules for global markets set? In this book, we focus on rule-making in private bodies, each of which is, in its particular issue area, largely uncontested as the forum for setting international standards—a form of governance that is tremendously important for global product and financial markets but has so far attracted little sustained analytical attention. We take seriously the distinctive institutional features of this *nongovernmental* form of global governance but also recognize, and indeed emphasize, its fundamentally conflictual, and hence political, nature.

To put this form of private regulation in context, we distinguish four modes of global rule-making, based on whether standards are developed in public or private settings—and whether multiple standard-setters compete or there is a single dominant body that is the focal point for developing international standards in a given issue area.[1] We refer to the former distinction as the institutional setting for rule-making (the horizontal axis in figure 2.1). It captures whether those who write a set of rules for a given issue come together in a public setting, such as a government agency or intergovernmental organization, or in a private setting, such as a firm or transnational standard-setting organization. The second dimension— the vertical axis in figure 2.1—draws attention to the process through which one set of rules becomes dominant as the global standard for a given issue. When multiple (public or private) standard-setters compete, then the selection process through which one set of rules achieves market dominance and thus becomes the single global standard follows the rule-making. We call this "market-based" selection. In contrast, when a single institution is already internationally recognized as the predominant forum

[1] As explained in the introduction, we use the terms *international rules* and *standards* interchangeably.

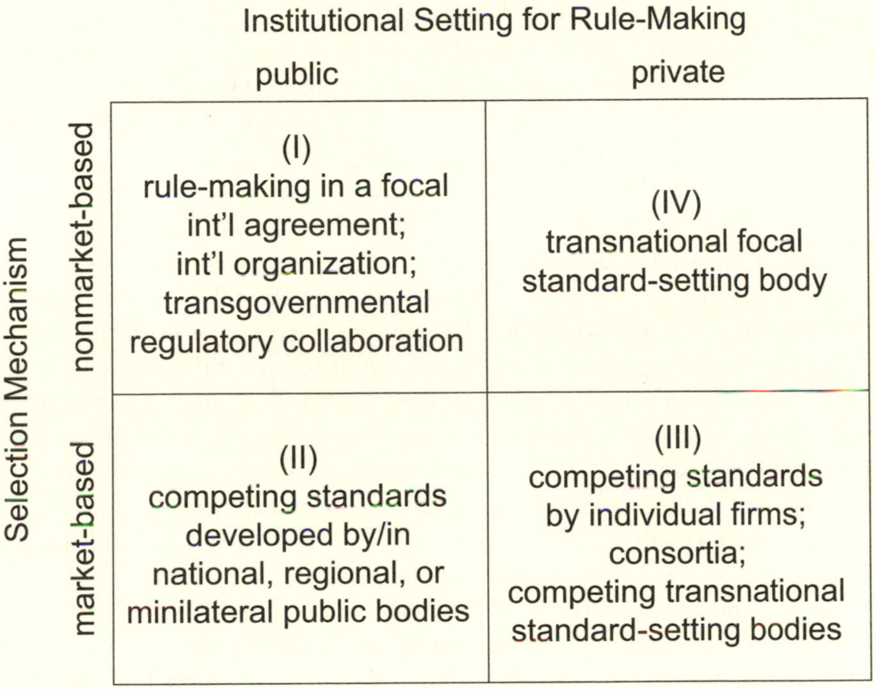

Institutional Setting for Rule-Making

	public	private
nonmarket-based	**(I)** rule-making in a focal int'l agreement; int'l organization; transgovernmental regulatory collaboration	**(IV)** transnational focal standard-setting body
market-based	**(II)** competing standards developed by/in national, regional, or minilateral public bodies	**(III)** competing standards by individual firms; consortia; competing transnational standard-setting bodies

Selection Mechanism (row axis label)

Figure 2.1 Typology: Modes of Global Regulation

for writing rules in the issue area, any particular standard that it develops becomes the global standard not through market selection but by virtue of having been promulgated by this focal institution.[2] We refer to this as the nonmarket-based process of establishing global regulations. Distinguishing these two dimensions yields four types, depicted in figure 2.1.

This typology allows us to delineate as a clearly distinct phenomenon the type of global regulation that is the focus of our book: standard-setting in private international institutions, which does not entail market competition (top right, cell IV). This mode of rule-making plays a prominent role in the international political economy. The international private standard-setting bodies IASB, IEC, and ISO, for instance, have set many of the key standards for global product and financial markets. Each of these bodies is essentially uncontested as the global rule-maker—it is what we call a focal institution—for its respective area of expertise. Until

---

[2] The existence of a focal institution implies a prior selection of one institution as the predominant one.

19

very recently, however, these standard-setting bodies have been largely overlooked by social scientists, who have tended to focus on standard-setting in traditional intergovernmental organizations (cell I) or private market-based standard-setting (cell III). We therefore focus in this study on rule-making in private focal institutions.

Our typology also identifies another mode of global rule-making that has received little analytical attention, namely marketlike competition between public standard-setting bodies (bottom left, cell II). We discuss the key characteristics of such competition among national or regional governmental bodies in this chapter, but comprehensive analysis of this type of international standard-setting is beyond the scope of this book.[3]

We next describe each of the four types, counterclockwise from top left. We then turn to the key analytical issue—the politics of rule-making. As illustrated by the examples in the introduction, the international harmonization of standards for product and financial markets entails great benefits as well as substantial adjustment costs—at least for some of those who have a stake in the content of the standard. What determines the winners and losers in the resulting distributional conflicts? What gives some stakeholders greater power than others in each type of global rule-making? In this chapter, we offer summary answers for types I, II, and III. Type IV—nonmarket private standard-setting—is analyzed in chapter 3.

Four Types of Global Rule-Making

Type I: Public (Governmental) Nonmarket Standard-Setting

Writing rules that organize and control economic or social behavior has traditionally been a key domestic policy function of governments. Such public regulation has been considered particularly important and desirable when economic activities have national security implications or affect

---

[3] The purpose of a typology is to be analytically useful rather than descriptively precise in every detail; see Lijphart, "Typologies of Democratic Systems" (1968). Our four types are therefore Weberian "ideal types." Some actual standard-setting bodies might be more accurately described, for instance, as hybrid public-private bodies, as discussed by Mattli, "Public and Private Governance in Setting International Standards" (2003), and Salter, "The Standards Regime for Communication and Information Technologies" (1999). If one such organization is the predominant rule-maker in its area of expertise, we would expect it to exhibit a mix of the characteristics discussed for nonmarket institutions below, depending on the relative power of public and private actors in the organization. For a useful alternative typology that complements ours, see Abbott and Snidal, "International 'Standards' and International Governance" (2001).

salient and hence politically sensitive areas of public policy, such as health, the environment, or consumer protection. In these areas, government control of rule-making has often been deemed necessary, for example, because standards for health and safety resemble "public goods," which markets will undersupply (see Type III below).[4]

Governments also have a long tradition of collaborating internationally to regulate public and private behavior. Such international collaboration has traditionally focused on activities that are inherently transnational, such as the operation of diplomatic emissaries, or on the consequences of international interdependence. International trade, for instance, increases the risk of disease in port cities when traded goods or foreign merchants hail from countries with poor sanitary conditions. Such mutual dependence on other countries' policies spurred international collaboration among government agencies responsible for human and animal health, starting in the nineteenth century.[5] In the last three decades, rapid market integration fueled by revolutionary advances in transportation, telecommunication, and information technologies has intensified the need for coordination of rules, regulations, and policies. Such coordination can take place through (1) ad hoc agreements among governments, (2) transgovernmental collaboration among specialized regulatory agencies, or (3) new or existing international (governmental) organizations (IGOs). Ad hoc agreements are international treaties or similar documents that codify an understanding between the governments of two or more countries. The Kyoto Protocol, for instance—an environmental treaty signed in 1997 to reduce greenhouse gas (GHG) emissions and global warming—sets standards for permissible ways of achieving the agreed reductions in GHG emissions.[6]

Transgovernmental collaboration involves public officials from two or more countries, charged with similar tasks. These government officials (possibly mid-level bureaucrats) form transgovernmental networks when they establish regular contacts directly with each other, without going through the traditional channels and political hierarchies of international

---

[4] Mattli, "Public and Private Governance in Setting International Standards" (2003), 208–10; see also Kindleberger, "Standards as Public, Collective and Private Goods" (1983), and Sykes, *Product Standards for Internationally Integrated Goods Markets* (1995).

[5] See, e.g., Cooper, "International Cooperation in Public Health as a Prologue to Macroeconomic Cooperation" (1989); Leive, *International Regulatory Regimes* (1976), vol.1; Zacher and Keefe, *The Politics of Global Health Governance* (2008), esp. 25ff.

[6] For a brief history of the Kyoto Protocol, see Oberthür and Ott, *The Kyoto Protocol* (1999), and Victor and Coben, "A Herd Mentality in the Design of International Environmental Agreements?" (2005). Regarding nontreaty international agreements, see Martin, *Democratic Commitments* (2000), 53ff.

diplomacy.[7] These networks often have set international standards. Central banks and banking system regulators from thirteen countries, for instance, in 1974 institutionalized their informal meetings by forming the Basel Committee on Banking Supervision. In direct collaboration with each other, they developed a series of "capital adequacy" standards, which specify a level of financial reserves that should be kept by each bank to safeguard against the collapse of a financial institution. The participating regulators then required the banks in their respective countries to implement these standards. They also recommended their standards to banking regulators in the rest of the world. Numerous public regulators who had no voice in setting these capital adequacy standards thus ended up adopting them.[8] Similarly, government space agencies from thirty countries in 1982 formed the Consultative Committee for Space Data Systems. This transgovernmental committee then set standards for data exchange among information systems supporting space research.

Notwithstanding the importance of some transgovernmental networks, traditional international—that is, intergovernmental—organizations (IGOs) are the most prominent kind of public international (nonmarket) standard-setting body. Standard-setting IGOs vary considerably in their age, breadth of activities, membership, and decision-making procedures.[9] Three examples illustrate this diversity.

The Universal Postal Union, founded in 1874, sets standards for international mail processing and delivery, as well as standards for technologies to detect and prevent mail fraud and crime. Adopting a standard requires at least a two-thirds majority of the 172 member states at the end of a multistage process. The International Labor Organization (ILO), founded in 1919 and today comprised of 182 member states, sets labor standards and gathers related statistics (based on its standards for defining and measuring labor conditions). Each member state can send four delegates to ILO meetings: two government representatives, one representative of employers (usually selected by the country's most prominent employers' association) and one representative of workers (usually selected by labor unions). Standards are adopted by a simple majority of all the

---

[7] Keohane and Nye, *Power and Interdependence* (1977; 1989), 34; see also Slaughter, *A New World Order* (2004), esp. 36ff; Eberlein and Grande, "Beyond Delegation" (2005).

[8] Oatley and Nabors, "Redistributive Cooperation" (1998); Singer, *Regulating Capital* (2007).

[9] See, e.g., Murphy, *International Organization and Industrial Change* (1994); Reinalda and Verbeek, eds., *Decision Making Within International Organizations* (2004); see also Barnett and Finnemore, *Rules for the World* (2004).

votes cast by individual delegates. Finally, the International Monetary Fund (IMF), established in 1944, sets standards for national governments and statistical offices, specifically for data dissemination, current account reporting, as well fiscal and monetary policy transparency. It adopts these standards through weighted majority voting, where rich countries generally have vastly greater voting weights than developing countries, mostly based on the capital that they have made available.[10]

Type II: Public Standard-Setting Bodies in Market Competition

Some standards that address global problems or achieve global reach nonetheless originate in regional or domestic rule-making bodies. What we call market-based public international standard-setting involves competition between such bodies—legislatures or regulatory agencies of individual states and regional or minilateral standard-setting bodies.[11] Such geographically limited standards can come into competition with each other—sometimes after coexisting independently for many years—when changes such as a lowering of tariffs or the lifting of restrictions on cross-border financial transactions increase interdependence and thus create functional or political-economic incentives for a single common standard.

There are many empirical examples of marketlike international competition between standards developed by public regulatory agencies or governmental international organizations. Standards for determining the structure of a market, established by the European Union (EU) Commission to decide whether a merger would imperil competition, for instance,

---

[10] The standard-setting procedures of the Universal Postal Union are specified in Universal Postal Union (UPU), *General Information on UPU Standards* (2007); specific examples are discussed by Codding, *The Universal Postal Union: Coordinator of the International Mails* (1964), and Jones and Lubenow, "Universal Postal Union (UPU) International Postal Addressing Standards" (2008). For more detailed discussions of the ILO standard-setting process, see International Labour Office, *International Labour Standards* (1998), 29ff; Hughes and Haworth, *The International Labour Organisation* (2010); Mosley, *Labor Rights and Multinational Production* (2011); and Vosko, "Standard Setting at the International Labour Organization." (2004). The importance of the capital made available to the IMF by member states arises from its central function of giving loans to countries with balance-of-payments problems; see Vreeland, *The International Monetary Fund* (2007), and Helleiner, *States and the Reemergence of Global Finance* (1994). For more detailed information about the IMF standard-setting process, see the various documents posted on the IMF's website, e.g. the "IMF-SDDS Home Page" (http://dsbb.imf.org/Applications/web/sddshome/, last accessed 8/2/2009), and Mosley, "Constraints, Opportunities and Information: Financial Market-Government Relations around the World" (2006).

[11] Each of them may internally be characterized by collaboration of the public nonmarket type.

23

differ from the standards used by competition watchdogs in the United States and other jurisdictions.[12] Not only have these differences contributed to divergent decisions that regulators have reached in some cases involving multinational companies, but the standards also compete for voluntary use by companies when they contemplate or structure mergers.[13]

For consumer goods, government agencies have established standards for products ranging from pesticides, drugs, and cosmetics to chlorofluorocarbons in spray cans and vehicle emissions. From the 1960s to the 1980s, American regulators such as the U.S. Environmental Protection Agency (EPA) established these standards with domestic consumer and environmental protection as their predominant concern, leaving the United States with substantially more stringent standards than the EU and many other countries.[14] But as more and more of these products became internationally traded, U.S. standards increasingly competed with European ones (and occasionally other standards), often resulting in a "race to the top," where the more stringent standard became the de facto global standard.[15] By contrast, competition in "flagging standards," which shipowners must meet to register their ships in the countries whose flag they are flying, resulted for a long time in a race to the bottom,[16] though some scholars note a more recent convergence at intermediate levels of stringency[17] or even a broad race to the top with a permanent divergence by a small group of countries with weak domestic political and legal institutions and little concern for their international reputation.[18]

Finally, states sometimes delegate standard-setting tasks to multiple intergovernmental organizations—or different groups of states delegate to different public bodies—whose standards then compete. One example of such a public body is the Codex Alimentarius Commission, an international organization co-sponsored by the Food and Agriculture Organization and the World Health Organization. The Codex has set relatively permissive food safety standards for genetically modified organisms, which its 180 member states are supposed to use as the technical basis of

---

[12] Damro, "Transatlantic Competition Policy" (2006).

[13] Büthe, "The Politics of Competition and Institutional Change in the European Union: The First Fifty Years" (2007), and Büthe, "Institutional Change in the European Union" (2008).

[14] Vogel, "The Hare and the Tortoise Revisited" (2003), 558ff. Only in cosmetics were American standards for consumer protection less stringent than European ones, see Bach and Newman, "Governing Lipitor and Lipstick" (2010).

[15] Vogel, *Trading Up* (1995). See also Heyvaert, "Globalizing Regulation" (2009).

[16] Murphy, *The Structure of Regulatory Competition* (2004), 45ff.

[17] DeSombre, *Flagging Standards* (2006).

[18] Barrows, "Racing to the Top . . . at Last: The Regulation of Safety in Shipping" (2009).

their domestic regulations, according to the WTO's Agreement on Sanitary and Phytosanitary Measures.[19] Yet, for live plants and animals, these standards compete with more stringent standards for living modified organisms adopted under the Cartagena Protocol of the Convention on Biological Diversity, which operates as a suborganization of the UN with 190 member states.[20]

Private Governance

International standard-setting by public bodies is an important part of global regulation. With the onset of economic globalization, however, international rule-making led by governments or public agencies has come under considerable pressure, particularly in product and financial markets. Globalization has laid bare serious procedural inadequacies and organizational limits of public international governance, notably the excruciatingly slow pace of standards production and, in some cases, lack of technical expertise and financial resources to deal with ever more complex and demanding standards issues. These limitations and failures have reinforced the rapid privatization of international standard-setting.[21] Such private rule-making, to be sure, still takes place in political and legal contexts at the domestic and international level, which are shaped by governments. Yet, while we recognize private global governance as not fully autonomous, we emphasize its distinctive characteristics.

Private rule-making leads to global standards via a market-based or a nonmarket-based path. We first discuss the former (Type III); in the next subsection, we introduce the undertheorized private nonmarket mode of global regulation (Type IV), which is our focus in the remainder of the book.

Type III: Market-Based Private International Standard-Setting

Market-based private standard-setting has been the primary focus of economists.[22] In recent years, it also has attracted analytical attention from

---

[19] Trebilcock and Howse, *The Regulation of International Trade* (2005), 207ff; Büthe, "The Politics of Food Safety in the Age of Global Trade" (2009).

[20] Drezner, *All Politics Is Global* (2007), 149ff; Pollack and Shaffer, *When Cooperation Fails* (2009).

[21] See, e.g., Abbott and Snidal, "The Governance Triangle" (2009).

[22] See especially, David and Steinmueller, "Economics of Compatibility Standards" (1994); Farrell and Saloner, "Installed Base and Compatibility" (1986); Katz and Shapiro, "Network Externalities, Competition, and Compatibility" (1985). For comprehensive reviews of this literature, see Blind, *The Economics of Standards* (2004); Matutes and Regibeau, "A

other social scientists.[23] There is consequently now an extensive literature on this mode of standard-setting. It entails rule-making by firms or other nongovernmental bodies, competing individually or in small groups to establish their preferred technical solutions as the de facto standard. A firm may seek, for instance, to make its copyrighted business model an essential component of service provision. Alternatively, a firm may seek to make a technology the starting point for further product development if it has patented the technology, its engineers have great expertise in that technology, or the technology is more compatible with the firm's existing line of products than an alternative technology. One firm's proprietary solution may become the global de facto technical standard if that firm attains a dominant position in the market or if most of its competitors decide to adopt its technology as the standard, often under license. Market competition between competing private standards, however, can persist for a long time.[24]

A classic example is the nineteenth century standardization of the gauge and generally the operation of the railroads—according to Alfred Chandler "the greatest force for economic change," including the "beginnings of modern corporate finance."[25] As late as 1861, U.S. railway companies used numerous different gauges—ranging in width from four and a half feet to six feet—fragmenting the U.S. transportation system. As the decline in transport costs, the policies of the federal government, and the consolidation of the railroad industry forged truly national markets, self-contained local railroad networks based on rail widths that differed from those used by the largest network operators became unsustainable by the 1880s. In a remarkable case of the transnational operation of historical legacies, the market-dominant U.S. railroad companies settled on four feet eight and a half inches—the gauge established in 1825 in the United Kingdom by George Stephenson, one of Britain's commercial railroad

Selective Review of the Economics of Standardization" (1996); Swann, *The Economics of Standardization* (2000); and Vogel, "Private Global Business Regulation" (2008).

[23] See, e.g., Abbott and Snidal, "The Governance Triangle" (2009); Bartley, "Certifying Forests and Factories" (2003); Baron, "Private Politics, Corporate Social Responsibility, and Integrated Strategy" (2001); Gereffi et al., "The NGO-Industrial Complex" (2001); Haufler, "Globalization and Industry Self-Regulation" (2003); Zysman and Newman, eds., *How Revolutionary Was the Digital Revolution?* (2006).

[24] See, e.g., Besen and Farrell, "Choosing How to Compete " (1994); Gabel, ed. *Competitive Strategies for Product Standards* (1991); and Gauch, "+ vs. –" (2008).

[25] Chandler, *The Railroads* (1965), 9, 43ff, 108–17.

pioneers, and by the end of the 1880s, four feet eight and a half inches was the de facto U.S. standard.[26]

Market-based private standard-setting has been very prominent in the information and communications technology (ICT) sector. Microsoft, for instance, succeeded in establishing its Windows operating system as a de facto global standard thanks to its market dominance and strong "network effects," that is, substantially increased benefits from adopting a technology also adopted by many others.[27] Other prominent examples include JVC's VHS format winning out over Sony's Betamax as the standard for videocassettes, and most recently the Blu-ray standard for optical disc formatting winning out over the HD-DVD format.

In market-based private standard-setting, firms need not act independently as in ideal models of market competition but often form consortia—ad hoc strategic alliances of two or more firms, usually in the same industry, created to develop a new standard.[28] Established by a private contract, they usually require unanimous approval from all current members before any new members can join the consortium, since the individual participating firms share the often substantial costs of research and development in exchange for a stake in the intellectual property rights of the new technology. This allows a small and often exclusive group of firms to move fast in developing a common technological solution (particularly important where compatibility is desired)—which they then "deliver for de facto ratification to the market."[29] Thus, for example, Sony, Philips, and Panasonic cooperated via a consortium, created in 2000, to develop the Blu-ray optical disc format—in competition with a consortium led by Toshiba, which developed the alternative HD-DVD format. After a "standards war" that raged from 2006 to 2008, the Blu-ray format effectively became the global standard after enough computer manufacturers, movie

[26] See Bensel, *The Political Economy of American Industrialization* (2000); Kindleberger, "Standards as Public, Collective, and Private Goods" (1983), 384f; Kirkland, *Industry Comes of Age* (1961), esp.46–51; Stover, *American Railroads* (1997), 143ff; and Taylor and Neu, *The American Railroad Network, 1861–1890* (1956), esp.12ff, 58ff.

[27] E.g., Grewal, *Network Power* (2008), 198ff, though cf. Liebowitz and Margolis, *Winners, Losers and Microsoft* (1999).

[28] Originally primarily a U.S. phenomenon, consortia are today often very multinational, though many lack institutionalization or permanence and there is great variation since each consortium is set up for a particular purpose, see Büthe and Witte, *Product Standards in Transatlantic Trade and Investment* (2004), 32f, and Mattli, "Public and Private Governance in Setting International Standards" (2003), 223f. For an extensive list of consortia, see Gesmer and Updegrove, "Standard Setting Organizations and Standards List" (2009).

[29] Mattli, "Public and Private Governance in Setting International Standards" (2003), 223.

studios, and retailers (especially Walmart) switched from supporting HD-DVD to supporting Blu-ray, thus "tipping" the market in favor of the latter standard.

Market-based private regulation is not limited to the ICT sector, and the rule-makers for this type of regulation vary from individual firms and consortia to civil society organizations.[30] Corporate Social Responsibility (CSR) standards, "fair trade" standards, and environmental sustainability standards also fall into this category of rule-making.[31] In all of these issue areas, standards developed by civil-society-based NGOs compete for consumers' or purchasing managers' allegiance with alternative standards, often developed defensively by firms.[32]

The Forest Stewardship Council (FSC), the earliest of the sustainable forestry standard-setting bodies, for example, can be traced back to proposals by high-end woodworking firms who sought to differentiate their products by assuring their customers that the wood used in their products had been harvested in an ecologically sustainable way. The FSC certificate for compliance with its standard for sustainability made this assurance more credible. The FSC achieved its breakthrough as a global standard-setting body when media-savvy lobbying from environmentalist NGOs and the threat of consumer boycotts led major retailers like Home Depot in the United States and B&Q in the United Kingdom to demand FSC certification from their suppliers all over the world.[33] The success of the NGO-driven FSC standards in the marketplace allowed it to prevail over attempts by governments to set sustainable forestry standards through an intergovernmental organization.[34] At the same time, it spurred the

---

[30] See e.g. Ronit and Schneider, *Private Organizations in Global Politics* (2000). Like firms, NGOs vary greatly in their internal structures; see Ahmed and Potter, *NGOs in International Politics* (2006); Meidinger, "The Administrative Law of Global Public-Private Regulation" (2006), 61ff. And NGOs often compete as shown by Cooley and Ron, "The NGO Scramble" (2002), even when the NGOs have normatively principled rather than material objectives; see Keck and Sikkink, *Activists Beyond Borders* (1998); Lauterbach, "The Costs of Cooperation" (2007).

[31] CSR standard-setting is discussed inter alia in Kirton and Trebilcock, eds., *Hard Choices, Soft Law* (2004), esp.189ff, and Vogel, *The Market for Virtue* (2005). Fair trade standards are discussed inter alia in Jaffee, *Brewing Justice* (2007); Levi and Linton, "Fair Trade" (2003); Raynolds et al., eds., *Fair Trade* (2007); Renard, "Fair Trade: Quality, Market, and Conventions" (2003); and Taylor, "In the Market But Not of It " (2005).

[32] Cashore, "Legitimacy and the Privatization of Environmental Governance" (2002), calls this type of private regulation "non-state market-driven governance" if the competing standards are linked to certification schemes that verify compliance.

[33] Bartley, "Certifying Forests and Factories" (2003), 443–45, and Bartley, "Institutional Emergence in an Era of Globalization" (2007), 315ff.

[34] Bartley, "Institutional Emergence in an Era of Globalization" (2007), 319f.

creation of alternative industry-driven standard-setters at the global and national level, such as the Programme for the Endorsement of Forest Certification and the Sustainable Forestry Initiative, with which it competes to this day.[35]

In sum, market-based private international standard-setting is a type of regulation of growing significance in today's global economy. Nevertheless, it is susceptible to weaknesses and inefficiencies. For example, de facto standardization is often praised for its speed, yielding a single leading standard after as little as two years of intense market contest among competing standards. However, when a standard is chosen too early in the development of a new technology, it may unintentionally lock the industry into an inferior standard.[36] In addition, uncoordinated standard-setting—typical of market-driven standardization—can give rise to wasteful duplication in the development and promotion of standards.[37] Valuable resources could be saved if producers pooled their resources and worked collectively in nonmarket private regulatory forums at the global level, as discussed next.

Type IV: Nonmarket Private International Standard-Setting

Market-based competition among firms and NGOs has resulted in hundreds of international de facto standards spanning many industries. Nonmarket private bodies, however, are responsible for the bulk of global private-sector rules; they have developed literally thousands of standards. In contrast to market-based private regulation, nonmarket private standard-setting entails rule-making by an international nongovernmental organization that is viewed by public and private actors alike as the obvious forum for the issue in question; in other words, it is *the* focal institution.

Two prominent bodies of this type are the International Organization for Standardization (ISO) and the International Electrotechnical Commission (IEC), introduced above and analyzed in detail in chapters 6 and 7. Jointly, they account for about 85 percent of all international product

---

[35] See Cashore et al., *Governing Through Markets* (2004) and Rupert, *Forest Certification Matrix* (2004).

[36] E.g., Arthur, "Competing Technologies, Increasing Returns, and Lock-in by Historical Events" (1989); David, "Clio and the Economics of QWERTY" (1985).

[37] Grindley, *Standards, Strategy, and Policy* (1995). For accounts of additional problems with market-driven standardization, see Farrell and Saloner, "Standardization, Compatibility, and Innovation" (1985), and Matutes and Regibeau, "A Selective Review of the Economics of Standardization" (1996).

standards. ISO's standards include standards for freight containers, paints and varnishes, screw threads, corrosion protection, thermal performance, and air quality measurement, as well as the "ISO 9000"-series management standards. IEC standards specify, for instance, safe and effective radiation dosages for x-ray machines, the standard dimensions and other characteristics of audio CDs and battery sizes, as well as methods to measure electromagnetic interference and thresholds to safeguard against it, so that the operation of one piece of electric equipment, such as a vacuum cleaner or microwave, does not interfere with the operation of other crucial equipment such as pacemakers or computerized security systems. For most industries, either ISO or IEC is clearly the focal point for setting international product standards, and where their areas of expertise overlap, they collaborate closely.[38] Credit and bank card dimensions, for instance, are specified by a joint ISO-IEC standard.

The stakes in ISO and IEC standardization are high: their product standards often determine market access, due to demands from purchasers or due to government regulations. Countries that adopt more and more ISO/IEC standards as domestic standards without modification include not only advanced industrialized countries such as Germany and Sweden, but also recently industrialized countries such as Singapore and South Korea and developing countries such as India and Brazil. A Japanese white goods manufacturer, for instance, who had long successfully exported washing machines made to Japanese domestic standards, lost its entire Asian export market for those machines when the importing countries switched to international standards.[39]

Moreover, governments in developing countries increasingly incorporate these standards into laws and regulations by reference (as governments of industrialized countries have done for some time), thus making compliance with the current version of a standard the regulatory requirement. China's Product Quality Law, for instance, calls on government agencies at all levels to use international standards for certification. Similarly, South Africa's Occupational Health and Safety Act refers to standards rather than writing specific technical requirements into the legislation.[40]

---

[38] Informal coordination and joint committees ensure a cooperative rather than competitive relationship between ISO and IEC.

[39] De Vries, "Standards for Business" (2006), 131.

[40] ISO/IEC, *Using and Referencing ISO and IEC Standards for Technical Regulations* (2007), 20, 22. See also Gormann, "Conformity Assessment, Standards and Trade" (2009); Hamilton, "The Role of Nongovernmental Standards" (1978); and U.S. Department of Commerce, *Standards and Competitiveness* (2004), 16–22.

ISO and IEC standards are also widely recognized as codifying "best practice," which has boosted compliance by firms and retailers that seek to reduce product liability risks and insurance costs. Last but not least, codification of a particular technical solution as an international standard often affects the value of intellectual property rights and competitors' costs.[41]

Another salient private global regulator is the International Accounting Standards Board (IASB). Based in London, it sets standards for financial reporting. As discussed in greater detail in chapter 4, IASB is the clear focal point for setting international financial reporting standards—which specify how to calculate profits and liabilities and thus have a substantial effect on the financial results that a company can report at the end of the quarter or year.[42] Senior managers, employees with share-based compensation or bonuses, investors, and regulators who are responsible for systemic risk to the financial markets all have a substantial stake in these standards.

Nonmarket private standard-setters often enjoy the privilege of tacit or explicit endorsement by governments, safeguarding their jurisdictional domains against competitive pressures. ISO and IEC standards, for instance, are referenced in many laws and government regulations, which enable governments to allow for technological change without the need to change the regulatory measures—a practice actively encouraged by ISO and IEC.[43] And in many countries, public financial market regulators now require the use of IASB reporting standards for the consolidated financial statements that companies with publicly traded stocks or bonds must issue regularly.[44]

ISO/IEC and IASB are the most prominent focal private standard-setters at the global level. Yet, for most observers, these important global rule-makers remain black boxes. Social-scientific analyses and even

---

[41] For the multinational Tyco Electronics, for example, a change in the international standards for optical connectors in commercial telecommunications increased market share, margins, and licensing income, generating *additional* profits of $50 million–$100 million during the first ten years after Tyco succeeded in shifting the standard away from a specification that favored a competitor's intellectual property toward a specification favoring its own; see de Vries, "Standards for Business" (2006), 132f; Schaap and de Vries, *Wat levert normalisatie u op?* (2005), 74–77. The competitor was Lucent Technologies. We discuss the increasing economic and political salience of international product standards in chapter 6.

[42] Mattli and Büthe, "Accountability in Accounting?" (2005).

[43] ISO/IEC, *Using and Referencing ISO and IEC Standards* (2007).

[44] Deloitte, *IAS in Your Pocket* (2008); Jo, "Diffusion of International Accounting Standards" (2009).

empirical accounts of standard-setting by these organizations are rare.[45] We therefore focus in this book on ISO/IEC and IASB. They are, however, not the only private standard-setters that are uncontested in their respective realms. The International Swaps and Derivatives Association (ISDA), for example, founded in 1985 as the International Swap Dealers Association, develops standards for financial transactions. Its ISDA Master Agreement, a standard contract for "over-the-counter"—that is, private—sales and purchases of derivatives is used in derivatives markets throughout the world.[46] For many years, ISDA was uncontested, though its standard contract has attracted some regulatory attention, along with the entire OTC market, in the aftermath of the financial crisis of 2008–9. Another example is the joint initiative of the World Resources Institute (WRI) and the World Business Council on Sustainable Development (WBCSD), which resulted in the Greenhouse Gas Protocol—a standard for measuring and reporting greenhouse gas (GHG) emissions, used for internal GHG emissions "accounting" by many multinational corporations and for emissions trading on the Chicago Climate Exchange. The institutionalized collaboration of WRI and WBCSD made them the uncontested global standard-setter for reporting GHG emissions at the level of companies or corporations (rather than at the level of individual plants, projects, or nation-states).[47] In sum, for major parts of the international political economy, nonmarket private standardization is the predominant mode of setting international standards today.

Figure 2.2 summarizes some of the key illustrative empirical examples of the four types of global rule-making discussed in this section.[48] In the next section, we examine what determines winners and losers when distributional conflicts arise in setting standards for global markets.

[45] Notable exceptions are Heires, "The International Organization for Standardization (ISO)" (2008), and Murphy and Yates, *The International Organization for Standardization (ISO)* (2008), tracing the history and increasing scope of ISO standardization; Büthe, "Private and Public Politics in International Market Regulation" (2009), and Büthe, "The Power of Norms; the Norms of Power" (2010), examining the evolution of IEC; and Mattli and Büthe, "Setting International Standards" (2003), analyzing ISO/IEC standard-setting.

[46] Feder, "Deconstructing Over-the-Counter Derivatives" (2002); Partnoy, "The Shifting Contours of Global Derivatives Regulation" (2001); and Partnoy, "Second-Order Benefits from Standards" (2007), 185ff. See also the discussion between Riles, "The Anti-Network" (2008), and Auer, "The Anti-Network: A Comment" (2008).

[47] Green, "Private Standards in the Climate Regime" (2010). WRI-WBCSD has in the meantime established a relationship with ISO that makes the GHG standard an ISO standard.

[48] If an organization develops standards for more than one industry or issue area, it may be uncontested in one area but face competition from other standard-setters in another. The placement of any particular organization in figure 2.2 might therefore differ by issue area.

Institutional Setting of Rule-Making

	public	private
nonmarket-based	**(I)** Kyoto Protocol; Universal Postal Union, ILO, IMF, ITU; Basel Committee on Banking Supervision	**(IV)** International Accounting Standards Board (IASB), Int'l Organization for Standardization (ISO), Int'l Electrotechnical Commission (IEC)
market-based	**(II)** EU Directorate General Competition vs. U.S. Dept of Justice/FTC; Codex Alimentarius vs. Cartagena Protocol	**(III)** Microsoft (Windows); Sony *et al* vs. Toshiba *et al* (Blu-ray); Forest Stewardship Council (FSC) and competitors, CSR standard-setters

Selection Mechanism (left vertical axis label)

Figure 2.2 Examples of the Four Types of International Standard-Setting

THE POLITICS OF INTERNATIONAL STANDARD-SETTING

When standards have distributional implications, one should expect conflicts of interest over which standard will be chosen.[49] Such conflicts are pervasive in international standard-setting since cross-national differences in standards often reflect differences in traditions or culture, such as the difference between a bank-based and an equity-market-based system for financing industry.[50] Genuine compromise—splitting the difference—is in such cases often impossible, as is establishing the superiority of one tradition based on what both sides would accept as objective criteria. And since the choice of a seemingly technical standard can "lock in"

[49] Krasner, "Global Communications and National Power" (1991). See also Knight, *Institutions and Social Conflict* (1992), esp. 21ff.
[50] Zysman, *Governments, Markets, and Growth* (1983).

33

commercial or political advantages for a long time to come, the ensuing global standards "battles" tend to be fierce.[51]

The International Telecommunications Union (ITU) is a good example of a nonmarket public (type I) organization that has set numerous technical standards with significant distributional implications. Created in 1865 to set standards for interconnectivity between national telegraph networks to enable international communications, it also coordinates member states' allocation of radio spectrum—so that commercial or entertainment use of the airwaves in one country does not interfere with the use for emergency communications in a neighboring country. Such coordination entailed effectively foreclosing the use of parts of the radio spectrum for each country and hence brought economic and political adjustment costs, raising the question of how these costs would be distributed. More generally, interconnectivity of networks tends to affect the commercial value of patents and technology, with clear distributional implications.[52]

In the realm of data privacy for e-commerce, regional standards developed in Europe at the EU level largely won out over U.S. standards as the global standards after a period of type II competition among public regulators, because firms that are engaged in transnational e-commerce were ultimately more concerned with adopting a single set of privacy standards for their increasingly global operations. United States databases with consumer information whose commercial use was illegal under EU standards thus lost most of their value.[53] Similar distributional consequences follow when a firm or other private standard-setter succeeds in establishing its technology as the market-dominant de facto standard (type III regulation). When Sony's Blu-ray format won over Toshiba's HD-DVD to become the new global standard for optical discs, it left more than a million owners of HD-DVD players with orphan technology. Blu-ray's

[51] Fearon, "Bargaining, Enforcement, and International Cooperation" (1998), and Moe, "Power and Political Institutions" (2005) discuss in greater detail how locking in advantages for one side can increase the difficulty of reaching agreement; see also Conybeare, "International Organization and the Theory of Property Rights" (1980), 322f.

[52] Codding and Rutkowski, *The International Telecommunications Union in a Changing World* (1982); Cowhey, "The International Telecommunications Regime" (1990); Krasner, "Global Communications and National Power" (1991); Wallenstein, *Setting Global Telecommunications Standards* (1990).

[53] Shaffer, "Globalization and Social Protection" (2000); Newman, *Protectors of Privacy* (2008). See also Bignami, "Transgovernmental Networks vs. Democracy" (2005); Farrell, "Constructing the International Foundations of E-Commerce" (2003); Farrell, "Regulating Information Flows" (2006); Heisenberg and Fandel, "Exporting EU Regimes Abroad" (2003).

victory also forced Toshiba to write off $1.1 billion of investments in the HD-DVD technology—and it led to a rise in Sony's share price in an otherwise declining stock market on the expectation of a long-term increase in licensing fee income for Sony.[54]

Distributional conflicts also often occur within standard-setting bodies that are unambiguously the focal point for standard-setting at the international level. In the process of setting international standards for shipping containers in ISO in the 1960s, for instance, there clearly was the prospect of substantial benefits from international standardization. Yet, American truckers, railroads, and shipowners pushed for the standards to specify a width of 8 feet—the maximum that could be readily accommodated by existing U.S. truck beds, railroad cars, tunnels, and ships—whereas European shippers pushed for wider "standard" containers, because existing containers for comparable volumes of freight in metric system-based Europe were slightly wider than 8 feet. For either side, giving in or compromising meant writing off investments often worth millions for a single company.[55]

As these examples illustrate, the commercial and political stakes in global standard-setting can be enormous. But who wins and who loses? Why do some have greater influence than others? What defines power in global rule-making and how does it operate? In the remainder of this chapter, we provide brief answers to these questions for the first three types of global rule-making. In chapter 3, we will answer these questions for nonmarket private regulation.

Power and Influence in Public Nonmarket Standard-Setting

Existing research suggests that outcomes of conflicts of interest in public, nonmarket standard-setting organizations are often well explained by the international distribution of power in the sense of *state power*, emphasized by the "Realist" tradition in international relations theory.[56] Generally, large, wealthy countries may be able to buy the support of smaller or poorer countries.[57] Specifically, an economically powerful country may link foreign aid, access to its markets, or other benefits sought by smaller

---

[54] *Financial Times*, "Sony and Blu-ray" (2008); Sanchanta, "Sony Wins Next-Generation DVD Battle" (2008); Soble, "Toshiba Counts Cost of HD Defeat" (2008).

[55] Egyedi, "The Standardized Container" (2000); Levinson, *The Box* (2006), esp. 137ff.

[56] Krasner, "Global Communications and National Power" (1991), esp. 351ff, 360ff.

[57] Cox and Jacobson, *The Anatomy of Influence* (1974).

or poorer countries to the latter countries' support for the international standards preferred by (the government of) the economically powerful country. Militarily powerful states may also be able to use their leverage over client states to get the latter to support them in other realms, including in formal votes in international organizations on technical matters such as standard-setting.[58] Finally, the formal decision-making rules within international organizations may be weighted by GDP or otherwise skewed in favor of powerful states. Drezner shows, for instance, that such deviations from the traditional one-country-one-vote norm have at times helped the United States and the EU to dominate rule-making in the IMF and the World Bank.[59]

Nonetheless, even in traditional intergovernmental organizations, influence may not simply be a function of the current distribution of power among states, as suggested by Realist accounts. Decision-making procedures of international organizations may not reflect the contemporary distribution of power but rather the international distribution of power at the time of the organization's inception, or it may reflect the equality principle that underpins—however imperfectly—the notion of state sovereignty.[60] The less international institutions reflect the contemporary international distribution of power among states, the more costly it is for powerful states to dominate day-to-day affairs in those institutions. Moreover, if domestic stakeholders from a small or developing country are better able to act jointly than their counterparts from ostensibly more powerful countries, the former may be able to have substantial influence vis-à-vis the latter.[61] Finally, international bodies may develop organizational interests of their own, different from those of powerful member states and more closely aligned with the interests of less powerful states. Powerful states may then find it difficult to reassert control over the international organization.[62]

[58] Krasner, "Global Communications and National Power" (1991), 364, though cf. Keohane, "Big Influence of Small Allies" (1971), and Risse-Kappen, *Cooperation among Democracies* (1995).

[59] Drezner, *All Politics Is Global* (2007), 119ff. See also Stone, "The Scope of IMF Conditionality" (2008), and Vreeland, *The International Monetary Fund* (2007).

[60] Hinsley, *Sovereignty* (1966); Krasner, ed. *Problematic Sovereignty* (2001); Lake, "Delegating Divisible Sovereignty" (2007).

[61] ITC (UNCTAD/WTO), *Influencing and Meeting International Standards* (2003). Key issues here are the ability to overcome collective action problems or information asymmetries.

[62] Barnett and Finnemore, "The Politics, Power and Pathologies of International Organizations" (1999); Bradley and Kelley, "Special Issue: The Law and Politics of International Delegation" (2008); Büthe, "Review of Hawkins et al., *Delegation and Agency in International Organizations*" (2007) and "The Dynamics of Principals and Agents: Institutional Persis-

Power and Influence in Public Market-Based Standard-Setting

International competition among public standard-setting bodies has received limited analytical attention, but existing studies suggest a political-economic explanation for who wins and who loses when alternative public standards compete. Standards set by government agencies and international (governmental) organizations often determine market access. For any good or service with economies of scale in production, producers have an incentive to comply with those standards to gain market access, and the incentive is proportional to the size of the regulated market. Consequently, a country's market size should be an important power resource when public standard-setters compete—conditional on the government's (i.e., the public regulator's) ability to control market access.[63]

Numerous examples from the regulation of manufactured goods illustrate this political logic of market-based competition between public regulators. From the 1960s through the 1980s, for instance, manufacturers from Europe and Asia often ended up implementing the stringent U.S. consumer and environmental protection standards for their entire production, because the U.S. (and sometimes just Californian) market was too important for them, and producing to a different standard for each market would have forced them to forego valuable economies of scale.[64]

Power and Influence in Market-Based Private Standard-Setting

Firms, consortia, and other private standard-setters often seek to establish their own solution to a technical problem as the de facto standard. Who prevails when their standards compete in the market? Economic analyses suggest that power is here primarily a function of market share, that is, the size of the market controlled by those who support the standard and, most importantly, strategic decisions of the standard-setting firm (or other body), that is, its mix of political and commercial strategies. The famous "standards war" between Sony's Betamax video-cassette format

---

tence and Change in U.S. Financial Regulation, 1934–2003" (2010); Hawkins et al., eds., *Delegation and Agency in International Organizations* (2006).

[63] Bach and Newman, "The European Regulatory State and Global Public Policy" (2007); Drezner, "Globalization, Harmonization, and Competition" (2005); Simmons, "The International Politics of Harmonization" (2001).

[64] See Vogel, *Trading Up* (1995); DeSombre, *Domestic Sources of International Environmental Policy* (2000).

and JVC's VHS format illustrates the point: Sony initially established a lead by bringing consumer video recorders with Betamax technology to the market in April 1975, many months before any competitor. By 1978, however, it was losing out to the VHS technology, launched only in October 1976, even though Sony had not only been first-to-market but also had the arguably superior technology. The remarkable failure of Sony's standard has been attributed to Sony's attempt to dominate the market by maintaining near-monopolistic control over the technology. JVC, by contrast, made its VHS standard publicly available and encouraged competing electronics manufacturers to license it on favorable terms. The resulting competition among VHS players from multiple manufacturers accelerated the introduction of features valued by mass market consumers (variation in playing time, preprogramming, smaller sizes of the recorders), drove down prices for VHS machines, and fostered the availability of prerecorded video tapes in the VHS format. Betamax technology remained on the market until the mid-1980s, but once the market had tipped in favor of VHS, VHS became the de facto standard.[65]

States can, of course, intervene in private market-based standard-setting.[66] Yet, if they do so after a de facto standard has already been established through market-based mechanisms, such interventions tend to be costly and may well fail. The recent attempt by the Chinese government to establish a distinctly Chinese mobile phone standard, on behalf of China's leading telecoms manufacturers and operators, appears to be destined for such a failure: so far, the interest of consumers as well as Chinese and foreign handset manufacturers in the new, exclusively Chinese standard is minimal, and forcing the adoption of the new standard would render the mobile phones of millions of Chinese worthless—an action that even an authoritarian government appears hesitant to undertake.[67]

In sum, power matters in private market-based standard-setting. The kinds of resources required to influence global outcomes, however, differ markedly from those in traditional international politics. Strategies for market competition play a very important role. These include licensing, pricing a new technology temporarily below cost to establish market dominance early on, or establishing strategic alliances with content providers, makers of peripherals, or other market participants that can

---

[65] Grindley, *Standards, Strategy, and Policy* (1995), 75–98.

[66] See, e.g., Austin and Milner, "Strategies of European Standardization" (2001).

[67] Dickie, "China's Phone Standard Fails to Win Gold" (2008), and Hille, "4G Focus Behind China Mobile Deal" (2009). See also Kennedy et al., "Standards, Stakeholders, and Innovation" (2008).

generate positive network externalities. Since market share is a key determinant of markets "tipping" in favor of one technology or another, firm
size also should be an important power resource in market-based private
regulation.

Power and Influence in Nonmarket Private Standard-Setting

The politics of private rule-making in nonmarket settings have been studied little until quite recently, arguably because this mode of global regulation has not been fully recognized as distinctive. Some scholars effectively
subsume private nonmarket regulatory institutions under public ones.
Daniel Drezner, for instance, draws on the so-called Realist tradition in
international relations theory to argue that states dominate global governance to the point where nongovernmental organizations do little more
than their bidding. According to his account, the same logic drives outcomes in both public and private international organizations. Standards
developed by organizations such as ISO and IEC, Drezner claims, reflect the international distribution of power among states and hence predominantly the interests of the "great powers."[68] Similarly, Beth Simmons
treats standard-setting in the private transnational IASB just as standard-
setting in transgovernmental organizations like the Basel Committee
or ad hoc collaborations among governments, such as the G-7, though
she emphasizes market size rather than "great power" status.[69] We argue
that these scholars fail to properly assess the political implications of the
nongovernmental status of private standard-setters, discussed in greater
detail in the next chapter.

Others explicitly or implicitly assume that the logic of market-based
private rule-making also applies to nonmarket private standard-setting.
Aseem Prakash and Matthew Potoski, for instance, discuss ISO standardization based on their insightful analysis of ISO's 14000-series environmental management standards. However, these management standards,
which regulate elements of the process of production rather than characteristics of products, are among the few standards where ISO competes
with other standard-setters. In the larger universe of the thousands of
ISO product standards, 14,000-series standardization is therefore highly

---

[68] Drezner, *All Politics Is Global* (2007), 91ff.
[69] Simmons, "The International Politics of Harmonization" (2001). See also Posner, "Sequence as Causes" (2010), who comes to a different assessment about the relative power of
the EU and the United States, based on market size and regulatory capacity.

unusual.[70] We would not expect business strategies for market competition to play the same role when ISO is clearly the focal institution for setting international standards.

While the studies noted above have not sufficiently recognized the distinctiveness of private nonmarket standard-setting, a few others have, in our assessment, gone too far by asserting that this mode of governance is not only different but devoid of politics. Drawing on ideal notions of science and engineering, sociologists Thomas Loya and John Boli see standard-setting essentially as a scientific optimization problem: a search for the objectively best standard, given a clearly defined technical problem or objective. They argue that neither "the competitive struggle between states"[71] nor the commercial interests of individual firms affect the process of standard-setting in nonmarket private governance, since the specialized technical expertise of the participants in the transnational standard-setting organizations and their joint/shared social status as scientific experts grants them a high degree of autonomy.[72] Due to the universal nature of scientific method and rationality, as pointed out by Loya and Boli, everyone can agree on what the optimal solution is, as long as there is an explicit exchange of information about the measurements and scientific procedures used. We do not doubt that technical expertise is important for exerting influence in transnational standard-setting organizations. We see little reason, however, to expect that science and technology can simply dissolve the conflicts of interest among competing stakeholders in this mode of global governance.

In the next chapter, we present an analytical framework that takes account of the distinctive elements of nonmarket private governance and recognizes its fundamentally political and hence conflictual nature. We

---

[70] Prakash and Potoski, "The ISO as a Global Governor" (2010). See also McDermott, Noah, and Cashore, "Differences that Matter?" (2008); Kollman and Prakash, "Green By Choice?" (2001). The only other ISO standards that are seriously contested are ISO's new corporate social responsibility standards (26,000-series, see Tamm Hallström, "International Standardization Backstage" (2005)) and some standards for information technology. In addition, as pointed out by the ISO itself, ISO 14,000-series standards are "generic" in that they "can be applied to any organization, large or small, whatever its product or service, in any sector of activity, and whether it is a business enterprise, a public administration, or a government department," which leads to the involvement of an exceptionally diverse set of stakeholders and public attention, whereas "the vast majority of ISO standards are highly specific to a particular product, material, or process"; see ISO "What's Different about ISO 9001 and ISO 14001" (2009).

[71] Loya and Boli, "Standardization in the World Polity" (1999), 196.

[72] See also Schofer, "Science Associations in the International Sphere, 1875–1990" (1999).

argue that the politics of global rule-making in these private settings systematically follow an institutional logic that differs from public governance as well as market-based private governance.

CONCLUSION

In this chapter, we have developed a typology of global regulation. We have identified the key characteristics of each type and analyzed the implications of differences between the four types for the political dynamics in each setting. Drawing on our typology and previous empirical studies, we have found that in public standard-setting, the traditional power resources of states—especially market size and the ability to control access to that market—play a far greater role than in private standard-setting. Studies of market-based regulation also show that strategic decisions of standard-setters can play a key role in shaping outcomes. As we will discuss in the next chapter, in nonmarket private standard-setting, technical and financial resources are important but the explanation of outcomes turns largely on institutional factors.

Those who set standards wield influence. Standard-setting is thus an inherently political activity. Politics, however, need not be governmental. A growing share of international rule-making takes place in private rather than public fora. The resources required to wield influence in private standard-setting bodies differ from those required in traditional governmental international organizations. In the next chapter, we develop an analytical approach, institutional complementarity theory, to provide a systematic understanding of the politics in focal private institutions for setting standards for global markets.

CHAPTER THREE

Institutional Complementarity Theory

INTERNATIONAL STANDARDIZATION almost always entails distributional conflicts. As the examples in the previous chapters illustrate,
standardization implies the harmonization of differing prior practices
and therefore adjustment costs, at least for some. Consequently, it involves
conflicts of interest over the distribution of those adjustment costs—even
when the benefits of convergence on a single international standard clearly
exceed the adjustment costs for each country or even each affected user.[1]
Moreover, standardization can increase or decrease the value of patents
and open up profitable business opportunities for some while foreclosing them for others. When the member bodies of ISO voted to adopt
Microsoft's "open XML" standard as an ISO standard, for instance, they
greatly improved Microsoft's chances of winning and retaining government contracts worth billions. That decision simultaneously reduced the
chances of Microsoft's competitors to establish their alternative solution
to cross-platform document compatibility as a de facto standard.[2] In
sum, for any given standard, the economic and sociopolitical stakes are
real and often high.

---

[1] International standardization thus often resembles what game theorists call a coordination game with distributional conflict. See Snidal, "Coordination versus Prisoners' Dilemma" (1985); Stein, "Coordination and Collaboration" (1982). See also Morrow, "Modeling the Forms of International Cooperation" (1994). For applications to international
standardization see Krasner, "Life on the Pareto Frontier" (1991), and Mattli and Büthe,
"Setting International Standards" (2003). For how long the losers in such games incur adjustment costs may vary, as discussed below.

[2] To achieve ISO adoption, Microsoft had to commit to disclosing and licensing its XML
code, and future revisions of the standard are subject to ISO technical committee review
and voting, but Microsoft retained full intellectual property rights; see Financial Times,
"Software Wars" (2008); Lohr, "OpenDocument Format" (2006); Palmer, "Microsoft Wins
Key ISO Certification" (2008).

In this chapter we seek to explain the distributional consequences of shifting rule-making to the international private and nonmarket sphere. We ask: Who wins, who loses, and why, when international standard-setting takes place in private focal institutions? What is distinctive about the politics of rule-making in these transnational institutions? What defines power in these organizations, and how does it operate? We develop institutional complementarity theory to offer general answers to these questions.

Institutional complementarity theory posits: When one international organization is the clear focal point for setting global rules, the ability of firms and others to influence the specific outcomes of private rule-making is a function of the fit between these stakeholders' domestic institutions and the international organization—as well as their technical expertise and economic resources. Specifically, given common features of the private rule-making organizations at the international level, domestic institutions need to provide timely information to allow those who have a stake in the content of the standard to influence that content in the early stages of standards development. Further, domestic institutions need to enable effective, uncontested representation of these stakeholders at the international level. In this chapter, we flesh out the argument to develop a general understanding of this important type of global rule-making. In chapters 4 and 6, we then derive more specific answers to the above questions in the particular empirical contexts of global financial and product markets, respectively.

THE INSTITUTIONAL SETTING OF NONMARKET PRIVATE GOVERNANCE: ACTORS AND SOURCES OF POWER

A defining characteristic of nonmarket private governance is that governments are excluded from this type of rule-making in that they are not directly represented in the transnational private standard-setting organizations. Even the affiliated or member organizations at the national/domestic level are, for advanced industrialized countries, generally nongovernmental. And the international standard-setters have strong incentives to keep governments at bay. Standard-setting organizations, like other public and private bodies, generally want to safeguard their own autonomy. Moreover, the scientists, engineers, and other technical experts who cooperate in these settings often attribute the efficiency and effectiveness of private standard-setting to the nongovernmental status of the transnational organizations, based on experience or ideology. Allowing direct government influence in anything more than truly exceptional circumstances would risk the willingness of these experts to contribute to international standardization efforts.[3] In sum, the nongovernmental status of nonmarket private standard-setters is not just coincidental but consciously and sometimes adamantly maintained by organizations such as IASB, IEC, and ISO.

This insistence on no more than a marginal role for governments has important implications for who holds power and how it is exercised in private international rule-making organizations. Traditional power resources of states are not likely to be useful for influencing the specific content of international standards, except in extraordinary cases—unlike in intergovernmental standard-setting organizations.[4] Yet, given the stakes involved, "governance without governments"[5] is bound to be a conflictual and political rather than merely a technical process. In other words, power matters, but technical expertise, financial means, good and timely information, and especially effective mechanisms of interest representation—rather than the size of the economy or the military might of a stakeholder's home state—we argue, are the crucial resources that give some greater influence than others in international private standard-setting.

We first discuss the significance of technical expertise and financial means. Their importance has been noted in other studies of product standard-setting. We go a step further, however, and argue that these resources are necessary but not sufficient for successful involvement in global private-sector standardization. Given certain institutional features that are common to international private rule-makers, timely information and effective interest representation will determine which actors—among those possessing technical expertise and good financial resources—are likely to gain a key advantage in the rule-making process and significantly shape the content of global standards. We discuss the analytical importance of timely information and interest representation in the next section and also explain how they flow from what we call institutional complementarity.

---

[3] Büthe, "The Power of Norms; the Norms of Power" (2010).

[4] E.g., Krasner, "Global Communications and National Power" (1991); Drezner, *All Politics is Global* (2007), esp. 119ff, 149ff.

[5] Rosenau and Czempiel, eds., *Governance without Government* (1992).

Technical Expertise and Economic Resources

Private standard-setters generally have strong norms or formal rules that require technical, scientific reasoning from anyone who seeks to have a voice in the development of a standard. There are two main reasons for this insistence on technical language. It reinforces the transnational standard-setting body's legitimacy, which is based on technical expertise.[6] And in rendering other (political or economic) arguments impermissible and illegitimate, it safeguards the transnational body against overt political and especially government interference. The requirement to provide technical arguments for any proposal or demand thus also helps—and is intended to—retain the nongovernmental character of these expert bodies.[7]

Given this requirement for technical reasoning, the pertinent expertise should be an important resource for exerting influence in international standardization. The requirement can render the politics of setting standards different from traditional international politics insofar as the requirement to frame proposals in scientific language or as a technical improvement constrains what arguments get made,[8] and it might even change some participants' view of their self-interest.[9] Yet, it does not render the process of standard-setting apolitical: scientific knowledge and technical expertise can be employed strategically—and as the example of the audio CD standard illustrates (see box 3.1), commercial interests often create strong incentives to do so in international standardization.

Having the requisite technical expertise is not enough. Those who have a stake in the specific provisions of a standard also must be able to afford the time and expense to follow the substantive discussions in the international standard-setting organization, determine how their interests are affected by the proposals at hand, and take action, if they want to have a chance to influence the outcome of those discussions. This may require international travel, for instance, to provide oral testimony or to coordinate with similarly affected stakeholders in other countries. In short, exerting real influence in international private nonmarket standard-setting also requires significant material resources.

[6] Murphy and Yates, *The International Organization for Standardization* (2008), 25–42; Porter, "Private Authority, Technical Authority, and the Globalization of Accounting Standards" (2005). See also Avant, Finnemore and Sell, eds., *Who Governs the Globe?* (2010).

[7] Büthe, "The Power of Norms; the Norms of Power" (2010), 312–15.

[8] Schmidt and Werle, "Technical Controversy in International Standardisation" (1993).

[9] Loya and Boli, "Standardization in the World Polity" (1999).

BOX 3.1

The Audio CD Standard:
Art and Science in the Service of Commercial Strategy

The standard for audio CDs—since 1987 recognized and maintained as ISO standard 60908—was originally jointly developed by two multinational corporations: the Japanese Sony Corporation and the Dutch manufacturer Philips. The "red book" standard specifies the dimensions of an audio CD, the structure of the data, how a CD is to be read (from the center out, in contrast to vinyl records), etc. The Sony-Philips collaboration, launched in 1979, proceeded under intense competitive pressure from other electronics giants, such as Matsushita/JVC, Mitsubishi, and Hitachi. Starting in the mid-1970s, each of these firms had sought to develop viable technological solutions for mass-market audio discs, and the race was on to bring discs and players to the market first. The engineers in the Sony-Philips consortium therefore largely worked cooperatively, which enabled them to license the technology starting in January 1981 and bring commercial CD players on to the market in October—November 1982, beating their competitors decisively.[i] But even under these conditions, technical and scientific reasoning was often used strategically.

One of the more mundane but critical elements of the new technology that had to be standardized was the diameter of the discs. Prior to the beginning of the collaboration, Philips managers had decided that the diameter of the discs should equal the diagonal dimension of compact cassettes—115mm—on the belief that it would allow "compact discs" to emulate the great commercial success of cassettes as a portable medium for sound recording.[ii]

Sony had initially preferred a smaller diameter, but soon after the beginning of the collaboration started to argue vehemently for a diameter of 120mm. Sony's argument was simple and compelling: to maximize the consumer appeal of a switch to the new technology, any major piece of music

[i]The Sony-Philips collaboration was motivated in large part by each firm having separately developed crucial components of the new technology but not yet having solved technical problems already solved by the other firm. Kretschmer and Muehlfeld, "Co-opetition in Standard-Setting: The Case of the Compact Disc" (2004), 5–9.
[ii]See Schouhamer Immink, "The CD Story" (1998), 460; Lauterslager, "Interview with Schouhamer Immink" (2001).

(Continued)

needed to fit on a single CD so as to eliminate the need to switch CDs. Beethoven's Ninth Symphony was quickly identified as the point of reference—according to some accounts, it was the favorite piece of Sony vice-president Norio Ohga's wife. And thorough research identified the 1951 recording by the orchestra of the *Bayreuther Festspiele* under Wilhelm Furtwängler, at seventy-four minutes, as the slowest performance of the Ninth Symphony on record. And so, according to the official history, Sony and Philips top executives agreed in their May 1980 meeting that "a diameter of 12 centimeters was required for this playing time."[iii]

It is a charming story of the marriage of art and science in determining the dimensions of the new technology—but not quite true. According to Philips' lead electronics engineer on the project, Kees Schouhamer Immink, the information density of the discs had not yet been decided in May 1980. It was therefore impossible to deduce any "necessary" or technically optimal diameter from a desired playtime. In fact, the density on which Philips' and Sony's engineers settled one month later would have allowed a playtime of 97 minutes with a diameter of 120mm or a diameter as small as 100 mm for a playtime of 74 minutes. The real reason for Sony's insistence on 120mm was that Philips' subsidiary PolyGram had already developed manufacturing capacity for 115mm discs as prototypes for Philips prior to the start of the collaboration. Sony, with a stake in PolyGram's competitor CBS, had no such facility. As Schouhamer Immink notes, "If Sony had agreed on the 115mm disc, Philips would have had a significant competitive edge in the music market."[iv] Beethoven had been employed strategically.

[iii]Philips, "Optical Recording: Beethoven's Ninth Symphony of Greater Importance than Technology" (2007).

[iv]Schouhamer Immink, "Shannon, Beethoven, and the Compact Disc" (2007), 45.

The importance of technical and financial resources has implications for who has power and who succeeds in global private governance. Within countries, large commercial entities are far more likely than consumers or individual private investors to have the pertinent expertise and material resources. Representatives from industry therefore vastly outnumber other stakeholders in international standard-setting, even when formal procedures, such as public notice-and-comment periods, create a nominally even playing field.[10] Consequently, we focus on firms as the most influential stakeholders.[11]

Across countries, both of these resources are generally relatively abundant in advanced industrialized countries but often scarce in developing countries. We therefore generally expect stakeholders from advanced industrialized countries to play a more prominent role in private transnational standard-setting organizations than stakeholders from developing countries.[12] There are, however, few reasons to assume that stakeholders from developed countries have identical preferences—and, in fact, they often differ amongst themselves.[13]

INSTITUTIONAL COMPLEMENTARITY, EFFECTIVE REPRESENTATION, AND TIMELY INFORMATION

Global private governance entails rule-making at the international level. Some scholars therefore discount domestic standard-setting institutions in their analysis of who wins and who loses from this shift of authority to the international level.[14] We argue, to the contrary, that domestic institutions are crucial in interaction with international institutions. Specifically, countries differ in how well their historically conditioned domestic institutions fit with international standards institutions, most of which have grown to prominence only recently as a result of globalization. Cross-national

---

[10] Mattli and Büthe, "Global Private Governance" (2005).

[11] See also Gregory Shaffer's discussion of the centrality of business in transnational rule-making in "How Business Shapes Law" (2009), 149f, 151f, 162ff. Other stakeholders differ by specific issue area, but tend to include groups such as labor, consumers, government regulators, etc.

[12] While most developing countries generally play a marginal role in ISO and IEC (see, e.g., Clapp, "The Privatization of Global Environmental Governance" (1998)), a developing country may of course play an important role in an issue area where it has an exceptionally high stake and therefore is able or willing to muster the necessary resources. Malaysia, for instance, as one of the most important producers of natural rubber, holds the chair and secretariat of ISO TC45, responsible for developing standards for "rubber and rubber products." Similarly, the importance of technical and material resources does not necessarily imply the centrality of large powerful countries, which dominate traditional accounts of international politics. Stakeholders from small but wealthy advanced industrialized countries, such as Finland and Sweden, may play a prominent role and be among the winners in international standards battles if they have complementary domestic institutions, as discussed below.

[13] Similarly, analyses of international standard-setting should be cautious about treating developing countries as if they were a monolithic bloc.

[14] E.g., Drezner, "The Global Governance of the Internet" (2004).

differences in what we call institutional complementarity between domestic and international standard-setting organizations affect the ability of stakeholders to influence the *content of international standards* and hence the *distribution of costs and benefits*. Specifically, high institutional complementarity enables stakeholders to (1) obtain good and timely information about international standardization initiatives and developments, enabling them to get involved where necessary, and (2) project their technical preferences without being contested by domestic rivals. Early involvement due to timely information, combined with uncontested representation, makes for highly influential participation in international standardization of the type that is the focus of this book.

Institutional Complementarity

Two institutions are complementary—from the perspective of, for instance, a firm—when their combination yields greater benefits than the firm can attain from either of them separately. This concept has proven analytically useful in explaining the operations of individual firms and of national economies but has not been used to explain international political-economic phenomena. It is a key element of our explanation of outcomes in global private governance.[15]

Domestic institutions that are more complementary with a particular international institution confer on stakeholders with access to such domestic institutions a strategic advantage by amplifying their voices in the international standardization process. Such actors thus attain a greater benefit through the international institution than they could have attained in the absence of these domestic institutions. At the same time, international institutions that are complementary with a particular domestic system confer on the stakeholders in that domestic system the

[15] Our definition is adapted from Hall and Soskice, "An Introduction to Varieties of Capitalism" (2001), 17ff and Höpner, "What Connects Industrial Relations with Corporate Governance? Explaining Institutional Complementarity" (2005). Notions of institutional complementarity were introduced in economics to analyze the fit between organizational structure and work practices within firms; see Chandler, *Strategy and Structure* (1962), and Milgrom and Roberts, "Complementarities and Fit" (1995). In comparative political economy, notions of complementarity play an important role in the varieties of capitalism literature, especially in the work of Aoki, "The Contingent Governance of Teams" (1994); Amable et al., "How Do Financial Markets Affect Industrial Relations?" (2005); and Hall and Gingerich, "Varieties of Capitalism and Institutional Complementarities in the Macroeconomy" (2002). They are also implicit in many second image reverse arguments in international political economy, such as Katzenstein, ed. *Between Power and Plenty* (1978). See also the additional discussion of institutional complementarity in chapter 8.

advantages of greater effectiveness and legitimacy in establishing a truly global standard. These actors with access to highly complementary domestic and international institutions thus attain a greater benefit than they could have attained through their domestic institutions in the absence of the complementary international institutions.

This core idea of institutional complementarity theory implies that we need to know the institutional structure and procedures at the international level to determine which characteristics of domestic institutions would put a country's stakeholders in the strongest position to influence international standard-setting. We therefore conduct detailed analyses of the international and domestic institutions for financial and product standardization in chapters 4 and 6, respectively. The key features of the international institutions in these two domains, however, can be sketched briefly.

For most manufacturing industries, there is a single global body (either ISO or IEC) that is the clear focal point for setting international product standards. Similarly, IASB is the focal point for international financial reporting standard-setting. While operating within a broader political and legal context shaped by governments, these international institutions as such are strictly private. Each body develops its international standards in a multistage process, in which the fundamental issues are decided at the outset and the technical specification then becomes successively more detailed. In developing its standards, each international body aims for a broad consensus and thus seeks to accommodate the stakeholder preferences of as many countries as possible—based on a system of national but nongovernmental representation. At the same time, each also has ultimately a majoritarian decision-making procedure for adopting—or rejecting—the resulting technical specification as an international standard.

Given these characteristics of the institutions at the international level, those who seek to influence international standards will need good and timely information about the standardization agenda at the international level, and they need to have institutional mechanisms at their disposal for projecting their preferences effectively from the domestic to the international level. What domestic institutional features are most likely to provide the greatest institutional complementarities and hence an advantage for influencing the content of the international standards? We focus on the degree to which the institutional structure of domestic systems of standardization is hierarchical and differentiate two ideal types.

In countries with what we call hierarchical domestic institutions, the domestic system of standard-setting looks like a pyramid (see figure 3.1). At the apex of the national system, there is a single peak-level standards

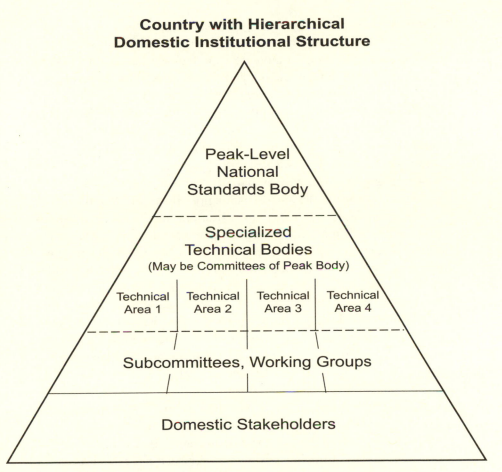

Country with Hierarchical
Domestic Institutional Structure

Peak-Level
National
Standards Body

Specialized
Technical Bodies
(May be Committees of Peak Body)

| Technical Area 1 | Technical Area 2 | Technical Area 3 | Technical Area 4 |

Subcommittees, Working Groups

Domestic Stakeholders

Figure 3.1   Hierarchical Institutional System

body, which is uncontested as the focal point for standard-setting activities at the national level. Underneath, the technical work takes place in specialized bodies and is in that sense decentralized. These bodies may be committees of the national standards organization or formally autonomous, specialized standards-developing organizations. Beneath this second tier, there may be further levels to allow for even more differentiated technical work in subcommittees or working groups. All of these groups, however, operate under the guidance of a national peak-level body, which functions like a central coordinating mechanism for the entire system. It coordinates the activities of the specialized technical bodies and ensures that only a single national standard is developed for each technical issue.

All stakeholders, including industry associations, professional associations, consumer groups, government regulatory agencies, and specialized domestic standard-setters (if any) are expected to pursue their interests through participation in, or submissions to, the specialized expert group dealing with the issue that concerns these stakeholders. Contestation is thus restricted to the technical work; the issue-specific standards-developing bodies do not compete with each other. In sum, these systems are characterized by institutional hierarchy and coordination.

In non-hierarchical domestic systems, by contrast, multiple standards-developing organizations exist in parallel and compete with each other (see figure 3.2). Each of them has separate procedures and committees for developing standards, and there is no institutional mechanism in countries with such a system for coordinating the rule-making of these competing bodies. For a given technical issue, multiple standards may therefore exist—simultaneously and often in competition with each other. In non-hierarchical systems, one of the domestic standard-setters or a neutral third party may be designated as the country's representative at the international level, but such a body has no authority over the genuinely autonomous organizations at the domestic level. Non-hierarchical systems are therefore characterized by institutional fragmentation and contestation.

Importantly, we do not argue that hierarchical domestic institutions are inherently superior to fragmented institutions. In the absence of international economic integration, either may serve a country well; competition among multiple standard-setters, for instance, may hasten technological advance. Rather, economic globalization in conjunction with institution-alized rule-making at the international level, which increases everyone's stakes in global standard-setting, changes the costs and benefits of having hierarchical or fragmented domestic institutions, due to differences in institutional complementarity. Specifically, the differences between hierarchical and non-hierarchical domestic institutions have important implications for the timeliness of the information available to a country's stakeholders, for the timing of their involvement, and more broadly for their ability to exert influence at the international level. As discussed in greater detail below, organizational hierarchy ensures the representation of national technical preferences at the international level without contestation and facilitates the flow of information between the domestic and the international level. Consequently, given the characteristics of the international standard-setting organizations sketched above, we expect that stakeholders who seek to influence international standards will be more successful the more hierarchical their domestic institutions.

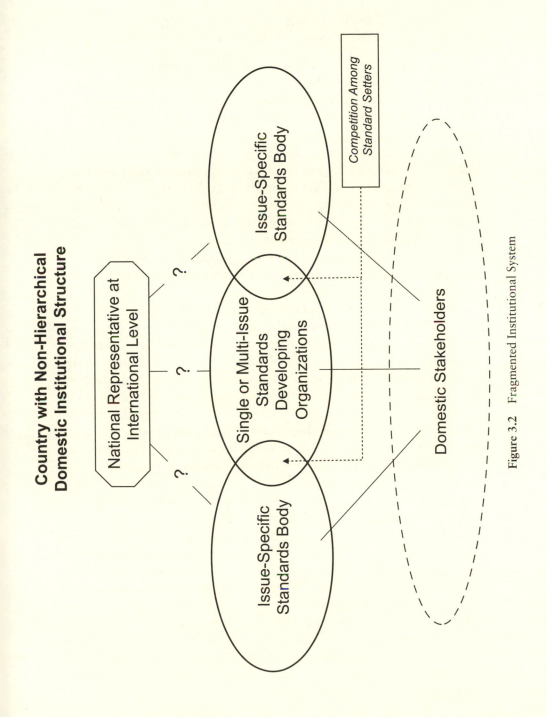

Figure 3.2 Fragmented Institutional System

Institutional Complementarity and the Effective Representation of Domestic Interests at the International Level

International harmonization of standards affects a heterogeneous set of interests. In the absence of domestic institutions that ensure a single common standard, firms within a given country may differ in their prior practices, even in the same industry. In addition, they may face different adjustment costs. Consequently, they may well have conflicting preferences. Domestic institutions govern whether any such conflicts are projected onto the international stage and hence determine the effectiveness of the country's stakeholders in international standardization. The critical distinction is between hierarchical and fragmented domestic institutions, since, we argue, the former exhibit greater institutional complementarity with international standard-setting institutions.

Hierarchy entails clear procedures for aggregating preferences. Having a hierarchical system of standardization makes it more likely that a single national technical standard exists prior to the globalization of standard-setting, and that the preferences of the country's stakeholders are closely aligned. Moreover, regardless of the similarity or diversity of domestic prior preferences, a hierarchical system aggregates those preferences from the bottom up into a single national position and unambiguously designates a person or body to present that position at the international level with a single voice. Organizational hierarchy thus ensures that the country's representative (and substantive position) is uncontested at the international level, even when the process of aggregating preferences takes place in the private realm. This increases the coherence of the country's stakeholders and should increase the effectiveness of the international representation of their interests.

By contrast, countries with non-hierarchical national systems of standardization, characterized by institutional fragmentation, lack a mechanism for aggregating diverse domestic preferences. This makes it more likely that prior practices, and hence preferences, differ. Most importantly, the lack of an aggregating mechanism undermines the chances that a country's stakeholders will take a common position internationally, since each competing domestic standards body has an incentive to advance only its own position and to emphasize differences. The result is the simultaneous, additive representation of competing positions from the same country, each contesting the others' claim to represent the country's stakeholders, which we expect to undermine the country's ability to influence standard-setting at the international level.

Specifically, we hypothesize domestic institutions to be a source of power (for some relative to others) because hierarchical domestic institutions exhibit a better fit with the institutional structure at the international level, that is, because of greater institutional complementarity. As noted above, international standard-setting organizations have "consensus" norms to maximize legitimacy and standards adoption. Notwithstanding the private nature of the organizations, these norms call for accommodating stakeholder preferences *by country*, to the greatest possible extent.[16] Consequently, if a country's domestic organizational structure makes it hard or impossible for stakeholders from that country to project a single position onto the global stage, the effectiveness of its stakeholders should suffer. And open contestation of the positions taken by the country's representatives internationally directly undermines their ability to benefit from the international consensus norm, as it suggests that no modification of a draft standard would accommodate the country's stakeholders as a whole.

Institutional Complementarity and the Timeliness of Involvement and Information

Cross-national differences in technical standards often reflect historical legacies more than a "failure" of one or more countries to adopt an objectively superior technical solution. For most practical purposes, a sheet of paper that measures 8.5 by 11 inches (216×279cm) is neither superior nor inferior to a sheet of paper that measures 210 by 297 centimeters (8.3×11.7 in). The former complies with the U.S. standard for "letter size" paper; the latter with the metric "A4" paper standard, which is based on a "practical and aesthetic idea" developed by German physicist Georg Christoph Lichtenberg in 1786. It was made a technical standard by the German standards institute (DIN) in 1922, and since 1975 has been the "ISO 216" paper size standard that is used virtually everywhere outside of the United States, Canada, and parts of Mexico.[17] Similarly, differences

---

[16] The consensus norm is conditional on compliance with the norm that any proposal be supported by technical arguments, as discussed earlier in this chapter.

[17] Kuhn, "International Standard Paper Sizes" (2006). The U.S. standard, nominally established in 1921 though universally used only since the 1980s, traces its origins to the late 1600s when, according to the American Forest and Paper Association, "the Dutch invented the two-sheet mold. The average maximum stretch of an experienced vatman's arms was 44". Many molds at that time were around 17" front to back because the laid lines and watermarks had to run from left to right. . . . To maximize the efficiency of paper making,

in American and European solutions to engineering problems or divergent preferences regarding rules versus principles in accounting standards are often attributed to differences in "engineering traditions," corporate "cultures," or financial systems.

It is difficult if not impossible to find a genuine compromise on such issues, and since these differences must nonetheless be addressed in the early stages of developing any standard, exerting influence during those early stages is likely to be crucial. More generally, those who voice their preferences early, for instance, at the agenda-setting stage, should have greater influence, since the specificity of a draft standard increases successively during the multistage process, and the more detailed, later drafts are more difficult to change. Latecomers are unlikely to have more than a marginal impact and therefore pay more of the switching costs.[18]

Global governance institutions differ in how exactly stakeholders can gain access to the decision makers and what lobbying methods are considered legitimate.[19] The specific ways in which stakeholders can exert influence at the various stages of standards development therefore may vary across global private bodies, but regardless of the format, early involvement requires having *good and timely information* about the standardization agenda at the international level. How does this information reach domestic stakeholders? How do the domestic producers and users of standardized or to-be-standardized physical or financial products learn of international standards proposals that affect them?

We posit that the domestic institutional distinction that we have emphasized above also affects the timeliness of information. Hierarchical

---

[two sheet were made in each 44" × 17" mold], and then [each was] quartered, forming four 8.5" × 11" pieces." See American Forest & Paper Association (2009).

[18] Switching costs may entail a simple one-time change in procedures or technology. Those who benefit from international harmonization through the integration of markets should be willing to absorb those costs as long as they take a sufficiently long-term perspective in calculating costs and benefits. In a highly competitive market, however, these costs matter even if a firm can derive a long-term benefit, and there are numerous examples where international standardization has threatened the commercial viability of firms before they could achieve the long-term benefits. Moreover, since differences in standards can be due to fundamental differences regarding, for example, the role and autonomy of financial markets or engineering philosophy, adjustment costs may persist for a long time, putting the losers of international standardization at a lasting disadvantage. The realization that such losses will persist and hence will accumulate can make the initial coordination on a single common solution far more politically contentious, as James Fearon has shown in "Bargaining, Enforcement, and International Cooperation" (1998).

[19] E.g., Cutler et al., eds., *Private Authority and International Affairs* (1999); Jordana and Levi-Faur, eds., *The Politics of Regulation* (2004); Mattli and Woods, eds., *The Politics of Global Regulation* (2009).

BOX 3.2

The Persistence of Domestic Institutions with Suboptimal Complementarity

The logic of institutional complementarity raises the question: Once governance shifts to the international level, if a country's domestic institutions do not serve that country's interests well any more, why do such suboptimal institutions persist? Why would we not expect all countries to convergence rapidly on the most efficient institutional arrangement?

We do not expect such convergence because institutions are often created by specific historical events but then become entrenched in self-reinforcing ways. Consequently, as work in the historical institutionalist tradition has shown, the institutions one encounters at a given point in time may be better explained by institutional legacies than by their current functionality.[*] Due to the historical predominance of domestic economic activity, national systems of standardization in advanced industrialized countries developed and solidified (with entrenched interests privileging a path-dependent evolution) long before institutionalized international cooperation in this realm became a major issue. Moreover, institutional change is slow and incremental, so that institutional differences may persist even when the institutions clearly differ in how well they are suited to their current functions.[‡] A given standardization system therefore need not constitute an optimal institutional arrangement at a particular point in time.

[*]E.g., Büthe, "Taking Temporality Seriously" (2002); Pierson, "Increasing Returns, Path Dependence, and the Study of Politics" (2000), and "The Limits of Design" (2000); and Thelen, "Historical Institutionalism in Comparative Politics" (1999).

[‡]Campbell, *Institutional Change and Globalization* (2004); Streeck and Thelen, *Beyond Continuity* (2005); Wimmer and Kössler, *Understanding Change* (2006).

organizations are designed to pass information up and down the hierarchy, which should ensure the flow of information about standards proposals and activities from the international level to those at the domestic level who are most likely to be affected by it. In countries whose domestic system of standardization is characterized by hierarchy, domestic stakeholders should therefore enjoy good and timely information about the international standardization agenda. We expect information about international standardization to reach domestic stakeholders less promptly in countries with fragmented domestic institutions because of the weak institutional links between a country's representatives at the international level and stakeholders at the domestic level. In fragmented systems where multiple standard-setting bodies compete, each domestic body has incentives to treat information as a commercially valuable proprietary asset and restrict its dissemination to its members/customers. Competition among domestic standards bodies thus should lead to inferior (later and/ or poorer) knowledge about the international standards agenda among domestic stakeholders in countries characterized by institutional fragmentation. In sum, stakeholders from countries with hierarchical institutions are more likely than stakeholders from countries with fragmented institutions to have timely information and hence better opportunities to influence the content of international standards.

These benefits of hierarchical domestic institutions are a consequence of the increased importance of global governance. The institutional differences matter because domestic standardization systems characterized by hierarchy exhibit greater complementarity with the private nonmarket institutions at the international level than domestic systems characterized by institutional fragmentation and competition.

Conclusion

Institutional complementarity theory offers an explanation for who wins and who loses in global private nonmarket governance. Fundamentally, we argue that decisive power in this form of transnational rule-making is a function of institutions and specifically a function of the complementarity between international and domestic institutions, which may vary across countries. In this chapter, we have discussed specific structural-institutional reasons why—given key institutional characteristics of international standard-setting—stakeholders from countries with hierarchical domestic institutions should be better able to influence international standards than stakeholders from countries with domestic standardization systems characterized by fragmentation and competition among multiple domestic standard-setters.

Our analytical framework suggests that domestic standardization systems characterized by institutional hierarchy facilitate the accommodation of the new institutional layers of standardization activity above the national level. Offering greater complementarity with international standards institutions, a hierarchical structure eases the adaptation of national standard-setting bodies and their domestic constituencies (firms and other actors interested in standards) to the changed circumstances of economic globalization, in which economic and political imperatives push toward setting standards in focal institutions (rather than through market competition) at the international level.[20] It also eases the search and identification by the international institution of domestic actors authorized to speak on behalf of a country's stakeholders. By contrast, systems characterized by institutional fragmentation and contestation among commercially competing domestic standard-setters exhibit low complementarity with international standards institutions and impede adaptation and identification. To put it simply: hierarchies can accommodate another level of aggregation—another layer in the pyramid—with relative ease; hierarchies and markets do not mix well.

In parts II and III of the book, we analyze the politics of international standards for international financial reporting (chapters 4 and 5) and global product markets (chapters 6 and 7). We begin, in chapters 4 and 6, respectively, with an overview of the economic and political dynamics that have driven the globalization of standard-setting. We then examine the contemporary international and domestic institutions for setting standards. The specific information about these governance institutions allows us to develop more detailed hypotheses about the ways in which stakeholders can exert influence, given the nature of global rule-making in each issue area, and about the consequences of institutional complementarity for the international standards that are developed by the IASB and ISO/IEC, respectively. Next, we put our argument to the test in chapters 5 and 7. For each issue area, we present a series of statistical/quantitative analyses of data that we have gathered through business surveys among hundreds of firms with a stake in international standardization. We supplement these analyses with qualitative information drawn from interviews, documents from the standard-setting organizations, open-ended questions embedded in our surveys, and secondary sources (news reports and academic analyses). In chapter 8, we put our analysis in the context of the broader literature, before we conclude with a summary of our main findings and a discussion of policy implications.

---

[20] The specific economic and political dynamics that have driven the globalization of standard-setting for manufactured goods and financial reporting are discussed in the empirical sections. Regarding the ability of some types of domestic institutions to provide resources that help actors adopt to change while others inhibit change, see Hall, "The Movement from Keynesianism to Monetarism" (1992).

CHAPTER FOUR

Private Regulators in Global Financial Markets

INSTITUTIONAL STRUCTURE AND COMPLEMENTARITY
IN ACCOUNTING REGULATION

IN APRIL 2009, as the global financial crisis was quickly deepening, the leaders of the G-20 group of industrialized and developing nations met in London to take urgent steps to prevent a further downward spiral of the world economy and avert a new Great Depression. Among the measures on which they agreed at the conclusion of their meeting was to call on the International Accounting Standards Board, IASB, "to improve standards on valuation and provisioning and achieve a single set of high-quality global accounting standards" to bring greater stability to global financial markets and thus lay the foundation for the resumption of economic growth around the world.[1] Why were these seemingly technical rules for calculating assets, liabilities, and profits of firms attracting the attention of world leaders? And why were they calling on a small private-sector regulatory organization rather than finance ministers or government regulators to take the lead in improving these rules?

The G-20 leaders understood that accounting, or "financial reporting," standards were crucial to the efficient operation of global financial markets. At the height of the crisis, financial markets had frozen and the values of complex financial products plunged, sometimes regardless of the credit quality of the underlying assets. The leaders turned to the IASB because it had established itself as the focal organization for such rule-making, offering the only viable mechanism to enhance market efficiency through a common set of international standards in the near future.

The issue remained on the agenda of international high politics. Five months later, at their Pittsburgh Summit, the G-20 leaders admonished

---

[1] Final communiqués signed by the leaders of the world's largest economies: G20, "The Global Plan for Recovery and Reform" (2009) and "Declaration on Strengthening the Financial System" (2009).

the private rule-makers "to redouble their efforts to complete global convergence in accounting standards by June 2011."[2]

The international harmonization of financial reporting rules is, however, anything but a harmonious process of determining objectively optimal solutions to technical problems. Consider the heated debate about "fair value" accounting. Also known as "mark to market," it refers to the practice of valuing assets at current prices. Supporters of "fair value" accounting argue that it provides the most transparent view of a firm's account and best serves investors. Opponents vehemently disagree. "Mark to market," they claim, weakens financial and economic stability. When markets freeze and prices plunge, lenders demand more collateral against their loans, forcing heavily leveraged firms to sell assets which pushes prices down further and thereby deepens a crisis. These critics favor a different approach: amortized cost. Here, valuation is based not on current market prices but expected cash flow. Such valuation is less volatile as it provides a view of an asset's worth over a longer period of time. Those opposed to amortized costs, however, call it a method of financial obfuscation; it offers no transparency and thus fails investors.

In this standards controversy, as in many others, a "middle way" does not exist. Cars drive either on the right side of the road or the left. But who prevails in such controversies and why? In this chapter and the next, we examine this question in the critically important area of global accounting.

We begin with an overview of the historical evolution of accounting governance up to the creation of the IASB in 2001. This is followed by a description of the institutional structure of the IASB and the international standard-setting process. The next section offers a detailed examination of the striking domestic institutional differences between the American system of standardization in accounting and the European system. In the final section, we analyze the implications of these differences in terms of institutional complementarities and discuss testable implications.

A Brief History of Accounting Governance

Accounting, defined as the recording and summarizing of commercial transactions, is an ancient practice. Much of our knowledge about bygone people and civilizations in fact comes from the records they kept of inventories, sales, lending, and hiring. The methods of accounting varied across

[2] G-20, *Leaders Statement* (2009).

cultures and improved over time. They included simple tokens, such as Sumerian clay balls of various shapes dating as far back as the fifth millennium BC;[3] Babylonian clay tablets;[4] Peruvian *quipus,* or knotted strings;[5] Grecian *abax,* or sand trays; Roman stone tablets; and Egyptian bead-and-wire abacus.[6]

A milestone in the development of modern accounting methods was the publication in 1494 of a treatise entitled *Summa de Arithmetica, Geometrica, Proportioni et Proportionalita* by Luca Pacioli, a Franciscan monk and teacher of mathematics.[7] The book contained a detailed description of the mechanics of double-entry bookkeeping as developed in the fourteenth century by the merchants of Genoa and Venice—key port cities for the profitable trade between Europe and the Near East.[8] John Edwards explains that its "specific advantages . . . were the greater care and correctness it demanded from clerical staff; the increased difficulty of falsifying the books to conceal fraud or theft, particularly where duties were divided among a number of personnel; and the arithmetic check provided by periodically balancing the books and extracting a trial balance."[9] Unsurprisingly, the treatise found an avid readership in commercial circles throughout Europe and remained popular as a reference book for more than four hundred years. It laid the foundation of a system of accounting that, remarkably, "remains intact to this time."[10]

Major developments in the world of accounting occurred in the wake of the industrial revolution. New sources of power, in particular steam power based on coal, gas, and then electricity, combined with new technologies, such as the Bessemer steel making process and the Siemens open hearth process, to give rise to vast business ventures requiring unprecedented amounts of capital. To meet these needs, the large-scale limited-liability (joint stock) company was developed to enable entrepreneurs to

[3] Mattessich, *The Beginning of Accounting and Accounting Thought* (2000), 3.

[4] Keister, "The Mechanics of Mesopotamian Record-keeping" (1965).

[5] Locke, *The Ancient Quipu: A Peruvian Knot Record* (1923), 325.

[6] Smith, *History of Mathematics* (1958), 160.

[7] Translated as *Review of Arithmetic, Geometry, Ration, and Proportion.*

[8] See also Mills, "Early Accounting in Northern Italy: The Role of Commercial Development and the Printing Press in the Expansion of Double-Entry from Genoa, Florence and Venice" (1994), and Green, "Brief Resume of the Life of Luca Pacioli and His Book Entitled 'Summa de Arithmetica, Geometria, Proportioni et Proportionalita'" (1930). Double-entry bookkeeping introduced debit and credit entries for each transaction.

[9] Edwards, *A History of Financial Accounting* (1989), 11.

[10] Buckley and Buckley, *The Accounting Profession* (1974), 3; Lee et al., eds., *Accounting History from the Renaissance to the Present* (1996).

raise capital from a substantial number of investors.[11] This form of business organization separated management from ownership by 'absentee' shareholders. The principal function of accounting now became to "fill gaps in knowledge which occur[red] . . . as [a] result of physically separating managers from the shopfloor and shareholders from the company in which they ha[d] invested."[12] In sum, accounting began to change in the wake of the industrial revolution away from bookkeeping for internal purpose to financial reporting for persons outside the firm. This usually took the form of a balance sheet summarizing the firm's assets and liabilities, an income statement reporting the firm's gross proceeds, expenses, as well as profits and losses.

The rise of the joint stock company led to a rapid increase in demand for financial reporting and audit expertise, which in turn led to the emergence of the accountancy profession.[13] William Deloitte founded an accounting services firm in London in 1845, followed by William Cooper in 1854, William Peat in 1867, and Edwin Waterhouse and Samuel Price in 1865. By the 1840s, there were 107 accountants in London; ten years later, the number had risen to 264. In 1860, it stood at 310, and in 1870 at 467.[14] A similar trend could be detected in the United States and continental Europe toward the end of the nineteenth century.[15]

Accountants soon formed their own professional organizations. The Society of Accountants was established in England in 1873, morphing in 1880 into the Institute of Chartered Accountants in England and Wales. The American Association of Public Accountants was incorporated under New York state law in 1887.[16] On the European continent, accountants began to establish professional organizations around the turn of the century.[17] Over time, these organizations evolved quite differently in

---

[11] Limited liability of shareholders means that shareholders only lose what they subscribe to in shares should the firm become insolvent. This reduces the risk for potential shareholders, thereby increasing the number of willing investors as well as the sums invested. See Hunt, *The Development of the Business Corporation in England 1800–1867* (1936); Cooke, *Corporation, Trust, and Company* (1950); and Conard, *Corporations in Perspective* (1976).

[12] Edwards, *A History of Financial Accounting* (1989), 91.

[13] The appointment of the professional accountant as independent auditor dates in England from the 1840s; see Edwards, *A History of Financial Accounting* (1989), 265; see also Power, *The Audit Society* (1997), 17.

[14] Brown, *A History of Accounting and Accountants* (1905), 234.

[15] Brown (1905).

[16] Brown (1905), 232–52 and 271–80.

[17] An early exception is Italy where Colleges and Gilds of Accountants were formed in most provinces shortly after the 1879 National Congress of Accountants. See Brown (1905), 281–301.

different countries, as discussed below, but they served similar purposes: to educate the next generation of accountants and certify their qualifications through examinations, disseminate information about the purpose and use of accounting throughout society, and generally promote the interests of the profession.[18] During the first half of the twentieth century, the professional organizations came to assume another key function within their respective countries: they began to identify and encourage the adoption of best accounting practices and sought to advance accounting *standards* by narrowing the difference and variety in those practices to achieve greater comparability of accounts.

Standardization of financial reporting practices at the *national* level made sense in an era where the overwhelming number of business transactions occurred within the boundaries of each country. The integration of financial markets at the international level in recent decades, however, has led to a rapid increase in foreign stock ownership and even listings of a company's shares on several countries' stock exchanges, as illustrated by the information from the two main American exchanges and the German stock exchange in table 4.1.[19]

The international integration of financial markets thus raised the problem of multiple and conflicting financial reporting standards. Infamously, when the German Daimler-Benz Corporation sought a listing on the New York Stock exchange and hence had to publish its accounts under two different systems, it reported for 1993 a profit of $373 million under German accounting rules but a loss in excess of $1.1 billion under U.S. GAAP.[20] And a 2002 Forbes study showed at least twenty-six different accounting standards in use among what it considered the 500 top international (non-U.S.) companies.[21] This lack of international harmonization came at a cost: when a major international corporation such as Daimler reported, for the same year, large profits under one set of accounting standards but large losses under another, it raised doubts for

---

[18] These interests were broadly defined to include the "improve[ment of] social status and financial rewards by achieving control over the supply of a particular service within the market for skilled labour." Edwards, *A History of Financial Accounting* (1989), 276; see also West, "The Professionalisation of Accounting" (2000).

[19] Karolyi, "Why Do Companies List Shares Abroad?" (1998), 9. See also Sarkissian and Schill, "The Overseas Listing Decision" (2004); Baker et al., "International Cross-Listing and Visibility" (2002); and Pagano et al., "The Geography of Equity Listing" (2002).

[20] Radebaugh et al., "Foreign Exchange Listings" (1995). The authors report the amounts in German Marks (profit of DM615 million versus losses of more than DM1.8 billion); the exchange rate stood at about 1.65 DM/US$ in 1993.

[21] See also Maiello, "Tower of Babel" (2002).

TABLE 4.1

Foreign Listings on U.S. and German Stock Exchanges

	New York Stock Exchange	Nasdaq	Frankfurter Börse+
1986	59	244	181
1987	67	272	409
1988	76	271	474
1989	86	267	535
1990	95	256	555
1991	104	254	578
1992	120	261	594
1993	158	301	633
1994	216	309	801
1995	246	395	944
1996	304	389	1,290
1997	355	454	1,996
1998	392	441	2,784
1999	405	429	3,847
2000	433	488	4,789

Note: Source: *Deutsches Aktieninstitut Factbook 2009*, Table 02-4, supplemented for German listings by information from *Deutsche Börse Factbook* for 1999, 2000. Germany figures are for all German exchanges, including the unregulated "Freiverkehr," which accounted for more than 90% of the increase in foreign share listings.

investors about both results, increasing the cost of capital for everyone as investors demand higher risk premiums. It also threatened to undermine trust in both sets of standards and in financial markets more broadly.

Companies operating in overseas markets stood to gain large savings from reduced transactions costs if they could advance a single set of accounts accepted by all exchanges. First, the work of corporate accountants who prepared and consolidated financial statements would be much simplified if statements from multiple markets were prepared on the basis of a single set of international standards. Second, the evaluation of foreign companies for potential takeovers would be facilitated. Third, greater comparability and reliability in accounting would bring down the cost of raising capital by reducing the risk to investors.[22] In addition, for multinational corporations, the task of preparing comparable internal information for the appraisal of performance of subsidiaries in different countries would be made easier.[23] For all of these reasons, the pressure from internationally oriented firms and multinationals for transnational harmonization of accounting rules became acute.

An early attempt at harmonizing financial reporting rules occurred in Europe as part of the EU's project to achieve a common market.[24] The Fourth Directive of 1978 established acceptable formats for financial statements for all public and private limited liability companies operating in the EU.[25] It also set out minimum disclosure and auditing requirements and enjoined particular accounting and auditing principles on preparers and examiners of financial statements.[26] The next major directive dealing with accounting issues, the so-called Seventh Directive of 1983, produced standards governing the preparation of consolidated statements for business

---

[22] Nobes and Parker, *Comparative International Accounting* (2004), 78.

[23] Recent research in fact suggests that these theoretical expectations are borne out by real benefits from international accounting standards harmonization. Barth et al. for instance find evidence of more accurate and comparable reporting of earnings (less "earnings management") and more timely disclosure of losses after firms adopt IFRS, though it may be too early for drawing firm conclusions on that issue. Barth et al., "International Accounting Standards and Accounting Quality" (2007), and Brüggemann et al., "How Do Individual Investors React to Global IFRS Adoption?" (2009) report information suggesting that not only institutional but also individual investors consider IFRS-based accounts more easily comparable; and Rezaee et al., "Convergence in Accounting Standards" (2010), 148, find that both academics and practitioners see IFRS as improving internal reporting and oversight within multinational corporations.

[24] See Jupille et al., *International Institutional Choice for Global Commerce* (2008); Thorell and Whittington, "The Harmonization of Accounting Within the European Union" (1994).

[25] A directive is a form of legislation in the European Union, which obliges member states to achieve the specified results but leaves it to each member state to pass what it considers the requisite implementing legislation or regulatory measures; only the domestic measures, not the directives themselves, create rights and obligations for citizens or legal persons such as firms. Banks and insurance companies were excluded from the provisions of the Fourth and Seventh Directives. However, the Directive of 8 December 1986 extended the scope to banks and other financial institutions.

[26] These principles include what in accounting lingo are called historical cost, going concern, prudence, accrual accounting, and consistency.

groups.[27] Prior to the Seventh Directive, many EU countries had few if any rules requiring consolidated accounts or governing their preparation. For example, as late as 1983 only about 75 percent of French listed companies published consolidated statements, and they were not legally bound to do so until 1986. Consolidated statements were still rare in the early 1980s in countries such as Italy, Spain, Greece, and Luxembourg.[28] It took more than a decade to negotiate just these two directives. Widely varying practices among EU member states made negotiations difficult, and conflicts ensued over issues such as which forms of business should be covered by the directive's provisions.[29]

Agreement on European harmonization in the Fourth and Seventh Directives was eventually made possible by problematic compromises. First, the directives have many options and exemptions.[30] Second, the directives concern themselves with broad issues rather than detailed guidance, which has the advantage of making the standards politically palatable but the drawback of leaving great latitude to national legislatures when implementing the directives—latitude that compromised cross-country comparability of financial statements.[31]

Important issues remained untouched by the directives, including leases, pensions, taxation, and currency transactions. This experience led many experts to question whether directives, which involve years of difficult political negotiations among governmental officials, were the proper regulatory mechanism for harmonizing accounting standards.[32] Critics of the European approach also noted that the scale of the problem was

---

[27] The Seventh Directive requires consolidation where either the parent or a subsidiary company is a limited liability company, regardless of the location of its registered office. The principle of legal power of control determines the consolidation obligation. The Fourth and Seventh Directives are the main legal acts dealing with financial reporting among the set of EU company law directives.

[28] Nobes and Parker, *Comparative International Accounting* (2004), 374.

[29] Haskins et al., *International Reporting and Analysis* (2000), 58f.

[30] For example, in the area of valuation, member states were relatively free to choose whatever form of valuation they most preferred; or they could decide to write different reporting requirements for small- and medium-size firms.

[31] Except for consolidated accounts, now governed by IFRS throughout the EU, neither asset valuation, nor formats, nor disclosure have been completely standardized due to diverging implementation legislation in the EU member states. See Nobes and Parker, *Comparative International Accounting* (2004), 99; Emenyou and Gray, "EC Accounting Harmonization" (1992); and Walton, "Harmonization of Accounting in France and Britain" (1992).

[32] See Van Hulle, "Harmonization of Accounting Standards in the EC" (1993); Hopwood, "Some Reflections on 'The Harmonization of Accounting Within the EU'" (1994); Hegarty, "Accounting Integration in Europe" (1993); and Wilson, "Harmonisation" (1994). In 1990, the EU established a forum of European standard-setters to discuss accounting issues not

global. Regional harmonization would inevitably lead to interregional incompatibilities in financial reporting and undermine progress in global harmonization by diverting resources from the global to the regional level. Global challenges, they argued, needed global solutions.

This point was underlined—in dramatic fashion—by the Asian financial crisis of 1997–98. It laid bare not only major deficiencies in national accounting systems and their enforcement mechanisms but also highlighted the problematic lack of transparency and comparability of financial accounts due to the absence of global standards. Governments around the world came to realize that a solid international accounting regime was much needed to ensure the stability and efficient functioning of international capital markets and enhance the protection of investors. The Asian financial debacle firmly put the arcane matter of accounting standards on the agenda of the Group of Seven (G-7) leading industrial nations.[33] A common accounting language would benefit not only firms by reducing the cost of raising capital and enhancing market stability but also investors and shareholders by improving the transparency and comparability of financial statements. But who would provide international accounting standards of high technical quality?

The call was answered by the International Accounting Standards Committee (IASC)—a London-based private-sector organization that had emerged in the late 1980s as the focal point for financial reporting standard-setting at the global level.[34] Founded in June 1973 by sixteen accountancy bodies from nine countries (US, United Kingdom, Canada, Australia, Netherlands, Germany, France, Japan, and Mexico), its stated mission was to "formulate and publish in the public interest . . . standards to be observed in the presentation of audited accounts and financial statements, . . . promote their worldwide acceptance and observance," and work generally for the improvement and harmonization of procedures, standards, and regulations relating to the presentation of financial statements.[35]

---

covered by the two directives, such as lease accounting and foreign currency translation. However, little progress was made and the forum closed down in 2001.

[33] Martinez-Diaz, "Private Expertise and Global Economic Governance" (2001), 60. See also G-7, *Final Report to the G-7 Heads of State and Government on Promoting Financial Stability* (1997); G-7, *Strengthening the Architecture of the Global Financial System* (1998); Walter, *Governing Finance* (2008).

[34] See Camfferman and Zeff, *Financial Reporting and Global Capital Markets* (2007); Jupille et al., *International Institutional Choice for Global Commerce* (2008).

[35] See *Text of the 1973 Agreement and Constitution* in Camfferman and Zeff (2007), 500–503 (Appendix 1). The IASC replaced the Accountants International Study Group, a forum

The IASC lived a relatively quiet existence during its first two decades, incrementally broadening its membership and expanding its institutional remit.[36] In 1982, the IASC entered into an agreement with the International Federation of Accountants (IFAC) under which IFAC recognized the IASC as the sole official source of international accounting standards and promised to promote the use of international standards in all IFAC member countries.[37] In return, the IASC recognized the IFAC as the authorized representative of the accounting profession worldwide, accepted all members of the IFAC as members of the IASC, and gave the IFAC authority to nominate candidates for membership on the governing Board of the IASC.

In the early years, the IASC strove to produce a small number of basic international accounting standards (IAS) and get them accepted—a difficult task given its lack of enforcement power.[38] The typical IAS contained considerable flexibility, prescribing a particular accounting method but allowing alternative treatments provided they were adequately disclosed and their effects noted.[39] The 1990s, however, saw the IASC shift focus toward improving international standards—eliminating options, filling

---

created in 1966 by British, Canadian, and American accountancy bodies to discuss harmonization issues in accounting. According to Anthony Hopwood, a leading figure in the European accountancy scene: "A key impetus for the establishment of the IASC was given by the impending entry of the United Kingdom into the European Economic Community. The imminence of this had brought fear to the British accounting bodies who were worried by the potential consequences of what they saw as the imposition of continental European statutory and state control on the much more discretionary relationship between corporate management and the auditor in the United Kingdom. The British bodies mobilized an active and quite extensive political campaign . . . [and] the IASC was established." Hopwood, "Some Reflections on 'The Harmonization of Accounting Within the EU'" (1994), 243. See also Benson, "The Story of International Accounting Standards" (1976); Nobes and Parker, *Comparative International Accounting* (2004), 81; and especially Camfferman and Zeff (2007).

[36] See Cairns, ed. *The IASC* (1999); and Camfferman and Zeff, *Financial Reporting and Global Capital Markets* (2007).

[37] The IFAC was formed in 1977 and comprises today some 140 professional organizations from over 100 countries. It promulgates guidelines for the accounting profession in the areas of auditing, ethics, management accounting, and professional education. IFAC is headquartered in New York. Its roster of member organizations reveals important cross-national differences in the organization of the accounting profession: for the United States, with the largest number of accountants by far, there is a single member organization; for Germany and France, there are two IFAC member bodies each; for the United Kingdom, there are five.

[38] IASC's first standard was approved in 1974. By 1991 it had adopted 31 standards.

[39] Choi and Mueller, *International Accounting* (1992), 29.

gaps, and narrowing differences between IAS and national requirements. These improvements were in part motivated by a desire to render the standards more acceptable to capital market regulators and achieve public recognition.[40]

The strategy worked, and the IASC was rewarded with public endorsements by key governmental organizations. The first came in 1995 when the International Organization of Securities Commissions (IOSCO)—an organization of governmental financial market supervisory institutions from 105 countries, regulating 90 percent of the world's financial securities markets—reached an agreement with the IASC, committing stock market regulators to accept a set of "core standards" to be completed by the IASC.[41] The member states of the WTO, which had started to take an interest in the issue because of its effect on "trade in services," backed this endorsement at the conclusion of the Singapore Ministerial Meeting of 1996. In their statement, they "encourage[d] the successful completion of international accounting standards . . . by the International Federation of Accountancy (IFAC) . . . [and] the International Accounting Standards Committee."[42] Joel Trachtman has argued that this statement signaled the WTO's willingness to delegate regulatory authority (at least in political as opposed to legal terms) to the IASC.

> The WTO [thus] has . . . "delegated" to specific functional organizations the task of establishing standards to facilitate the free movement of accountancy services. This particular delegation is not inconsistent with prior practice in other particular areas, such as food safety standards (Codex Alimentarius Commission) and general product standards (International Organization for Standardization). . . . We begin to see some evidence of a common institutional

---

[40] Cairns, ed. *The IASC* (1999), 6; Camfferman and Zeff, *Financial Reporting and Global Capital Markets* (2007), 253ff. When the IASB was founded, it retained the International Accounting Standards (IAS) developed by the IASC but has revised most of them. For new issues, it has developed IFRS. We generally subsume current (that is revised) IAS whenever we speak of IFRS in this book.

[41] See IOSCO, *Annual Report* (1995), 13. Under the agreement, IOSCO was allowed to monitor the IASC standard-setting process as a nonvoting observer at steering committee and board meetings. This agreement built on informal support from IOSCO for the IASC going back to 1987/88, see Cairns, *International Accounting Standards Survey* (2001), 26–34. In 2000, IOSCO endorsed 30 extant international accounting standards and generally recommended the use of IAS for cross-border offerings and listings.

[42] WTO, "Singapore Ministerial Declaration" (1996). The IFAC writes auditing standards only.

solution . . . utilizing informal "delegation" to specialized functional international organizations.[43]

In 1998, the G-7 finance ministers and central bank governors followed suit, issuing a declaration endorsing the work of the IASC and calling on the committee to "finalize by early 1999 a proposal for a full range of internationally agreed accounting standards."[44] Together with explicit support by the World Bank, IMF, and the Basle Committee on Banking Supervision (BCBS), these statements provided the IASC with a firm mandate to produce global financial reporting rules.[45] As a result, the number of countries permitting foreign companies to prepare their consolidated financial statements using IAS started to grow in the late 1990s.

Under the IASC structure and decision-making, however, those who opposed the elimination of particular options or alternative accounting treatments for the benefit of greater uniformity of rules could resort to institutional blockage. Timely completion of a full set of global accounting rules necessitated institutional reform. In 1999, the IASC Board of Trustees therefore agreed to replace the IASC with a new organization, the International Accounting Standards Board (IASB)—described below.[46]

The IASB began operations in April 2001. Since then, two events, in particular, have enhanced its status as an international financial regulator. First, the EU passed legislation in 2002 requiring all firms listed on a stock exchange in the EU to use IFRS for their consolidated accounts, causing more than seven thousand businesses to switch accounting rules by January 2005.[47] This "unprecedented privatization" of the authority to

---

[43] Trachtman, "Addressing Regulatory Divergence Through International Standards" (2003), 30f.

[44] See also G-7, *Final Report to the G-7 Heads of State and Government on Promoting Financial Stability* (1997); and G-7, *Strengthening the Architecture of the Global Financial System* (1998).

[45] See G-7, *Declaration of G-7 Finance Ministers and Central Bank Governors* (1998); IMF, *Report of the Management Director on Strengthening the Architecture of the International Financial System* (1999); International Bank for Reconstruction and Development, *Financial Accounting, Reporting and Auditing Handbook* (1995); Wolfensohn, "Accounting and Society" (1997); Basel Committee on Banking Supervision, *Report to G-7 Finance Ministers and Central Bank Governors on International Accounting Standards* (2000); and Financial Stability Forum, *Issues Paper of the Task Force on Implementation of Standards* (2000). The World Bank now includes international accounting standards as a condition of its loan agreements.

[46] For a political history of the IASC restructuring process, see Jupille et al., *International Institutional Choice for Global Commerce* (2008), chap. 3; and Camfferman and Zeff, *Financial Reporting and Global Capital Markets* (2007), 447–99.

[47] European Communities, "Regulation (EC) No. 1606/2002" (2002), esp. Art. 3.

set mandatory standards was largely driven by purely European policy objectives.[48] The EU Commission, having failed to bring about effective harmonization of accounting rules and practices across Europe via the Fourth and Seventh Directives, reckoned that requiring listed companies to comply with international standards would now be the quickest and most effective way to achieve harmonization in financial reporting. Such harmonization, in turn, was seen as an essential stepping stone toward the creation of a truly single financial market in Europe.

The European decision to follow IFRS prompted major countries such as China, Japan, Brazil, India, Canada, and South Korea to set out timetables to adopt or converge with IFRS. By 2008, more than one hundred countries were using IFRS or had committed to start using them soon. These developments prompted the U.S. financial regulator, the Securities and Exchange Commission (SEC) to start deliberations on a timetable for switching from U.S. Generally Accepted Accounting Principles (GAAP)—long viewed by many as the gold standard in accounting—to IFRS. The SEC's "Roadmap to IFRS adoption" of November 2008, discussed in the introduction, envisioned intensified monitoring of the progress toward convergence between IFRS and U.S. GAAP, leading to a review and confirmation in 2011. The Roadmap was followed in February 2010 by the SEC "Work Plan" which reaffirms 2011 for committing to a specific timetable for mandatory adoption by 2015 or 2016 of IFRS for all companies whose shares are listed and publicly traded on a U.S. stock exchange.[49] As the United States switches to IFRS, even more countries are likely to follow. These countries will have a strong incentive to adopt IFRS because compliance with such standards will give them easy access to the large U.S. capital market.

Endorsements by key players, such as the EU and the United States, have increased not only the salience of IASB but also the pace and breadth of standards production. Until 2005, the IASB was largely focused on revising standards inherited from the IASC. Since then, it has moved to producing a rapidly growing number of new standards on a wide range of topics. These topics include business combinations, segment reporting, joint

---

[48] Chiapello and Medjad. "An Unprecedented Privatisation of Mandatory Standard-Setting" (2009).

[49] The Roadmap is published in the Federal Register as "proposed rule" # 33-8982/34-58960, File # S7-27-08 of Nov. 14, 2008. For the Work Plan, see SEC, Office of the Chief Accountant, *Work Plan* (2010). See also SEC, "Commission Statement in Support of Convergence and Global Accounting Standards" (2010).

ventures, intangible assets, leases, revenue recognition, consolidations, impairment, credit risk in liability measurement, fair value measurement guidance, hedging, emission trading schemes, insurance contracts, and financial reporting for small and medium enterprises.

INSTITUTIONAL STRUCTURE AND THE STANDARDIZATION PROCESS

The institutional pillars of the new global accounting regime are the Board (IASB), the Interpretations Committee (formerly called the International Financial Reporting Interpretations Committee, IFRIC), the Advisory Council (formerly known as the Standards Advisory Council, SAC), and the Trustees of the IFRS Foundation (formerly called the International Accounting Standards Committee Foundation, IASCF).[50]

The central body, the Board, currently counts fifteen members; it is set to increase to sixteen members by 2012. The Board is charged with leading the development and deciding about the final adoption of the international financial reporting rules, IFRS. The members "comprise a group of people representing . . . the best available combination of technical skills and diversity of international business and market experience in order to contribute to the development of high quality, global financial reporting standards."[51] By custom, at least five members have a background as practicing auditors, three as preparers of financial statements (i.e., representatives of firms), and another three as users of financial statements (i.e., investors and financial analysts); one Board member traditionally hails from academia. In appointing Board members, the Trustees also

---

[50] The changes in the names of the key bodies were the result of the 2008–10 "Constitutional Review" of the IASCF, now IFRS Foundation. The changes were approved by the Trustees on 26 January 2010 and became effective 1 March 2010. The review also created a new body, the Monitoring Board, to "provide a formal link between the Trustees and public authorities." The Monitoring Board consists of one representative each of the SEC, the EU, and the Japan Financial Services Agency, two representatives of IOSCO—and the chair of the Basel Committee as an observer. It has the power to request meetings with the Trustees and "participate" in their appointment but has no authority directly vis-à-vis the IASB. The effect of this new body on the politics of international standard-setting remains to be seen, but our analysis below leads us to expect that the change is mostly cosmetic (see also Richardson and Eberlein, "Legitimating International Standard-Setting" (2010)). The Foundation is a not-for-profit corporation registered in Delaware.

[51] IFRS Foundation, "Constitution" (2010), 11f, paragraph 25. Up to three board members may be part-timers; all others must be full-time members.

aim for geographic diversity.[52] Each Board member has one vote, and a majority of 9 out of 15 (or 10 of 16) votes is required for the adoption of a standard.

The IASB is supported in its work by the Interpretations Committee. This committee issues authoritative interpretations on financial reporting matters where conflicting interpretations and practices have developed in countries using IFRS. Fourteen voting members serve on the Interpretations Committee, but their decisions are subject to IASB approval—after which they have the same authority as standards issued by the Board.[53] The Board also consults the IFRS Advisory Council, a forum that meets three times a year and comprises about fifty representatives from a wide range of groups, including preparers, auditors, investors, and financial analysts.[54]

Providing general oversight of the IASB are the twenty-two Trustees of the IFRS Foundation.[55] The Trustees monitor IASB's effectiveness and have the power to change the rules governing the international rule-making structure. They also appoint the members of the IASB, and the advisory bodies. The trustees discharge another key role, namely fundraising for the IASB. In its first year of operation, the IASCF received in voluntary contributions about $11 million from 125 companies, $5 million from the 'Big Five' accounting firms, and between $1 million and $2 million from central banks and bodies such as development banks.[56] By 2009,

[52] Starting in 2012, there are to be at least 4 members from Asia/Oceania, 4 members from Europe, 4 members from North America, 1 member from Africa, and 1 member from South America.

[53] The members of IFRIC are appointed by the Trustees for once-renewable terms of three years.

[54] SAC members serve (renewable) terms of three years.

[55] The appointment of the trustees is organized as follows: the Trustees nominate candidates upon consultations with international organizations of auditors, preparers, users, and academics (with an especially prominent role for the International Federation of Accountants). Six trustees must be selected from the Asia/Oceania region, six from Europe, six from North America, one from Africa, one from South America, and another two from any region. These nominations are subject to the approval of the Monitoring Board, whose members may, however, only object on the basis of an individual nominee's expertise or the group's overall balance of "professional backgrounds." (IFRS Foundation, "Constitution" (2010), 6f).

[56] In theory, IASB's independence is ensured by the separation of the Board from the fundraising by the trustees. However, such separation may in practice fail to fully shield standard-setters from business pressure. Indeed, the chairman of IASB, David Tweedie, complained only one year after the IASB was launched that powerful donors were threatening to withdraw their financial support and "perhaps [even] destroy the organization" if the Board failed to show greater sensitivity to their policy preferences; see Hill and Parker, "Standard-Setters Are Targeting Stock Options Again" (2002). See also Mattli and Büthe,

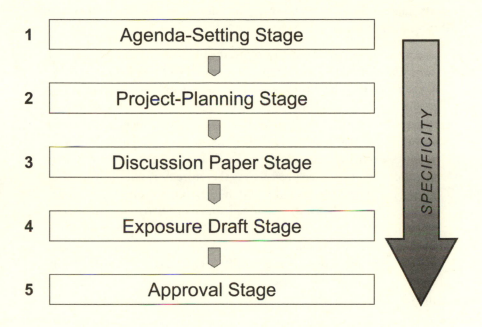

Figure 4.1   Stages of the IASB Standardization Process

the IASB was still largely funded by the private sector, and its budget had grown to some $30 (£18.4) million—80 percent covered by the funds raised by the trustees and 20 percent through the sale of standards and related documents.[57]

Last but not least, the new global accounting regime depends critically on the technical, logistical, and financial support of the standard-setting bodies at the domestic level. Domestic standard-setting bodies play a particularly important role early during the IASB standardization process, which has five main stages (see figure 4.1): the proposal or agenda-setting stage, the project-planning stage, the discussion paper stage, the exposure

---

"Global Private Governance" (2005); Büthe, "Technical Standards as Public and Club Goods" (2009).

[57] See IASCF, *Who We Are and What We Do* (2009); Büthe, "Technical Standards as Public and Club Goods" (2009). An increasing amount of funds is of late coming from mandatory fees imposed on listed and/or private companies by exchanges, business associations, and national authorities.

draft stage, and the approval stage. We summarize the key developments during each of the stages.[58]

1. During the agenda-setting stage, the IASB discusses proposals for new international financial reporting standards (or revisions to existing standards). These proposals may come from national standard-setting bodies, members of the Board, IASB staff, or occasionally other interested parties. The IASB staff screens all such requests and identifies the key issues raised. The Board may decide that an item requires extensive preliminary research that exceeds the IASB staff resources and time. Such research is therefore normally delegated to a national standard-setting body under the supervision of, or in collaboration with, the IASB. A simple majority of Board members then is required to add an item to the IASB's agenda. In making this decision, the members of the Board are supposed to take into account, above all, whether developing an IFRS to address the issue raised by some stakeholders will "meet the . . . needs of users across different jurisdictions," as communicated by national standards bodies.[59]

2. During the project-planning stage, the Board first has to decide whether to conduct the project alone or jointly with a national standard-setter. A working group or project team from the technical and research staff of the IASB (and staff from the national body in the case of joint projects) then works out a timetable for developing the new standard, outlines the major elements or the standard, and makes specific recommendations, building on the earlier preliminary research.

3. The IASB then tends to publish a discussion paper, written by a research team at the IASB or a national accounting standard-setter in the case of joint projects.[60] The discussion paper offers a comprehensive overview of the proposed new standard and notes the major issues identified by the working group/project team responsible for drafting the particular standard. The IASB uses the discussion paper to explain its own position on the issues raised by the new standard and launches an initial notice-and-comment period, during which it solicits comments from national standard-setters, industry groups, the

---

[58] For details, see IASCF, *Due Process Handbook for the IASB* (2006), esp. 4–7.
[59] See IASCF (2006), 8.
[60] The third stage is not mandatory but the IASB must explain a decision to skip the discussion paper and the opportunities for stakeholder input that it provides.

IFRS Advisory Council, and others on what is effectively an interme-diate draft. During this stage, the IASB may also seek additional feed-back through field tests, public hearings, or round-table meetings.[61]

4. During the fourth stage, the IASB and its staff develop what is known as the "exposure" draft. An exposure draft sets out specific proposals. The members of the Board take the lead at this stage in that they decide the major issues raised by the discussion paper and by the comments received from stakeholders during the previous stage. IASB staff (some of whom are temporarily seconded to the IASB from national standards bodies) flesh out the details. The IASB then publishes the resulting document as an Exposure Draft and invites feedback, typically allowing 4 months (120 days) for com-ments.[62] This is the main notice-and-comment period of the IASB standard-setting process.

5. During the final stage, the IASB considers the issues that arise from comments received on the exposure draft and makes changes to the provisions of the standard that the Board members consider warranted.[63] The IASB is required to take specific decisions about controversial issues in public Board meetings; the staff then drafts the final IFRS. This document is put to a ballot of the members of the Board for their approval.[64] Upon approval as an IFRS, the new standard is published by the IASB.[65]

In sum, IASB standardization has two key characteristics. First, the essen-tial principles for each standard are selected early during the rule-making

---

[61] Field tests are conducted to assess the cost of new standards or changes to existing stan-dards. The tests require collaboration with interested firms. IASB staff closely works with these firms in preparing financial reports according to the new standard and evaluating the results of the tests. Field tests may also be organized after the publication of an exposure draft.

[62] An internal ballot precedes publication of the Exposure Draft. Approval of the staff-written draft by 9 of the 15 members of the board (10 of 16 after the 2012 increase) is required for publication.

[63] The IASB may decide to issue another Exposure Draft instead, thus repeating stage 4.

[64] Should the draft fail to get approved (by at least 9 out of 15 or 10 out of 16 affirmative votes), it is subject to further discussion or revisions by the IASB and its staff.

[65] Some suitable time after the new standard has become mandatory and has been imple-mented by users, the IASB usually consults with national standard-setters and other groups to assess whether further work on an IFRS is needed, for example, due to unintended con-sequences of the standard or changes in the financial reporting environment or regulatory requirements. The IASB calls this "stage 6" of the standard-setting process. These informal consultations may re-start the rule-making process (this time as a revision of an existing standard) in stage 1.

process. The exposure draft stage, when a detailed draft is widely circulated, is designed for marginal improvements rather than a reconsideration of the fundamental principles underpinning the draft. Second, while the global standard-setter has a small permanent staff, which allows for a limited pursuit of its organizational self-interest, the IASB—similar to ISO/IEC, as shown in chapter 6—critically depends for its operational viability and effectiveness on technical expertise and other resources voluntarily offered by national standard-setters.[66] The importance of national accounting standards organizations also is explicitly recognized in the IFRS Foundation Constitution and in the IASB *Due Process Handbook*, which states, "close coordination between the IASB . . . [and] accounting standard-setters [at the national level] is important to the success of the IASB." At its inception, the IASB established formal liaison relationships with standard-setters in Australia and New Zealand, Canada, France, Germany, Japan, United Kingdom, and the United States.[67] The number of liaisons grew over time and the IASB currently seeks relationships with "[national] accounting standard-setters throughout the world."[68] Not all national standard-setters are equal, however. The *Handbook* notes that "the extent and depth of liaison . . . depends on the organization involved."[69]

It therefore is of central importance, as suggested by our analytical framework, to investigate national organizational capabilities and structures and the manner in which national standard-setters interact with the IASB. This will enable us to assess differential abilities to influence the standardization process.

The remainder of this chapter turns to this task by first examining the institutional structures for standard-setting in accounting at the domestic level. We focus on the differences between the two main players in accounting—the United States and Europe—and discuss the implications of such differences for the ability of American and European stakeholders, respectively, to influence the content of the international financial reporting rules during the standard-setting process. This focus is warranted due

[66] Mattli and Büthe, "Global Private Governance" (2005).

[67] The Technical Expert Group of the European Financial Reporting Advisory Group (EFRAG) was given the same rights as those bodies formally designated as national liaison standard-setters. EFRAG is discussed in the next section.

[68] IASCF, *Due Process Handbook for the IASB* (2006), 20f.

[69] IASCF (2006), 21.

to the predominance of American and European interests in global accounting rule-making, which has changed little since the establishment of the IASB. As the share of the Asia-Pacific region in global GDP continues to grow—reaching an estimated 34 percent by 2014, up from 27 percent in 2004—the region's desire for greater involvement and representation will undoubtedly increase.[70] As Noriaki Shimazaki, a Japanese member of the Board of Trustees of the IASC Foundation, recently noted: "Japan has to work with nations in Asia and Oceania to form a third force to challenge Europe and the United States and raise its voice in accounting issues."[71] However, building a common front on accounting issues is likely to prove elusive given the enormous regional diversity in accounting traditions and structures as well as differences in economic development. So far, Asia largely remains an insignificant player, as evidenced, for example, by the fact that the overwhelming majority of comment letters, submitted during the due process of IASB rule-making, come from America and Europe.[72]

DOMESTIC INSTITUTIONAL VARIATION AND INSTITUTIONAL COMPLEMENTARITY

In accounting, the United States has a single, well-established, and uncontested private-sector standard-setting organization, which produces accounting rules for the large U.S. financial market. In its institutional structure and its uncontested status as the focal point for domestic standard-setting in the United States, this well-established body resembles the hierarchical ideal type of a domestic institution. The institutional structure in Europe, by contrast, is characterized by high levels of fragmentation and contestation at the national and regional levels.

[70] Bruce, "Asian-Oceanian Standards Setters Group Created" (2009).

[71] Noriaki Shimazaki, quoted in Finbarr Flynn and Takako Taniguchi, "Japan Urges to Form Third Force on Accounting Standards" (2010).

[72] The composition of the IASB Board similarly reflects continuing Western dominance. In 2001, the Board counted 14 members—11 hailed from the United States and Europe. Asia had only one representative—a Japanese national. The other two members were from Australia and South Africa. As of early 2010, the Board had 15 members of which 10 were from the United States and Europe. The remaining 5 came from Japan, Australia, South Africa, Brazil, and China.

The American System of Standardization in Accounting

In the United States, federal regulation of financial reporting began after the onset of the Great Depression and the Stock Market Crash of 1929, which was blamed in part on "deceptive and misleading financial reporting practices" and ended the deference to individual U.S. states to regulate financial markets.[73] In the Securities Act of 1933 and the Securities Exchange Act of 1934, Congress mandated "full and fair disclosure" in the flotation of financial securities and the filing of periodic financial statements by the issuers of publicly traded securities. The 1934 legislation also created the Securities and Exchange Commission (SEC), charged with specifying and enforcing all obligations arising from the two acts. In 1938, the SEC—a public agency—delegated regulatory authority in accounting to a private-sector standard-setting body established by the accounting profession: first the Committee on Accounting Procedure (1934–59), then the Accounting Principles Board (1959–72), and since 1973 the Financial Accounting Standards Board, commonly known by its acronym: FASB.[74] The members of the actual Board, who collectively set the standards, are appointed and paid by the trustees of the Financial Accounting Foundation (FAF), a private-sector body registered in Delaware as a not-for-profit corporation.[75] Most of the fourteen to eighteen FAF trustees come from the private sector; a few have always been former financial officers or elected officials of state or local governments (with accounting experience). Trustees serve for single five-year terms.[76]

FASB—the Board itself—has seven members, including a chairman with special agenda-setting powers. The chairman serves at the pleasure of the FAF Trustees; the other Board members serve staggered 5-year terms, renewable once, ensuring a high degree of continuity over time. Members of the Board are usually certified public accountants (CPAs) or experts from other relevant disciplines who "in [the] judgment of the Trustees,

---

[73] Ripley, *Main Street and Wall Street* (1927), 198.

[74] The history of this delegation of regulatory authority is covered in greater detail by Büthe, "The Dynamics of Principals and Agents" (2010); Miller et al., *The FASB* (1998), 55–58; and Van Riper, *Setting Standards for Financial Reporting* (1994), 3–11.

[75] The trustees of the FAF also oversee the Governmental Accounting Standards Board (GASB), which was created in 1984 to set standards of financial accounting and reporting for state and local governmental units.

[76] The chair of the Board of Trustees can be reelected to successive terms. See FAF, "By-Laws of the Financial Accounting Foundation" (2010), Chapter A, Article I-A, Section 3.

each have a concern for the investor and public interest in matters of financial accounting and reporting, and shall, collectively, have knowledge of and experience in investing, accounting, finance, business, accounting education and research."[77]

The primary and exclusive responsibility of the Board is "establishing and improving standards of financial accounting and reporting for nongovernmental entities by defining, issuing, and promoting such standards and by issuing other communications with regard to nongovernmental accounting and reporting."[78] The members of the Board are assisted in this task by FASB's research and technical staff, two permanent bodies, and at any given time various project-specific ad hoc committees—usually called task forces or advisory groups—which include numerous stakeholders.

One of the permanent bodies is the Financial Accounting Standards Advisory Council (FASAC). It is supposed to be broadly representative of groups interested in or affected by accounting standards, though representatives of publicly listed companies have long played a particularly prominent role in FASAC. The members of FASAC, appointed by the FAF Trustees, meet quarterly. As a group and individually, they are supposed to advise the Board on issues ranging from its overall agenda to specific technical details of draft standards.[79] The other permanent body, created in 1984, is the Emerging Issues Task Force (EITF). Its members are appointed by and serve at the pleasure of the FASB chairman, subject to the stipulation that EITF include representatives of accounting firms, preparers, and investor-users of financial reports. The remit of the ten to fifteen EITF members is to identify, discuss, and resolve "emerging issues affecting financial accounting and reporting . . . for nongovernmental entities"

---

[77] By-Laws of the Financial Accounting Foundation, Chapter A, Article II-A, section 2, as amended 26 February 2008, when the FAF also reduced the number of members of the FASB Board from seven to five; see FAF, "Trustees Approve Changes" (2008). For coverage of the controversial "downsizing" decision, see, e.g., Reader and Leone, "Downsizing FASB" (2007); Leone, "FASB Parent: Five Is More than Seven" (2008); Heffes, "FAF Proposed Changes" (2008); and Chasan, "Investor Group Says FASB's Independence has Eroded" (2009). In August 2010, the FAF Trustees reversed the change in the size of the Board.

[78] FASB, "Rules of Procedure" (2010), 6.

[79] When FASAC was first established in 1973, it was composed of 20 experts from the fields of finance, accounting, industry, education, banking, and law. Today, the IFRS Advisory Council usually has some 30 members, drawn from the ranks of CEOs, CFOs, senior partners of accounting firms, executive directors of professional organizations, and senior members of the academic and analyst communities, with representatives of "preparers," i.e., publicly listed companies, accounting for about half of the members. See FASB, "FASAC Members" (2010); Miller et al., The FASB (1998), 44–47.

with a view to "reducing diversity in practice."[80] When the identified issue is "narrow" and EITF members can achieve consensus on what they consider the appropriate accounting treatment, they issue a "guidance" document, which becomes an amendment to FASB accounting standards if approved by a simple majority of the Board.[81]

A central role in FASB is played by its full-time staff of some sixty research and technical experts, who are the envy of the IASB and other national accounting standard-setters.[82] Based at the FASB headquarters in Norwalk, Connecticut, FASB staff experts conduct background research, gather and analyze the input from various constituencies, prepare recommendations, and draft the various documents issued by the Board. Most of this work is specific to a particular project on FASB's technical agenda at any given point in time and may therefore be assigned to individual staff members or small teams coordinated by a project manager.

To develop standards (U.S. GAAP) and arrive at their positions on other matters—including topics on the international standardization agenda—FASB has put in place "due process" procedures that provide numerous opportunities for stakeholder input beyond direct participation in EITF, FASAC, and ad hoc task forces and advisory groups.[83] Stakeholder-input is often responsible for putting issues on FASB's agenda and may come in the form of a proposal from regular participants, such as members of EITF or FASAC, representatives of major private sector groups, such as the Chartered Financial Analysts (CFA) Institute or Financial Executives International (FEI), public agencies or political leaders, such as the SEC or members of Congress, or from individual stakeholders, including investors. When an issue is raised for possible rule-making by the FASB, members of the staff are usually asked to conduct preliminary examinations of the proposal.

---

[80] FASB, *Rules of Procedure* (2010), 13; *Emerging Issues Task Force Operating Procedures* (2005), 1. Representatives of the SEC and other "constituency" groups of the FASB, as well as FASB staff directors, also regularly attend EITF meetings as nonvoting observers.

[81] By custom, a "consensus" is deemed to exist when no more than two EITF members oppose the proposed "guidance."

[82] In addition to the research and technical staff, FASB has office assistants and other administrative and clerical staff, resulting in a total staff size of about ninety, not including staff working for the Financial Accounting Foundation or GASB (private communications with FASB Technical Director Russell Golden, 21 and 28 July 2010, and with Ron Lott, FASB Research Director, 28 July 2010).

[83] See also Mattli and Büthe, "Accountability in Accounting?" (2005), and Zeff, "'Political' Lobbying on Proposed Standards" (2002), which provide illustrative examples of the political use of the due process and other informal procedures.

Based on the initial staff assessment and consultations with the members of the Board, the chairman of the Board decides whether to add a corresponding "project" to FASB's technical agenda.[84] FASB staff then conducts more extensive background research. On major issues, FASB often invites outside experts from various stakeholder groups to serve with FASB employees on project-specific advisory groups or task forces.[85] Next, the Board discusses the key issues identified by the staff. These early deliberations are to take place, at least in part, in public meetings and may result—at the Board's discretion—in a published Discussion Paper. Based on further work of the staff and task forces and taking into account possible comments from other stakeholders, the Board then issues an Exposure Draft and invites comments on that draft, which may also be discussed at a FASB "public forum."[86] The project staff then analyzes comments received in writing, at public meetings, and through other avenues and prepares a recommendation or penultimate draft. Adoption of an accounting standard (update) or other significant document then requires a simple majority of the Board, that is, support from at least four of the seven members.

In sum, the domestic institutional structure in the United States closely resembles the prototype of a hierarchical system discussed in chapter 3

---

[84] Agenda-control prerogative for the chairman, which includes the power to change the priority level of each project, was part of the 2008 reforms. Previously, the Board admitted a proposal to the technical agenda by majority vote. FASB chairmen are nonetheless likely to continue the tradition of putting an issue on the agenda only when it has broad significance for financial reporting *and* there is a high probability that at least the required majority of the members of the Board will achieve a common position; see Miller et al, *The FASB* (1998), 69. All Board members retain the individual right to propose changes to the FASB agenda.

[85] Being a member of the Board is considered a full-time position, for which FASB pays salaries comparable to the salaries of senior financial executives in the private sector (and thus far more than the commissioners and the chief accountant of the SEC). To "provide at least the appearance of independence . . . and avoid an appearance of conflicts of interest" (Miller et al. 1998, 48), members of the Board and the regular full-time staff must sever their relationships with previous employers. All others participants in FASB rule-making, however, retain their relationships with their sponsoring companies or groups. Employers pay, for instance, for travel and related costs of the participants in task forces and advisory groups (including the EITF) and, via the FAF, pay the salary of employees who are temporarily (usually for two years) seconded to the FASB staff as FASB "Fellows." This financial arrangement contributes to the predominance of major corporations and the relative scarcity of representatives of investors and public agencies; see Mattli and Büthe, "Accountability in Accounting?" (2005).

[86] Some of the steps in FASB's "due process," such as announcements and formats for Public Forums are specified and discussed in great detail in FASB's *Rules of Procedure* (2010), 14f.

and illustrated in figure 4.2. A single, private rule-maker is essentially uncontested as the focal point for all standardization activities at the national level, and while FASB's decisions may be occasionally controversial, no other body is in a position to credibly claim to be representative of U.S. stakeholders. This puts FASB in a strong position to speak with a single voice on behalf of U.S. interests vis-à-vis the IASB, which has recognized FASB as the representative of U.S. interests, and its well-established linkages to domestic stakeholders put it in a strong position to know the preferences of those stakeholders.

The European System of Standardization in Accounting

In Europe we find contrasting styles and orientations of financial reporting practices, reflecting differences in legal systems, the relative importance of capital markets, and the role of government in capital and other markets. In the United Kingdom and the Netherlands, for example, where stock markets have long been the main source of capital, the needs of investors have been the main consideration in the development of accounting standards. In Germany and several other continental countries, the main purpose of statements of account has long been tax assessment and the protection of creditors. In these countries, the basis of accounting has traditionally been highly legalistic. Private shareholding has until quite recently been less widespread than in the United Kingdom and the Netherlands; individual investors traditionally have preferred bonds to equity. The key providers of capital to firms have thus been banks. These financial institutions are often represented on the boards of companies to which they lend. As such they are assumed to be privy to inside information; legal disclosure requirements are therefore less important for them than for British or Dutch holders of financial securities.[87]

Besides different purposes and traditions of accounting, Europe displays highly fragmented and frequently contested regulatory authority in

---

[87] German accountants, for example, seek to comply with strict legal rules and reduce the tax liability of a corporate client. British accountants heavily rely on judgment and do not let rigid rules get in the way of presenting a "true and fair view" of a company's financial statements: "The 'true and fair view' suggests a culturally conditioned distrust of rules—a skepticism of their efficacy unless they are subordinated to human judgment—and a belief in an abstract fairness that can never be completely codified" (Haskins et al., *International Reporting and Analysis* (2000), 53). See also Ordelheide, "True and Fair View" (1993); Alexander, "A European True and Fair View?" (1993); and Perry and Nölke, "The Political Economy of International Accounting Standards" (2006).

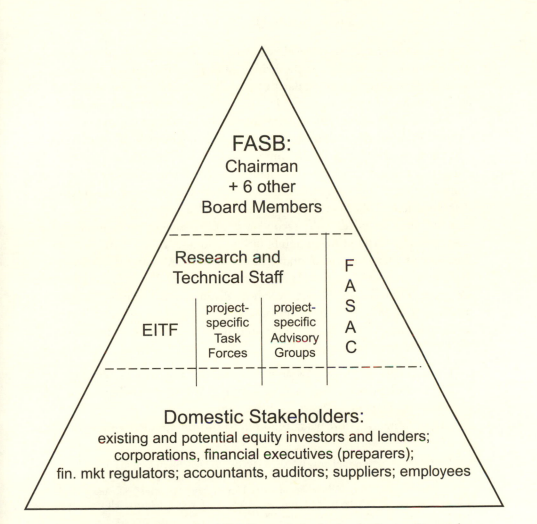

Figure 4.2 FASB: Hierarchical U.S. Domestic Institution for Setting Financial Reporting Standards

• • • • • •

EITF is the Emerging Issues Task Force, a permanent group of technical experts, mostly representing domestic stakeholders. FASAC is the Financial Accounting Standards Advisory Council, the other permanent body. All other advisory groups and task forces are formed on an ad hoc basis to work with the research and technical staff on specific projects as they arise.

accounting at the domestic level, *regardless* of accounting tradition. Particularly informative here is the British case, since the United Kingdom is in many respects most similar to the United States and may therefore appear to be the least likely case for significant institutional differences.

The United Kingdom has a capital market-based financial system where regulatory authority has long resided with the accounting profession, as in the United States. Unlike in the United States, however, legislators in Britain have until most recently not believed it necessary to have a public regulatory agency with jurisdiction over financial reporting.[88] Rule-making has been left in the hands of six professional accountancy bodies, including three founded in the second half of the nineteenth century: the Institute of Chartered Accountants in England and Wales (ICAEW), the Institute of Chartered Accountants of Scotland (ICAS), and the Association of Chartered Certified Accountants (ACCA).[89] These bodies have different traditions, developed over time distinctive accounting philosophies, and often have different priorities reflecting in part their different constituencies.[90] Christopher Nobes and Robert Parker describe the ensuing problem as follows:

> The structure of the profession reflects historical events rather than any overall planned coverage of membership and distribution of functions. The existence of six professional bodies seems unnecessary, with major effort being required to coordinate their views and

[88] The Financial Services Authority (FSA), an independent nongovernmental body, was created only in 2000 by the Financial Services and Markets Act. Similar to the SEC, it is responsible for regulating the financial services industry. However, until the 2007–8 financial crisis, its approach had largely been hands-off, i.e., it strongly favored industry self-regulation. See Moran, *The British Regulatory State* (2003).

[89] The history of these three organizations through the early 1970s, with a focus on their accounting standards and "guidance," is discussed in Zeff, *Forging Accounting Principles in Five Countries* (1972), 1–57. See also Gordon and Gray, *European Financial Reporting: United Kingdom* (1994). The three other bodies are the Chartered Accountants Ireland (formerly the Institute of Chartered Accountants in Ireland, founded in 1888 and operating as both an Irish and British professional association headquartered in Dublin and Belfast), the Chartered Institute of Management Accountants (now "CIMA Global," founded in 1919 and headquartered in London), and the Chartered Institute of Public Finance and Accountancy (which traces its roots back to the 1885 Corporate Treasurers' and Accountants' Institute).

[90] Some British accountants are members of several bodies, and no organization has a purely geographically delimited base anymore, but overlap in membership is limited and long-standing differences persist. ICAEW, for instance, has long been seen as taking positions that advance the interests of large international auditing firms and major corporations, for which many of their members work as accountants; ACCA is widely seen as closer to small- and medium-sized firms, where most of its members work.

resolve conflict, which in a unified structure would perforce occur as part of the internal policy process of the profession. However, all attempts to integrate the six bodies . . . have so far failed.[91]

The British accountancy bodies continue to compete for members, on whom they bestow their professional titles based on tests, and they compete for status.[92] They therefore regularly contest each other's claims to be speaking on behalf of the profession as a whole and engage in "internecine bickering" on anything from accounting principles to the details of accounting education in Britain.[93] Hence, in May 2010, when ACCA's and ICAS's marketing managers and ICAEW's director of member services issued a joint response to a British accounting magazine's critique of their contribution to UK accounting education, the editor quipped "ACCA, ICAEW and ICAS all talking with one voice—that's got to be a first."[94]

This institutional fragmentation of the British accountancy profession has also affected British accounting governance more broadly. In 1970, the ICAEW established an Accounting Standards Steering Committee— later renamed the Accounting Standards Committee (ASC) and joined by the other professional accountancy bodies—in an effort to streamline accounting practices in the United Kingdom.[95] ASC's specific remit was to develop Statements of Standard Accounting Practices (SSAPs). However, disagreements among the six bodies remained widespread, and since each body retained veto power, the ASC frequently failed to produce common standards. The ASC had little authority—a fact reflected in its confederate method for setting standards: all member bodies had to adopt each SSAP before it could be issued in final form.[96] ICAEW and the other professional associations retained their full independence, perpetuating

---

[91] Nobes and Parker, eds., *Comparative International Accounting* (2008), 146. The difficulty that the United Kingdom has encountered in replacing its fragmented domestic structure with anything resembling a hierarchical organizational structure is similar to the problems that Americans have had in trying to streamline their domestic institutions for product standard-setting, as discussed in chapter 6.

[92] See, e.g., Percy, "ICAEW Grows Slower than Rivals" (2007); Sikka and Willmott, "The Power of 'Independence'" (1995).

[93] Perry, "Competition or Merger?" (2005).

[94] Hambly, "Editor's Note" (2010).

[95] The effort has been variably attributed to the unexpected and high-profile financial collapses of several UK companies in the 1960s (Roberts et al., *International Financial Reporting* (2005), 446) or the impending UK membership in the EEC (Zimmermann et al., *Global Governance in Accounting* (2008), 24).

[96] Zimmermann et al., *Global Governance in Accounting* (2008), 46.

the institutional fragmentation of, and the contestation among, the British accounting bodies. In fact, it soon became readily apparent that this structure impeded the British ability to speak with a single voice on specific accounting matters at the international level. During the negotiations for the Fourth Directive in the mid-1970s, for instance, the European Commission complained repeatedly that it was hearing as many voices as there were British accountancy bodies. But with accounting still mostly a domestic affair, calls for a merger of the six bodies fell on deaf ears.[97]

In 1990, the ASC was replaced by the Accounting Standards Board (ASB), a private-sector organization modeled on FASB in the United States.[98] The ASB has a full-time chairman, a full-time technical director, and eight part-time members.[99] Unlike its predecessor, the ASB has the power to issue accounting standards on its own authority, and many in the United Kingdom have accepted it as the domestic standard-setter and follow its standards.[100] Companies must generally comply with the spirit and reasoning of individual British standards and the ASB's statement of principles for financial reporting.[101] However, companies are allowed to depart from the required accounting standards if following those rules does not yield a "true and fair" view of their accounts. In such exceptional circumstances, companies can devise their own appropriate alternative rule.[102] This "true and fair override" is said to be a legacy of the multiple approaches to financial reporting in the past; it "can be explained only by [the country's] laissez-faire [accounting] history."[103]

For the representation of domestic interests at the international level, the ASB remains a relatively weak institution and does not enjoy unwavering support from the UK accounting bodies, although it is recognized by the IASB as the primary UK representative. In September 2005,

---

[97] A merger remains a contentious issue whenever it is suggested; see, e.g., CIMA Discussion Board discussion "Consolidation of Accountancy Bodies" (6/4/2009). A merger between ICAEW and ICAS was voted down by the membership.

[98] The ASB was created as part of the Financial Reporting Council, the UK's government-empowered but independent regulator for corporate governance and financial reporting, which is financed jointly by the accountancy profession, business firms (through a mandatory direct levy), and the government, but operates mostly like a private-sector not-for-profit corporation.

[99] In contrast, ASC's members were all part-time volunteers.

[100] Not-for-attribution interview with a British accounting expert, 16 July 2010.

[101] Listed companies are required to comply with IFRS rather than UK (ASB) accounting standards. This option is also available to all UK companies other than charities. Chopping and Stephens, *Accounting Standards 2010–11* (2010), 6.

[102] See Stephens (2010), esp. 170.

[103] Zimmermann et al., *Global Governance in Accounting* (2008), 48.

for instance, Richard Martin, the ACCA Head of Financial Reporting, warned that, if ASB is to retain its official role as the representative of British interests vis-à-vis the IASB, it would "need to be more actively engaged with those groups."[104] When British stakeholders—individually or organized through bodies such as ICAEW, ICAS, or ACCA—seek to influence international standard-setting, they might work through the ASB, but also might approach the IASB directly; ASB is not the clear focal point. Without an accepted institutional mechanism for aggregating domestic preferences, a multitude of British voices are often heard at the international level.[105]

In sum, the United States and the United Kingdom are not just, as the saying goes, "divided by a common language."[106] Notwithstanding the importance of capital markets, which has long been comparable, the British system of rule-making is strikingly different from the American. It resembles closely the fragmented type, as illustrated by figure 4.3.

Domestic institutional fragmentation also characterizes accounting governance in Germany and France, although the specific institutional arrangements are a function of each country's political-economic history and traditions of market regulation. In Germany, accountants' influence on rule-making has been weak compared with that of their counterparts in the United States or United Kingdom.[107] Tax rules and the *Handelsgesetzbuch* (HGB commercial code) have been the main sources of guidance for accounting. Other sources, however, are important too. German generally accepted accounting principles (*Grundsätze ordnungsgemäßer Buchführung*) are made up of jurisprudence, regular practice, and professional opinions.[108] The main professional accountancy body, the Institut der Wirtschaftsprüfer (IdW), gets involved in consultations during the formal process of rule-making in accounting, and it discharges the role of filling gaps in the law by issuing "standards" in the form of recommendations

---

[104] ACCA, "ACCA Urges ASB to Get On with IFRS Convergence" (2005). The statement was made in the context of a heated multi-months exchange between the ACCA and the ICAEW over whether the ASB should continue to push for the convergence between UK GAAP for nonlisted companies and (the principles of) IFRS.

[105] E.g., not-for-attribution interview with British accountancy expert, 17 July 2010. In addition to listed companies and accountancy organizations, other bodies sometimes lay claim to representing UK interests, such as the Association of Corporate Treasurers.

[106] On the issue whether the United Kingdom and the United States speak a common "Anglo-Saxon" language in accounting, see, e.g., the exchanges between Alexander and Archer (2000, 2003) and Nobes (2003).

[107] For a good historical overview, see Schneider, "The History of Financial Reporting in Germany" (1995).

[108] Zimmermann et al., *Global Governance in Accounting* (2008), 51.

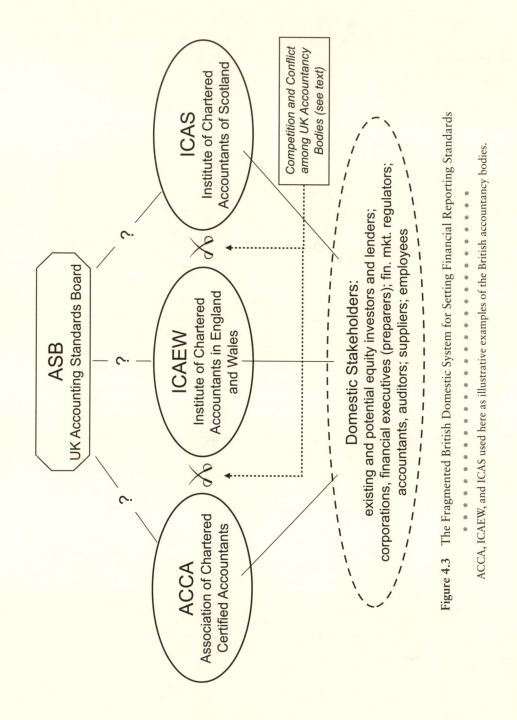

ASB
UK Accounting Standards Board

ICAS
Institute of Chartered Accountants of Scotland

ICAEW
Institute of Chartered Accountants in England and Wales

ACCA
Association of Chartered Certified Accountants

Competition and Conflict among UK Accountancy Bodies (see text)

Domestic Stakeholders:
existing and potential equity investors and lenders; corporations, financial executives (preparers); fin. mkt. regulators; accountants, auditors; suppliers; employees

Figure 4.3 The Fragmented British Domestic System for Setting Financial Reporting Standards

ACCA, ICAEW, and ICAS used here as illustrative examples of the British accountancy bodies.

and nonmandatory releases. It also exerts influence in a roundabout way by pronouncing standards for auditing, which in turn, are informative for balance sheet preparers and relevant in court decisions.[109]

The diffuse and fragmented governance structure in accounting has long been a source of confusion for outside observers. FASB member Gerhard Mueller, for example, noted in the mid-1990s:

> We would really like to have a US-German dialogue about accounting standards, but with whom? There is no German 'Standard Setting Body' and indeed there seems to be no-one who really feels responsible for accounting standards. The *Institut der Wirtschaftsprüfer* passes, noting the prerogative of the legislature, the Ministry of Justice refers you to various working groups in some room on the upper floor—or in the basement.[110]

Large German firms lobbied in the second half of the 1990s for consolidation and greater centralization of rule-making authority in accounting. The effort had some success, leading in 1998 to the passage of a law on control and transparency in business (*Gesetz zur Kontrolle und Transparenz in Unternehmensbereich*). The law created preconditions for recognition of a private-sector accounting standards body. In the same year, the private-sector German Accounting Standards Committee (Deutsches Rechnungslegungs Standards Committee, GASC) was founded by representatives of leading German industrial and accounting firms as well as financial services.[111] Its objectives are (i) to develop accounting standards for application in the areas of consolidated financial reporting (not for individual company financial reporting);[112] (ii) to represent German interests on international accounting committees; and (iii) to act in a consultative role in relation to the development of accounting legislation. Despite its formal legal independence, GASC remains "hostage to

---

[109] Zimmermann (2008), 51. See also Schruff, "Die Rolle des Hauptfachausschusses (HFA) des IdW" (2006). A second organization, the Wirtschaftsprüferkammer (Chamber of Accountants) was introduced by the law regulating the accountancy profession (*Wirtschaftsprüferordnung*) of 1961. Their members check compliance of corporate financial reports with legal requirements and accounting practices. In this process, they often exercise considerable judgment with respect to valuation matters and application of accounting principles.

[110] Quoted in Anonymous, "Bilanzen aus der Provinz" (1997), authors' translation.

[111] Walton et al., *International Accounting* (2003), 93.

[112] Accounting consolidation is the process of aggregating financial information from a group of companies (or a parent company and its subsidiaries) into a single financial statement for the entire economic entity.

its political overlord, the Ministry of Justice."[113] Indeed, even though part of the rule-making process in accounting has now been outsourced to the private sector, the ministry's seal of approval is required if the rules are to be binding on German firms, although some observers have noted that "the [approval] process is of a rubber-stamping nature."[114] In short, the German accounting governance structure is complex and diffuse, with several institutions—private and public—claiming authority in the setting of standards. When it comes to accounting and financial reporting rules, Germany thus lacks any clear, broadly accepted mechanism for aggregating preferences and representing the interests of German domestic stakeholders in private governance at the international level.

In France, as in Germany, accounting rules originate from a variety of sources, and accounting governance is diffuse and fragmented.[115] The French state issues general accounting rules via the Commercial Code and Companies Act. In addition, tax laws play an important role in shaping financial statements of companies. Another source of accounting rules is the national accounting plan (*Plan Comptable Général*)[116] which is the responsibility of the Conseil National de la Comptabilité (CNC),[117] a mixed public/private-sector body of fifty-eight civil servants and accountants.[118] This plan is an authoritative detailed manual on financial reporting, first published in 1947 and revised several times since.[119] It exists in many versions for different industries and comprises a chart of accounts, definitions of terms, model financial statements, and rules for measurement and valuation.[120] The CNC also issues technical "opinions" (*avis*) that become either voluntary "best accounting practices" or binding regulations if endorsed by yet another mixed public/private-sector body, the Comité de la Réglementation Comptable (CRC)—the accounting regulatory authority.[121] The CRC's main responsibility is to issue rules relating

---

[113] Anonymous, "Reform in Germany," (2000).

[114] Zimmermann et al., *Global Governance in Accounting* (2008), 52.

[115] See Raybaud-Turillo and Teller, "Droit et Comptabilite" (2009).

[116] Scheid and Walton, *European Financial Reporting: France* (1992).

[117] Translated as the national accounting council.

[118] The CNC was established in 1957 and extensively reformed in 1996.

[119] See Standish, "Origins of the Plan Comptable Général" (1990); and Richard, "De l'histoire du plan comptable français" (1992). Revised versions of the plan were issued in 1957, 1982 (as partial implementation of the Fourth Directive), 1986 (to include the Seventh Directive), and 1999. The 1982 plan, unlike previous plans, was made compulsory for all industrial and commercial companies. An early plan of 1942 never became operational. See Mikol, "The History of Financial Reporting in France" (1995), 107–119.

[120] Nobes and Parker, *Comparative International Accounting* (2004).

[121] The accounting regulation committee. The CRC dates from 1996.

to consolidated financial accounts. The members of the CRC include the minister of economy and finance, the justice minister, budget minister, a judge each from each of the highest courts—the Conseil d'Etat and the Cour de Cassation—and the head of the Financial Markets Authority (Autorité des Marchés Financiers, AMF). Representatives from industry and the presidents of the two main professional accountancy bodies, the Ordre des Experts Comptables (OEC)[122] and the Companie Nationale des Commissaires aux Comptes (CNCC) also serve on the CRC.[123]

The accounting profession was first organized in the Société de Comptabilité de France in 1881. Over the years, other organizations emerged. The government decided in 1945 to regulate the profession, establishing the OEC and placing it under the supervision of the Ministry of Economy and Finance. The institution of the Commissariat aux Comptes similarly hails from the nineteenth century. The CNCC in its modern form was established in 1969 by government decree. It operates under the authority of the Ministry of Justice. Besides participating in the CRC regulatory process, OEC and CNCC may issue their own "accounting guidance" in the form of *avis* for the benefit of their sixteen thousand members. Like the British professional accounting institutes, OEC and CNCC have not succeeded in putting their differences aside and forging coordinated and single positions on accounting issues. In the words of French accounting expert Edouard Salustro: "It is evident today that despite almost twenty years of commendable efforts at coordination, the two professional organizations are pursuing distinct paths, not without a certain overlap in . . . [their functions]."[124]

As in Germany, influential business groups have sought to simplify the rule-making process in French accounting, pressing for an overhaul of the domestic institutional structure. In response, legislation has been proposed in 2007 to merge the CNC and CRC, creating a single national accounting standards board able to directly issue accounting standards and speak on behalf of French domestic interests at the international level. As explained by French financial reporting expert Christian Hoarau: "How can an EU member state exercise a real influence in international accounting bodies? . . . [It needs to speak with] a common voice . . . and [make] robust contributions that are submitted as far upstream as possible in the

[122] Order of Chartered Accountants.

[123] Nobes and Parker, *Comparative International Accounting* (2004). The CNCC is the national association of auditors. The OEC is the equivalent to the German Institut der Wirtschaftsprüfer; and the CNCC is similar to the Wirtschaftsprüferkammer.

[124] Salustro, "France: Two Overlapping Paths of Progress" (2003).

process of international standard-setting."[125] The objective of the 2007 reform proposal thus "was that the national accounting standard-setter should have greater efficacy and ability to react in an international context marked by the general growth of . . . IFRS and competition between countries to influence their evolution."[126]

The reform was envisaged in two steps: first, the creation of an efficient decision-making body within the CNC through the creation of a *collège* of sixteen members replacing the old board of fifty-eight members; and, second, the merger of the CRC and reformed CNC into a single National Standards Authority (Autorité des Normes Comptables, ANC). The first reform stage was completed quickly in 2007; the merger idea, however, remains a proposal. Those with a stake in the old regulatory system resist the idea of a merger. The final outcome and effectiveness of the reform of the French standard-setting system in accounting thus is uncertain.[127]

A Transnational Accounting Standard-Setting Structure in Europe?

Domestic institutions for setting accounting rules are thus fragmented in each European country. Can EU-level coordination provide a substitute for hierarchical institutions? Well before the creation of the IASB, Karel Van Hulle, the Belgian head of the financial information unit at the Commission, admonished his fellow Europeans: "When you have a European market that operates with one currency you need common European thinking on accounting and regulation of accounting and financial markets. . . . We must get our act together in Europe—there is no alternative."[128] To achieve this objective, he proposed the creation of a European Accounting Standards Board (EASB). The British expressed clear opposition to such plan, and the proposal went nowhere. A few years later, the Commission made another attempt "to give a more forceful voice to European concerns"[129] by creating the so-called 'E5+2' group, comprising the European Board members of the IASC, as well as the EU and the Fédération des Experts Comptables Européens (FEE). This attempt, too, foundered on the many incompatibilities of the various national practices

[125] Hoarau, "The Reform of the French Standard-Setting System" (2009), 140.
[126] Hoarau (2009), 127.
[127] Moody, "Institutes Present a Combined Front: French Audit Industry" (2008), 18; Hoarau (2009).
[128] Cited in Anonymous, "Europe Sets Out Its Stall" (1987), 9.
[129] Anonymous, "G4+1 Gets a Rival" (1998), 8.

and the organizational segmentation of the accountancy profession in Europe.

After the establishment of the IASB, the Europeans made a fresh attempt to forge a regional coordination mechanism. The impetus came from the EU's 2002 endorsement of IFRS.[130] As a condition for endorsing international standards, the EU retained authority to exercise regulatory oversight and correct any perceived material deficiencies or concerns regarding these standards. The body designated by the EU to conduct such review is the European Financial Reporting Advisory Group (EFRAG)—a private-sector organization established in 2001 by seven industry groups.[131]

EFRAG's official role is "provid[ing] ... opinions in order for the Commission to take a view on endorsement of any IFRS ... [and] issues related to the development and the improvement of the standards and their effective implementation in the European area."[132] Not content with a mere reviewing role, EFRAG soon set its sight on becoming the regional focal institution in accounting and the promoter of European interests at the international level—that is, to become a European Accounting Standards Board. Stig Enevoldsen, CEO of EFRAG, explained:

> It is important for Europe to get involved in the deep technical work on accounting standard setting and participate in the global debate with the highest degree of technical expertise. EFRAG is now in a position to claim to be the European technical voice vis-à-vis the IASB and therefore we will be ready to ... get more closely involved in the work of the IASB Board itself. ... Some argue that the US had too big an influence ... and there is need for a counterbalance. We in EFRAG are ready to be involved.[133]

---

[130] EU Regulation 1606/2002 providing that firms listed on an exchange within the EU must prepare their consolidated accounts in accordance with international accounting standards as of January 2005.

[131] The founding groups of EFRAG were the European Business Federations, Federation of European Accountants, European Insurance Organization, European Banking Federation, European Savings Banks Group, European Association of Co-operative Banks, and the European Federation of Accountants and Auditors.

[132] EFRAG and EC, "Working Arrangement" (2006), 1.

[133] EFRAG, *Annual Review* (2004), 6. Enevoldsen has also been chairman of the Technical Expert Group of EFRAG since 2001. In the same Annual Review, Göran Tidström, chairman of the EFRAG Supervisory Board, noted: "It is important that we work closely together in Europe with all parties involved, including the standard setters, to coordinate the European views and thereby give solid and robust input to the IASB" (2004), 3.

What then are the prospects of EFRAG emerging as a "European FASB"? They are slim for many reasons: first, Europe remains divided on accounting issues; it is unlikely that the various member states will overcome deep disagreements on accounting rules and practices that reflect idiosyncratic national traditions. Second, several national standard-setters resent EFRAG; they view it as a parvenu perilously treading on their turf. Unsurprisingly, cooperation between EFRAG and national rule-makers has been weak.[134] Third, EFRAG's resources are tiny compared to those of FASB. In 2005, for example, EFRAG had a budget of €1 million and a full-time staff of eight.[135] In the same year, FASB had a budget of $34 million and a staff of about seventy professionals.[136]

Fourth, since the launch of EFRAG, the EU has introduced ever greater complexity in accounting governance, replicating to some extent the fragmented institutional structure present in several member states. For example, the Commission established in 2006 a Standards Advice Review Group (SARG) "to ensure objectivity and proper balance of the European Financial Reporting Advisory Group's opinions."[137] In addition, the Commission changed the EU regulation on IFRS to give the European Parliament a role in the endorsement process. The Commission's own Accounting Regulatory Committee also claims authority in this area, and more generally in IFRS/IASB-related matters. As a result, regulatory competencies have become rather diffuse and sometimes contested.

And fifth, while large European multinational companies strongly support a forceful single European voice in global standardization, they take a rather dim view of EFRAG's main stated role of IFRS reviewer. This role, they fear, may lead to "carve-outs" and exemptions that risk undermining the very goal they have been fighting for, namely the creation of a common set of global standards in accounting.

To summarize, the Europeans have not succeeded in superimposing an effective coordinating mechanism or centralized regulatory structure on the fragmented institutional arrangements at the national level. Long-

---

[134] See lament expressed by Stig Enevoldsen in EFRAG, *Annual Review* (2006), 8.

[135] EFRAG's budget has grown to only €1.8 million by 2008. Insistent demands by EFRAG for big increases seem to have fallen on deaf ears. Most funding comes from EFRAG's founding organizations. However, EFRAG has been hoping to receive sizable additional funding from the EU Commission.

[136] FASB raised approximately $20 million from fees paid by 8,300 registered companies and $14 million from the sale of publications and subscriptions.

[137] Anonymous, "Accounting: New Commission Expert Group" (2006), 1.

standing differences in national accounting traditions and institutions have surfaced at the regional level, shaping Europe's new regional accounting governance. A "European FASB" remains, for the time being, an elusive goal.

Differences in Institutional Complementarity and Implications for Global Governance

At the international level, the institutional structure for setting financial reporting standards gives pride of place to coherently presented national positions. Taking such unambiguous national preferences into account allows the IASB to claim that its standards have widespread support and legitimacy. Hierarchical domestic institutions, such as in the United States, therefore exhibit high institutional complementarity in financial standard-setting. The fit between IASB and their domestic institutions should put American firms in a strong position for exerting influence at the international level. By contrast, divisions within the accounting profession in individual European countries, combined with a highly fragmented governance structure in most EU member states and at the regional level, should make it difficult for Europe to speak with a single voice since these institutions found in Europe exhibit low complementarity with the IASB. And such low institutional interoperability between national and international standard-setting structures should, according to our theory, put Europeans at a disadvantage relative to Americans in global rule-making in accounting.

The high complementarity between FASB and IASB is reinforced by an institutional linkage formalized through the so-called Norwalk Agreement of 2002. The stated objective of the Norwalk Agreement is to achieve convergence of American standards, the Generally Accepted Accounting Principles (U.S. GAAP), and IFRS, and to coordinate future work programs.[138] At the time of the Norwalk Agreement, the IASB was a fledgling institution with eighteen staff members and a modest budget.[139] The agreement gave it much needed access to the extensive technical resources of a key national standard-setter. Europeans have criticized the agreement, arguing that it has given American interests undue influence in

---

[138] See FASB-IASB, *Memorandum of Understanding* (2002).
[139] IASB staff grew to 109 by 2009.

international accounting processes. Yet the lack of uncontested standard-setters at the national or European level has rendered them unable to offer a real counterweight to U.S. influence.

In sum, then, our argument about varying degrees of institutional complementarity, presented in chapter 3, leads us to expect American firms to be more successful than their European counterparts in getting the IASB to take their technical views and regulatory preferences into account. European stakeholders are likely to be disadvantaged by the lack of institutional hierarchy at the national and regional levels, which compromises their ability to speak with one voice at the global level. And to the extent that Europeans are aware that it is domestic institutional fragmentation that puts them at a disadvantage (as we have argued), the importance of institutions should be reflected in their responses to survey and interview questions that probe the institutional logic of our argument. We would also expect low levels of satisfaction with domestic standards institutions relative to Americans' satisfaction with FASB. As a consequence of all this, we also expect American firms to have more favorable views of the IASB rule-making process than their European counterparts. The next chapter puts these hypotheses to the test.

CHAPTER FIVE

The Politics of Setting Standards for Financial Reporting

IASB'S SHORT HISTORY provides ample anecdotal evidence for the predominance of U.S. interests and the crucial role of FASB in ensuring U.S. influence in international rule-making. In several recent projects, for instance, the IASB has adopted U.S. standards as international standards virtually without change, even in the face of European opposition. Such U.S. predominance is all the more remarkable since "Realist" scholars have argued that the EU increasingly equals the United States on various measures of raw economic power, such as GDP and market capitalization; some other scholars even argue that the EU has governmental regulatory power over financial markets that now exceeds the power of the United States.[1] Yet, in IASB rule-making U.S. interests appear to be clearly dominant.

A telling example is IFRS 8, adopted by the IASB on 30 November 2006 as a successor to IAS 14, effective 1 January 2009, against vehement opposition from European interests, including investors and civil society groups. IFRS 8, like its predecessor, specifies what information a corporation must disclose to investors, regulators, and others in its consolidated financial statements. Specifically, IAS 14 required each reporting entity to provide key information—such as expenses, revenues, assets, and liabilities—separately for each kind of business activity in which the entity was engaged (business segments) and separately for each political jurisdiction in which it operated (geographic segments). By contrast, IFRS 8 has more detailed rules for disclosure but requires separate reporting only for whatever each corporation internally treats as a separate "operating segment" for its allocation of resources and assessment of performance.

---

[1] Drezner, *All Politics Is Global* (2007), esp. 36; Posner, "Making Rules for Global Finance" (2009), and "Sequence as Explanation: The International Politics of Accounting Standards" (2010).

IFRS 8 was the result of a joint project of IASB and FASB, under-taken to advance the convergence with U.S. GAAP under the Norwalk Agreement, which reinforces FASB-IASB institutional complementarity as described in chapter 4. "Convergence" here consisted of IASB copy-ing "almost line-for-line . . . a standard already in force in the U.S."[2] The project generally escaped the attention of European interests until IASB published the exposure draft (ED8), which in four months elicited 182 comment letters, including numerous highly critical ones. The IASB-FASB juggernaut, however, pushed ahead without "practically any conceptual debate," even in the face of "dissent . . . by a significant minority of IASB members," since critics had allegedly failed to show any problems in practice with the application of the standard in the United States.[3]

Institutional investors and other users of financial reports, in particular from the United Kingdom and continental European countries, expressed concerns that IFRS 8 would reduce comparability and generally lower the quality of financial reports, making them less useful for analyses of corporate financial and management performance—and less helpful for the detection of tax avoidance through transfer pricing.[4] During the IFRS notice-and-comment period, however, these European stakeholders were undermined by their inability to speak with a single voice, and by the lack of institutional mechanisms for weighing their interests at the na-tional or European level against the interests of European preparers who supported the new standard. Many of the European critics even missed the deadline for submitting comments during the Exposure Draft period altogether, again consistent with what the low institutional complemen-tarity for Europeans leads us to expect.[5]

When the IASB adopted the draft standard virtually unchanged as IFRS 8, European critics escalated the fight through direct appeals to the European Commission, national governments, and the European Parlia-ment.[6] They succeeded in getting a cross-party group of members of the UK House of Commons to call for the "totally unacceptable" standard to be rejected or altered by the EU for use in Europe; the Economic and

[2] Jopson, "UK Investors in Plea to Brussels" (2007).
[3] Deloitte Audit, "Segment Reporting: Why the Controversy?" (2010); Jopson, "UK Inves-tors in Plea to Brussels" (2007).
[4] Neveling, "EU Delays IFRS 8 Ratification in Shock Move" (2007); Stokdyk, "FRRP Un-happy with IFRS 8 Dodgers" (2010); Alvarez, "IFRS 8" (2009), 58–60; Véron, *The Global Accounting Experiment* (2007), 38.
[5] Neveling, "EU Delays IFRS 8 Ratification" (2007).
[6] Jopson, "UK Investors in Plea" (2007).

Monetary Affairs Committee of the European Parliament warned against "import[ing] into EU law an alien standard" and forced the Commission to conduct a drawn-out analysis.[7] The Commission, however, was powerless. It had learned of European stakeholders' opposition only during the final stages of the standard-setting process; as a public body, it had no formal, legal way to intervene in that private process. After much agony, the Commission therefore adopted IFRS 8 for use in the EU at the end of November 2007.[8]

This account of IFRS 8 nicely illustrates the fundamentally political nature of technical rule-making and provides a concrete example of institutional complementarity as a source of power. Ultimately, however, it provides only anecdotal support for our argument without allowing us to assess how generalizable the findings are.[9] Do institutional complementarities generally determine the ability of the key stakeholders to influence international financial reporting standards? Specifically, is it true that institutional fragmentation of accounting governance in Europe, documented in chapter 4, impedes the effective aggregation of European interests and their projection onto the international stage, while the close institutional fit between IASB and FASB significantly facilitates the representation of American interests?

---

[7] Hanney, "MPs Attack IFRS 8" (2007); Neveling, "EU Delays IFRS 8 Ratification" (2007).

[8] Commission Regulation 1358/2007 of 21 Nov 2007, *OJ* L 304/9. As Nicolas Véron notes, based on other cases, "experience . . . prove[s] that the endorsement process gives the EU only limited leverage" (*The Global Accounting Experiment* ((2007), 37).

[9] In addition, determining the extent to which institutions mattered vis-à-vis other factors in this particular case would require more (and more reliable) information about the communications and negotiations among the members of the IASB. One might argue, for instance, that this particular standard pitted the interests of firms, for which the new standard increased management discretion and lowered record-keeping costs, against the interests of investors and tax assessors, and that the switch was a function of unobserved but successful lobbying by EU-based preparers, who had also prompted the positive assessment by EFRAG. Conducting research on the internal negotiations within the IASB, however, would be difficult even for the historian, precisely because such a private body does not have the record-keeping requirements of traditional public bureaucracies, and Board members have every incentive not to disclose fully the information in interviews. In our analyses below, we therefore "control" for such an alternative explanation by restricting our survey to senior financial managers of publicly listed companies, though we return to the issue of the balance between corporate, investor, and societal interests in the conclusion.

TESTING THE ARGUMENT SYSTEMICALLY THROUGH AN INTERNATIONAL BUSINESS SURVEY

In this chapter, we provide a systematic empirical investigation of our hypotheses, in large part based on data from a multi-industry business survey among senior financial executives in France, Germany, the United Kingdom, and the United States.[10] Using social-scientific research methods described in greater detail in appendix 3, we asked these executives about international financial reporting standards (IFRS) and their ability to affect standard-setting in the IASB. The survey allowed us to gather detailed and directly comparable information about companies whose financial securities (stocks and bonds) are traded on these countries' financial markets.[11] These companies are the primary "targets" of corporate financial reporting rules since they are required by financial market regulators to issue financial reports at regular intervals.[12]

With 749 respondents, distributed across the four countries as shown in table 5.1, our survey yields the most comprehensive and cross-nationally comparable information to date about how companies affected by international financial reporting standards (IFRS) assess these standards, and to what extent they are able to influence the decisions of the global private rule-maker, the IASB.

In the next section, we provide background information about our survey participants and show that the American and European firms in our samples are comparable on various dimensions that might affect their assessment of international financial reporting rules or their ability to exert influence. The second section discusses our respondents' assessments of various aspects of IFRS and of IASB governance. The third section, on Power and Influence in International Standard-Setting, provides the cen-

---

[10] The survey was targeted at financial executives of publicly traded companies. It was supplemented by interviews conducted with a broader range of stakeholders, including current and former CEOs and CFOs, academic corporate finance experts, senior partners of accounting firms, public and private financial market regulators, and representatives of institutional investors, as well as current and former staff and participants/members of standard-setting bodies at the national level and the IASB.

[11] To ensure the specific applicability of our theoretical framework, which emphasizes the complementarity between a stakeholder's domestic institutions and the institutional structure at the international level, we restricted our sample for each country to companies that have actual business operations, with separate financial reporting, in the country in question.

[12] We conducted the survey over several months in 2007–8 and achieved a response rate of about 25 percent—about ten times the rate of typical CFO surveys.

TABLE 5.1
Respondents by Country

Country of respondent company	Number of responses	Percentage of total sample
U.S.	208	28%
Germany	194	26%
France	135	18%
UK	212	28%

tral statistical analysis. The concluding section draws on additional data from the survey and other sources to shed further light on the importance of institutional complementarity.

RESPONDENTS OF THE INTERNATIONAL ACCOUNTING STANDARDS SURVEY

Most of our survey respondents were chief financial officers (CFOs), chief accounting officers (CAOs), and functionally equivalent corporate financial managers, or controllers, as shown in figure 5.1. In some cases, chief executive officers (CEOs) took charge of responding to our survey. The remainder of our respondents were other financial executives. We asked each respondent to answer the survey questions on behalf of his or her company, rather than in a personal capacity. We therefore allowed only one response per company.[13]

Before drawing attention to some of the similarities between American and European firms in our sample, it is worth noting one difference between them. The U.S. firms in our sample are on average larger than European firms: 87 percent of U.S. firms in our sample have more than 1,000 employees; 7 percent have less than 250. Of our European respondent firms, 58 percent have more than 1,000 employees; 23 percent have fewer than 250. This reflects real differences between U.S. and European

---

[13] Responses to open-ended questions and e-mail exchanges with respondents revealed that in several cases more than one financial executive contributed to the company's survey response—perhaps an indication of the importance that firms attach to the topic.

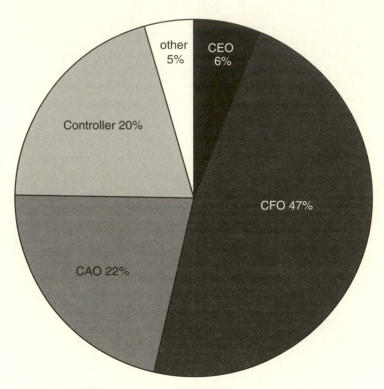

Figure 5.1 Survey Participants by Title

• • • • • •

Responses to survey question: "About you and your firm: What best describes your primary responsibility?" N = 747.

corporations: companies traded on the major U.S. stock exchanges are on average larger than firms traded on the European exchanges. Differences in size, however, are not driving any key differences between U.S. and European firms, as we show when we take this difference in size into account in our analyses.[14]

In many other respects, the firms in our European and American samples are very similar, most importantly in their international orientation as well as in their perception of the growing significance of IFRS. The new rules should therefore matter to both: growing internationalization of

[14] Specifically, in the statistical analyses reported below, we include size as a control variable and/or we repeat the analysis for only the largest firms as a robustness check, to ensure that the size difference between U.S. and European firms does not bias our findings.

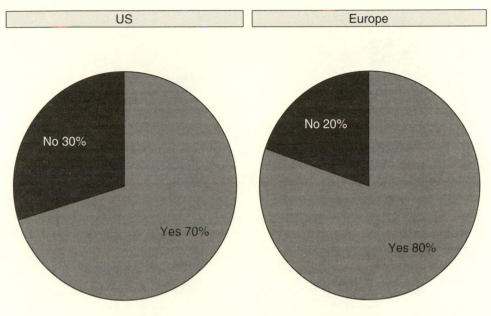

Figure 5.2 Multinational Respondent Company

• • • • • •

Responses to survey question: "Does your company itself have subsidiaries abroad?" N = 749.

business creates ever stronger pressure to comply with international accounting rules. Both European and American firms thus have an interest in shaping these rules to minimize the cost of switching to them.

Similarity in international orientation is reflected by the following data: 70 percent of U.S. firms and 80 percent of European firms reported having subsidiaries abroad (see figure 5.2). And 16 percent of U.S. firms are listed on at least one foreign exchange in addition to being listed on their main domestic exchange (NYSE or Nasdaq); 14 percent of European firms are also listed outside their respective home countries.[15]

The U.S. and European firms in our sample also rely on capital markets to a comparable extent, giving them a similar stake in the specific provisions of financial reporting standards: for most firms surveyed, capital

---

[15] The survey question was: "Does your firm have financial securities listed on any of the following exchanges? Please check all that apply." Unlike for most survey questions, European responses here differed: the percentages for British, German, and French firms are 19 percent, 12 percent, and 8 percent respectively.

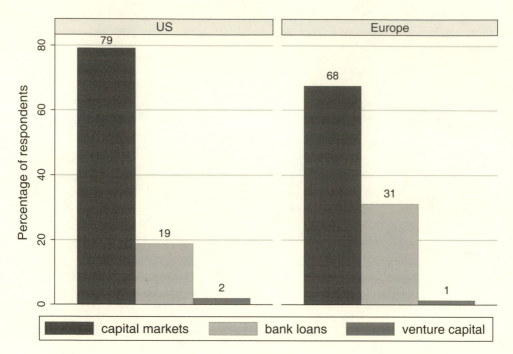

Figure 5.3 Percentage of Firms for Whom . . . Is Most Important Source of Capital

• • • • • •

Responses to survey item: "Please rank the following sources of capital in order of importance for your firm." Survey allowed respondents to designate only one source as "most important." N = 719 respondents who made a "most important" selection.

markets are the most important source of capital (see figure 5.3),[16] and many of them rely on *foreign* capital markets. When we asked how important access to foreign capital markets is for the firms' ability to raise capital, 58 percent of U.S. firms and 60 percent of European firms said

[16] As shown in figure 5.3, reliance on capital markets is higher and reliance on bank loans notably lower among American respondent firms, consistent with long-standing differences in the relative importance of capital markets for corporate finance; see Vitols, "Are German Banks Different?" (1998); Vitols, "Changes in Germany's Bank-Based Financial System" (2004); Zysman, *Governments, Markets, and Growth* (1983). We also conducted the analyses below conditional on the importance of capital markets for the companies. When the analyses are restricted to firms for which capital markets are the most important source of capital, the differences between U.S. and European firms with respect to assessment of IASB/IFRS or ability to influence generally remain unchanged or become even more pronounced; in the statistical analyses, firm size becomes insignificant.

TABLE 5.2

Shift of Governance to the International Level

Please indicate whether you agree or disagree with [...] the following statement:		Agree or strongly agree	Disagree or strongly disagree
"Standards will increasingly be developed at the international level."	U.S. firms	96.5%	3.5%
	European firms	97.7%	2.3%

Note: Percentage of respondents who selected the indicated response option, excluding the 5% of respondents (identically among U.S. and European respondents) who selected "neither agree nor disagree." N = 654.

foreign markets play some role; and 20 percent of United States as well as 33 percent of European respondents indicated that access to foreign markets is "equally," "more," or even "much more important" than access to their home market.[17] And while most respondents indicated that their firms intended to keep "the share of capital raised on foreign capital markets" the same as during the prior year, notable minorities—14 percent of U.S. firms and 18 percent of European firms—indicated the intent to increase their reliance on foreign capital markets.

U.S. and European respondents also proved remarkably similar in another respect. Due to differences in the present regulatory environment, current use of IFRS within respondent firms was naturally higher in Europe than in the United States. Yet, more than 60 percent of Americans and most Europeans reported being "familiar" or "very familiar" with IFRS.[18]

Finally, the importance of IFRS is clearly perceived as increasing on both sides of the Atlantic: American and European survey respondents overwhelmingly agree that governance in financial reporting is indeed moving from the domestic to the international level, as shown in table 5.2.

In sum, the U.S. and European firms in our samples are very comparable, especially with respect to their international orientation and their understanding of the significance of the trend toward international financial reporting rules. We would therefore expect U.S. and European firms to

[17] Responses were heavily concentrated in the "equally as important" response category.

[18] At the time of our survey, European corporations were generally required to use IFRS (see chapter 4) whereas the SEC only had plans but did not yet allow IFRS-based filing for U.S. filings of U.S. firms. Current U.S. users were mostly U.S. multinationals and some firms using IFRS internally.

have similar stakes in the specific provisions of these global rules. The challenge that these firms then face is to find ways to effectively shape the global rules in a way to minimize the cost of adopting them.

Assessing IFRS and IASB

How do publicly listed companies in the United States and Europe assess IFRS and IASB? We asked survey participants to rate several aspects of the international standards, including quality, complexity, and effectiveness. The responses reveal striking differences, consistent with our argument about institutional complementarity. The technical quality of international standards is rated more highly by Americans than Europeans: 84 percent and 68 percent, respectively, consider the quality of IFRS to be "high" or "very high."[19] Similarly, U.S. respondents' assessment is more favorable regarding the complexity of IFRS: 64 percent of American firms versus 95 percent of European firms consider complexity to be high or very high. Moreover, American respondents who were familiar with both U.S. GAAP and IFRS generally report lower costs of implementation and compliance for IFRS than for U.S. GAAP. These responses suggest that, to the extent that the specific provisions of IFRS differ from the corresponding provisions of U.S. GAAP, U.S. firms will gain from the switch in the long term.

American firms are also more sanguine about the effectiveness of IFRS, as conveyed by their responses to the question: "Please rate the effectiveness of IFRSs in achieving each of the following objectives of financial reporting standards:"[20]

- increasing the comparability of corporate financial information
- providing a level playing field internationally for companies

[19] The wording of the question was: "Please assess the following aspects of IFRSs or revised IASs: Quality." Cf. Myers, "The Development of International Accounting Standards" (1999), 11f. IASs were developed by the predecessor of the IASB. The IASB has issued new standards, IFRS, or has revised the IAS. All of our survey questions referred to both IFRS and revised IAS, but we omit the "or revised IASs" hereafter.

[20] Most of the stated objectives are widely recognized in the accounting literature as important objectives of financial reporting standards or the international harmonization of these standards; others appeared to be important to corporate financial executives in our preliminary interviews. Survey participants selected between "not effective," "somewhat effective," "effective," and "highly effective" for each of the following objectives of IFRS.

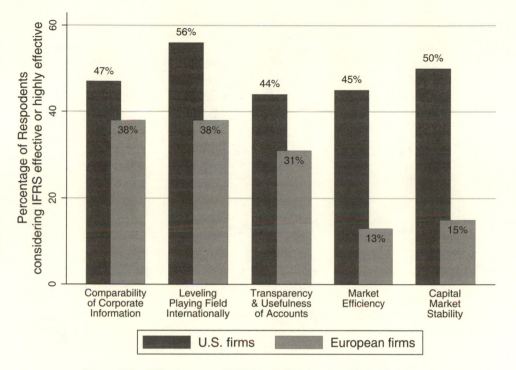

Figure 5.4 Effectiveness of IFRS in Achieving Specified Objectives

• • • • • •

Survey question: "Please rate the effectiveness of IFRS in achieving each of the following objectives of financial reporting standards." Figure shows percentage of respondents rating IFRS as "effective" or "highly effective." The specified objectives were: increasing the comparability of corporate information; providing a level playing field internationally for companies; improving the transparency and usefulness of accounts to shareholders, investors, and creditors; enhancing market efficiency; and increasing the stability of capital markets. See table 5. A.2 in the chapter appendix for additional information.

• improving the transparency and usefulness of accounts to shareholders, investors, and creditors
• enhancing market efficiency
• increasing the stability of capital markets

While strong majorities on both sides of the Atlantic consider IFRS at least somewhat effective in achieving the various stated objectives, there is a striking divergence between European and American respondents in

TABLE 5.3
Assessment of IASB Standard-Setting

Aspect of IASB standardization	U.S. respondents rating IASB "good" or "very good"	European respondents rating IASB "good" or "very good"
Due process, in general	88%	65%
Transparency	80%	51%
Accessibility	69%	52%
Inclusiveness	72%	44%
Accountability	75%	38%
Timeliness of updating; cancellation of superseded standards	73%	55%
Up-to-date availability of IFRS*	80%	60%

Note: The number of respondents (N) ranged between 641 and 651 for the questions in table 5.3.

* In the German survey, the availability question read "aktuelle Verfügbarkeit in deutscher Sprache"; in the French survey: "Disponibilité des normes les plus récentes en français." 75% of UK respondents reported good or very good availability, whereas 57% of German respondents and only 41% of French respondents reported good or very good availability in German and French, respectively.

how effective they deem IFRS to be in attaining these objectives, as illustrated in figure 5.4 (see also table 5.A.2 in this chapter's appendix). The differences are particularly wide with respect to enhancing market efficiency, where 45 percent of Americans but only 13 percent of Europeans think IFRS play an effective or highly effective role, and increasing capital market stability, where 50 percent of Americans yet only 15 percent of Europeans hold similarly positive views.[21]

These striking differences between European and American assessments also extend to IASB governance: in a separate battery of questions, we

[21] In the responses to these questions, exceptionally, we observed differences among the Europeans, with British and French respondents generally more skeptical about IFRS effectiveness than the European average and German firms generally more favorable than the European average (but less favorable than American firms).

asked U.S. and European companies to assess the most important aspects of the international standard-setting process.[22] Participants rated the IASB on each aspect by choosing from one of four response options: very bad, bad, good, and very good. Table 5.3 reports, for the U.S. and Europe separately, the percentage of respondents with favorable assessments.

The differences here are again striking. On literally every aspect of IASB governance, European firms have less favorable views than U.S. firms. And the differences are large and statistically significant in every case, supporting our hypothesis that better institutional fit between U.S. domestic standard-setting institutions and the institutional structure at the international level puts U.S. firms into a much stronger position for exerting influence in international standardization. Among European firms, unfavorable responses even exceed favorable ones when it comes to accountability, where 62 percent rate IASB governance as "poor" or "very poor," and inclusiveness, where 56 percent rate IASB similarly unfavorably. These are exactly the aspects of global private governance where the disadvantage from a poorer fit between European domestic institutions and the IASB—discussed in chapter 3—should be most notable and put European interests at a disadvantage.

POWER AND INFLUENCE IN INTERNATIONAL STANDARD-SETTING

We now turn to a statistical analysis of successful involvement in the IASB standard-setting process, which allows for a more rigorous test of our core hypothesis by also taking into account a broad range of factors that may explain different levels of success. The results corroborate the tentative evidence presented above in support of the institutional complementarity hypothesis.

As our measure of successful involvement, we use the responses to the question: "When you try to affect the specific provisions of a new international standard, how frequently do you succeed?"[23] Respondents were offered five response options: (1) rarely/never, (2) sometimes, (3) about half of the time, (4) often, and (5) very often/always. Average success rates are not high, but significantly higher for U.S. firms, with a notably

---

[22] The survey question asked the participants to "assess the process by which the IASB develops international standards (IFRSs or revised IASs)."

[23] The meaning of success, clarified in the survey question, was that the standard adopted in the end is closer to the respondent's preferences than the initial proposal.

different distribution across the two regions. Among U.S. responses, "rarely/never" and "sometimes" were evenly balanced, with numerous firms more frequently successful. Among European firms, by contrast, the number who reported being rarely or never successful exceeded the number who reported being successful at all higher frequencies combined. In short, U.S. firms are more frequently successful when they seek a voice in international standard-setting, and a simple t-test shows that the difference is statistically significant. This finding supports our argument, but should only be taken as suggestive, given that this test does not control for other factors and does not take into account that the responses are ordinal.[24]

To analyze more systematically differential rates of successful involvement (our dependent variable), we test four statistical models (see table 5.A.1 in Appendix).[25] Our key explanatory variable is differential institutional fit, based on our institutional analysis of the international rule-making process in chapter 4: whereas American firms are embedded in a domestic institutional system conducive to successful involvement at the international level, we expect European firms to be handicapped by institutional fragmentation, since domestic fragmentation results in poor institutional complementarity.[26] Our models control for other factors likely to affect success, including several specific ways in which firms may seek to influence IASB standard-setting (each of which is discussed in more detail below):

- firm size
- direct contacts with the expert group (within IASB) developing the standard

---

[24] Ordinal responses are ranked ("very often" clearly indicates a higher frequency than "often") but otherwise not necessarily mathematically related in the same manner as the numerical values assigned to them ("often" is not necessarily twice as frequent as "rarely/never"). Ordered logit, used below, takes this into account by estimating separately for each response category the likelihood that a respondent is successful at the specified frequency. A t-test simply assesses whether the difference in the average success rate might be due to random chance, given the distribution of responses around the mean. This test estimates that the probability of the observed difference occurring by chance is less than 0.0072 ($N = 356$), which makes the difference highly statistically significant. Note that the question about success was only asked of respondents who had earlier in the survey told us that they had at least some experience with attempting to influence international standards (they had tried more often than "never"). The number of observations is correspondingly smaller for the analyses of success than for the questions discussed above.

[25] We use multivariate maximum likelihood regression for ordinal dependent variables (ordered logit).

[26] U.S. FIRM is a dummy variable coded 1 for each American firm and 0 for each European firm.

- attempted influence via government(s)
- attempted influence via "comment letters" submitted to the IASB through the notice and comment procedures during the discussion paper or exposure draft stage
- timing of information received about a pertinent standard-setting effort at the international level
- frequency of influence attempts

We start by taking into account FIRM SIZE. As noted in chapter 3, any attempt to influence the content of international standards requires material resources as well as specialized expertise. Larger firms are more likely to have both of them. As expected, we find that larger firms are generally more successful. This effect is statistically significant, though it becomes weaker once we control for several other factors (see table 5.A.1 in the appendix to this chapter).[27]

In addition, we control in all analyses for the frequency of CONTACT WITH THE EXPERT GROUP DEVELOPING THE STANDARD within the IASB, since such contacts presumably constitute the most direct avenue of influence, given the IASB standard-setting procedures.[28] We find that such direct contacts—with the working group or project team that develops the standard—boost a company's success in influencing the provisions of a standard. This effect is initially statistically highly significant but also becomes weaker as we consider a broader set of factors. Controlling for firm size and contacts with the IASB expert group, we still find that U.S. firms are more successful than European firms in influencing international standardization, given the better fit between U.S. domestic institutions and the IASB.

The third possible explanation for success—arguably the most important alternative to our institutional explanation—is government involvement and state power. To examine this issue systematically, we asked firms how frequently they request governments to act on their behalf:

---

[27]Throughout this section, when we say "more successful" we technically are saying that there is a higher probability of being more frequently successful. FIRM SIZE is based on the question "How many employees does your company have?" with seven response options (size categories): "less than 50"; 50–100; 101–250; 251–500; 501–1000; 1001–1500; and "more than 1500." The thresholds were a function of the definitions for small- and medium-sized enterprises by the U.S. Department of Commerce and its European counterparts, which vary by industry.

[28]This measure is based on the reported frequency with which a firm "communicate[s] directly with experts on the IASB steering committees or working/advisory groups involved in writing discussion papers or preliminary drafts of a proposed standard."

US survey: We contact the SEC or another agency of the U.S. government and ask them to take action on our behalf.

UK survey: We contact a ministry or agency of the British government and ask them to take action on our behalf.

French survey: Nous contactons le Ministère de l'Économie, des finances et de l'industries pour leur demander d'intervenir en défense de nos intérêts.

German survey: Wir wenden uns an die Bundesregierung oder ein Bundesministerium bzw. eine Bundesbehörde und bitten, daß sie in unserem Sinne aktiv werden.[29]

The results show (see figure 5.5) that firms rarely even attempt to get governments to intervene with IASB on their behalf. Moreover, firms generally deem governments ineffective in promoting their regulatory preferences at the global level in private regulation: when we asked firms about the effectiveness of government support for influencing IASB rule-making, 59 percent of Europeans and 67 percent of Americans told us that such government support was categorically "not effective"; only 6 percent of each group consider government involvement "highly effective."[30] Overall, for private-sector stakeholders on both sides of the Atlantic, turning to government to influence private governance is not common, and few consider it effective, consistent with our argument about the primary importance of institutional complementarity in private standard-setting. We nonetheless test directly for the possibility that firms might influence international standards with the support of their governments by including in our statistical analyses the option of ATTEMPTED INFLUENCE VIA GOVERNMENT based on the above question (responses summarized in figure 5.5). We find that the factor is statistically insignificant and thus cannot be said to explain success rates.

[29] This option is one of several options offered in response to the following question: "When you try to get involved, how often do you do so by each of the following methods?" The immediately preceding question on the questionnaire defined "get involved" as trying to influence the specific provisions of a forthcoming standard.

[30] Excluding respondents who had indicated that their firms had never attempted to get governments to act on their behalves vis-à-vis IASB. U.S. firms, of course, have the alternative option of asking their representatives in Congress to take action on their behalf, but few do so, and only 10 percent believe that it is a highly effective method to exert influence; more than 71 percent believe that it is not effective at all. Europeans have the option of turning to the EU, but we find that this route is also rarely taken, and while 16 percent believe it is highly effective, 51 percent consider it not effective.

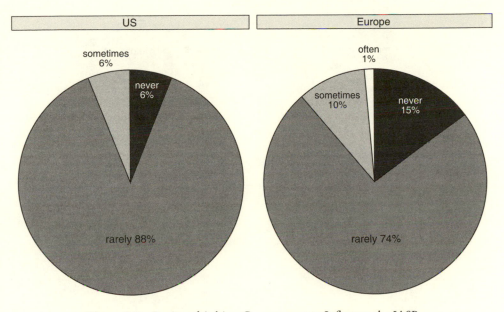

Figure 5.5   Rarity of Asking Government to Influence the IASB

• • • • • •

Responses to survey question: "When you get involved, how often do you do so by each of the following methods?" The option for U.S. respondents was: "We contact the SEC or another agency of the U.S. government and ask them to take action on our behalf." The option for European respondents was: "We contact the [country-specific ministry and/or agency] of the government and ask them to take action on our behalf." *N* = 391.

Our fourth control variable is *ATTEMPTED INFLUENCE VIA COMMENT LETTERS*. As described in chapter 4, the IASB "due process" procedures provide for notice-and-comment periods, during which stakeholders can submit written comments, endorsing or criticizing any aspect of a proposed rule or standard. The IASB commits to read and consider all comment letters submitted by the stated deadline for any given standards project, though it has no obligation to explain its reasons for acting on the concerns raised in some such letters while rejecting others.[31] We find that such comment letters increase firms' success in influencing IASB decisions. The statistically estimated effectiveness of these letters declines

---

[31] See also Mattli and Büthe, "Global Private Governance" (2005).

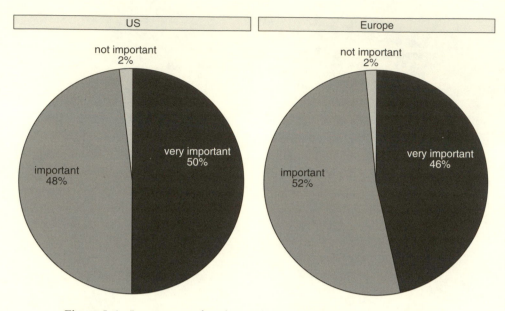

Figure 5.6 Importance of Early Involvement for Firm's Ability to Exert Influence

• • • • • •

Responses to survey question: "How important are these factors for a firm's ability to affect a proposed standard? . . . Timing (getting involved early)." Excluding respondents who selected the "don't know" option: N = 333.

when we subsequently take other factors into account, but it remains clearly significant.[32]

In chapter 3, we argued that timing is very important in a multistage standard-setting process, such as the one used by the IASB, where the crucial decisions are made early and only marginal changes are made later on. The importance of early involvement in IASB standardization has also been recognized, for instance, by Mike Metcalf, technical partner at KPMG who noted that "at [the] exposure draft stage it's rather late to turn round the IASB supertanker,"[33] and David Tweedie who, speaking at a conference, admonished IFRS stakeholders: "Get in at the beginning.

---

[32] The exact wording in the survey questionnaire was: "We write comment letters, alone or jointly with other firms in our industry." The bivariate correlation between attempted influence via government and via comment letters is 0.18, suggesting that there is no reason to be concerned about multicollinearity.

[33] As quoted in Bolton, "Recipe for Dissent" (2006), 91.

That's the time to change things."[34] When asked about the relative importance of timing in affecting the content of a proposed standard, respondents on both sides of the Atlantic overwhelmingly considered timing "important" or "very important."[35]

Good timing requires early INFORMATION about international standards proposals, which financial executives may obtain from domestic standards organizations, industry or professional associations, customers and colleagues in the industry, the firm's auditors, or the general media. Due to the nature of the standard-setting process, where the most important decisions are taken early on (as described in chapter 4), timely information should be particularly important. Differences in the timing of information are captured by the responses to the following survey question: "At what stage do you usually hear about a forthcoming new or revised international standard that may affect your firm's accounting or financial reporting practice?" In the response options for this question, we differentiated four stages:[36]

1. during the first deliberations and drafting of the initial standards proposal in the IASB working/advisory groups or project teams
2. when an exposure draft has been issued and is open for comments
3. during the final development and adoption of the new IFRS or revised IAS
4. after the standard has been adopted

When we include the responses in our main statistical analysis, we find that having early information boosts the likelihood of success in international standardization. This effect is strongly statistically significant when information is added by itself to the baseline model (model 1 in table 5.A.1), but becomes insignificant when the specific means of attempting influence are directly controlled for.

---

[34] As quoted by Bolton, "IAS—Best Chance?" (2003), 16.

[35] Of those who expressed an opinion ($N = 333$), 98 percent selected "important" or "very important," with about half selecting the latter. The extent of uncertainty (i.e., the share of respondents who selected "don't know") was higher in Europe.

[36] Given that the exposure draft stage is the first stage during which IFRS projects become widely known to stakeholders irrespective of institutional linkages, we simplified the survey options by combining the first three stages of the IASB standard-setting process (agenda-setting through discussion paper).

TABLE 5.4

Influencing International Financial Reporting Standards:
Change in Predicted Probability of Successfully Influencing Technical Specification

	Rarely or never	Sometimes	Half of the time	Often	Very often or always
U.S. firms compared to European firms	−16%	+13%	+1.4%	+0.8%	+0.2%

Note: Difference in predicted probabilities of success for U.S. versus European firms in influencing the technical specification of international financial reporting standards, at specified levels of frequency, based on ordered logit model, controlling for (and holding at their means): firm size, contact with expert group, attempted influence via government, attempted influence via comment letters, timing of information, and frequency of attempts. $N = 349$.

Finally, we include in our statistical analyses the responses to the question: "When new international standards projects are considered or launched by the IASB, which may impact your firm, how frequently do you try to affect the specific provisions of such standards?"[37] We find, as one would expect, that a higher FREQUENCY OF ATTEMPTS TO INFLUENCE IASB standard-setting increases the reported frequency of success.[38]

In addition to these control variables, we included in all of our statistical models an indicator of whether the respondent firm is a U.S. FIRM.[39] The positive and statistically highly significant coefficient on this variable (see chapter appendix, table 5.A.1) reveals that U.S. firms are more successful than European firms in their attempts to influence IASB standards, even after taking into account all the other possible explanations discussed above.

In conclusion, the key finding of our statistical investigation is that U.S. firms are significantly more successful in international standard-setting than European firms, regardless of the control factors included in the analysis. To provide an easily understandable measure of U.S. success, we

---

[37] The seven response options ranged from never to always, anchored again by a middle option "about half of the time."

[38] Causality may run either way here, as more successful firms may therefore get involved more frequently, but any such endogeneity does not affect our main result regarding U.S. vs. European firms.

[39] The indicator variable U.S. Firms is a dichotomous ("dummy") variable coded 1 for U.S. firms and 0 for non–U.S. firms.

report in table 5.4 the change in the likelihood (so-called "predicted probabilities") of success for each of the specified levels of frequency. The results show, for example, that for firms which seek to influence the specific provisions of an IFRS, the probability of rarely or never succeeding is 16 percent *lower* among U.S. firms than among European firms, after controlling for all the variables discussed above; and the probability of succeeding "sometimes" is 13 percent *higher* for U.S. firms.[40]

INSTITUTIONAL COMPLEMENTARITY AFFECTING SUCCESS: ADDITIONAL EVIDENCE

Our theory suggests that firms from countries with domestic institutions that are characterized by fragmentation and contestation should be less likely to rely on their domestic standard-setter to pursue their interests in international standardization on their behalf than firms from countries with hierarchical and coordinated standard-setting institutions. As explained in chapter 4, the specific expectation for accounting standards is that Americans should be able to rely greatly on FASB to make their voices heard, thanks to FASB's hierarchical structure supplemented by FASB's tradition of staff support for the IASB and joint projects, especially under the Norwalk Agreement for U.S.GAAP-IFRS convergence. Europeans, by contrast, should rely less on their domestic standard bodies and find them less effective than Americans relying on FASB. We find that American firms ask their domestic standard-setter only slightly more frequently for assistance in influencing the specific provisions of standards. However, when asked to what extent they agree with the statement that involvement in the standard-setting process is not necessary *because their domestic standards organization already represents their interest adequately (or better)*, we find 68 percent of U.S. respondents agreed or strongly agreed that FASB indeed does so. Only 51 percent of European respondents agreed or strongly agreed with corresponding statements about their domestic standards organizations.

Comments and observations from a wide range of additional sources further corroborate the importance of the institutional logic underpinning

---

[40] The reported changes in probability were calculated using the software *Clarify* by Tomz, Wittenberg, and King; see also King et al., "Making the Most of Statistical Analyses" (2000). Table 5A.2 in the chapter appendix provides more detailed information, including for the other variables included in the full statistical model.

our theory. For example, it is remarkable how consistently business leaders as well as policymakers in Europe, aware of the weakness of effective involvement in global regulatory processes and unable to remedy the problem, have lamented the institutional fragmentation of European accounting governance. Vested interests in existing domestic accounting rules and institutional arrangements do seem to have resisted change with considerable success.

As early as 2002, Daniel Bouton, chairman of the French bank Société Générale, warned: "Europe needs to speak with a strong and single voice to avoid the risk that regulation be carried out . . . by the United States."[41] A year later, Jonathan Sysmonds, finance director of the British pharmaceutical giant AstraZeneca, spoke for many when he voiced his grave concerns about Europe's inability to overcome institutional divisions: "I am concerned about fragmentation . . . I've had calls from CFOs of Nestle and Philips saying, 'How can we coordinate our concerns about specific issues in international accounting standards?' I think we are going to have to find ways of linking up. Fragmentation is a big issue now."[42]

No progress was made, however, prompting *The Independent on Sunday* to write: "The problem is that while the EU squabbles, America is busy creating international rules."[43] In 2006, the European Federation of Accountants published a report warning that Europe needed to be more coordinated in its approach to convergence of financial reporting standards to be an effective player on the global stage.[44]

This warning was echoed two years later in a remarkably trenchant report by the EU Parliamentary Committee on Economic and Monetary Affairs. It concluded that "the [institutional] tools the Community has for making its views known . . . do not allow it to deal on an equal footing with those states whose structures are founded on the centralized powers of regulators . . . e.g., FASB."[45] It went on to express the view that "creating a more streamlined EU structure, taking into account national structures for accounting issues could, *especially if . . . some existing bodies*

---

[41] Daniel Bouton quoted in "French Launch Stricter Rules for Companies," *Financial Times*, 24 September 2002.

[42] Interview with Johnathan Sysmonds, in *Financial Director*, 1 November 2003.

[43] "Force Isn't with FRC," *The Independent on Sunday* (London), 28 March 2004.

[44] Fédération des Experts Comptables Européens, *Financial Reporting*, FEE Position Paper (March 2006).

[45] European Parliament, Committee on Economic and Monetary Affairs, *Report on International Financial Reporting Standards (IFRS) and the Governance of the International Accounting Standards Board (IASB)*, A6-0032/2008, 5 February 2008, 7.

were abolished, contribute to simplification and thereby also strengthen the role that the EU should play at the global level."[46]

Low institutional complementarity resulting from the fragmented institutional accounting structure in Europe is seen as a problem even for the IASB—as noted for instance by David Tweedie, IASB chairman: "We go to the regions and try to organize meetings, but always the problem is: who do you talk to? We've learnt our lesson, because you get people coming forward who say they represent industry X but then industry X repudiates them."[47]

This problem has been recognized by some European companies. As a French financial executive put it in his response to one of our open-ended questions, asking respondents to elaborate on their experience with IASB standard-setting: "Our firms are too poorly organized to be effectively represented. [And if and when we organize ourselves] it often is too late: at the exposure draft stage, the basic principles have been defined and the IASB is unwilling to reverse course and start from scratch."[48]

While the Europeans face great difficulties in the getting their act together, Americans seem well served by the existence of FASB—an institution of unrivaled cohesion and strength, and the natural rallying point for American interests in the IASB regulatory processes. As one respondent notes: "FASB [well] represents US positions."[49] It generally enjoys solid support from industry and is wont to sending staff members to partake in IASB working groups charged with developing specific standards, guidelines, and recommendations.

Tricia O'Malley, a Canadian accountant who was a member of the Board of IASB from 2001 to 2007, noted in 2005 how much more effectively FASB interacted with IASB than other national standard-setters. "There was concern, therefore, that standards development could be

---

[46] European Parliament, *Report on IFRS* (2008), 7 (emphasis added). Consistent with this description of ineffectual European governance, we found that EFRAG, the regional body established in the hope that it may grow into the main representative of European interests at, and interlocutor with, the IASB (see chapter 4), is rarely consulted or used by firms seeking to influence IASB regulation. Only 2 percent of surveyed British firms, 9.7 percent of French companies, and 4.4 percent of German firms said they often contact EFRAG and ask it to get involved.

[47] Here as quoted in Bolton, "Tweedie's Best of Breed" (2008), 27.

[48] Authors' translation. The original comment was: "Entreprises sont mal organisées pour être représentées. Il est souvent trop tard: à la phase ED [the public enquiry stage of the IASB process], les grands principes sont définies et compte tenu du travail fourni, l'IASB n'a pas l'intention de revenir en arrière.» French Controleur financier Groupe (f0617bv).

[49] Controller (u0615bq). This general representativeness of FASB is acknowledged even by those who might oppose FASB's position on some issues, such as fair value accounting.

skewed in favor of the U.S."[50] Similar views have been expressed several times by Europeans. To quote the head of the influential British Group of One Hundred [finance directors]: "There is some concern that the strength of the relationship between IASB and FASB means we are heading down a US path without adequate debate."[51]

Consistent with these general impressions, we find that our American respondents generally are content with the present institutional structure. Many feel they are well served by it, as conveyed by respondent comments such as: "Communicating with the staff at the FASB can be the most effective way to get our voice heard";[52] and "We feel confident our opinion would be considered by both the FASB and IASB."[53] Finally, the institutional "intertwining" of IASB and FASB can offer cost-saving advantages to firms seeking to influence international regulation, as expressed by the following respondent: "Although not very familiar with the IASB standard-setting process, we have seen that joint projects between the IASB and the FASB as part of the convergence efforts of the two standard setting groups solicit input in the form of comment letters on all Exposure Drafts issued by the FASB regarding new accounting pronouncements or amendments and interpretations of existing ones."[54] This obviates the need for U.S. firms to directly submit comment letters to the IASB; FASB will take care of U.S. comments in its dealings and deliberations with the IASB.

[50] Tricia O'Malley, quoted in "Board Faces US Backlash," *Accountancy Age* (1 September 2005).

[51] Jonathan Sysmonds quoted in "UK's Top Groups in U-Turn on Accounts," *Financial Times* (26 August 2005).

[52] Chief Accounting Officer/Audit Manager (u0309zf).

[53] Controller (u0055rx).

[54] Controller (u0055rx).

Appendix

Table 5.A.1
Maximum Likelihood Regression Estimates, Models of Success in Attempts to Influence International Financial Reporting Standards

	Model 1	Model 2	Model 3	Model 4
US firms	0.500**	0.594**	0.667**	0.659**
	(.251)	(.256)	(.262)	(.262)
Firm size	0.242***	0.179**	0.154*	0.181**
	(.0767)	(.0779)	(.0793)	(.0823)
Contact with expert group developing the standard	0.823***	0.458**	0.397*	0.349*
	(.176)	(.196)	(.203)	(.205)
Attempted influence via government		0.352	0.377	0.286
		(.248)	(.250)	(.253)
Attempted influence via "comment letter"		0.655***	0.598***	0.461**
		(.167)	(.171)	(.180)
Information (time of obtaining)			0.250	0.157
			(.159)	(.161)
Frequency of Attempting Influence				0.204**
				(.0841)
N	351	351	349	348
pseudo-R^2	0.0719	0.1016	0.1056	0.1157

Note: Estimated coefficients based on logistic regression (ordered logit); standard errors in parentheses. * $p < 0.1$; ** $p < 0.05$; *** $p < 0.01$, two-tailed tests. All estimates in Stata version 10.1.

TABLE 5.A.2
Effectiveness of IFRS in Achieving Specified Objectives

		Not effective	Somewhat effective	Effective/ highly effective
Increasing [the] comparability of corporate financial information (N = 667)	U.S. firms	5%	48%	47%
	European firms	16%	46%	38%
Providing a level playing field internationally for companies (N = 666)	U.S. firms	7%	37%	56%
	European firms	13%	48%	38%
Improving the transparency and usefulness of accounts to shareholders, investors, and creditors (N = 665)	U.S. firms	4%	51%	44%
	European firms	33%	37%	31%
Enhancing market efficiency (N = 657)	U.S. firms	5%	50%	45%
	European firms	37%	51%	13%
Increasing [the] stability of capital markets (N = 659)	U.S. firms	3%	48%	50%
	European firms	32%	54%	15%

Note: Based on responses from all respondents who answered the question "Please rate the effectiveness of IFRSs in achieving each of the following objectives of financial reporting standards." Percentages may not sum to 100 due to rounding.

TABLE 5.A.3

Change in Probability of Success in Attempts to Influence the Technical Specification of Proposed International Standards

	Rarely or never	Sometimes	Half of the time	Often	Very often or always
Region (European → U.S.)	**-0.16** (.063) [-.28 -.032]	**0.13** (.053) [.027 .23]	**0.014** (.0082) [.0020 .033]	**0.0082** (.0057) [.0047 .023]	**0.0022** (.0028) [.0001 .010]
Firm size (min → max)	**-0.21** (.082) [-.35 -.025]	**0.19** (.074) [.022 .31]	**0.014** (.0073) [.0019 .030]	**0.0077** (.0050) [.00007 .019]	**0.0020** (.0027) [.0001 .009]
Contact with expert group developing std (No → Yes)	**-0.25** (.14) [-.50 .025]	**0.21** (.11) [-.021 .41]	**0.024** (.018) [-.0015 .067]	**0.014** (.011) [-.0019 .042]	**0.0036** (.0050) [-.0002 .018]
Attempted Influence via government (min → max)	**-0.19** (.17) [-.52 .13]	**0.16** (.13) [-.11 .40]	**0.020** (.021) [-.0095 .073]	**0.011** (.013) [-.0054 .045]	**0.0031** (.0072) [-.0015 .019]
Attempted Influence via "comment letter" (min → max)	**-0.30** (.11) [-.50 -.063]	**0.26** (.094) [.056 .43]	**0.024** (.013) [.0043 .054]	**0.014** (.0092) [.00040 .035]	**0.0037** (.0051) [.0002 .017]
Timing of Information (early → late)	**-0.099** (.11) [-.30 .12]	**0.087** (.093) [-.10 .27]	**0.0073** (.0089) [-.011 .026]	**0.0040** (.0052) [-.0062 .016]	**0.0011** (.0022) [-.001 .007]
Frequency of attempted influence (min → max)	**-0.28** (.11) [-.49 -.048]	**0.23** (.091) [.041 .39]	**0.027** (.016) [.0026 .064]	**0.15** (.011) [.00077 .043]	**0.0042** (.0059) [.0002 .020]

Note: Columns represent the five response categories of the dependent variable (frequency of success when the respondent attempts to influence the IASB's specification of an IFRS or revised IAS). Larger bold numbers indicate, based on the estimates from Model 4, the change in the probability that a firm is successful at the specified frequency, resulting from switching the independent variable on the left from its minimum to its maximum value while holding all other variables at their means. Standard errors in parentheses; 95% confidence intervals in brackets (based on *Clarify* simulations).

Private Regulators in Global Product Markets

INSTITUTIONAL STRUCTURE AND COMPLEMENTARITY IN PRODUCT REGULATION

Iɴ Aᴜɢᴜsᴛ 2000, the American National Standards Institute issued a stern warning: "*The standardization world has changed*. We can't assume that U.S. technology and practices will automatically be adopted everywhere [anymore]."[1] The concern was in fact not new. A decade earlier, the Office of Technology Assessment of the U.S. Congress had observed: "Many American companies . . . have yet to recognize the implications of international [product] standards in a global economy. By the time they come to appreciate the potential consequences, the damage to the national economy may already have been done."[2]

To illustrate what was at stake, the office pointed to the U.S. machine tools industry, a backbone of manufacturing production, described by Ronald Reagan as a "vital component of the U.S. defense base."[3] For years, this industry had been able to thrive without regard to international standards. Until the early 1980s, more than 80 percent of U.S. machine tool production was for the domestic market,[4] which was so large that industry practices often "became de facto [global] standards."[5]

Globalization, however, brought new realities. Key growth opportunities shifted to foreign markets, especially developing industrial nations like Brazil, Russia, India, and China, where customers and sometimes government regulations demand international rather than American standards.[6] In the words of the CEO of Milacron, a Cincinnati-based major machine

---

[1] ANSI, *National Standards Strategy for the United States* (2000), 3, italics added.

[2] OTA, *Global Standards* (1992), 12.

[3] Reagan statement of 26 May 1986, as quoted in McCormack, "U.S. Machine Tool Industry Is On the Brink" (2009).

[4] Kalafsky and MacPherson, "The Competitive Characteristics of U.S. Manufacturers in the Machine Tool Industry" (2002), 357.

[5] OTA, *Global Standards* (1992), 8. See also McClure et al., *The Competitive Status of the U.S. Machine Tool Industry* (1983), 44.

[6] Kawasaki, *Industry Assessment: Machine Tools and Metalworking Equipment* (2009).

tools company founded in the mid-nineteenth century: "[Our] competitors [now] are global. [Our] suppliers, standards, designs, . . . all must become global."[7] Yet, many in the U.S. machine tool industry failed to adapt to these changes and did not involve themselves effectively in the rule-making for global product markets.[8]

The consequences were severe: having been the world's largest producer of machine tools from the end of World War II through the early 1980s, the United States declined to fourth by the early 1990s and seventh by 2009—after China, Germany, Japan, Italy, South Korea and Taiwan; just ahead of Switzerland.[9] Long gone are the "golden years" when the United States was the number-two exporter in the world and "dominated global machine tool production."[10] Hundreds of U.S. firms went out of business,[11] leaving a domestic industry now described as "a shadow of its former self . . . on the verge of oblivion."[12] The decline, moreover, was far from inevitable, as evidenced by the continuing strength of the industry, notably in Germany and Italy, which—unlike the United States—have actively been shaping the rules of the "new standardization world."

We will show that the failure of the U.S. machine tools industry is far from an isolated case, and that our institutional complementarity theory offers a compelling explanation of why the Europeans are today more effective players in shaping rules for global product markets than the Americans. We begin in this chapter with an historical overview of how the International Organization for Standardization (ISO) and the International Electrotechnical Commission (IEC) became the focal institutions for setting international product standards for most industries. We then examine the institutional structure and decision-making procedures of these global private regulators, followed by an investigation of domestic systems of standardization, where we concentrate on the contrast between the institutional structure for setting product standards in the United States and Europe. In contrast to the financial realm, the institutional

[7] "Cincinnati Milacron Chairman Issues Stern Warning to U.S. Manufacturers," *New Technology Week*, 18 November 1991, 4; as quoted in OTA, *Global Standards* (1992), 8.

[8] OTA, *Global Standards* (1992), 8. See also U.S. House of Representatives (Hearing), *Standards-Setting and United States Competitiveness* (2001).

[9] Carlsson, "Small-Scale Industry at a Crossroads" (1989); Finegold et al., *The Decline of the U.S. Machine-Tool Industry* (1994); McCormack, "U.S. Machine Tool Industry Is On the Brink" (2009).

[10] Albrecht, *The American Machine Tool Industry* (2010), passim.

[11] Carlsson, "Small-Scale Industry at a Crossroads" (1989), 246; Kawasaki, *Industry Assessment* (2009).

[12] McCormack, "U.S. Machine Tool Industry Is On the Brink" (2009).

complementarity between the U.S. domestic system for setting product standards and the standards institutions at the global level is low, whereas complementarity between the domestic systems of standardization in Europe and the institutions at the global level is high. In the last section of the chapter, we discuss the implications of these differences in institutional complementarity for who is most likely to influence the content of product standards in ISO and IEC and by what means—and who is most likely to pay the adjustment costs.

A Brief History of Global Market Governance Through Product Standards

The world's first international private standard-setting organization, the IEC, was established in 1906, at the end of a remarkable century of scientific breakthroughs that fundamentally transformed economic, social, and political life in the Western world and beyond. Many of these breakthroughs occurred in the area of electro-technical engineering. Alessandro Volta's invention of the so-called voltaic pile, an early battery, allowed for electric energy to be stored; Michael Faraday's work on electromagnetic rotary devices set in motion the development of electric generators and motors; Heinrich Hertz's invention of ways to measure and receive electromagnetic waves paved the way for radio communication; and Thomas Edison—inventor and businessman—developed the telegraph, phonograph, and the first commercially successful incandescent light bulb.[13] This steady stream of inventions and innovations, combined with rapidly growing interest in their industrial application and commercialization, led to the creation of national electro-technical societies in the 1870s and 1880s. Representatives of these societies, meeting in so-called International Electrical Congresses, soon started to discuss standardization of terminology and matters relating to safety and testing. The driving force was largely commercial: the lack of standardization impeded achieving economies of scale in the production of goods ranging from electrically powered machinery to light bulbs.[14]

---

[13] See Frary with Tunbridge, "The World of Electricity: 1820–1904" (2006).

[14] The early history and institutional development of the IEC is discussed in greater detail in Büthe, "The Power of Norms; the Norms of Power" (2010) and "Engineering Uncontestedness?" (2010), and Yates and Murphy, "The Formation of the ISO" (2006), 8–11.

At the first such congress, in 1881 in Paris, the delegates of the national electro-technical societies agreed on a series of standard measurement units that exist to this day: they selected Ampere from no fewer than ten different units of electric current, Volt from twelve units of electromotive force, and Ohm from fifteen units of resistance. Despite such early achievements, glaring gaps remained in international standardization, particularly in the area of electrical equipment, where national differences had become "a worldwide problem" by the end of the nineteenth century,[15] and international standardization was proving difficult without an institutional structure to facilitate the exchange of proposals and to aggregate technical preferences.

The issue was addressed at the 1904 International Electrical Congress in St. Louis. In a concluding resolution, the delegates pledged to take steps "to secure the co-operation of the technical societies of the world [for] the appointment of a representative Commission to consider the question of the standardization of the nomenclature and ratings of electrical apparatus and machinery."[16] These scientist-businessmen had concluded that the market mechanism was neither effective nor efficient, especially transnationally, to achieve standardization—but they also sought to keep the "bureaucratic influence" of governments at bay and hence sought to create a nongovernmental body.[17] Two years later, delegates from thirteen national electro-technical societies convened in London at the invitation of the British Institution of Electrical Engineers (IEE) to establish a new standard-setting organization, the International Electrotechnical Commission.[18] The IEC's first meeting, attended by representatives from fifteen countries, took place in October 1908 in London, where its secretariat was housed at the IEE until it relocated to Geneva in the aftermath of World War II.[19]

---

[15] Frary with Tunbridge, "The World of Electricity: 1820–1904" (2006).

[16] Quoted in Ruppert, *Brief History of the International Electrotechnical Commission* (1956), 1. For further discussion of the 1904 Congress, see Erdmann, "The Appointment of a Representative Commission" (2009).

[17] IEC, *Report of Preliminary Meeting* (1906), 10.

[18] The countries were Austria, Belgium, Canada, France, Germany, Great Britain, Hungary, Italy, Japan, Netherlands, Spain, Switzerland, and the United States. For details, see Büthe, "The Power of Norms; the Norms of Power" (2010), 297–302.

[19] Ruppert, *Brief History* (1956), 6. IEC's secretary-general was Charles Le Maistre, a British engineer who held the position until his death in 1953. On the key role played by Charles Le Maistre in international standardization, see Yates and Murphy, "Charles Le Maistre: Entrepreneur in International Standardization" (2008).

IEC's sister organization, the ISO, is the product of a 1946 merger between the International Federation of National Standardizing Associations (ISA) and the United Nations Standards Coordinating Committee (UNSCC). The ISA was established in New York in 1926 and administered from Zurich, Switzerland. While the IEC focused on only one (albeit broad) domain, ISA's jurisdiction was general and wide-ranging, covering potentially all other technical areas. Demand for international standards grew with the steady resumption of world trade in the 1920s. The stock market crash of 1929 and the ensuing downward spiral of global trade, however, had an immediate dampening effect on ISA activities. The ISA faced another difficulty: tensions between countries that used metric measurements in their standards and countries that followed the British imperial tradition of measurements in inches, pounds, gallons, etc. The "metric" countries—Austria, Belgium, Czechoslovakia, France, Germany, Italy, Japan, Netherlands, Sweden, and Switzerland—constituted a majority; "inch" countries—primarily Canada, Great Britain, and the United States—a small minority. The latter countries participated rarely, and ISA's work ended up being largely confined to continental Europe.[20]

The outbreak of World War II brought activities within IEC and ISA to a standstill. The need for standardization, however, did not cease during the war. In fact, the war effort sometimes dramatically illustrated the costs of the lack of *international* standards, as experienced by the British Eighth Army, fighting Rommel's forces in 1941–42. British replacements for worn-out parts on their American-made tanks reached the British armed forces just in time—only to be unusable due to literally incompatible nuts and bolts. Differences in British and American threading standards—established in the 1840s and 1860s, respectively—thus forced the British commanders to abandon tanks and equipment in the North African desert![21] According to American sources, the difference in British and American standards for screw threads alone added some £25 million to the cost of war.[22] Unlike in the pre–World War II period, Americans now took great interest and a leading role in transnational standardization. They organized a meeting in 1943 in New York, attended by the directors

---

[20] Kuert, "The Founding of the ISO: 'Things are Going the Right Way'" (1997), 15.

[21] Robb, "Significance of Company and National Standards" (1956), 296; Surowiecki, "Turn of the Century" (2002).

[22] The number is reported in *Economist*, "UNSCC" (1945), 286. Reports such as this one coincided with a generally increased appreciation of the economic benefits of standardization for industrial production and sustained economic growth, see, e.g., *Economist*, "Standard Production" (1945); Ord, *Secrets of Industry* (1945).

of the American, British, and Canadian national standards institutes—all private-sector organizations—to discuss the possibility of establishing "an agency for inter-allied cooperation in standards work."[23] A year later, they set up the United Nations Standards Coordinating Committee (UNSCC)—not as an intergovernmental organization but as a private-sector institutional arrangement with offices in New York and London.[24] UNSCC membership grew to eighteen countries by early 1945; neutral countries and enemy countries were barred from membership.[25] *The Economist* observed: "It may be a coincidence that the countries thus [excluded] all belong to the metric bloc and that on the new body the Anglo-Saxon countries must have, if not a numerical majority, at least an overwhelming economic preponderance."[26]

The urgent need to rebuild the devastated economies after Allied victory, however, militated against continuing exclusion and required "the honest desire to make the new standards serve the economic interests of all nations instead of strengthening existing differences for use as protective barriers or instruments of economic imperialism."[27] Talks on merging the UNSCC and ISA began in 1946, resulting in a London conference later that year, convened by the UNSCC and attended by representatives of twenty-five national standards institutes—many of them ISA members. Willy Kuert, a Swiss delegate, noted: "The atmosphere at first was . . . uncertain. We were sizing each other up. We feared that the UNSCC didn't want an organization like the ISA had been, but an organization . . . dominated by the winners of the war. . . . There was an inch bloc and a metric bloc. We did not talk about it."[28]

In the end, the UNSCC leadership agreed to merge with the ISA, creating a new institution, the International Organization for Standardization (ISO).[29] The representatives of the American Standards Association (ASA) sought to secure a key position in the new organization by selecting

---

[23] Minutes of the meeting of 10 December 1943, quoted in Yates and Murphy, "The Formation of the ISO" (2006), 21.

[24] The term *United Nations* was generally used as early as 1942 to refer to Allied countries; Yates and Murphy, "The Formation of the ISO" (2006), 22–23.

[25] The member countries were Australia, Brazil, Belgium, Canada, Chile, China, Czechoslovakia, Denmark, France, Great Britain, Mexico, Netherlands, New Zealand, Norway, Poland, South Africa, the U.S., and the USSR.

[26] *Economist*, "UNSCC" (1945), 286.

[27] *Economist* (1945), 287.

[28] Kuert, "The Founding of the ISO" (1997), 18.

[29] About two-thirds of the initial 67 ISO technical committees were based on ISA committees.

Henry St. Leger, an American, to be secretary-general—a position he held until 1965.[30] The ISO conducted its first official meeting in Geneva in June 1947, where it established its permanent secretariat, sharing a building with the IEC.

Increasing Scope and Importance of International Product Standardization

The scope of international standardization broadened in the post–World War II period for both IEC and ISO. IEC had, in the early years, focused mostly on measurements, symbols, terminology, and ratings for electrical current, as well as electricity-producing equipment. During the interwar years, IEC started to develop standards for transformers, insulation, circuit breakers, and a broad range of electrical equipment for industry, as well as a few early consumer products, such as household electrical lamps. After WWII, IEC expanded into new areas, such as safety standards for household electrical appliances and design and performance standards for electronic devices and later audio, video, and multimedia equipment. In the 1970s, it added, for instance, laser equipment; in the 1980s, fiber optics, superconductivity, and wind turbines; in the 1990s, fuel cell technology.[31]

ISO standardization was originally mainly concerned with basic issues of mechanical engineering, such as screw threads, ball bearings, pipe sizes, shafts, couplings, and power transmission. By the 1970s, however, standards from the mechanical field represented only about 20 percent of all ISO standards.[32] The ISO had quickly moved into new areas, such as chemical technology, construction materials, nuclear and solar energy, ergonomics, as well as air and water quality. More generally, the ISO moved away from producing standards covering basic test methods and terminologies toward standards related to the design or performance, as

---

[30] Yates and Murphy, "The Formation of the ISO" (2006).

[31] See Raeburn "IEC Technical Committee Creation" (2006) and "Development and Growth of IEC Technical Committees" (2006). See also Büthe, "Engineering Uncontestedness?" (2010), and "The Power of Norms; the Norms of Power" (2010), 302f, 305f. The IEC mission statement on the official website now reads: "The IEC charter embraces all electrotechnologies including electronics, magnetics and electromagnetics, electroacoustics, multimedia, telecommunications, and energy production and distribution, as well as associated general disciplines such as terminology and symbols, electromagnetic compatibility, measurement, and performance, dependability, design and development, safety and the environment" (IEC, "Mission and Objectives" (2009)).

[32] Latimer, ed. Friendship Among Equals (1997), 36.

well as safety and health aspects, of industrial and consumer products (including sports and recreation equipment, as well as clothing). This trend coincided with the rapid growth of the consumer movement in industrialized countries starting in the late 1960s, leading to increased demand for health and safety standards. More recently, the ISO has expanded into a wide range of new domains, including information technologies, nanotechnology, biometrics, health care, e-commerce, fisheries and aquaculture, and—most famously—quality management (ISO 9000-series) and environmental management (ISO 14,000-series standards).[33]

The number of international standards produced by ISO and IEC increased substantially in the 1950s, 1960s, and 1970s, and the organizations slowly but decisively established themselves as *the* truly international standard-setters for manufactured goods. Yet, they lived in relative obscurity—mostly unknown outside the world of engineering experts—until the increase in nontariff barriers and other developments in global markets raised the economic and political stakes in international standardization. When Robert Baldwin wrote his seminal study *Nontariff Distortions of International Trade* in 1971, technical standards and regulations for health and consumer safety were still a minor issue, discussed along with customs procedures and antidumping in one short chapter.[34] By the end of the 1970s, however, technical standards had become important nontariff barriers to trade. Member states of the GATT thus devoted a separate agreement to the issue during the Tokyo Round negotiations, which ended in 1979.[35] The so-called Code on Technical Barriers to Trade obliged signatories to avoid technical standards that "unnecessarily" restrict market access and to use international harmonized standards rather than divergent domestic ones whenever possible.[36] The 1979 protocol, however, was optional, and even a decade later had attracted less than forty signatories and few beyond advanced industrialized

---

[33] Unlike the vast majority of ISO standards, which are highly specific to a particular product, material, or process, ISO 9001 and ISO 14001 are "generic management system standards," meaning that they can be applied to any organization, whatever its product or service, in any sector of activity, and from the private sector to public administration. See Guler et al., "The International Spread of ISO 9000 Quality Certificates" (2002); Prakash and Potoski, *The Voluntary Environmentalists* (2006), and Tamm Hallström, *Organizing International Standardization* (2004), 52–74 and 98–118. For a good summary of the growth of ISO standardization, see Murphy and Yates, *The International Organization for Standardization* (2008), 17–23 and 46–88.

[34] Baldwin, *Nontariff Distortions of International Trade* (1971).

[35] For a discussion of the early history of the agreement, see Groetzinger, "The New GATT Code and the International Harmonization of Product Standards" (1975).

[36] E.g., Middleton, "The GATT Standards Code" (1980).

countries. It also remained vague about signatories' obligations and had no enforcement mechanisms. It was therefore generally considered ineffective.[37]

Product standards continued to become more and more important in the 1980s, a time of increasing international integration of product markets, partly enabled by the reduction in long-distance transport costs due to the global introduction of ISO-standardized shipping containers,[38] and partly due to the success of GATT trade negotiations in lowering the tariffs for manufactured goods—from an average of about 40 percent to less than 10 percent by the end of the Tokyo Round. These changes led to what Robert Baldwin has called the "draining of the swamp" effect: cross-national differences in product standards became more visible (and economically important) because they now impeded trade in goods that few had even thought of exporting or importing previously, when transport costs and tariffs had made trade prohibitively costly. And standards often differed, because the vast majority of product standards were until the 1980s still developed by each country on its own, without much regard for what others were doing. Setting standards at the domestic level had been sensible and efficient when the standards were intended to solve local or at most national issues of compatibility or serve as the technical basis of laws and regulations that sought to address purely domestic health, consumer safety, or environmental concerns. With economic globalization, however, technical standards that differed across countries became prominent nontariff barriers to trade.[39]

Product standards not only became more visible but also increased in number and diverged further as consumer-voters became generally more sensitive to environmental, health, and safety issues, yet differed in their specific concerns and preferred solutions.[40] In response to public concerns about the chemical industry in the 1960s and 1970s, for instance, the U.S. Congress enacted with bipartisan support strict regulations that went far beyond the regulations of that industry in any European country. In recent years, by contrast, consumer concerns have sparked far more

---

[37] Grieco, *Cooperation Among Nations* (1990), esp. 76f, 86ff, 113ff, 156f, 185ff.

[38] The history of the ISO standard for shipping containers is covered in some detail by Egyedi, "The Standardised Container" (2000); Grey, "Setting Standards: A Phenomenal Success Story" (1997); Levinson, *The Box* (2006); and Murphy and Yates, *The International Organization for Standardization* (2008), 46–67.

[39] E.g., Bhagwati and Hudec, eds., *Fair Trade and Harmonization* (1996); Trebilcock and Howse, *The Regulation of International Trade* (2005).

[40] E.g., Dalton et al., "Electoral Change in Advanced Industrial Democracies" (1984).

stringent regulations of the chemical industry in Europe than in the United States, where these concerns are not even prominent among consumer safety advocates.[41] Cross-national differences in these standards thus often reflect accidents of history in the sense that the reasons for these differences long precede the present era of international interdependence and global governance.

Most countries, however, also clearly raised some standards (and enshrined them in regulations that made compliance mandatory) with the intent of creating or raising NTBs in order to protect domestic producers, usually in declining or uncompetitive industries.[42] Technical standards as protectionist devices were politically attractive: the international orientation of industry had created by the 1970s a domestic constituency against raising tariffs because such protectionism risks retaliation.[43] But disguised protectionism via technical standards is harder to prove and less easily results in retaliatory protectionism. A Japanese product standard, for example, adopted in 1986 by the Consumer Product Safety Association (CPSA) at the request of the nascent Japanese ski manufacturing industry, required that skis sold in Japan would have to comply with particular product design specifications in order to get a consumer safety seal. None of the major foreign manufacturers met the standard. The CPSA sought to justify the introduction of the ski standard by arguing that Japanese snow is "different" from snow in other (ski-exporting) countries.[44]

[41] Vogel, "The Hare and the Tortoise Revisited" (2003) and *The Politics of Precaution* (2011).

[42] E.g., Mansfield and Busch, "The Political Economy of Nontariff Barriers" (1995); Motaal, "The Agreement on Technical Barriers to Trade, The Committee on Trade and the Environment, and Eco-Labeling" (2002); Ray and Marvel, "The Pattern of Protection in the Industrial World" (1984).

[43] Milner, *Resisting Protectionism* (1988).

[44] Established international competitors' skis did not have the required "safe" thickness and width because these manufacturers had already found technologically superior ways of achieving stability and flex simultaneously without making the skis as thick and heavy as their new Japanese competitors. Foreign ski manufacturers, however, had been excluded from the meetings of the committee that developed the standard. The standard was withdrawn during the preliminary consultation phase of a GATT Standards Code dispute, launched by the U.S. and European governments on behalf of their ski manufacturers, but not until the 1986/87 ski sales season was effectively over; see Rappoport, "Japanese Ski Makers Freeze out the Opposition" (1986), and "Skiing Dispute Goes to GATT" (1986); Rodger, "Japanese in Flurry over Ski Standards Protest" (1986); and Sykes, *Product Standards for Internationally Integrated Goods Markets* (1995), 76f. See also Lecraw, "Japanese Standards: A Barrier to Trade?" (1987). Others raised standards to force all producers to face production costs similar to their high-end domestic producers. Thus U.S. car manufacturers supported higher emissions standards for all cars sold in the United States after they had found cost-effective ways of meeting the environmental standards initially enacted

Even when they do not completely close markets to foreign produc-ers, product standards and related technical regulations that differ across countries inhibit efficient mass production ("economies of scale") and increase the cost of foreign goods—equivalent to a tariff of 2 percent to 10 percent according to an OECD study.[45] At the same time, increasing international trade meant that the level of technical standards and quality of regulation in countries in which manufactured goods were produced increasingly affected consumers in other countries.[46] In sum, national regulatory autonomy has been increasingly replaced by regulatory in-terdependence. To address many of the concerns about interdependence without sacrificing international economic integration, governments and private actors who expected to benefit from further economic integration sought common "international" standards for an increasingly wide range of goods.

ISO and IEC, well-established by the 1980s, were an easy focal point for developing such harmonized international standards. Their importance and visibility was particularly boosted by the adoption of the Agreement on Technical Barriers to Trade (TBT-Agreement), negotiated during the Uruguay Round of the GATT, 1986–94. Unlike the 1979 Standards Code, the TBT-Agreement is an integral part of the Agreement Establishing the World Trade Organization and hence binding on all WTO member states. It stipulates that "where technical regulations are required and relevant international standards exist or their completion is imminent, Members shall use them . . . as a basis for their technical regulations" (Article 2.4).[47]

---

solely for the state of California. DeSombre, *Domestic Sources of International Environ-mental Policy* (2000); Vogel, *Trading Up* (1995).

[45] Kawamoto et al., "Product Standards, Conformity Assessment and Regulatory Reform" (1997). To put this price differential into perspective: average tariff levels for manufactured goods are now (post-Uruguay Round) between 3 percent and 4 percent for advanced in-dustrialized countries. Regarding the trade-inhibiting effect of cross-national differences in product standards for developing countries, see Chen et al., "Do Standards Matter for Export Success?" (2006).

[46] This remains an important issue to this day. As more and more countries import a grow-ing share of their food supplies, poor sanitary standards or lax enforcement of the related regulations for farms and food products manufacturers in one country threaten health and safety of foreign consumers who have often no direct recourse to the food producers; see Coglianese et al., eds., *Import Safety* (2009).

[47] The agreement is reproduced, for example, in Sykes, *Product Standards for Interna-tionally Integrated Goods Markets* (1995). Similar provisions for health and food safety standards are specified in the Agreement on the Application of Sanitary and Phytosanitary Measures (SPS-Agreement); see Büthe, "The Globalization of Health and Safety Standards" (2008) and "The Politics of Food Safety in the Age of Global Trade" (2009).

Regulations that use international standards are rebuttably presumed to be consistent with the country's WTO obligations, whereas the use of a standard that differs from the pertinent international standard may be challenged through the WTO dispute mechanism as an unnecessary non-tariff barrier to trade and thus a violation of international trade law. And while the TBT-Agreement does not define international standards exclusively as the products of ISO and IEC standardization, it assigns these private organizations (and only them) a prominent role that amounts at least to an implicit delegation of regulatory authority.[48]

The consequently increased importance of international product standards resulted in an explosive growth—and inevitably some degree of politicization—of standard-setting activity in both ISO and IEC. To date the ISO has produced more than eighteen thousand standards and IEC more than fifty-five hundred—approximately 85 percent of all known international standards and more than four times as many ISO and IEC standards as existed in the early 1980s.[49] And while none of these standards are legally binding as such, they are increasingly referenced in, or incorporated into, government regulations, which effectively makes them mandatory.[50] Moreover, manufacturers have a range of incentives to comply with product standards, including consumer demand and insurance/liability incentives: "For business purposes, what is legally voluntary may be financially necessary."[51] And, crucially, ISO and IEC standards are adopted not only in advanced industrialized countries. Many recently industrialized countries, such as South Korea and Singapore, and numerous developing countries—including large, fast-growing ones such as Brazil, China, and India—adopt many ISO and IEC standards without change as domestic standards, if only to forestall "becom[ing] the dumping ground for noncompliant products."[52] In sum, the international integration of

[48] E.g., Marceau and Trachtman, "TBT, SPS, and GATT" (2002).

[49] By 1980, ISO had produced 4,269 standards; IEC's output stood at about 1,500 standards. See ISO, "The ISO Timeline" (2007).

[50] E.g., ISO/IEC, *Using and Referencing ISO and IEC Standards for Technical Regulations* (2007).

[51] Anonymous, "Product Positioning" (2009), 1. For a discussion of the range of business motivations for compliance with "voluntary" domestic and international standards, see Büthe and Mattli, "International Standards and Standard-Setting Bodies" (2009), 441–43.

[52] Gormann, "Conformity Assessment, Standards and Trade" (2009). On the adoption of ISO/IEC standards by developing countries, see, e.g., EOS, "Harmonization of Egyptian Standards" (2009); SPRING Singapore, "Standardisation for Market Access and Competitiveness." (2005); and U.S. Department of Commerce, *Standards and Competitiveness* (2004), 16.

markets as well as governments' implicit or explicit delegation of regulatory authority to ISO and IEC have in recent decades greatly increased the stakes in international standards. We therefore turn next to an analysis of ISO and IEC standard-setting.

INSTITUTIONAL STRUCTURE AND THE STANDARDIZATION PROCESS

> Most influence to shape regulation globally is accumulated in thousands of obscure technical committees
> of . . . private standard-setting bodies like the ISO.
> —*John Braithwaite and Peter Drahos, Global Business Regulation*

The IEC started forming specialized committees to write standards as early as 1911. In 1926, it pioneered the practice of allocating the secretariat of a given technical committee (TC) to a national standards organization. The national body provides the administrative support to the work of the committee, thereby reducing the IEC's cost of organizing and managing the TC. This institutional innovation brought great financial relief to the IEC and permitted it to accelerate the international standards production.[53] The practice of closely involving national standard-setters was later copied by other international standard-setters, including the ISO, and has had a lasting impact on the politics of standardization, as we explain below.

The ISO—and its predecessor, the ISA—built their organizational structure on the IEC model. The members of ISO are national standard-setting bodies. Each country can be represented only by one body, namely the "most broadly representative [organization] of standardization in [the] countr[y]."[54] For the vast majority of industrialized countries, such national standard-setting bodies are—again in the IEC tradition—private-

---

[53] Former IEC secretary-general Louis Ruppert noted in the mid-1950s: "This proved to be a most successful arrangement which has since made it possible for the IEC to handle a large number of subjects at the minimum of cost." See Ruppert, *Brief History of the IEC* (1956), 3.

[54] Article 3.1.1 of the Statutes of ISO. IEC membership is governed by Article 4 of the IEC Statutes, which requires national member bodies to be "fully representative of national interests in the fields of activity of the [IEC]." A country's IEC and ISO member bodies may differ or be the same.

sector organizations, largely funded by industry.[55] They select experts to serve as their countries' representatives in ISO technical committees and fund 60 percent of the operating costs of the ISO central secretariat in Geneva through membership fees.[56]

ISO has 107 full voting member bodies; IEC has 59. Both organizations offer other kinds of membership for countries of modest resources, mostly developing countries and very small countries (see table 6.1). In exchange for lower or no membership fees, these countries have limited participation rights. For ISO, the decision to offer such alternative types of membership was taken in the 1970s by the Swedish secretary-general of ISO, Olle Sturen, in order to boost membership beyond the developed world, thereby solidifying ISO's credibility and legitimacy as a truly global organization.[57]

The prodigious technical output of the ISO is carried out within the ISO by a large network of 210 technical committees, 509 subcommittees and 2,443 working groups;[58] IEC standardization is conducted in 174 technical committees and subcommittees and 1,118 working groups (see table 6.1). In these highly specialized fora, some 60,000 experts gather to tackle standardization issues.[59] Most of these experts come from industry, and their firms cover their travel and related costs; a few others come from academic and not-for-profit research institutes, regulatory agencies,

[55] For some developing countries, the national ISO member bodies are governmental or hybrid public-private organizations.

[56] The individuals who directly participate in ISO/IEC standardization officially do so as representatives of a member body. National member bodies therefore often constitute mirror committees or working groups at the domestic level to provide input. The remaining 40 percent of the budget comes from the sale of publications, see *ISO in Figures* (2010). ISO estimates that, in addition to contributing to the 33 million Swiss Francs annual operational costs of the central secretariat, the 39 member bodies that staff technical committee and subcommittee secretariats spend about 120 million Swiss Francs annually on these additional operational (administrative) expenditures of ISO standardization. In the IEC case, about 40 percent of its 23 million Swiss Franc budget comes from membership fees; the rest comes from sales of standards and conformity assessment systems operations, see IEC, *Annual Report 2008* (2009).

[57] Sturen, "The Expansion of ISO" (1997), 65f. Sturen served as secretary-general of ISO from 1968 until 1986. IEC already counted India, China, South Africa, Egypt, and Argentina among its pre–World War II members, but was slower to broaden its membership in more recent decades, see Büthe, "The Power of Norms; the Norms of Power" (2010).

[58] Every working day of the year about seven ISO technical meetings take place around the world, and between meetings, the experts may continue the standards developing work by correspondence.

[59] This is an official estimate. Some interviewees have argued that the number is as high as 100,000.

TABLE 6.1
ISO/IEC Organizational Structure and Output

	ISO	IEC
Membership	107 "Member bodies"	59 "Full members"
	45 "Corresponding members"	22 "Associate members"
	11 "Subscriber members"	81 "Affiliate members"
Countries represented (total)	163	162
Central secretaria	1	1
Full-time staff	153	30
Technical committees (TCs)	210	94
Subcommittees (SCs)	519	80
Working groups	2,443	1,118
Individual participants/ year	ca. 50,000	ca. 10,000
Total Standards (current)	18,083	5,520

Sources: "ISO in Figures" (2010); "ISO Members" (2010); "IEC in Figures" (2010); "Members of the IEC" (2010); and authors' calculations from data provided by ISO and IEC. Information about structure, participants, and number of standards developed is current as of 31 December 2009; membership information is current as of 31 August 2010; Total number of countries represented includes countries represented by bodies with limited participation rights (corresponding/associate members, subscriber/affiliate members). Working groups includes for IEC project/maintenance teams. Number of individual participants is based on ISO/IEC estimates, not including technical experts who are involved in national "mirror" committees, only.

consumer organizations, and other NGOs. Their work is coordinated by the Geneva secretariats. This coordination ensures consistency and the creation of only a single ISO or IEC standard for any given product or technical issue.[60] The international institution thus is characterized by decentralization of the detailed technical work *combined with* a high degree of coordination and organizational hierarchy, though agenda-setting within that hierarchy occurs mostly from the bottom up rather than from the top down.[61]

The International Standardization Process for Products

In chapter 3, we emphasized the importance of early involvement in multistage standardization processes. What are the stages of this process for setting international product standards? After a "preliminary" stage, during which often informal discussions within and among member bodies explore the level of interest in developing a new standard at the international level, if one or more stakeholders consider it desirable, the ISO and IEC standard-setting process (governed by a joint document) has five stages, followed by publication of the final product as an ISO or IEC standard: the proposal stage, the preparatory stage, the committee stage, the enquiry stage, and the approval stage. We describe each stage in brief:[62]

1. The submission of a formal proposal to develop a new standard starts the standardization process in the Proposal Stage. Such proposals are virtually always preceded by formal deliberations within a

---

[60] ISO and IEC have established a series of joint committees in areas of overlapping jurisdiction to ensure a cooperative rather than competitive relationship.

[61] The presentation of the institutional structure of ISO and IEC would be incomplete without mention of the ISO and IEC Councils. The councils set policy and long-term strategic and financial objectives. The ISO Council meets twice a year and is chaired by the president—a prominent person from the standardization or business community elected for two years. Council proposals are put to the ISO members who meet annually at the General Assembly. The IEC Council meets during the IEC "General Meeting," the annual gathering of members. The role played by the Councils and related advisory committees may best be described as auxiliary to the expansive committee structure. See Frontard, "Standards-Related Activities" (1997), 56.

[62] Essentially the same process is followed for revising an existing standard. The rules are specified in the *ISO/IEC Directives*, Part 1 (7th ed., 2009), esp. 20ff; as explained below, the Directives describe actual ISO/IEC standard-setting practice. For further discussion of the ISO process, see also Büthe and Witte, *Product Standards in Transatlantic Trade and Investment* (2004); for IEC, Büthe, "The Power of Norms; the Norms of Power" (2010).

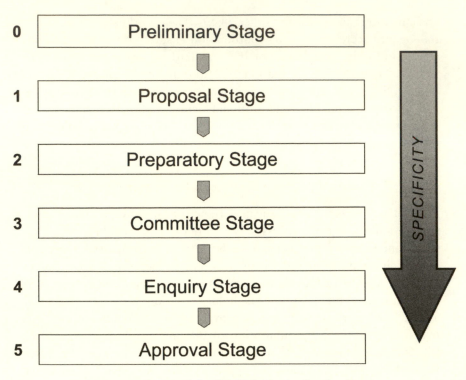

Figure 6.1 Stages of the ISO/IEC Standardization Process

national standard-setting body and often informal transnational de-liberations among ISO-participating standards experts from several countries during what we call the preliminary stage.[63] One ISO member body, based on internal decision-making procedures that may vary from country to country, then typically proposes a new "work

[63] The ISO and IEC standardization processes are virtually identical. There are only two notable differences, which do not affect our analysis. First, the staff of national member bodies play a larger role as technical committee secretaries and sometimes even chairs in ISO than in IEC (where TC chairs and secretaries almost always come from firms with a stake in the matter—usually as suppliers or industrial customers). Second, in ISO, each standard is subject to review every five years; in IEC, each standard has its own "maintenance schedule," which provides for review and possible revision anywhere from two to twenty years after the initial adoption; see Büthe, "The Power of Norms; the Norms of Power" (2010), 317f. For simplicity, we refer only to ISO here, but always mean "ISO or IEC, respectively."

item" to ISO.[64] The relevant technical committee or subcommittee considers the request and must approve it with a simple majority for the proposal to move forward.

2. During the Preparatory Stage, a working group of experts—usually assembled by a leader appointed by the committee or subcommittee—develops a first working draft of the standard. This first draft specifies the technical scope of the future standard and elaborates general technical solutions and takes into account initial submissions made by the members of the technical committee in charge of the new item. The experts participate as national delegates, chosen by their ISO national member bodies. As such, they are asked to speak not only on behalf of the firms or sectors in which they are employed but for other national stakeholders, too.[65] The preparatory stage ends, and the work moves to the committee level, when the working group circulates a first draft of the standard.

3. During the Committee Stage, the full technical committee or subcommittee discusses and further develops the standard. At this stage then, only the "P-members" of the pertinent committee—that is, those member bodies whose representatives regularly "participate" in the committee—have a voice in the process.[66] The standard often goes through several drafts during this stage, with increasing specificity, until a consensus is achieved among the members of the (sub)committee. The resulting technical document is then issued as a "Draft International Standard" (in ISO) or "Committee Draft for Voting" (in IEC).

4. During the Enquiry Stage, the central secretariat circulates the committee draft to all ISO member bodies (regardless of committee representation) for comments and a preliminary vote. The comment period typically takes five months. Member bodies may submit technical comments in lieu of a vote; negative votes must be accompanied

---

[64] Senior officers of ISO and IEC also have the right to propose new work items.

[65] The national delegates are usually supported by national mirror committees in domestic standards bodies to which the delegates report.

[66] National member bodies may be P-members of any number of TCs and SCs (those in reduced-fee membership status are limited to a small number). Any P-member, however, can be downgraded to observer (O-member) status if the member body's representative fails to participate for two consecutive meetings of the TC or SC, where participation is defined as a substantive (technical) contribution in person or by correspondence. Having the resources to make such regular contributions is thus effectively a prerequisite for retaining a voice at this stage of the standardization process.

by technical reasons for objecting to the committee draft. If the draft passes the vote,[67] the committee considers objections and requests for changes submitted by stakeholders via the national standards organizations, then produces a final draft international standard (FDIS).

5. The Approval Stage begins when the FDIS is circulated among all ISO member bodies for a ballot. Approval requires support from two-thirds of the members of the committee that developed the standard *and* from 75 percent of all member bodies that choose to submit a vote.[68] If the final draft is approved, it becomes an ISO standard, which is then published by the Central Secretariat within two months.

Interviews with participants have confirmed that these stages describe not only the de jure but also the de facto standardization process. The stages matter because they make standardization an iterative process of working through successively more specific technical solutions in various working drafts and committee drafts, before the Draft International Standard and then the Final Draft International Standard are drawn up. The "consensus" decision-making procedures are intended to ensure broad support for new standards but also make it successively more difficult to change already settled elements of draft standards as they move through the stages (see also box 6.1).

In sum, ISO and IEC are best described as centrally coordinated global networks comprising hundreds of technical committees spread all over the world, involving tens of thousands of experts representing industry and other groups. The institutional backbone of these networks is formed by standards bodies at the national level. Domestic bodies thus are part and parcel of the institutional structure for rule-making for global product markets. Although membership is organized by country, however, ISO and IEC are private-sector organizations, and states and governments as

---

[67] Passing the vote requires the same 2/3 + 3/4 majorities as adoption of the final draft, described below. If the committee draft fails the vote during the Enquiry Stage, the project may be returned to the committee (re-starting the process at stage 3).

[68] More precisely, approval requires that two-thirds of the submitted, nonabstention votes from the "P-members" of the committee that developed the standard are in favor *and* that no more than 25 percent of all vote-casting member bodies vote against it. If these conditions are not met, the standard is sent back to the committee for reconsideration in light of the technical reasons submitted in support of the negative votes. See discussion of Committee P-membership above (stage 3).

BOX 6.1

Consensus Standard-Setting

Rule-making in ISO and IEC (as well as many product standard-setting bodies at the national level) is often described as voluntary "consensus" standard-setting. As much is made of the consensus norm,[i] it is important to clarify what consensus means in ISO and IEC.[ii]

According to the consensus norm, the specialized technical committees, subcommittees, and working groups that conduct the actual standardization work must conclude each stage of the ISO/IEC process by consensus to move forward, and any objections to draft standards prior to the votes in the final stages are supposed to be resolved through consensus rather than a (super-)majority vote. Consensus, however, does not mean achieving unanimity, but striving for the greatest feasible agreement among the technical preferences of the member countries that have taken a position on the (draft) standard.

Consensus may be achieved through marginal changes to achieve a compromise. Anecdotal evidence suggests that this is common at the final stage, which might explain why final draft standards are often approved with fewer negative votes than were submitted during the enquiry stage.[iii] The consensus norm at the international level has important implications for institutional complementarity in a system of national (and nongovernmental) representation: if representatives from a given country are divided at the international level, accommodating the technical preferences of any one faction against another does not achieve greater consensus. Fragmented domestic institutions thus exhibit low complementarity with an international institution characterized by national representation and consensus norms.

---

[i]E.g., Loya and Boli, "Standardization in the World Polity" (1999). Murphy and Yates provide a nuanced and richly historical discussion in *The ISO* (2008), 5–25.

[ii]The private standards are "voluntary" in that implementation is never mandated by the standard as such, though market forces, political-legal incentives, legislation, or government regulations may require implementation of the private standard (see chapter 1, box 1.1). The standard-setting *process* is "voluntary" insofar as there are no legal requirements for firms to participate (this applies even in most democratic corporatist and nondemocratic countries)—though as Braithwaite and Drahos aptly observe "in a global economy, no country, [firm, or industry] can afford to leave the table for fear that its [competitors] will set standards that advantage them" (*Global Business Regulation* (2000), 281).

[iii]See Büthe and Witte, *Product Standards in Transatlantic Trade and Investment* (2004), 39; Büthe, "Engineering Uncontestedness?" (2010).

(Continued)

(Continued)

Consensus, moreover, need not mean compromise at all, but can also be achieved by concluding that it is technically not feasible to accommodate opposing views (which allows moving forward if the current draft has the support of a supermajority) or by rejecting objections as lacking justification. This even applies at the voting stages, where negative votes, when submitted without technical reasons that could be accommodated through changes in the standard, can be discarded. General opposition to international standardization for a given issue, no matter how principled, is not a permissible reason for opposing a specific proposal once the process has been launched. This reinforces the importance of early involvement, for which again institutional complementarity is crucial.

such cannot be members, and the national member bodies are also mostly private.[69]

We now turn to an investigation of the domestic institutional structures for setting product standards in two key markets, the United States and Europe, followed by an examination of the effectiveness of these structures in defending and promoting domestic interests in global standardization.

DOMESTIC INSTITUTIONAL VARIATION AND INSTITUTIONAL COMPLEMENTARITY

The characteristics of the international standard-setting institutions and processes, as described above, have important implications for the actions and resources required to influence the content of international standards. The decentralized nature of ISO/IEC standard-setting suggests that early and direct *involvement* in the right working groups and technical committees is crucial. This requires that stakeholders receive *early and good information*, to allow them to determine the implications of a proposed new standard for their products and production processes (that is,

---

[69] This need not imply that states can never intervene in international private-sector standardization through the use of traditional means of state power; however, such intervention would be markedly more costly and hence rarer than in traditional intergovernmental organizations. Even in countries where the national product standards body is nominally public, such as China and Korea, most of the technical experts come from private industry.

to determine what their interests are) in order to influence the technical specification accordingly.[70]

But as we have argued in chapter 3, successful participation not only requires good information but also the ability to speak with a single national voice. Cohesiveness among the participants from a given member body is helped by extensive consensus procedures within uncontested domestic standard-setters.[71] If a country is unable to speak with a single voice, it undermines the credibility of its stakeholders' claims that accommodating the preferences expressed by the national member body or any other stakeholder constitutes an accommodation of the country's preference. In other words, effective global participation also requires *effective mechanisms for broad preference aggregation at the domestic level.*

We argue below that the quality and speed of information flows and the effectiveness of preference aggregation vary between the United States and Europe. Both Americans and Europeans are key players in international product standardization; they possess the financial and technical resources to be actively involved in global standardization. Their domestic systems, however, are strikingly different. The American system of product standardization is fragmented, with substantial overlap among multiple, competing standard-setters. The European system, by contrast, is hierarchical and characterized by a high degree of coordination.[72] These systems date back to the nineteenth and early twentieth centuries and have changed little since.[73] In the pre-globalization era, both systems served their domestic economies similarly well.[74] But with the onset of globalization,

[70] We assume that participants in international standardization pursue their self-interest strategically. For representatives of firms, most of which face intense competition in international markets, self-interest is primarily materially defined. Interviews and numerous responses to open-ended questions on our survey support this assumption.

[71] In our empirical analysis (chapter 7) we are only concerned with the ability of domestic institutions to aggregate the preferences of firms, since these commercial stakeholders are the predominant participants in the international rule-making process (with an ability to undermine a country's nominal representative). In the concluding chapter, we discuss variations in the inclusion and exclusion of other, noncommercial interests, such as consumer groups.

[72] This is not to say that the domestic institutions for standardization are identical across Europe (for a rich discussion, see Tate, "National Varieties of Standardization" (2001)), but the difference between the US and the Europeans is much larger than any difference among the Europeans.

[73] For a comprehensive discussion of the services provided by national standardization organizations, see de Vries, *Standards for the Nation* (1999).

[74] We are *not* arguing that any one system is superior in general. As Hendrik Spruyt shows historically, welfare-enhancing standardization does not require a single mode of governance for the standardization process; see Spruyt, "The Supply and Demand of Governance

domestic systems have been confronted with new challenges, and their ability to cope with them and effectively advance national interests has varied across systems. In this section, we offer an overview of the U.S. and European systems, highlighting their differences. This prepares the ground for the next section, where we discuss the implications of these differences specifically for information flows and the effectiveness of preference aggregation.

The American System of Standardization

The U.S. system has its roots in the industrialization process in the late nineteenth and early twentieth centuries and reflects a strong cultural and political bias in favor of market solutions.[75] It continues to be decentralized and characterized by extensive competition among many standard-setting bodies, operating with little government oversight and no public financial support. The U.S. private-sector standards community comprises some 300 trade associations, 130 professional and scientific societies, 40 general membership organizations, and at least 150 consortia which together have set more than 50,000 standards.[76] It includes such influential and internationally respected standards organizations as the American Society for Testing and Materials (ASTM), producer of the largest number of nongovernmental standards in the United States; the American Society of Mechanical Engineers (ASME), famous for its Boiler and Pressure Vessel Code;[77] and the Institute of Electrical and Electronics En-

---

in Standard-Setting" (2001), 382f. Similarly, we have found few systematic differences in firms' assessments of the technical quality of U.S. and European countries' domestic standards *per se*.

[75] On this bias, see, for example, Sutton et al., *The American Business Creed* (1956); Vogel, *Kindred Strangers* (1996), esp. 29–72; and Büthe, "The Political Sources of Business Confidence" (2002). On the broader legacies of American economic and political development, see Bensel, *The Political Economy of American Industrialization, 1877–1900* (2000), esp. 124ff, 293f, 457ff; Chandler, *The Visible Hand* (1977); Gourevitch, "International Trade, Domestic Coalitions, and Liberty" (1977), and "Corporate Governance" (2003); Katznelson and Shefter, *Shaped by War and Trade* (2002); and Lake, "The State and American Trade Strategy in the Pre-Hegemonic Era" (1988). See also Büthe and Witte, *Product Standards in Transatlantic Trade and Investment* (2004), 27–30.

[76] Toth, ed. *Standards Activities of Organizations in the United States* (1996); U.S. Department of Commerce, *Standards and Competitiveness* (2004), 5. Representatives of NIST (the U.S. Department of Commerce Technology Administration's National Institute of Standards and Technology), report minimal changes in recent years.

[77] See Greene, *History of the ASME Boiler Code* (1955); Ling, "The Evolution of the ASME Boiler and Pressure Vessel Code" (2000).

gineers (IEEE), which is responsible for the National Electrical Safety Code. Spurred by competition, these organizations have developed numerous standards of the highest technical quality, but the fragmentation also comes at well-known costs. Most importantly, fragmentation results in conflicting standards and hence poor interoperability, as well as duplication and waste.[78] John Milek offers a telling illustration:

A given grade of copper-silicon rod stock may be produced and stored under any of the following standard designations: MIL-B-15939; AST B-150, Alloy No.1; SAE 701-B; AMX 4632B; [. . .] Army-Navy Aeronautics Specification AN-B-11; Navy Specification 46B17, Grade B; and many proprietary or trade designations. . . . Should the metal be purchased at different times . . . by different engineers in different departments, each one of the purchases might be carried in the stockroom and on the records as a separate item.[79]

The shift of rule-making to the international level turns this fragmentation into a problem for the effectiveness of American interests in the global market place. Coordination and cooperation do not arise spontaneously among competing standard-setters, and American standard-setting organizations have a long tradition of keeping government at arm's length. In fact, attempts at governmental interference in the workings of the private standards system have been few, and at an April 1990 hearing by the National Institute of Standards and Technology (NIST) to determine whether the federal government should become more active in standard-setting, especially in the international arena, the response of those testifying was an emphatic "No."[80] The few subsequent proposals

---

[78] As a consequence of incompatible communications equipment, for instance, local and federal police and emergency service providers were unable to communicate with each other, sometimes for days, after the 1995 Oklahoma City bombing, the attack on the World Trade Center in 2001, and after Hurricane Katrina in 2005; U.S. House of Representative (Hearing), *Interoperability of Public Safety Communications Equipment* (2010).

[79] Milek, "The Role of Management in Company Standardization" (1972), 142. The long tradition of fragmentation and partial competition among U.S. standardizers is also nicely illustrated by the list of 31 standard-setting bodies for the chemical industry alone, including 24 nongovernmental ones, compiled in the early 1950s by Cedric Flagg and Robert Ware in "Standards and Specifications" (1954).

[80] See NIST's Transcript of Hearing on Improving U.S. Participation in International Standards Activities in OTA, *Global Standards* (1992). See also presentation by James Thomas, President of ASTM, in Leight and Leuteritz, *Toward a National Standards Strategy* (1998), 3.

for increasing the coordination among U.S. standard-setters have been similarly rejected.[81]

In the absence of government control or any other central monitoring and coordinating agent, the American system for product standardization is characterized by extreme pluralism and contestation. Attempts to inject a measure of unity into the system have largely failed. In the early 1960s, Francis LaQue, vice president of the International Nickel Corporation, proposed the creation of a national coordinating institution, leading to the establishment of a private-sector organization called the American National Standards Institute (ANSI). Commenting on the system in 1971, the Stanford Research Institute (SRI) observed:

> Up to the mid-1960s, a favorable solution appeared possible under the guise of ANSI. . . . Reportedly, however, ANSI now has less support and less probability of succeeding as the nominal national voluntary standards coordinating agency than it did . . . [half] a decade ago. . . . In fact, fragmentation is becoming worse. . . . A leadership conflict exists and will probably persist for some time.[82]

This prediction proved correct. Some forty years later, the U.S. standards system remains fragmented, and ANSI remains a weak institution, even though it formally is the sole representative of U.S. interests in international standards organizations.[83] The main reason for this weakness is that its status has not been fully accepted by major players in the American standards community, and a few organizations keep acting independently of ANSI.[84] Private U.S. standards organizations, which de-

[81] See e.g. Kammer, "Prepared Remarks at ANSI Board Meeting" (1998). See also Hanson, *CE Marking, Product Standards and World Trade* (2005), 190f. The structure of U.S. product standard-setting and a possible government role in its reorganization remains a current and contested issue, as evidenced, for instance, in the comments submitted by ANSI President Joe Bhatia in response to the 2009 initiative of the Office of Management and Budget to develop recommendations to President Obama for the new Executive Order on Federal Regulatory Review (74 FR 5977). See also the reactions gathered by Purcell, *A National Survey of United States Standardization Strategies* (2009).

[82] SRI, *Industrial Standards* (Menlo Park, CA: SRI, The Long Range Planning Service, 1971), 3. See also Garcia, "Standard Setting in the United States: Public and Private Sector Roles" (1993), 30f.

[83] ANSI, *Overview of the U.S. Standardization System* (2010), 4. See also ANSI, *National Standards Strategy* (2000), 11.

[84] Samuel Krislov describes ANSI as follows: "ANSI . . . is not a direct standards developer or standards enactor. It is rather a holding company that recognizes and validates standard-setting organizations. . . . Those who are recognized by ANSI . . . vary enormously in type of organization and emphasis. Some are trade associations, others professional expert groups or entrepreneurships. They must agree to ANSI's . . . procedures and promulgate standards

rive 50 to 80 percent of their income from the sale of their proprietary standards documents (with the remainder coming mostly from membership fees of individuals and firms) fear that a more centralized system would rob them of these revenues and eclipse their power and autonomy. As a result, the U.S. system of standardization, as illustrated in figure 6.2, remains characterized by contestation and fragmentation—a "hodgepodge of sources of standards rather than a neat pyramid with ANSI at the apex."[85]

The European System of Standardization

In stark contrast to the American system, standardization in European countries is hierarchical, coordinated, and regulated. As in the United States, the bulk of industrial activity in Europe is conducted and organized in sectors, and standards experts are organized in private sector-specific bodies. However, unlike their American counterparts, these bodies are not autonomous standardizers but constituent elements of a much larger and hierarchical institutional structure: the country's national standards institutes, such as BSI, the British Standards Institution (used as the illustrative example in figure 6.3); DIN, the German Institute for Standardization (discussed in greater detail in box 6.2); AENOR, the Spanish Association for Standardization; or SIS, the Swedish Standards Institute.

As in the U.S. case, the domestic systems of standardization reflect each country's political and economic history, but particularly striking are common elements that set European countries apart from the United States. And just as in accounting, the United Kingdom provides a useful illustration. The British Standards Institute (BSI), generally regarded as the first national standard-setting body, was founded in 1901 as the Engineering Standards Committee of the Institution of Civil Engineers, similar to many national standard-setting bodies, which also trace their origins to agreements among various societies of civil, mechanical, or electrical engineers.[86] It initially focused on drawing up technical specifications

---

in specific forms. . . . Thus ANSI standards . . . are actually secondhand products derived in accordance with ANSI's . . . procedures" (Krislov, *How Nations Choose Product Standards and Standards Change Nations* (1997), 101).

[85] Hamilton, "The Role of Nongovernmental Standards in the Development of Mandatory Federal Standards Affecting Safety or Health" (1978), 1343. See also Büthe and Witte, *Product Standards in Transatlantic Trade and Investment* (2004), esp. 26–35.

[86] See, e.g., de Vries, *Standards for the Nation* (1999). In 1918, the Committee became the British Engineering Standards Association; in 1931 it changed its name to BSI. Our discussion of BSI draws mostly on Hemenway, *Standards Systems* (1979); Lukes, *Überbetriebliche technische Normung in den Rechtsordnungen ausgewählter EWG- und EFTA-Staaten*

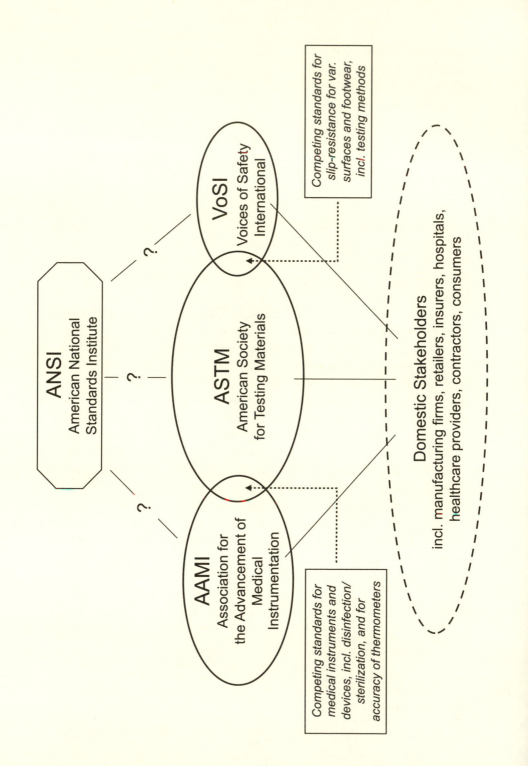

ANSI
American National
Standards Institute

VoSI
Voices of Safety
International

ASTM
American Society
for Testing Materials

AAMI
Association for
the Advancement of
Medical
Instrumentation

*Competing standards for
slip-resistance for var.
surfaces and footwear,
incl. testing methods*

*Competing standards for
medical instruments and
devices, incl. disinfection/
sterilization, and for
accuracy of thermometers*

Domestic Stakeholders
incl. manufacturing firms, retailers, insurers, hospitals,
healthcare providers, contractors, consumers

for sections of rolled iron and steel used in the construction of bridges, buildings, and various of the railways, but soon expanded to developing standards for a broad range of products.

While BSI may have been the first, it was not for long the only standard-setter in the United Kingdom; and as Robert McWilliam points out, Britain as an early industrializer with its wealth of engineering societies and powerful, independent trade and industry associations could easily have ended up with domestic institutional fragmentation akin to the United States. BSI, however, sought and gained recognition as *the* British standard-setter, a position cemented through Royal charters starting in the 1920s. To restrain BSI dominance, trade associations pushed for BSI to develop standards only for products and processes with a need for uniform specifications across multiple industries. Ironically, this only strengthened BSI by making it the only British standard-setter covering essentially the entire economy and naturally the British member body of ISO and the British National Committee of the IEC.[87] BSI thus increasingly became the focal point—not just for the British government seeking efficiency gains through standardization in times of war and during postwar reconstruction, but also for industry seeking a means to restore its international competitiveness in internationally integrated product markets. By the 1970s, the British standards system with BSI as "the principal standards writer in the United Kingdom" had become "strikingly

---

(1979); McWilliam, "Business Standards and Government" (2000), and *BSI: The First Hundred Years* (2001); Woodward, *BSI: The Story of Standards* (1972).

[87] The opposition from industry-specific standard-setters also prompted BSI to focus exceptionally early on generic quality management standards, which enabled it later to play a leading role in the eventual development of the ISO 9,000-series of standards.

Figure 6.2   The Fragmented U.S. Domestic System for Setting Product Standards

• • • • • • •

AAMI, ASTM, and VoSI are used here as illustrative examples of the hundreds of domestic standards bodies in the United States. ASTM has some 130 technical committees covering a broad range of materials and industries, including F04 (Medical and Surgical Materials and Devices) and F13 (Pedestrian/Walkway Safety and Footwear). AAMI is a hybrid professional and industry association with 36 technical committees with various subcommittees, all of which are concerned with medical instruments/devices (overlap with ASTM is therefore only partial). VoSI is an activist NGO that has developed a number of standards for public safety.

different" from the United States.[88] Well before the globalization of product markets took off in the 1980s, the United Kingdom had thus converged on most other European countries, each of which has one national standard-setting body that adopts technical specifications and represents national interests at the regional and international levels.[89]

Another distinctive feature of the European system is that most national standards bodies are subject to governmental regulation. In exchange for usually providing partial public funding, these rules require each national standards organization to have representatives from a wide range of interests on technical committees and to comply with comprehensive rules on public enquiry and publication.[90] Consequently, European national standard-setting organizations count among their members not only industry and trade associations as well as professional and scientific organizations, but also trade unions, consumer groups, various other types of socioeconomic interest groups, ministries, and public agencies. The number of experts involved in standardization at any given moment is in the tens of thousands.[91] The drafting of standards is the responsibility of specialized technical committees and working groups of the national standards bodies; and adoption of a standard is preceded by circulation of drafts for public comment. In short, a standard adopted in Europe typically is the result of the involvement of representatives of a broad range of societal interests, and it derives its legitimacy, in part, from extensive coordination and consensus-building (for an illustration, see DIN case below).

Such broad-based involvement, however, is neither easy nor automatic because participation in standardization can be quite costly and is nonremunerative. Representatives of noncommercial interests may find it difficult to be actively involved if not supported financially. Europeans therefore recognize a need for subsidies to weaker groups; such assis-

---

[88] Hemenway, *Standards Systems* (1979), 73; see also Woodward, *Story of Standards* (1972), 19–35, 42ff.

[89] The main national SDO may have a sister organization responsible for electrical and electronic standards.

[90] For details, see Falke and Schepel, eds., *Legal Aspects of Standardisation in the Member States of the EC and of EFTA* (2000). Often, this is based on an explicit contract between the government and the national nongovernmental standards body, such as the UK Government and BSI, "Memorandum of Understanding between the United Kingdom Government and the British Standards Institution" (2002).

[91] As of 2008, e.g., some 28,500 for DIN and 20,000 for BSI.

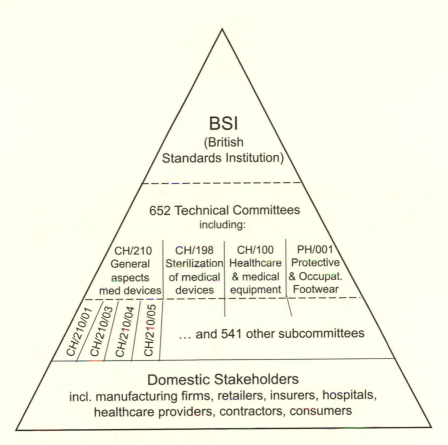

Figure 6.3   The British Standards Institution (BSI): Hierarchical Domestic System for Setting Product Standards

• • • • • •

BSI technical committee CH/210 has four subcommittees with specialized responsibilities: CH/210/01: Quality systems for medical devices; CH/210/03: General terminology and symbols (for medical instruments/devices); CH/210/04: Risk analysis; and CH/210/05: Small bore connectors for medical devices. In addition to the technical (standard-setting) committees and subcommittees depicted here, BSI has some twenty policy and general advisory committees. Committee structure as of July 2010. *Sources*: BSI Group Annual Report 2009; BSI website; and personal communications from Debbie Stead, head of BSI Committee Service Centre, 12–13 July 2010.

BOX 6.2

DIN: Exemplar of Hierarchical Domestic
Standard-Setting Institution

The German Institution for Standardization, DIN (Deutsches Institut für Normung), was founded in 1917. DIN is a private organization registered as a nonprofit association. Its members hail from industry, commerce, trade associations, service providers, consumer groups, research organizations, technical inspection institutions, and public authorities. Any member can submit a proposal for a new standard, and once a proposal has been accepted, participation in the standard-setting process is also open to interested parties that are not members.

The work is carried out in 77 DIN standards committees which, in turn, are divided into 3,439 working groups. In these various DIN committees and groups, approximately 28,500 experts contribute to more than 2,300 German national, European, and international standards each year. Draft standards are published for public comment, thus allowing an even broader public to become involved in the process.[i]

The 77 standards committees are responsible not only for national standardization but also for standards work at the international level. About 85 percent of DIN work is now international in nature. DIN experts serve on ISO and IEC committees but also national committees that "mirror" international committees, forging national positions on global projects. DIN standardization work is coordinated by a permanent staff of some 370, responsible for overall project management, as well as ensuring uniformity and consistency of the resulting standards.

The cost to DIN of this work amounts to 62 million Euros annually. Royalties from the sales of standards and related documents pay for 52 percent of the cost; 22 percent is financed by project funds from industry, 18 percent by public funding, and 8 percent by membership fees. The benefit of the DIN standards work has been estimated at 16 billion Euros annually for Germany. These benefits stem from improving the suitability of products, processes, and services for their intended purposes, reducing barriers to trade, and facilitating communications as well as technological cooperation.

[i]All figures are for 2008, from DIN, *Geschäftsbericht 2008*. For more detailed information about DIN's history and structure see Geuther, *Festschrift 75 Jahr DIN* (1992), and Büthe and Witte, *Product Standards* (2004), esp. 17–25.

tance is viewed as a prerequisite for genuine openness and due process.[92] In sharp contrast, most American standards organizations contend that willingness to pay is the best measure of interest in the process and see no need for financial assistance.

The European system of standardization is comprised not only of a national layer of standards organizations but also of a regional layer, created in the course of economic integration.[93] Two major regional standards organizations exist, the European Committee for Standardization (CEN) and the European Committee for Electrotechnical Standardization (CENELEC),[94] both partially funded by the EU Commission. CEN was established in 1961 as a nonprofit regional association producing voluntary European standards in a broad range of areas; it is the regional equivalent to ISO. CENELEC was set up in 1972 to produce electrotechnical and electronic engineering standards; it is the European functional equivalent of IEC. The members of CEN and CENELEC are the European national standardization organizations—the same domestic-level standards bodies that represent European countries in ISO and IEC. As part of their close working relationship with CEN/CENELEC, each national standards organization selects up to three experts representing the national technical preferences in a given regional standards committee and establishes a "mirror-committee" at the national level to keep all domestic interested parties informed and to decide on a national consensus position.[95] After the approval of a European standard, each national standards body implements the standard as a national standard, either

---

[92] None of this is to suggest that all interests are equally represented. As in financial standard-setting, industry and more generally commercial interests are virtually always at a substantial advantage vis-à-vis noncommercial stakeholders with respect to expertise and resources available to them for exerting influence during the standard-setting process; see Mattli and Büthe, "Global Private Governance" (2005). But other interests *do* have a seat at the table in European standard-setting organizations, and extended participation often allows them to acquire significant expertise; see Schulz, *Einflußmöglichkeiten des Arbeitsschutzes auf die ISO-Normung* (2005); Sterk, ed. *Beteiligung des Arbeitsschutzes an der Normung* (2009), esp.25f.

[93] For more detailed discussions, see Egan, "Regulatory Strategies, Delegation and European Market Integration" (1998); Egan, *Constructing a European Market* (2001); Hanson, *CE Marking, Product Standards and World Trade* (2005); and Vad, *The Europeanization of Standardization* (1998).

[94] The acronyms stand for Comité Européen de Normalisation and Comité Européen de Normalisation Eléctrotechnique.

[95] As of 30 November 2009, CEN, for example, has 291 technical committees, 62 subcommittees, and 1,399 working groups; it has produced 13,690 standards. See CEN, "Statistics" (2009).

by publication of identical texts or by endorsement; conflicting national standards must be withdrawn.

The presence of a single uncontested standardization institution at the regional level has made institutional links with the main international standards organization relatively easy. Examples of such links are the 1991 Vienna Agreement between the ISO and CEN and the 1996 Dresden Agreement between the IEC and CENELEC.[96] Under the Vienna Agreement, CEN and ISO have agreed detailed procedures for the exchange of information and their cooperation in the drafting and adoption of standards. For example, when a new international standards project is proposed, members in the relevant ISO technical committee decide by majority vote whether CEN or ISO should take the lead in developing the standard. In the majority of cases, ISO takes the lead, but voting on the final draft standard is parallel with CEN.[97] However, if specific requirements of European directives or regulations must be reflected in a standard, or the Commission mandates that a standard be written by a certain target date, or the affected businesses are primarily European, the lead usually goes to CEN. Voting on the draft standard then takes place in both CEN and ISO. If adopted by both, the European-made standard becomes an international standard without further technical discussion at the ISO. The agreement between the IEC and CENELEC contains similar procedures.[98] American critics of these agreements have argued that they serve as vehicles to unduly influence global standardization processes and discriminate against non-European interests—a charge dismissed by Europeans.[99]

In sum, the European system of product standardization is characterized by a high degree of coordination under the umbrella of a single

[96] ISO-CEN, "Vienna Agreement" (1991). IEC-CENELEC, "Dresden Agreement" (1996). The Dresden Agreement is a revision of the 1991 Lugano Agreement between IEC and CENELEC. A working agreement also exists between the IEC and the European Telecommunications Standards Institute (ETSI). Differences between the Vienna and Dresden agreements are discussed in Hilpert and Vomberg, "Wiener und Dresdner Vereinbarung" (2006).

[97] By 2005, ISO had taken the lead in a total of 685 work items, and CEN in 306. See Cornish, "ISO, CEN, and the Vienna Agreement" (2005), 2.

[98] As a result of the close intermeshing of European and international standardization activities and structures, about 55 percent of CEN standards and 70 percent of CENELEC standards are technically equivalent or identical to ISO and IEC standards respectively. See Hilpert and Vomberg, "Wiener und Dresdner Vereinbarungen" (2006).

[99] Both claims were made by some experts in interviews with the authors.

domestic institution with a hierarchical structure, supplemented by Europeanwide private-sector organizations that reinforce these structures. By contrast, the U.S. domestic institutions for product standardization are characterized by extreme fragmentation and competition among specialized standard-setters.

INSTITUTIONAL COMPLEMENTARITY IN PRODUCT REGULATION

Given the differences in domestic standardization systems just presented, what are the implications for information flow and preference aggregation—and for how well these different systems position their domestic firms for exerting influence in global standard-setting? What should we expect to observe in ISO and IEC rule-making based on the institutional complementarities approach?

In a fragmented system as embodied in the U.S. system of product standardization, competing private-sector bodies have incentives to treat information that they may have about international standardization as a commercial asset: a private benefit that they share only with their members. Moreover, the arms-length relationship with nonmember groups renders the institutionalization of information dissemination difficult. While a given firm may be a member of several such organizations (directly or via its employees), the institutional fragmentation should be expected to further impede efficient information flows about the standards agenda at the international level—information that may originate from any number of different sources. Moreover, U.S. firms frequently complain about the costliness of participating and paying fees in all the various domestic organizations that set standards for their industry (a cost they are often not willing to pay).

In contrast, subsidized national standard-setters in Europe, not facing any domestic competitor, have little incentive to hold back information. Quite to the contrary, being subjected to public scrutiny to justify the subsidies they receive, these organizations have strong incentives to legitimate their work through the institutionalized and timely dissemination of information from the central secretariat to industry associations, firms, and other domestic stakeholders. In addition, as hierarchical organizations, they have strong institutionalized lines of communication between the different levels of the hierarchy. They should therefore be much better at disseminating information about new standards proposals to firms potentially affected by the proposed new standard.

Hierarchical institutional structures are also geared toward preference aggregation, since they exist to produce a single set of standards. Standards organizations such as Germany's DIN or Britain's BSI are inherently geared toward coordinating a diverse set of actors in order to arrive at one aggregate national position. This national consensus, based on the involvement of a broad range of interests, can then be easily and authoritatively presented at the international level.

The process of aggregating technical preferences and projecting consensus standards to a higher level is considerably more difficult in the decentralized and uncoordinated standards system of the United States, where the nominal national representative for international standardization is a weak and contested institution. Institutional fragmentation provides no mechanism for speaking with a single voice internationally. This should put U.S. firms at a persistent disadvantage vis-à-vis their European competitors, without giving them any way to prevent the shift of standardization to the international level since launching new standards projects in ISO and IEC is easy—and the increasing use of international standards for regulatory purposes by developing countries, including large ones like India and Brazil, effectively forces U.S. firms to produce to these standards if they do not want to forego access to these fast-growing markets.

In sum, when standardization becomes an increasingly international process, the organizational structure of the European standardization system makes for a closer fit with international institutions than the structure of the essentially anarchic American system: cross-level hierarchies mix and match better than do hierarchies and market systems. As a result, we would expect European firms to possess better information about international standardization initiatives and pursue their interests more effectively than their American counterparts.

At the same time, if the advantage a firm enjoys derives from the standardization system to which it has access, we should see a notable difference between U.S. firms with subsidiaries in Europe and those without them. A U.S. multinational with a subsidiary in Germany, for instance, could send its standards experts via its subsidiary to sit on DIN technical committees and therefore also on CEN committees. Such subsidiaries, treated like European firms in the national and regional standardization processes, should allow U.S. firms with European subsidiaries to "play" the standardization game by European rules. By being an integral part of the European structure of standardization, such firms should not only receive up-to-date information about standards proposals from European

160

competitors, but also have privileged access to international standards bodies through CEN. As a result, we would expect relatively few differences between U.S. firms with subsidiaries in Europe and European firms, but marked differences between these two kinds of firms and U.S. firms without subsidiaries.

CHAPTER SEVEN

The Politics of Nuts and Bolts—and Nanotechnology

ISO AND IEC STANDARD-SETTING FOR GLOBAL PRODUCT MARKETS

P RIVATE RULE-MAKING for global product markets has much in common with private rule-making for global financial markets. The process of developing standards in ISO and IEC is in many respects similar to the process in IASB, especially in that ISO/IEC procedures similarly reward early uncontested involvement by a country's stakeholders. Given these international institutions, the argument that we developed in chapter 3 should also hold for ISO and IEC, the international organizations discussed in chapter 6. The logic of the argument leads us to expect that countries with domestic coordination and institutional hierarchy benefit from greater complementarity and hence have greater influence in ISO/IEC rule-making because such domestic institutions facilitate effective interest aggregation and information flows. Institutional fragmentation and competition, by contrast, impedes them and should put countries with such domestic institutions at a disadvantage for international rule-making in ISO and IEC. In product standard-setting, however, it is the United States that is characterized by fragmentation and competition, while standard-setting in Europe is characterized by hierarchy and coordination, as shown in the previous chapter. These institutional differences are the exact opposite of those in the case of financial reporting standards. We therefore expect European firms to exert greater influence over international product standards than their American counterparts.

Anecdotal evidence provides strong support for our argument. In 1988, for instance, the EU passed a general directive on the Safety of Toys, which left it to toy manufacturers to develop specific regional or international standards to meet the broad regulatory objective. European toy manufacturers, invoking the Vienna Agreement, proceeded to develop several toy standards entirely in CEN Technical Committee 52 instead of

ISO TC181, the ISO committee responsible for toy safety issues. With the Danish standards organization in charge of both committees, the Europeans easily succeeded in having the new European toy standards for mechanical and physical properties (EN71, part 1) and for flammability (EN71, part 2) accepted verbatim as ISO standards 8124-1 and 8124-2 shortly after the technical work was completed in CEN. Consequently, compliance with these new private regulations soon became not only a de facto requirement for exporting to the European market but also for exporting to many other international markets.[1] A few American toy manufacturers had been able to participate effectively in the European rule-making process via their European subsidiaries. The vast majority of U.S. manufacturers, however, learned about these new rules only after all opportunities had passed to take advantage of the ISO consensus procedures. Many did not even hear about the new European standards until after the ISO vote adopting them as international standards.[2] These U.S. manufacturers paid with the loss of market share or costly changes to their products for the poor institutional fit between their fragmented domestic system of standardization and the ISO rule-making process.[3]

In contrast, when American firms sought in the early 2000s to establish an ANSI/ASME standard as an ISO standard—imposing substantial switching costs on their European competitors—they failed almost completely. At issue in this case was the 17-part ISO 10110 standard, originally based on a German DIN standard, which specifies how to prepare technical drawings for optical elements and systems.[4] In 2001, when the standard came up for review in ISO TC 172 (Optics and Photonics),

---

[1] The ability of the EU to influence U.S. companies' safety and quality management practices (including product design) through international (ISO/IEC) standards has been increasingly widely observed; see, e.g., Manuele, "Global Harmonization of Safety Standards" (2005).

[2] In fact, due to divisions among U.S. standard-setters, with the Toy Manufacturers of America categorically opposed to the development of international standards in this field, the U.S. had until 1992 only observer status in ISO TC181.

[3] Before the adoption of the third CEN toy safety standard as an ISO standard, a coalition of non-European standards bodies forced the technical work into the ISO committee. For more details on the Safety of Toys case, see American National Standards Institute (ANSI), *American Access to the European Standardization Process* (1996), 18ff; Egan, *Constructing a European Market* (2001), 169ff. See also Frankel and Højbjerg, "The Political Standardizer" (2010).

[4] Technical drawings for optical elements of the type governed by ISO 20110 are used for R&D and internal communications within firms, in product specifications, on purchase orders, and in documents to establish compliance with government regulation: they matter commercially.

well-prepared U.S. representatives sought to bring it into line with ANSI/ ASME standard Y14.18, which was also used by the U.S. military. Their proposal would have allowed U.S. manufacturers to meet two standards at once and facilitated U.S. access to international markets. Thanks to effective and efficient institutions at the national level, however, European manufacturers quickly learned of this proposal and realized that the changes would impose on them costs estimated at several billion euros for German industry alone.[5] Their early active opposition paid off.[6] The revised parts of ISO 10110 (completed finally between 2006 and 2009) have been much closer to European preferences, and in 2009, ASME voted to withdraw its Y14.18 standard, and U.S. optics industry organizations started to adopt the ISO standard instead.[7]

The above anecdotes provide compelling illustrations of the importance of institutional complementarity in some particular cases of international standard-setting. But how representative are these cases?[8]

To go beyond anecdotes, we examine our hypotheses based on a business survey among standards experts in firms in the United States and four European countries: Germany, Spain, Sweden, and the United Kingdom.[9] We sought to include in our survey traditional and high-tech industries, and industries in which international trade is similarly important for U.S. and European firms in order to ensure that they have comparable stakes

[5] Personal communication from long-time German industry participant in ISO standardization (dn63), 20 April 2002 and 30 October 2010.

[6] Competitive gains or losses are of course not permissible as reasons to oppose a technical change in ISO. At the national level, European firms therefore developed a common line of technical argumentation against the proposed changes. The cost of this coordination was considered minuscule relative to the anticipated cost had the U.S. proposal succeeded.

[7] Aikens, "ANS OP1.110 Draft Specifications" (2009); *OEOSC Optical Standards News* online (June 2010).

[8] As Martin Weiss and Marvin Sirbu note: "When studying the process by which voluntary standards are developed, one is struck by the complexity and subtlety of the process. It is often the case that observations can be made about the standards process that are supported by one group of cases that are not supported by another group of cases." Weiss and Sirbu, "Technological Choice in Voluntary Standards Committees" (1990), 111f.

[9] In Europe, we thus included two large countries whose domestic standards have long played an important role in international commerce (Germany, United Kingdom), a medium-sized European country that went through the industrialization process more recently (Spain), and a typical example of a small country with internationally oriented industries (Sweden).

TABLE 7.1
Respondents by Country

Country of respondent company	Number of respondent companies	Percentage of total sample
U.S.	1011	73%
Germany	188	13.5%
Spain	41	3%
Sweden	63	4.5%
UK	82	6%

in the international standardization process.[10] We selected five industries for inclusion in our study:[11]

- chemicals
- rubber and plastic products
- medical instruments and medical devices
- petroleum products
- iron and steel products

With 1,385 responses across the four countries (see table 7.1), our survey offers the most comprehensive and cross-nationally comparable information to date about how companies affected by international product standards assess these standards and to what extent they are able to influence rule-making in ISO and IEC.[12]

---

[10] Due to the size of their domestic market, U.S. firms are generally less trade-oriented than European firms (when their national market, rather than the EU, is taken as the domestic market, as it should be for assessing the trade effect of international standards). There also is a notable difference in the industries chosen for our analysis, but we sought to avoid industries where only a small number of firms is engaged in international trade. For firms engaged in manufacturing medical instruments and devices, for instance, OECD trade statistics show that exports constituted the following share of production in 2003: Germany: 71%; Spain: 51%; United Kingdom: 46%; Sweden: 65%; United States: 47%.

[11] For more detailed information about how we defined the industries and our survey methods, see appendix 3.

[12] We conducted the survey in three waves from October 2001 to September 2003, achieving a response rate of 32 percent—more than twice as high as typical business surveys. Contrary to our prior expectations, the response rate was as high among U.S. firms as among European firms, resulting in a larger number of American responses.

We first provide some background information about our survey participants, which shows that the European and American firms in our samples are comparable. We then examine their assessment of the standards and the rule-making process of ISO and IEC, before turning to the key investigation of what determines successful participation in international standard-setting for global product markets. This statistical analysis is followed by an analysis of additional qualitative evidence, which sheds further light on the importance of institutional complementarity for influencing the content of international standards.

RESPONDENTS OF THE INTERNATIONAL PRODUCT STANDARDS SURVEY

Most of our survey participants are engineers and technical experts working in research and development (R&D), production, or quality control; sometimes they are specifically designated as standards managers. Some respondents have primary responsibility for sales and marketing. In about one in ten cases, the chief executive officer (CEO) or another senior manager took charge of answering our questions, as shown in figure 7.1. The remaining respondents have responsibility for internal company communications or legal services, including patents and licensing issues ("other" in figure 7.1).

As in the accounting standards survey, each participant was asked to answer the survey questions on behalf of his or her company, rather than in a personal capacity. We therefore allowed only one response per company. The size of these companies ranged from very small specialist manufacturers to large global firms, with a similar distribution across the United States and Europe: 39 percent of European firms and 36 percent of U.S. firms in our sample have fewer than 250 employees; 35 percent of European and 45 percent of American firms have more than 1,000 employees.[13]

The companies in our sample also are similar in their international orientation and thus have similar stakes in the internationalization of product standards. As shown in figure 7.2, large majorities of firms on both sides of the Atlantic are multinational companies with subsidiaries abroad. Moreover, 94 percent of the European and 86 percent of the

---

[13] We nonetheless control for firm size in our analyses, as we do for accounting standards.

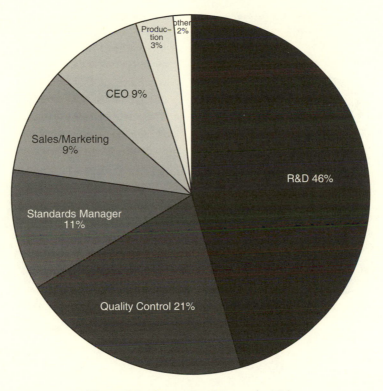

Figure 7.1 Survey Participants by Title

• • • • • • •

Responses to survey question: "About you and your firm: What best describes your primary responsibility?" N = 1372.

U.S. respondents export at least part of their production.[14] It is therefore hardly surprising that nearly all firms in our sample regularly use ISO or IEC standards in purchasing, internal quality control, or marketing of their own products.

At the same time, export-oriented firms are clearly affected by persistent cross-national differences in domestic standards. Asked about the current situation, 46 percent of U.S. firms as well as 45 percent of European

---

[14] Among the firms in our sample, as in the population of manufacturing firms generally, U.S. firm are on average less export-oriented than European firms, but the differences are small as we focused our research consciously on industries that are trade-oriented on both sides of the Atlantic.

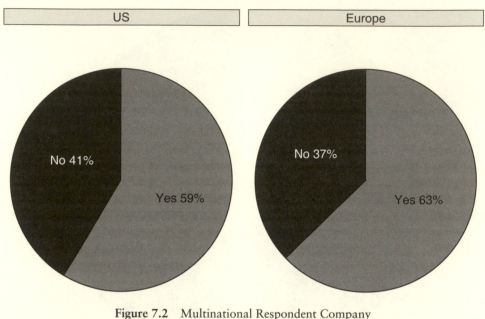

Figure 7.2 Multinational Respondent Company

• • • • • •

Responses to survey question: "Does your company have production sites or other subsidiaries abroad?" *N* = 1375.

firms report that domestic standards in foreign countries restrict their opportunities to export their products.[15] And strikingly large majorities on both sides of the Atlantic consider the ongoing harmonization of product standards at the international level a boost to their actual and potential export opportunities (see table 7.2).

Finally, American and European firms are remarkably similar in their perceptions of the growing importance of ISO and IEC. Overwhelming majorities of our respondents agree that the governance of product markets is indeed moving from the domestic to the international level, as shown in table 7.3.

In sum, U.S. and European firms in the five industries analyzed here have a similarly international orientation and a common understanding

[15] In the U.S. survey, the statement was "Foreign national and regional standards restrict our opportunities to export our products." In the European surveys, the statement was "Foreign national standards outside of Europe restrict our opportunities to export our products." The percentage reported is for respondents who selected "agree" or "strongly agree" (*N* = 1146).

TABLE 7.2
Product Standards as Nontariff Barriers to Trade

Please indicate whether you agree or disagree with [. . .] the following statement:		Agree or strongly agree
"The increasing international harmonization of standards improves our opportunities to export our products."	U.S. firms	84%
	European firms	91%

Note: Percentage of respondents who selected the indicated response option (remainder selected disagree or strongly disagree). N = 1182.

of the significance of the trend toward international rule-making in product markets and the long-term benefits of international standards. At the same time, switching from domestic to international standards comes at a cost in the short term. Given the comparability of the U.S. and European firms in our sample, they have similar incentives to seek to reduce the switching costs by promoting their respective domestic rules or technical preferences in the international standard-setting process. Successful involvement, however, is not simply a function of similar incentives. As we argued in chapter 3, we expect differences in institutional complementarity between the domestic and international levels to play a key role in determining success. In the case of product standard-setting, the institutional fit is strong on the European side but weak for Americans, leading

TABLE 7.3
Shift of Governance to the International Level

Please indicate whether you agree or disagree with [. . .] the following statement:		Agree or strongly agree
"Standards will increasingly be developed at the international level."	U.S. firms	87%
	European firms	95%

Note: N = 1195. 11% of U.S. and 10% of European respondents selected "neither agree nor disagree." Percentages reported above are calculated after excluding these neither-nor responses (remainder selected disagree or strongly disagree).

us to expect that European firms will be able to exert greater influence during the standard-setting process, and that U.S. firms will pay a greater share of the switching costs.

ISO, IEC, AND INTERNATIONAL PRODUCT STANDARDS

How do U.S. and European firms assess ISO, IEC, and their standards? We asked survey participants to rate ISO and IEC standards, as well as the domestic standards that they most frequently use. Their assessments of international standards were generally favorable, albeit usually slightly more so among the Europeans. For example, 87 percent of U.S. and 94 percent of European firms consider the technical quality of ISO and IEC standards to be high or very high.

What is striking about the responses, however, are the differences that emerge between European and American firms, consistent with our theoretical argument. Europeans, for instance, regard the international standard-setting process just as highly as their domestic standard-setting processes. Americans, by contrast, assess the international process far less favorably than the domestic process: 16 percent of U.S. firms consider the process by which *domestic* standards are developed as "bad" or "very bad," whereas 37 percent of them consider the process by which the *international* standard is developed "bad" or "very bad."[16]

In addition, initial proposals for new international standards tend to be substantially more favorable to Europeans, consistent with our expectations. When we ask firms how frequently an initial proposal for a new standard (which applies to the firm's products) differs from their current practice, 35 percent of American firms report that initial proposals for new standards differ from their current practice at least "half of the time," whereas only 18 percent of European firms report a similar divergence.

Why are these responses so different? A key reason may be the more effective involvement of European firms compared to American firms starting from the agenda-setting stage and throughout the rule-making

---

[16] U.S. comparison based on 556 U.S. firms that answered the assessment question ("process by which the standard is developed") for both U.S. domestic and international (ISO or IEC) standards; European comparison based on 196 European firms that answered the questions for both domestic and international standards.

process. We therefore turn next to statistical analyses of successful involvement in international standard-setting.

Power and Influence in International Standard-Setting: A Statistical Analysis

As our measure of success, we use the responses to the question: "When you try to influence the technical specification of a new international standard, how frequently do you succeed?" Respondents were offered five response options: (1) rarely/never, (2) sometimes, (3) about half of the time, (4) often, and (5) very often/always. We conduct a series of statistical analyses to determine the major factors affecting this measure of success.[17] Our primary interest in these analyses is the extent to which differences in institutional complementarity can explain differences in success. We use the nationality of a firm as our proxy for institutional fit and generally find that European firms are significantly more successful, as discussed in more detail below. To ensure that this finding is not spurious, we control for other factors that might affect success:

- firm size
- direct representation of the firm on a technical committee, subcommittee, or working group of a standards-developing organization
- attempted influence via government(s)
- attempted influence via contacts with the ISO or IEC during the standard-setting process
- timing of information received about a pertinent standard-setting effort at the international level
- frequency of influence attempts

Our statistical analyses ultimately consider all of these factors, but as in the case of international financial reporting standards we begin with a simple analysis (see model 1 in table 7.A.1 in the appendix to this chapter). We start by taking into account FIRM SIZE. Larger firms are more likely to have the material resources and specialized technical expertise required to influence international standard-setting, as discussed in chapter 3. As expected, we find that larger firms are generally more successful. This

---

[17] We conduct maximum likelihood regression analyses (ordered logit), as discussed in chapter 5.

effect is statistically significant, though it becomes weaker once we control for other factors.[18]

In addition, we control in all analyses for whether the firm has a REPRESENTATIVE IN THE EXPERT GROUPS OF STANDARDS-DEVELOPING ORGANIZATIONS (SDOs) at the international or domestic level, since such representation presumably constitutes the most direct avenue of influence, given ISO and IEC's standard-setting procedures.[19] We find that having such a direct link to the SDO technical committees, subcommittees, or working groups indeed boosts a company's success in influencing the provisions of a standard. The effect is highly significant and large. Most importantly, we find that, after controlling for firm size and SDO representation, European firms are notably more successful than U.S. firms in influencing international standardization, as we had expected, given the greater complementarity between the domestic and regional institutions in Europe and the institutional structure of the ISO/IEC.

We next take into account two specific methods used by firms to influence ISO/IEC standard-setting, drawn from responses to the survey question: "When you get involved, how do you do so? How frequently do you try to influence the technical specification of a newly proposed international standard by each of the following methods?"[20]

The main alternative to our institutional explanation of success in international standard-setting is one that emphasizes the role of governments and state power. As discussed in chapters 2 and 3, we are skeptical about the usefulness of state power in global private governance,

---

[18] Throughout this section, when we say "more successful" we technically are saying that there is a higher probability of being more frequently successful. *Firm size* is based on the question "How many employees does your company have?" with seven response options (size categories): "less than 50"; 50–100; 101–250; 251–500; 501–1000; 1001–1500; and "more than 1500." The thresholds were a function of the definitions for small- and medium-sized enterprises by the U.S. Department of Commerce and its European counterparts, which vary by industry.

[19] This measure is based on the question "Do you or other employees of your company (including parent company or subsidiaries abroad) participate in the work of a technical standards committee, subcommittee, or working group of a standards developing organization (SDO)?" The variable is coded 1 if the respondent selected "Yes, one or more employees of our company serve on such a committee."

[20] Respondents were instructed "Please check all that apply" and then were offered for each influence method three response options: (1) rarely, (2) sometimes, or (3) often—in addition to the option of leaving any particular method unchecked, which we coded as zero.

despite claims by some international relations theorists to the contrary.[21] To examine this issue systematically, we asked firms how frequently they request that governments act on their behalf. The results suggest that governments rarely play a role in international private rule-making for global product markets—most firms do not even try to get the government involved. Few American firms report contacting Congress, and even fewer rely on the Department of Commerce or other federal agencies for help. European firms also turn to their respective governments rarely if ever (see table 7.4).

These preliminary findings about the role of governments in international standard-setting are corroborated by our statistical analyses of success in which we use the reported frequency of requesting help from government agencies as our measure of ATTEMPTED INFLUENCE VIA GOVERNMENT. Remarkably, we find that recourse to government on average *decreases* the chances of success—a finding that is at least weakly statistically significant (models 2-4 in table 7.A.1).

We also consider ATTEMPTED INFLUENCE VIA CONTACTS WITH THE ISO/ IEC.[22] We would expect that actively making their voice heard vis-à-vis the ISO or IEC during the standard-setting process helps firms influence the standard. And indeed, we find that such contacts increase firms' success in influencing ISO and IEC standards, and the statistically estimated effect is clearly significant. Crucially, controlling for both methods of attempted influence as well as firm size and SDO representation, European firms remain clearly more successful in international standardization than U.S. firms (see model 2).

The survey responses allow an interesting additional test of our theory: since membership in European domestic and regional standards institutions is not based on nationality but on whether a firm has operations in Europe, U.S. firms with subsidiaries in Europe qualify for membership in these standards bodies. This should allow them to reap the benefits of better information and more effective interest aggregation that high institutional complementarity confers on European firms. We therefore

---

[21] These theorists base their claims on frequently retold anecdotes about highly unusual cases, concluding that firms regularly ask governments for help when they seek to influence international standards in private settings. See, for example, Drezner, *All Politics Is Global* (2007), 73f.

[22] The precise wording in the survey was "We directly contact the international SDO that is drafting the new standard and present our position to them." Such contacts are the functional equivalent in ISO/IEC to the submission of comment letters to the IASB.

TABLE 7.4
Influence via Government?

		Rarely	Sometimes	Often
[US:] We contact the Department of Commerce . . .	U.S. firms	67%	9%	0.2%
[Europe:] We contact our government agency [or] ministry . . .	European firms	60%	12%	1.6%
. . . and ask them to take action on our behalf				
We contact our representatives in Congress and ask them to take action on our behalf	U.S. firms	64%	12%	1.5%
	European firms		N/A	

Note: Based on responses to the question: "When you get involved, how do you do so? How frequently do you try to influence the technical specification of a newly proposed international standard by each of the following methods? Please check all that apply." In the German survey, the exact wording was "Wir kontaktieren die zuständigen Regierungsstellen (Ministerien, Ämter) und bitten Sie, in unserem Interesse aktiv zu werden." In the Spanish survey: "Contactamos a nuestro gobierno u organismo oficial competente para pedirle que participe en representación nuestra." The difference between the sum of percentages in each row and 100 is the percentage of respondents who did not make a frequency-of-use selection, indicating "never" or N/A. *N* = 1385 and 1011, respectively.

TABLE 7.5

Influencing International Product Standards:
Change in Predicted Probability of Successfully Influencing
Technical Specifications

	Rarely or never	Sometimes	Half of the time	Often	Very often or always
European firms compared to U.S. firms	–14%	+1.6%	+5.6%	+5.9%	+0.9%
U.S. firms with European subsidiaries vs. U.S. domestic firms	–10%	+1.8%	+3.9%	+3.9%	+0.6%

Note: Change in predicted probabilities of success in influencing the technical specification of ISO or IEC standards, at specified levels of frequency, based on ordered logit
model, also controlling for (holding at their means): firm size, representative on expert
group, attempted influence via government, and attempted influence via contact with ISO/
IEC (model 3; N = 1108). See Table 7.A.2 in this chapter's appendix for further details.

analyze *U.S. FIRMS WITH EUROPEAN SUBSIDIARIES* as distinct from other
U.S. firms and regular European firms.[23] The results offer strong support
for our hypothesis: U.S. multinationals with European subsidiaries are
substantially more successful than U.S. firms without European subsidiaries, even after controlling for size, representatives in the standards-
developing expert groups, and the specific ways of trying to influence
ISO/IEC standard-setting discussed above (models 3 and 4).[24]

To provide a concrete and easily understandable measure of how access
to more complementary institutions affects success, we report in table 7.5
the change in the likelihood of success in trying to influence ISO/IEC
standards.[25] According to these calculations, after taking into account
all the variables discussed above, the probability of being rarely or never
successful is 14 percent lower for European firms (and 10 percent lower
for U.S. multinationals with European subsidiaries) than for domestic

[23] We implement this by adding a dichotomous variable to our statistical model, coded 1
for U.S. firms with European subsidiaries (0 otherwise).

[24] At the same time, distinguishing between U.S. firms with and without European subsidiaries makes the difference between domestic U.S. firms and European firms even more pronounced and even more highly statistically significant, even while controlling for firm size.

[25] Technically, we estimate the statistically "predicted probabilities" of being successful at
the specified frequency.

U.S. firms. Conversely, the likelihood of being often successful is almost 6 percent higher for European firms than for U.S. firms and almost 4 percent higher for U.S. firms with European subsidiaries.

Another factor likely to affect a firm's ability to influence international standards is timely involvement in the standard-setting process. We have argued in chapter 3 that timing is very important in multistage standard-setting processes where the most fundamental decisions are taken early. And as discussed in chapter 6, ISO and IEC follow such a multistage procedure to set international product standards. The importance of being involved early during the ISO standard-setting process was underscored in many interviews and in responses to survey questions that allowed respondents to elaborate individually rather than be forced to choose from among response options. A U.S. chemical industry respondent, for instance, explained why his firm had repeatedly been unsuccessful in ISO standard-setting: "We were partly to blame because [we did not] participate in the beginning of the development of the standards."[26] Is there systematic evidence to suggest that timing matters? When asked how important timing is "for being able to affect the technical specification of [a] proposed standard before it is finalized," respondents on both sides of the Atlantic overwhelmingly considered it "important" or "very important" (see figure 7.3).

It should therefore matter greatly when firms get information about the standardization agenda at ISO and IEC. We examined this further by asking: "At what stage do you usually hear about a forthcoming ISO/IEC standard that may affect your products?" In the response options for this survey question, we differentiated five stages:

1. before an initial proposal is submitted to the ISO, during the informal planning stage

2. during the initial definition of the technical scope of the standard in the ISO working group

3. during the development of the new standard in the ISO technical committee

4. after it is registered and published as a Draft ISO standard (enquiry stage)

5. after the standard has been adopted

---

[26] Engineering/standards expert in R&D (am5082gd).

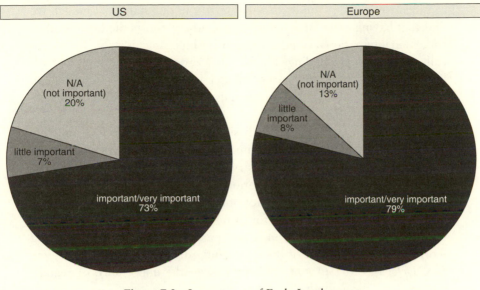

Figure 7.3   Importance of Early Involvement

• • • • • •

Responses to survey question: "When you succeed, how important are the
following reasons for being able to affect the technical specification of the
proposed standard before it is finalized? . . . Timing (getting involved early)."
N = 1004.

We have argued above that the better fit between European domestic
institutions and the institutional structure of ISO and IEC should provide European firms more quickly with the pertinent information about
the standardization agenda at the international level.[27] And indeed, we
find that European firms have better information at every stage of the
process.[28] Remarkably, more than 30 percent of U.S. firms first learn of
new ISO and IEC standards that affect their products only after the standard has been adopted—that is, when it is too late to influence it in any
way—whereas only 17 percent of European firms first learn of standards
at that late stage.

[27] Since information about new standards proposals—especially at the informal planning
stage and the beginning of the process—is generally not publicly available, it is difficult and
may be impossible to compensate for the institutional impediments.
[28] More precisely, at each stage prior to the final one, the share of European firms, which
know about a forthcoming standard that may affect their products, is higher than the share
of U.S. firms with such knowledge (N = 1295).

When we include TIMING OF INFORMATION in our statistical model, we find that having early information substantially boosts the likelihood of success in international standardization, and the effect is strongly statistically significant. The findings for the other variables persist after controlling for the timing of information (model 4 in table 7.A.1). In particular, European firms and U.S. multinationals with European subsidiaries remain significantly more successful.[29]

Finally, our institutional analysis suggests that, because ISO and IEC standard-setting takes place in technical committees and working groups where technical experts from industry can directly participate in the rule-making process, frequent participation or involvement should be crucial to being successful. The importance of regular involvement has also been noted by others. Roht-Arriaza, for instance, observes: "In practice, those who consistently attend meetings, and participate in the actual drafting work, decide the content of the ISO standard."[30] And ANSI's *Guide for U.S. Delegates to ISO and IEC* emphasizes the importance of regular participation throughout.[31]

Our theoretical argument suggests, however, that European firms should be more frequently involved than U.S. firms because the institutional structure in Europe facilitates such involvement. Including our measure FREQUENCY OF INVOLVEMENT in the statistical model should therefore diminish the difference between European and U.S. respondents. Indeed, we find that frequency of involvement greatly increases the chance of success (model 5 in table 7.A.1), and that including it in the statistical model reduces the statistical significance of the difference between European and U.S. firms (and several other variables).[32]

The finding that involvement statistically explains a large part of success begs the obvious question: *What explains involvement in international standardization?* We briefly address this question in the following, final part of our statistical analysis.

---

[29] Consistent with our argument, the magnitude of the statistically estimated effect for being a European firm (or having European subsidiaries) declines when we move from model 3 to model 4, as it should since TIMING OF INFORMATION directly captures one of the hypothesized reasons for why Europeans are more successful.

[30] Roht-Arriaza, "Shifting the Point of Regulation: The International Organization for Standardization and Global Lawmaking on Trade and the Environment" (1995), 524.

[31] ANSI, *Guide for U.S. Delegates* (2002), esp. 4f.

[32] FREQUENCY OF INVOLVEMENT is highly correlated with several explanatory variables (at above 0.4, indicating multicollinearity) and with FREQUENCY OF SUCCESS at above 0.6.

Institutional Complementarity and Involvement in
International Standard-Setting

The key issue in this analysis is whether European firms are in fact more frequently involved (and through involvement more successful) than their American counterparts, even after taking into account other factors that might explain involvement. We include many of the same factors considered in our analysis of success: firm nationality, timing of information, firm size, representative in SDO expert groups, and presence/absence of European subsidiaries of U.S. firms. In addition, we include three measures of a firm's economic stakes in international standardization to capture its incentive to get involved: EXPORTS AS A PERCENTAGE OF THE FIRM'S SALES measures the extent to which a firm relies on exports to turn a profit.[33] The FREQUENCY OF DIVERGENCE between proposals for new international standards and the firm's prior product specifications or production practices measures how frequently new international standards would impose adjustment costs if the initial proposals were adopted without change.[34] The final economic consideration included in our statistical model are the AVERAGE SWITCHING COSTS a company would incur if those initial proposals were adopted without change.[35]

The results of our statistical analyses about involvement confirm our theoretical prediction: European firms are more frequently involved than otherwise comparable U.S. firms, and the difference is highly statistically significant. Moreover, U.S. multinationals with European subsidiaries—which should be more involved in ISO and IEC standardization since they benefit via their subsidiaries from the greater complementarity between European and international institutions—are indeed more involved than other U.S. firms. Finally, when we test the informational argument directly, we find that early information significantly boosts involvement (see table 7.A.3 in the appendix to this chapter for details).

---

[33] The variable is based on the responses to the survey question: "What percentage of your company's total sales are exports?" Survey participants chose among eight response categories, ranging from "0 percent" to "more than 50 percent."

[34] Descriptive statistics for this measure are discussed above.

[35] This measure is based on the survey question: "When [a] newly proposed international standard differs from current practice, how costly would it usually be to comply with it if it were adopted as proposed?" with response options: very inexpensive, inexpensive, expensive, and very expensive.

TABLE 7.6
Involvement in International Standardization:
Change in Predicted Probability of Involvement

	Rarely or never	Sometimes	Half of the time	Often	Very often or always
European firms compared to U.S. firms	–11.5%	–1.2%	+2.4%	+6.9%	+3.3%
U.S. firms with European subsidiaries vs. U.S. domestic firms	–10.7%	–0.7%	+2.2%	+6.2%	+2.9%

Note: Change in predicted probabilities, based on ordered logit model (model 3; $N = 1167$). See table 7.A.4 in the chapter appendix for more details.

We report the key findings in table 7.6: after controlling for the other factors discussed above, the probability of being rarely or never involved is 11.5 percent lower for European firms (and 10.7 percent lower for U.S. multinationals with European subsidiaries) than for domestic U.S. firms. Conversely, the likelihood of being often involved is 6.9 percent higher for European firms and almost 6.2 percent higher for U.S. firms with European subsidiaries than for U.S. firms without European subsidiaries. The statistical analyses thus strongly confirm our theoretical expectations: the greater complementarity between European domestic institutions and the international standard-setting institutions facilitates European involvement in international rule-making and through better information flows and interest aggregation gives Europeans a significant advantage in international standard-setting. Otherwise comparable American firms are left paying a greater share of the adjustment costs.

INSTITUTIONS AS A SOURCE OF POWER IN PRIVATE STANDARD-SETTING: FURTHER EVIDENCE

Many survey participants provided copious comments based on their personal experiences with standardization in response to open-ended questions included in our survey. These comments offer valuable insights into the importance of institutions in international private rule-making.

They provide extensive direct evidence that the institutional logic and causal mechanisms of our theory indeed drive the statistical findings presented above.

Many American respondents lament domestic institutional fragmentation, which they see as undermining U.S. interests in international standardization. As a U.S. steel industry engineer puts it: "A better effort needs to be made to coordinate the . . . response for U.S. industries to international standards. . . . This is complicated by competing interests domestically [which] lead to multiple domestic views on an issue."[36] Another respondent complains that there are "too many standards organizations for Iron and Steel products [with] each organization put[ting out its] own standards."[37] An expert in another sector notes: "In the oil and gas measurement industry, standards are critical. At the same time, a lack of harmonization [among competing domestic standards bodies] has impacted the industry in a very negative fashion."[38] Similar views are voiced by many across all surveyed U.S. industries.

Several respondents specifically note how institutional fragmentation impedes information flows and thus puts them at a disadvantage in global governance. An American chemicals industry engineer, for instance, writes: "We are not made aware of international standard development for our industry. . . . The main problem is the lack of communication with international committees . . . it is [therefore] extremely difficult to find the information we are attempting to find."[39] Some American producers even report difficulty identifying the American representatives in international standardization.[40]

As a consequence of the poor institutional fit between U.S. domestic standard-setting and the rule-making institutions at the international level, the information often reaches U.S. firms too late to exert real influence. A quality control expert from a medical instruments manufacturer, for instance, explains: "There is no mechanism to bring to the attention of companies whose products may be affected [by an international standard] and who are not presently on a working committee . . . anything

---

[36] U.S. iron and steel industry engineering/R&D respondent (am2492b).
[37] U.S. iron and steel industry quality control respondent (am2349i).
[38] U.S. petroleum products industry sales/marketing participant (am8242fb).
[39] U.S. chemicals industry engineering/R&D respondent (am4537ns).
[40] See SASI Editorial Staff, "Conflicting Standards under Fire" (2007), 44, reporting on difficulties with European and international standards experienced by manufacturers of specialty equipment for firefighters.

[about the project] . . . until [the standard] is published."[41] And a CEO of a U.S. chemicals manufacturer comments: "We have sought to influence technical standards when one company or group seeks to change the standard only to give a specific product a competitive advantage. Usually, we only hear of it at the eleventh hour and have to assemble a mad dash to prevent such practices."[42] Many others get "involved too late" with the result that their "comments are essentially ignored."[43]

Unsurprisingly, U.S. firms rarely turn to ANSI, the weak official institutional representative of U.S. interests at the ISO (see chapter 6)—in contrast to European firms, which turn to their national ISO member bodies far more frequently, as we would expect given the greater institutional complementarity between ISO/IEC and AENOR, BSI, DIN, or SIS (see figure 7.4). ANSI even publicly recognized part of the problem in 2000, when it noted about the U.S. standardization system: "A sectorally based, decentralized system can sometimes lead to overlap in work programs and . . . conflicting standards."[44] It is still ANSI, however, which explicitly gets a lot of the blame for American firms' difficulties in international standard-setting. One respondent notes: "ANSI and other SDOs do a poor job in communicating international standards development actions to [users]."[45] Many others are less restrained in their criticism, noting for example that: "ANSI has been worthless in the area of plastics in international standards";[46] or "In my particular field, fire safety, the activities of ANSI are nil or counterproductive."[47]

It is telling that European respondents made more sparing use of write-in options in our survey. They seem largely content, and the few comments by Europeans tend to describe well-working institutional coordination mechanisms nationally as well as regionally. A Spanish respondent from a medical instruments manufacturer, for instance, comments on how: "Our involvement in IEC working groups has enabled us to propose changes while the standard was being developed and be informed of other international standards projects." And when time or resource constraints did not permit direct involvement in ISO technical committees, he "took part in discussions in committees of the Spanish

---

[41] U.S. medical instruments industry quality control expert (am1234pf).
[42] U.S. chemicals industry respondent (am5323se).
[43] U.S. rubber and plastics industry engineering/R&D respondent (am3446qk).
[44] ANSI, *National Standards Strategy for the United States* (2000), 11.
[45] U.S. rubber and plastics industry engineering/R&D expert (am3466sv).
[46] U.S. rubber and plastics industry quality control respondent (am3437nk).
[47] U.S. rubber and plastics industry engineering/R&D (am3222er).

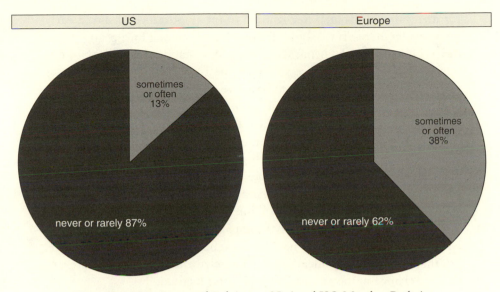

Figure 7.4 Frequency of Relying on National ISO Member Body in International Standardization

• • • • • •

Responses to survey question: "When you get involved, how do you do so? How frequently do you try to influence the technical specification of a newly proposed international standard by each of the following methods? . . . We ask [ANSI/DIN/AENOR/SIS/BSI] to get involved on our behalf."

standards institute (AENOR) that shadow the [for his firm relevant] IEC and ISO standards committees. In both cases, the Spanish position and proposals were discussed at the international level," allowing him to conclude: "Our company has successfully intervened in the development of [several international] standards" for medical instruments.[48] Similarly, a Swedish manufacturer reports how his company "got the wording" that they sought in a new international standard for pressurized gas cylinders

---

[48] Spanish medical instruments standards manager (em050ar). Similarly, a Spanish quality control expert, for instance, describes his company's strategy of forging a common position via multiple national standards bodies: "Una respuesta común a traves de nuestras filiales europeas que participan en sus ODEs nacionales" concerning an international standard for "uno de los productos de nueva creación en nuestra fábrica" (em006fr), and a German engineering standards expert (dn19) describes his company's success in influencing international standards through their involvement in domestic standards committees.

for medical equipment.[49] Recognition of the importance of direct, early involvement in ISO/IEC standardization is high among European respondents. Notes a British chemical engineer: "If a standard is critical [to our business], you cannot ignore it. . . . The best way to minimize its (negative) impact on our business is to be active in writing it."[50] Some note the benefits—especially new business opportunities—that their firms have derived from international (ISO/IEC) standardization, which most of the Europeans consider generally preferable to both national and European standard-setting.[51] Most importantly, though, regular and early involvement allows European firms to avoid paying massive switching costs by blocking in good time competitors' attempts to gain an advantage by shaping international standards.[52] For a German engineering firm, for instance, "an enormous amount of technical drawings would have had to be changed" had a proposed new standard been adopted without change, but thanks to the respondent's timely involvement "I was able to prevent a costly change in the permissible projection method."[53]

The perception that Europeans are better positioned to influence international product standardization is also widespread among Americans. Typical statements by American respondents include: "The U.S. position with regard to international standards is much weaker than in Europe . . . ANSI needs to develop a stronger international presence."[54] Or, "The EU has too much power in ISO standards making . . . the ISO committee is just an extension of the EU,"[55] and "ISO is controlled by European interests."[56] Other respondents sound resigned: "I believe that the U.S. has minimal involvement and influence on European and/or global standards. . . . As a result the [European] standards will dominate and the U.S. will follow."[57] The CEO of a U.S. chemicals industry firm similarly observes: "We are mostly the 'tail of the dog.' We seldom find ourselves

[49] Swedish medical instruments industry R&D expert (sm021fv).

[50] UK chemical industry standards manager (bc98h).

[51] E.g., German chemical industry information services expert (dac03ac); rubber and plastics industry quality control expert (dr005ia).

[52] E.g., response by a German medical instruments standards manager (dm002mk) concerning the standardization of ultrasound technology. Similarly, a German iron and steel industry quality control expert (di009bm) about a certification standard for metallic products: "Wahrung der Herstellerinteressen in wichtigen Punkten gelungen."

[53] German standards manager (dn20).

[54] U.S. rubber and plastics industry engineering/R&D expert (am3175kw).

[55] U.S. rubber and plastics industry engineering/R&D (am3018mr).

[56] U.S. chemicals industry engineering/R&D expert (am5167zb).

[57] U.S. rubber and plastics industry sales and marketing respondent (am3393xe).

even near the driver's seat. What is left is for us to follow the directives of the . . . European industries."[58]

The views on the U.S. side, however, are not all despairing and negative. For some firms the present institutional arrangement seems to work reasonably well. This is particularly true for American multinational corporations with operations in Europe—as predicted by our theory. A U.S. medical instruments manufacturer with several subsidiaries in Western Europe, for instance, notes: "Our company's ability to influence standards worldwide is due to an active coordinated . . . involvement with national and international SDOs in Europe."[59] A respondent working for a large U.S. chemicals firm similarly writes: "We have subsidiaries in most countries. Therefore, internal networking on standards is important . . . We can be involved in several countries at several levels simultaneously."[60] And the representative of a U.S. multinational company in the plastics industry explains: "We supported [European] technical committees with funding. . . . We supported persons to attend the meetings and we got standards close to our desires."[61]

Finally, in some particular U.S. industries, contestation among rival standards bodies is relatively weak, rendering the interface with international standard-setting organizations less problematic. As one respondent notes: "In my particular corner of the Petroleum industry (pipelines), . . . if an ISO standard is being revised and will be in conflict with the API/ ASTM, I hear about it and work with the U.S. standards organizations to develop the U.S. position for ANSI."[62] This is possible, he explains, due to the good institutional fit between API and ISO. This relationship "keeps us . . . informed of the status of the ISO [standards project]."[63] And when well-informed U.S. firms get involved in a timely fashion, they do quite well. As an American chemical industry respondent remarks: "Through my involvement, I feel that I was able to influence content."[64] Similarly, Robert Noth, manager of Engineering Standards for the U.S. multinational agricultural, construction, and forestry equipment manufacturer [John] Deere & Company testified before Congress that the exceptional commitment

---

[58] U.S. chemicals industry respondent (am5509bd).

[59] U.S. medical instruments industry standards manager (am1120sc).

[60] U.S. chemicals industry sales and marketing expert (am8914hk).

[61] U.S. rubber and plastics engineering/R&D respondent (am3240nt).

[62] API stands for the American Petroleum Institute; ASTM for the American Society for Testing and Materials.

[63] U.S. petroleum industry quality control respondents(am8026fq).

[64] U.S. chemicals industry engineering/R&D expert (am1208ps).

to international rather than domestic rule-making among firms in his industry had allowed Deere to overcome fragmentation and participate with considerable success "because of our early involvement."[65]

In other words, consistent with our theory, we find that in rare cases where domestic standardization governance is relatively hierarchical, American firms can effectively influence the content of international standards. The main problem for U.S. firms, then, remains that the domestic institutional fragmentation tends to impede their ability to take advantage of institutional procedures to exert influence at the international level. Conversely, European firms more often than not are empowered by greater institutional complementarity.

[65] U.S. House of Representatives (Hearing), *China, Europe, and Use of Standards as Trade Barriers* (2005), 25.

Table 7.A.1
Maximum Likelihood Regression Estimates, Models of
Success in Attempts to Influence International Product Standards

	Model 1	Model 2	Model 3	Model 4	Model 5
European firms	0.254*	0.474***	0.689***	0.385**	0.0171
	(.132)	(.135)	(.153)	(.159)	(.167)
U.S. firms with European subsidiaries			0.484***	0.406***	0.246
			(.146)	(.151)	(.157)
Firm size	0.118***	0.115***	0.0819***	0.0879***	0.0766**
	(.0256)	(.0259)	(.0281)	(.0289)	(.0300)
Representation on expert committee/ group of SDO	1.31***	1.08***	1.09***	0.949***	0.453**
	(.200)	(.203)	(.204)	(.209)	(.215)
Attempted influence via government		−0.253**	−0.252**	−0.225*	−0.0843
		(.118)	(.119)	(.121)	(.125)
Attempted influence via contact with ISO/IEC		0.912***	0.885***	0.716***	0.400***
		(.0767)	(.0771)	(.0801)	(.0846)
Timing of Information				0.540***	0.328***
				(.0524)	(.0552)
Frequency of Involvement					0.837***
					(.0600)
N	1113	1113	1108	1083	1067
pseudo-R^2	0.0307	0.0844	0.0871	0.1273	0.2076
Likelihood ratio test vs. previous model		χ^2=155.24***	χ^2=10.99***	χ^2=111.16***	χ^2=216.67***

Note: Estimated coefficients from ordered logit regressions with standard errors in parentheses. * $p < 0.1$; ** $p < 0.05$; *** $p < 0.01$. Pseudo-R^2 not fully comparable due to changes in sample size after listwise exclusion. Likelihood ratio tests (LR test) based on reestimation of the more restricted model for same sample as the unrestricted model. All estimates in Stata version 10.1.

TABLE 7.A.2

Change in Probability of Success in Attempts to Influence the Technical Specification of Proposed International Standards

	Rarely or never	Sometimes	Half of the time	Often	Very often or always
Region (U.S. → European)	-0.14 (.030) [-.20 -.078]	0.016 (.0074) [.0016 .031]	0.056 (.013) [.028 .083]	0.060 (.016) [.030 .094]	0.009 (0.0032) [.004 .016]
US firms w/ European subsidiaries (No → Yes)	-0.10 (.028) [-.15 -.044]	0.018 (.0063) [.0074 .032]	0.038 (.011) [.016 .060]	0.039 (.012) [.016 0.63]	0.0057 (0.0022) [.0021 .011]
Firm size (min → max)	-0.11 (.038) [-.18 -.034]	0.030 (.012) [.0079 .057]	0.038 (.013) [.012 .064]	0.036 (.012) [.011 .060]	0.0052 (0.0022) [.0014 .010]
Representation on SDO expert groups (No → Yes)	-0.26 (.049) [-.35 -.15]	0.12 (.031) [.057 .18]	0.070 (.011) [.047 .092]	0.060 (.0099) [.041 .081]	0.0083 (.0022) [.005 .013]
Attempted Influence via government (min → max)	0.17 (.085) [.0091 .34]	-0.057 (.033) [-.13 -.0022]	-0.055 (.026) [-.11 -.0032]	-0.052 (.024) [-.099 -.0032]	-0.0074 (.0038) [-.015 -.0004]
Attempted influence via contact w ISO/IEC (min → max)	-0.51 (.035) [-.58 -.44]	0.063 (.019) [.027 .10]	0.17 (.017) [.14 .21]	0.24 (.025) [.19 .29]	0.04 (.010) [.024 .064]

Note: Columns represent the five response categories of the dependent variable (frequency of success when the respondent attempts to influence the technical specification of an international standard in ISO or IEC). Larger bold numbers indicate, based on the estimates from Model 3, the change in the probability that a firm is successful at the specified frequency, resulting from switching the independent variable on the left from its minimum to its maximum value while holding all other variables at their means. Standard errors in parentheses; 95% confidence intervals in brackets (based on *Clarify* simulations).

TABLE 7.A.3

Maximum Likelihood Regression Estimates, Models of Involvement
in International Product Standard-Setting

	Model 1	Model 2	Model 3
European firms	0.433***	0.753***	0.576***
	(.139)	(.164)	(.169)
U.S. firms with European subsidiaries		0.545***	0.526***
		(.141)	(.147)
Timing of Information			0.673***
			(.0493)
Firm size	0.0549**	0.0151	0.0133
	(.0246)	(.0268)	(.0278)
Firm representatives on SDO expert committees/groups	1.96***	2.02***	1.86***
	(.197)	(.199)	(.206)
Frequency of divergence	0.124**	0.122**	0.138**
	(.057)	(.057)	(.0598)
Average switching costs	0.383***	0.402***	0.422***
	(.0903)	(.0907)	(.0952)
Exports as % of total sales	0.129***	0.106***	0.0782***
	(.0280)	(.0288)	(.0300)
N	1199	1195	1167
pseudo-R^2	0.0645	0.0690	0.1266
LR test vs. previous model		χ^2=14.91***	χ^2=198.81***

Note: Coefficients based on ordered logit estimation, with standard errors in parentheses. * $p < 0.1$; ** $p < 0.05$; *** $p < 0.01$. All estimates in Stata 10.1. Pseudo-R^2 not fully comparable across models due to changes in sample size. Likelihood ratio tests (LR test) based on reestimation of the more restricted model for same sample as the unrestricted model.

TABLE 7.A.4

Change in Probability of Firm Involvement in the Technical Specification of Proposed International
Standards at Given Level of Frequency

	Rarely or never	Sometimes	Half of the time	Often	Very often or always
Region (U.S. → European)	−0.11 (.031) [−.17 −.052]	−0.011 (.0081) [−.030 .0001]	0.024 (.0068) [.0105 .038]	0.069 (.021) [.029 .11]	0.033 (.011) [.013 .057]
U.S. MNC w/ European subsidiaries (No → Yes)	−0.11 (.028) [−.16 −.055]	−0.0063 (.0059) [−.021 .0032]	0.022 (.0061) [.011 .035]	0.063 (.017) [.030 .097]	0.029 (.0085) [.013 .046]
Timing of information (late → earliest)	−0.48 (.028) [−.53 −.42]	−0.087 (.017) [−.12 −.053]	0.064 (.0082) [.048 .080]	0.29 (.022) [.24 .33]	0.21 (.025) [.17 .26]
Firm size (min → max)	−0.017 (.035) [−.092 −.045]	0.0005 (.0019) [−.0024 .0052]	0.0036 (.0073) [−.0098 .019]	0.0090 (.018) [−.024 .047]	0.0039 (.0081) [−.011 .021]

Firm rep. on SDO committees/groups (No → Yes)	**−0.43** (.043) [−.51 −.34]	**0.15** (.027) [.097 .20]	**0.073** (.0091) [.056 .092]	**0.15** (.014) [.12 .17]	**0.058** (.0067) [.046 .073]
Frequency of divergence (min → max)	**−0.11** (.045) [−.20 −0.22]	**−0.0083** (.0085) [−.029 .0024]	**0.023** (.0094) [.0044 .041]	**0.065** (.028) [.013 .12]	**0.031** (.015) [.0053 .064]
Switching costs (min → max)	**−0.27** (.060) [−.39 −.16]	**0.016** (.012) [−.0052 .042]	**0.053** (.012) [.030 .076]	**0.14** (.030) [.082 .20]	**0.064** (.016) [.035 .098]
Exports as a % of firm's total sales (min → max)	**−0.095** (.037) [−.17 −.017]	**−0.002** (.0049) [−.014 .0060]	**0.020** (.0079) [.0037 .034]	**0.054** (.021) [.0097 .092]	**0.024** (.010) [.0042 .044]

Note: Columns represent the five response categories of the dependent variable (frequency of involvement in the technical specification of international standards). Larger bold numbers indicate, based on the estimates from Model 3, the change in the probability that a firm is involved with a given frequency, resulting from switching the independent variable on the left from its minimum to its maximum value while holding all other variables at their means. Standard errors in parentheses; 95% confidence intervals in brackets, based on *Clarify* simulations.

CHAPTER EIGHT

Contributions to the Theoretical Debates in Political Science, Sociology, Law, and Economics

Our empirical investigation of private rule-making in transnational focal institutions—based on quantitative analyses of hundreds of responses from two multi-industry business surveys, complemented by qualitative analyses of a wealth of additional sources—lends strong support to the institutional complementarity theory that we presented in chapter 3. In this chapter, aimed primarily at readers who are interested in the theoretical issues raised by our argument and analysis, we summarize what is distinct and novel about institutional complementarity, then discuss the contributions of our analytical framework to current scholarly debates in political science, sociology, law, and economics/business studies.

THE IMPORTANCE OF INSTITUTIONAL COMPLEMENTARITY

Throughout this book, we have emphasized the complementarity between domestic and international institutions. We have argued that power in private rule-making for global markets is a function of how well domestic institutions complement the pertinent international institutions, not simply a function of domestic institutions alone. It is important to emphasize this point because we have focused on two major issue areas in which the international institutions for rule-making are similar and only the domestic institutions differ. In international product and financial standard-setting, we have consistently found that stakeholders with hierarchical domestic institutions are better able to exert influence over global rules. We do not argue, however, that hierarchical domestic institutions are inherently superior, independent of context. Rather, we attribute these finding to the greater complementarity of hierarchical domestic institutions with the particular institutions that exist at the international level. We do so for three reasons.

First, the key features of the domestic rule-making institutions for both product and financial markets were largely established long ago. In the decades before they became important for domestic stakeholders' ability to influence international standard-setting, that is, well before the international integration of these markets, hierarchical and fragmented institutions served domestic stakeholders similarly well.[1] The international integration of product and financial markets in the last two decades of the twentieth century prompted a drive for regulatory harmonization. To achieve such harmonization, governments increasingly turned to international organizations of seemingly apolitical technical experts, which heretofore had promulgated only low-stakes, nonbinding rules. For large parts of the global economy, these focal points for international rule-making were private bodies. This delegation of regulatory authority, however, has transformed the domestic standard-setting institutions into conduits for the participation of domestic stakeholders in global processes of setting rules that now have real bite. Given this international context, domestic systems that leave standardization to an institutionally fragmented private sector tend to find themselves at a disadvantage relative to hierarchical systems. The advantage of hierarchical domestic institutions thus is not an inherent characteristic of these institutions but arises from their complementarity with the specific international institutions for setting standards for product and financial markets.

Second, economic integration need not entail institutionalized global rule-making. In some sectors, where technological change is particularly fast paced, including the information and telecommunication industries, particular technical solutions may become de facto global standards through international market competition. Here domestic institutional fragmentation is advantageous insofar as it stimulates innovation and provides a safeguard against early technological lock-in.[2]

---

[1] See, e.g., Spruyt, "Supply and Demand of Governance in Standard-Setting" (2001). Conversely, both systems had flaws. As illustrated by the near-simultaneous collapse of Enron and WorldCom in the United States and Ahold, Parmalat, and Vivendi in Europe, circumvention and abuse of accounting rules was equally feasible in both systems.

[2] E.g., Cargill, *Information Technology Standardization* (1989). See also Genschel and Werle, "From National Hierarchies to International Standardization" (1993); Genschel, "How Fragmentation Can Improve Co-ordination" (1997).

Third, international institutions vary. A cursory review of international *nongovernmental* organizations that play a role in setting standards for global markets—such as the International Chamber of Commerce or Consumers International—suggests that most of them use a model of national representation and some variant of majoritarian decision-making, reflecting the long-standing presumption of legitimacy for the nation-state as a sociopolitical unit. In those cases, hierarchical domestic institutions should be advantageous internationally for the reasons discussed above, and our analytical framework may therefore have wide applicability. Note, however, that here, too, the structure and decision-making procedures of the international rule-making determine which characteristics of domestic institutions give a decisive advantage to actors with access to such institutions. If, for instance, rule-making were to require unanimity in an international organization with national representation, efficient information flows to (and from) domestic stakeholders—one of the hallmarks of hierarchical institutions as discussed in chapter 3—may not bring substantial benefits, because each country's representative could maintain a veto until domestic stakeholders have come to a decision.[3]

Alternatively, international institutions need not be organized on the basis of national representation but instead may allow direct representation of individual stakeholders. Standards consortia (discussed in chapter 2) and transnational professional associations[4] often allow individuals to be equal members of the international organization without any mediation by their domestic member bodies. International civil society organizations (NGOs) and transnational industry or employer organizations often similarly have individual persons or firms as voting members. In such settings, domestic institutions may matter little, except insofar as they facilitate forming broad transnational coalitions. In fact, fragmented domestic institutions, in which individual stakeholders are accustomed to fending for themselves and seeking out others with whom they can form political coalitions, may be advantageous in such a setting. Consistent

---

[3] Such an institutional structure at the international level is more commonly found in traditional (governmental) international organizations. The Organization for Economic Cooperation and Development (OECD), for instance, has set standards for compiling macroeconomic statistics and tax information, as well as for fruits, vegetables and agricultural tractors. The technical specifications are developed in issue-specific expert committees, but require unanimous approval of all member governments before they become OECD standards, giving each member government a chance to block decision-making if domestic stakeholders are not yet ready to support (or decisively reject) a technical proposal.

[4] Such as the International Studies Association, which represents scholars of international affairs from around the globe (albeit disproportionately from the United States).

with this argument, a U.S. CEO, for instance, called for ISO to "operate on an individual [company] membership basis."[5] He considered this practice advantageous since he knew how to operate in such an environment, given that ASTM in the United States has long had individual firms as members.

CONTRIBUTIONS TO THE LITERATURE

Our study seeks to contribute to the literature in political science, sociology, law, as well as economics and business studies. We provide a brief overview of how our research may benefit these fields.

Political Science

In political science, we seek to engage, first, the institutionalist literature in International Relations (IR). In that literature, the debate has shifted from the early exchanges over whether institutions matter to the more fruitful analytical questions of how and under what conditions they matter.[6] We contribute to that debate through a systematic analysis of domestic and international rule-making institutions for global product and financial markets. Our theoretical argument builds on Robert Keohane's observation that institutions "do not merely reflect . . . the power of the units constituting them; the institutions themselves shape . . . that power."[7] Keohane, however, focused exclusively on international institutions, whereas other institutionalist IR scholars have focused on domestic institutions.[8] We focus instead on the interaction between domestic and international institutions and go beyond the literature on two-level games[9] by examining differences in institutional complementarity across the two levels.

[5] Write-in response from Product Standards Survey by U.S. chemical industry CEO (am5192rp).

[6] Martin and Simmons, "Theories and Empirical Studies of International Institutions" (1998).

[7] Keohane, "International Institutions: Two Approaches" (1989).

[8] E.g., Milner, "International Theories of Cooperation Among Nations" (1992); Milner, *Interests, Institutions, and Information* (1997); Martin, *Democratic Commitments* (2000); Dai, "Why Comply?" (2005); Ehrlich, "Access to Protection" (2007); Bernhard and Leblang, "Democratic Institutions and Exchange Rate Commitments" (1999); Jensen, "Democratic Governance and Multinational Corporations" (2003); Berger and Dore, eds., *National Diversity and Global Capitalism* (1996).

[9] Putnam, "Diplomacy and Domestic Politics" (1988); Evans et al., eds., *Double-Edged Diplomacy* (1993).

Specifically, we show that *even in the face of concerns over so-called relative gains*—that is, conflicts over who will pay the smallest adjustment costs and thus gain the greatest net benefit in international rule-making—institutions are an important determinant of outcomes at the international level and a source of power.

Second, we draw on and seek to contribute to the literature on historical institutionalism. Historical institutionalists recognize that establishing rules and enshrining them in a formal structure, such as a constitution or an international organization, has distributional consequences. Institutional forms should thus reflect—at least in part—the distribution of power among key stakeholders in the distributional conflict of interest that is implicit in creating an institution.[10] At the same time, historical institutionalists emphasize feedback loops that, more often than not, reinforce existing institutional arrangements or constrain subsequent institutional options ("path dependence"). As a consequence, institutional arrangements that we empirically observe at any given point in time might be far from what one might expect given the distribution of power at that time, but instead might reflect what we call historical (institutional) legacies.[11] While historical institutionalist ideas were a prominent (if largely implicit) element of seminal early works in International Political Economy (IPE),[12] they have received little attention in recent years as most of the literature in IPE has focused on comparative statics.[13] But when institutions persist even when they are no longer efficient, taking histori-

---

[10] Hall and Taylor, "Political Science and the Three New Institutionalisms" (1996), esp. 937–38; Mahoney and Thelen, "A Theory of Gradual Institutional Change" (2010), esp. 7–10. Some historical institutionalists emphasize cognitive and other limitations that may impede the correspondence between even the initial institutional design and the distribution of power at that time, see Pierson, "The Limits of Design" (2000). On institutions as the embodiment of distributional conflict, see especially Knight, *Institutions and Social Conflict* (1992).

[11] Büthe, "Taking Temporality Seriously" (2002); Immergut, "Historical-Institutionalism in Political Science and the Problem of Change" (2006); Mattli and Büthe, "Setting International Standards" (2003); Pierson, *Politics in Time* (2004), esp.17ff; Thelen and Steinmo, "Historical Institutionalism in Comparative Politics" (1992); Thelen, "How Institutions Evolve" (2003).

[12] E.g., Katzenstein, ed. *Between Power and Plenty* (1978). For an excellent review, see Fioretos, "Historical Institutionalism in International Relations" (2011).

[13] "Comparative statics" is the technical-methodological term for comparing two situations (or equilibria) before and after some change. The comparison is used to determine the effect of a change in an explanatory factor (for instance, a change in price) on the object of investigation (for example, the quantity of a good purchased), without an attempt to explain the dynamic process of change. For critiques, see, e.g., Büthe, "Taking Temporality Seriously" (2002), and Pierson, *Politics in Time* (2004).

cal legacies into account is crucial for understanding both the structure and the operation of institutions at any particular moment in time. This insight led us to explore theoretically and then analyze empirically the differences in institutional complementarity, which would not exist if institutional change were swift and efficient. We contribute to this literature by exploring the consequences of institutional legacies in specific, intrinsically important contexts and showing the analytical payoff of integrating insights from historical institutionalism into theories of IPE.

Third, we seek to contribute to the literature on nontariff or regulatory barriers to international market integration. Several recent analyses of trade policy have lent support to Bhagwati's earlier speculation about a "law of constant protection": if governments negotiate away any particular protectionist measure, such as a tariff, economic actors who feel threatened by foreign competitors seek to replace it with another, nontariff measure to achieve the same level of protection.[14] Product standards that differ across countries are a prime example of such measures in the trade realm. And even when there is no protectionist intent, standards that differ across countries impede the international integration of markets. The problem is not limited to product markets: differences in financial reporting standards are important barriers to the integration of financial markets.[15] The international harmonization of standards has been heralded as an ideal solution, allowing governments or private actors to develop standards that achieve legitimate objectives, such as keeping consumers or workers safe and investors informed, without impeding the efficient operation of markets across borders. Transnational nongovernmental organizations, in which technical experts develop standards for global use through "consensus" procedures, have enjoyed particular appeal; and WTO member states, G7 and G20 finance ministers, and others have implicitly and explicitly delegated regulatory authority to such bodies. But any assessment of international private standardizers—for analytical or policy purposes—requires understanding the process of international standard-setting, including the distributional consequences of this privatization of market regulation.[16] We offer an analytical framework for such an assessment, as well as specific empirical analyses of two

---

[14] Bhagwati, *Protectionism* (1988), 53. See also, e.g., Kono, "Optimal Obfuscation" (2006); Naoi, "Shopping for Protection" (2009). For a review of the earlier literature on nontariff barriers to trade, see Mansfield and Busch, "The Political Economy of Nontariff Barriers" (1995).

[15] See the discussion in chapter 4.

[16] We will return to this issue in the conclusion.

of the most important institutions for global private regulation, the IASB and ISO/IEC.

Our research thus also fills a gap in the broader literature on standard-setting as a form of governance. Most political analyses of international standards-developing organizations have focused on governmental international organizations, such as the ITU, or transgovernmental networks of regulators. The typology that we developed in chapter 2 offers a clearer analytical distinction between these two kinds of public regulation, but most importantly, it delineates an important phenomenon that warrants genuinely political analysis: private rule-making in international bodies that are recognized ex ante as the focal point for setting global standards. We offer a theoretical framework for such research, as well as the most comprehensive and rigorous empirical analysis of nonmarket private standard-setting to date.

Finally, we seek to contribute to the political science literature on nonstate actors in world politics,[17] and specifically the literature on private regulation and global private politics.[18] Contributors to this literature have built a compelling case that politics—the exercise of power by some over others—need not entail governments, even when influence crosses borders. Most of this literature, however, has focused on contestation among multiple private (would-be) regulators, such as when transnational NGOs and multinational corporations promote competing standards for sustainable forestry,[19] labor conditions,[20] or corporate social responsibility,[21] or when NGOs push firms in the diamond industry to self-regulate.[22] As important as contestation among separate institutional actors is, much of global private politics takes place *within* an institutional setting that is essentially uncontested as the place for rule-making in a given issue area. International standard-setting organization such as IASB, IEC, and ISO,

---

[17] See, e.g., Hall and Biersteker, eds., *The Emergence of Private Authority in Global Governance* (2002); Josselin and Wallace, eds., *Nonstate Actors in World Politics* (2001).

[18] Büthe, "Governance through Private Authority?" (2004); Cutler et al., eds., *Private Authority and International Affairs* (1999); Graz and Nölke, eds., *Transnational Private Governance and Its Limits* (2008); Haufler, *The Public Role of the Private Sector* (2001); Mattli, "The Politics and Economics of International Institutionalized Standards Setting" (2001).

[19] Cashore et al., *Governing Through Markets* (2004).

[20] Bartley, "Corporate Accountability and the Privatization of Labor Standards" (2005) and "Institutional Emergence in an Era of Globalization" (2007).

[21] Vogel, *The Market for Virtue* (2005).

[22] Haufler, "The Kimberley Process, Club Goods, and Public Enforcement of a Private Regime" (2009).

are key examples of such institutions. We provide the first comprehensive analysis of this type of nonstate, nonmarket regulation.

Sociology

Our research also contributes to the literature on standards and standard-setting organizations in sociology. Sociologists—attuned by the work of Emile Durkheim, Talcott Parsons, and Norbert Elias to the power of nongovernmental rules—have earlier than most political scientists recognized the importance of private transnational institutions in the global economy. John Braithwaite and Peter Drahos's *Global Business Regulation*, for instance, recognizes the central importance of international nongovernmental organizations, and private rule-makers play a prominent role in many of their case studies. Braithwaite and Drahos point out specifically that tremendous power "to shape regulation globally" is vested in "thousands of obscure technical committees of . . . private standard-setting bodies like the ISO."[23] Yet, their wide-ranging study of the nature and causes of the globalization—and often privatization—of regulation does not provide an analysis of the distributional consequences of these shifts of rule-making to private bodies such as ISO and IASB and therefore does not allow for a full assessment of global private regulation.[24] Similarly, Nils Brunsson and Bengt Jacobsson's insightful study of nongovernmental standards as means of governance requires an examination of why some win and others lose in the process of international standard-setting. Institutional complementarity theory provides a framework for such an analysis.

An alternative framework has been offered by sociologists Thomas Loya and John Boli in what was probably the first social-scientific study of nonmarket private standardization at the international level.[25] Their account of ISO and IEC standard-setting is based on the "World Society" approach pioneered by John Meyer and coauthors, a sociological institutionalist theory developed to explain organizational forms and behavior

---

[23] Braithwaite and Drahos, *Global Business Regulation* (2000), 28.

[24] To be sure, Braithwaite and Drahos note "large corporations" (especially American ones) and "business-dominated epistemic communities" (page 32) as wielding great power within the inter- and transnational "webs of influence," but they do not provide an analytical framework for understanding cross-national differences in such influence even among firms from advanced industrialized countries.

[25] Loya and Boli, "Standardization in the World Polity" (1999).

of collective and individual actors at the international level.[26] Meyer and his followers see the modern international system as comprising an increasingly homogenous "world society," which has at its core Weberian notions of rationality, modernity, and progress, as well as cognitive models that are "highly rationalized, articulated, and often surprisingly consensual."[27] One effect of this "world political culture" is the empowerment of transnational communities of scientists and other organizations of experts with a claim to "develop[ing] rationalized and universalistic knowledge."[28]

Loya and Boli portray the actual process of standardization in ISO and IEC as taking place in accordance with the standards bodies' principles and other, universal norms—most importantly "world-cultural conceptions of universalism, rational progress, and egalitarianism."[29] Consequently, international standardization appears as devoid of politics and contestation: technical rationality trumps power and dissolves distributional conflicts, as scientific knowledge, which "is everywhere the same," transforms standardization into a technical optimization problem.[30]

Loya and Boli's limited empirical analysis, however, is mostly based on the organizations' own pronouncements. It fails to take into account the conflicts between the multiple principles enshrined in international standards bodies such as ISO and IASB, as described by Kristina Tamm Hallström,[31] and the "struggle for control of the standards-making process"

---

[26] Meyer and Rowan, "Institutionalized Organizations" (1977); Meyer, "The World Polity and the Authority of the Nation-State" (1980); Meyer et al., "World Society and the Nation State" (1997). It is the assumed universality of the core ideas of world society that allows this approach to explain similar behavior by dissimilar actors or actors with different interests; see Finnemore, "Norms, Culture, and World Politics" (1996), esp. 334. For a comparative discussion of sociological institutionalism, see Hall and Taylor, "Political Science and the Three New Institutionalisms" (1996), 946–50.

[27] Meyer et al., "World Society and the Nation State" (1997), 144.

[28] Meyer, "The World Polity and the Authority of the Nation-State" (1980), 165. Meyer is very cautious, however, about the extent to which such universalism might be expected to determine actual behavior, given the ever-present possibility of divergence between proclaimed norms and formal structures on the one hand and actual behavior on the other. See Meyer and Rowan, "Institutionalized Organizations" (1977), 341, 355–59 and Meyer et al., "World Society and the Nation State" (1997), 149, 154–56. For an overview of recent work on such "decoupling," see Boxenbaum and Jonsson, "Isomorphism, Diffusion and Decoupling" (2008), esp. 85ff.

[29] Loya and Boli, "Standardization in the World Polity" (1999), 192f.

[30] Loya and Boli (1999), 188.

[31] Tamm Hallström, "Organizing the Process of Standardization" (2000), esp. 96–99, and *Organizing International Standardization* (2004), esp. 157ff, based on an analysis of the IASB's predecessor organization, IASC.

noted by Marc Olshan.[32] Our analysis of the experience of stakeholders that are directly affected by the distributional consequences of international standardization shows that the professional norms of engineering or accounting as "science," embodied in these "expert" organizations, shape and constrain *how* standards battles are conducted, but *not whether* such battles take place. These norms require technical arguments in pursuit of commercial interests, but they do not change firms' perception of the commercial stakes nor reduce their commitment to pursuing their economic interests strategically, whenever possible.[33] Our analysis thus calls into question the consensual image of technical expert organizations and supports Paul DiMaggio's argument that there are often severe conflicts of interest lurking beneath the surface of the structure and operation of any organization—interests that are obscured by the emphasis on culture, professional norms, technical expertise, or similar widely shared beliefs that have been internalized to the point that they are no longer subject to critical inquiry.[34]

While we reject the World Polity approach, because its idealizing assumptions about the nature of science and engineering lead to a flawed analysis of international standard-setting ignoring its distributional implications, we recognize the insightfulness of the broader sociological institutionalist tradition and seek to contribute to it. A major objective of that literature has been to explain why social or political institutions converge on common structures or procedures—a process known as "institutionalism isomorphism."[35] Early contributors to this literature, from Max Weber to Michael Hannan and John Freeman, focused on what might be called competitive isomorphism, where objectively superior performance or greater efficiency of a particular organizational form in a competitive environment leads to institutional convergence, because learning leads to institutional change toward the superior model(s), or because the inefficient forms are selected out.[36] By contrast, more recent key contributions

[32] Olshan, "Standards Making Organizations and the Rationalization of American Life" (1993), 319.

[33] See also Büthe, "The Power of Norms; the Norms of Power" (2010).

[34] DiMaggio, "Interest and Agency in Institutional Theory" (1988). See also Cox, "Gramsci, Hegemony and International Relations" (1983); Jacobsson, "Standardization and Expert Knowledge" (2000); and Lukes, *Power: A Radical View* (2004).

[35] For a recent review and critique, see e.g., Boxenbaum and Jonsson, "Isomorphism, Diffusion and Decoupling" (2008).

[36] Weber, *Wirtschaft und Gesellschaft* ([1921/22] 1972); Hannan and Freeman, "The Population Ecology of Organizations" (1977). These sociological models of institutional change are still largely compatible with rational choice institutionalists' models, see North,

by sociologists have sought to explain institutional convergence independently of whether the organization on which others converge exhibits any superior efficiency in fulfilling its official function. Organizational isomorphism might in fact entail a decline in economic efficiency, for instance when the headquarters of a diversified multinational corporation imposes a common accounting method on all of its subsidiaries or a philanthropic foundation demands standard operating procedures from any organization to which it provides funding; when employee migration among government agencies or the common advice of a consulting firm to multiple companies in the same industry leads to mimicry; or when "professionalization" leads to the hiring of increasingly homogenous experts who strive for behavior that is considered appropriate in light of their common training.[37] Nonetheless, underpinning all of these possible accounts of institutional change is the implicit notion that, in any particular context and at any particular moment in time, institutions differ in how well they serve the interests of certain stakeholders—an important, explicit component of our analysis of institutional complementarity in international rule-making.

As spelled out above, our analysis draws primarily on the historical institutionalist tradition in political science and the rationalist tradition in International Political Economy. As the preceding discussion shows, however, we also share a key assumption about institutional differences with sociological institutionalism, and our work may be read as a contribution to that literature: in a seminal article, Richard Scott and John Meyer called for organizational analysis to focus on "vertical linkages" among organizations at different levels and for going beyond studying organizations "within a narrowly delimited geographic area."[38] Our analysis of institutional complementarity in international standard-setting not only answers that call but also shows that variation in the relationship between domestic and international institutions can have a major impact on how well the interests of domestic actors *or organizations* can and will be served (bracketing here the question of whether those interests are

---

Institutions, Institutional Change and Economic Performance (1990), esp. 73ff. See also Hirschman, *Exit, Voice, And Loyalty* (1970) and Campbell, *Institutional Change and Globalization* (2004).

[37] DiMaggio and Powell, "The Iron Cage Revisited" (1983), esp. 150ff. These coercive, mimetic, and normative mechanisms in fact do not require the individuals who are the agents of institutional change to strategically pursue any explicitly recognized interests, see DiMaggio, "Interest and Agency in Institutional Theory" (1988), 3.

[38] Scott and Meyer, "The Organization of Societal Sectors" (1991), 110–14.

actively instrumentally pursued or not). Yet, rather than invoke differences in (vaguely defined) institutional isomorphism[39] to explain the differential level of influence at the international level, our analysis provides specific insights into *how and which* common and different institutional features have the stipulated effect.

Law

Our analytical framework and empirical examination of transnational private rule-making also contribute to positive and normative debates among legal scholars. And they matter for legal practitioners since private "technical" standards often play an important role in the law.

Traditionally, lawyers and legal scholars have been first and foremost concerned with rules that are legally binding and enforceable—acts of the legislature, maybe international treaties, government regulations, and judgments by courts of law. Here, private rules and rule-making matter for two reasons.

First, private rules are frequently incorporated into rules issued by public authorities, such as when the Canadian Medical Devices Regulation SOR/98-282 requires manufacturers of medical devices sold in Canada to comply with ISO standard 13485.[40] In some countries—including both common law countries such as the United States and civil law countries such as Germany—there is a long tradition of such ex post endorsements of private standards by public authorities, rendering voluntary standards mandatory.[41] In the United States, by 1981, about 80 percent of the standards developed by the private-sector member bodies of the American National Standards Institute (ANSI) had been included in local, state, or

---

[39] See Boxenbaum and Johnsson's critique "Isomorphism, Diffusion and Decoupling" (2008), 81–82.

[40] ISO 13485 specifies guidelines for risk management in firms that design or manufacture medical devices. Compliance with the then-current version is required under 32.0(2)f, 32.0(3)j, and 32.0(4)p of the Medical Devices Regulation SOR/98-292. These sections of the government regulation render obligatory the otherwise voluntary rules that are written by a private body with no power to require implementation.

[41] The U.S. practice is discussed in Büthe, "The Dynamics of Principals and Agents" (2010); Cheit, *Setting Safety Standards* (1990); Hamilton, "The Role of Nongovernmental Standards in the Development of Mandatory Federal Standards Affecting Safety or Health" (1978); Keating, "Standards: Implicit, Explicit and Mandatory" (1981); Rudder, "Private Governance as Public Governance" (2008); Russell, *Industrial Legislatures* (2007); and Salter, *Mandated Science* (1988). For the German case, see e.g. Geuther, ed. *Festschrift 75 Jahre DIN* (1992), esp. 89ff.

federal laws or regulations.[42] And for federal agencies, the use of technical standards developed by nongovernmental and usually private-sector
bodies has been required (whenever such standards are available) by the
National Technology Transfer and Advancement Act of 1996.[43] More recently, this practice has spread to many countries, and under international
trade law (such as the WTO's TBT-Agreement, discussed in chapter 6),
governments have now generally committed to using international and
thus often private standards as the "technical basis" for domestic regulatory measures.[44]

This trend toward private rules has been underscored by the shift from
ex post endorsement to ex ante delegation of public regulatory authority to private bodies. Increasingly, legislators and government regulators
no longer copy a private standard into laws or regulations but include a
general reference to the standard. If the private standard subsequently
changes, then the regulatory obligation is automatically transferred to the
revised standard. This flexibility is usually intended and considered desirable—such as when U.S. fire safety laws refer to the National Electrical
Code developed (and regularly updated) by the private-sector National
Fire Protection Association—because the prescribed technical solution
can thus be adjusted as technology or the scientific understanding of the
issue changes, without the need for new affirmative action by the legislature or executive.[45] And as economic globalization has undercut the

---

[42] Wines, "Should Groups that Set Standards Be Subject to Federal Standards?" (1981).

[43] Public Law 104-113. It was accompanied by the OMB Circular A-119, entitled Federal
Participation in the Development and Use of Voluntary Consensus Standards in Conformity
Assessment Activities.

[44] Braithwaite and Drahos, *Global Business Regulation* (2000). This is part of a wider trend,
to which scholars sometimes refer as the "hardening" of "soft law" see, e.g., Abbott and
Snidal, "Hard and Soft Law in International Governance" (2000); Kirton and Trebilcock,
eds., *Hard Choices, Soft Law* (2004).

[45] Such delegation has prompted extensive doctrinal controversy. In the United States, a
number of legal scholars and some courts have considered it unconstitutional, but many
state Supreme Courts have recognized it as a practical necessity, and the federal Supreme
Court has "not once since the New Deal . . . struck down a piece of federal legislation on
the grounds of unconstitutional delegation of legislative powers" (Schepel, *The Constitution of Private Governance* (2005), 259). In Europe, the accusation that reliance on private
standards constitutes impermissible legislative delegation has been avoided under the New
Approach by not actually making compliance with European (or international) standards a
legal requirement but extending to compliant products the automatic presumption of compliance with the EU regulatory requirements and thus guaranteeing such products market
access in all member states, whereas products made to different standards may have to
prove regulatory compliance on a country-by-country basis; for financial standards, the
controversy is moot due to EU adoption of each IFRS.

effectiveness of domestic rules, and international trade law encourages the use of international standards, such delegation has increasingly entailed referencing the pertinent standards of private transnational bodies, raising the economic and political salience of the IASB, IEC, ISO, and a few other bodies.[46] Under 47 CFR 15.109, for instance, the Federal Communications Commission requires radio equipment either to comply with domestic specifications written into the regulation "or with the standards contained in [a publication by the] International Special Committee on Radio Interference" (an IEC technical committee). As a consequence of these developments, to know what "the law"—classic black letter law—actually "says," one literally needs to determine what the private standards are and what changes in these global rules are likely and which ones are unlikely. Institutional complementarity theory provides a framework for such an analysis.

Second, judges frequently resort to privately developed product standards, disclosure rules, etc. to give meaning to general concepts in the law, such as "duty of care," "negligence," or "fairness"—and not just in common law countries.[47] Such judicial recognition can give binding effect to what are nominally voluntary private standards. As Jürgen Basedow explains: "The courts do not apply these private rules as such. Rather, the technical standards serve as guidelines when it comes to the determination of the required standard of care owed by producers and builders."[48] Importantly, in considering standards developed by firms or industry as a basis for their decisions, courts have generally taken the position that "compliance with technical standards . . . is not a [sufficient] defense but has evidentiary value, while violation of the privately defined technical standard is often conclusive because generally the standard of care runs higher than that defined by the industry."[49] Standards differ, however, in how broad or narrow the range of stakeholders is who had a voice in the standard-setting process. Whether a particular standard should be understood as

---

[46] Büthe, "The Globalization of Health and Safety Standards" (2008); Trachtman, "Addressing Regulatory Divergence Through International Standards" (2003); U.S. House of Representatives (Hearing), *The Role of Standards in Today's Society and in the Future* (2000). ISO/IEC now actively foster such referencing of their standards, as do some national standard-setters; see, e.g. BSI, "Enabling Lighter Touch Regulation" (2006) and ISO/IEC, "Using and Referencing ISO and IEC Standards for Technical Regulations" (2007).

[47] Glinski, "Corporate Codes of Conduct" (2007); Michaels and Jansen, "Private Law Beyond the State" (2006); Spindler, "Market Processes, Standardisation, and Tort Law" (1998).

[48] Basedow, "The State's Private Law and the Economy" (2008), 710.

[49] Cafaggi, "Private Regulation in European Private Law" (2009), 24.

the lowest common denominator or as the limit of technical feasibility requires an analysis of the standard-setting process.

In recent decades, legal scholars have increasingly gone beyond the study of only laws, regulations, and court decisions to ask what determines the content of laws and regulation and understand why the targets often comply even when the threat of enforcement is low. And scholars in the socio-legal tradition and in the law and economics tradition, in particular, have even more broadly examined the origin and effectiveness of systems of rules that govern human behavior, including "private law."[50]

In the socio-legal tradition, Janet Levit, for instance, examines how firms engage in "bottom-up [private] international lawmaking" through the International Chamber of Commerce to establish common rules for the issuance and acceptance of letters of credit and credit insurance for international trade.[51] In her accounts of transnational private rule-making, however, the preferences of firms (and other economic actors) appear to be closely aligned across countries; she does not consider situations where rule-making is transnational and highly institutionalized yet entails serious conflicts of interest. Institutional complementarity theory offers insights into how private law is formed when incentives for transnational collaboration coincide with distributional conflicts—a characteristic of most international commercial interactions.

In the law and economics (L&E) tradition, many scholars are normatively predisposed in favor of private rule-making, to which they frequently refer as "self-regulation." Debates, initially between L&E scholars and their critics, but increasing also within the L&E tradition, have focused on the extent to which private regulatory regimes impose negative externalities on some stakeholders as a function of the latter's exclusion from the rule-making.[52] This has led Gilian Hadfield and others to posit

[50] An important early work for this research was Macaulay, "Private Government" (1986). For a review and a synthetic argument in the socio-legal tradition see Shaffer, "How Business Shapes Law" (2009).

[51] See Levit, "A Bottom-Up Approach to International Lawmaking" (2005); Levit, "Bottom-Up Lawmaking Through a Pluralist Lens" (2008). See also Snyder, "Private Lawmaking" (2003).

[52] See e.g., Hadfield, "The Public and the Private in the Provision of Law for Global Transactions" (2009), 252f. In "Economic Analysis of Standard Form Contracts" (2007), Oren Gazal-Ayal, for instance, demonstrates the power of economic analysis by introducing a simple downwards sloping demand curve into the implicit model of the best-known work on private standard contracts, where the standard contract is designed by the seller. He thus

an autonomous sphere of relations between commercial actors, in which "providing the structure and regulation necessary for the operation of efficient markets" may be taken to be the sole function of the legal system.[53] In this commercial sphere, she argues, private rule-making yields superior outcomes.[54] This conclusion, however, depends crucially on the assumption that the private rules are Pareto optimal.[55] Our analytical framework provides scholars with tools to assess the likelihood that this assumption holds and more broadly contributes to a better understanding of the potential and limits of transnationally institutionalized private governance.

Finally, legal scholars and other social scientists have been actively engaged in normative debates over global governance and democracy, including global private governance.[56] A key issue here is the question whether global governance allows for broad-based, reasonably equal participation (at a minimum no less so than normal domestic politics) and whether opportunities for participation are real or exist only nominally procedurally. We will address these questions in greater detail in the conclusion.

Economics/Business

Our work also engages the literature in economics and business administration. Specifically, empirical analyses of the economic benefits of standardization for individual firms, individual industries, and entire national economies provide important evidence of the micro- and macro-economic

---

overturns the results of Schwartz and Wilde, "Intervening in Markets on the Basis of Imperfect Information" (1979) and Trebilcock and Dewees, "Judicial Control of Standard Form Contracts" (1981) by showing that the standard contract terms will under most conditions be biased against the interests of the buyer in socially suboptimal ways.

[53] Hadfield, "Privatizing Commercial Law" (2001). The "legal system" here refers to any system of rule-making, adjudication, and enforcement.

[54] Scholars in this tradition tend to rely exclusively on the Pareto efficiency criterion rather than a prior assumption of a normative desirability of inclusive stakeholder participation, which characterizes the work of scholars of democracy such as Robert Dahl in *A Preface to Economic Democracy* (1985); see our discussion in the conclusion.

[55] Some derive this assumption from the prior assumption (or empirical observation) of ideal-typical competition between systems of rule-making and enforcement (e.g., Hadfield, "Delivering Legality on the Internet" (2004)); for others, it follows from the assured enforcement by a hegemonic firm (e.g., Bernstein, "Opting Out of the Legal System" (1992)).

[56] Grant and Keohane, "Accountability and Abuses of Power in World Politics" (2005); Jansen and Michaels, "Beyond the State?" (2008); Kingsbury et al., "The Emergence of Global Administrative Law" (2005); Schepel, *The Constitution of Private Governance* (2005). See also Kaiser, "Das internationale System der Gegenwart als Faktor der Beeinträchtigung demokratischer Außenpolitik" (1969).

significance of the topic. Those findings motivated us to raise the political-analytical questions, introduced in chapter 1, about the distribution of the benefits (an issue assumed away by many economic analyses). Our theoretical framework and empirical findings, in turn, allow us to address concerns about innovation, lock-in, and the strategic use of standardization, which have played a prominent role in the economic literature on standards. Our work also has implications for the extent to which technical standards can help overcome information asymmetries.

A substantial empirical literature has sought to establish the economic consequences of standardization at the level of firms, industries, or national economies. Micro-economic empirical analyses of the use of product standards in individual firms show substantial cost savings from reduced inventory, better communication within a firm as well as with outside suppliers, greater economies of scale in production, and increased sales or profits from more effective marketing.[57] At the industry level, standards sometimes have literally created the market for the regulated products.[58] In addition, macro-economic studies of labor productivity and GDP growth in advanced industrialized countries have attributed up to 25 percent of the increases since World War II to technical standardization.[59] For financial reporting standards, comparable analyses are rarer, but there is substantial evidence that the introduction of explicit accounting standards has benefited both individual companies and national economies through greater market liquidity, lower costs of capital, higher investments, and more efficient allocation.[60]

[57] E.g., Blind, *The Economics of Standards* (2004), esp. 24–45; Price, "The Benefit of Standardization to Industry" (1972); Russell, "Industrial Legislatures" (2007); Töpfer et al., "Unternehmerischer Nutzen" (2000); Woerter, "Value of Properly Planned Standardization" (1972).

[58] The standardization of second-generation mobile phone technology in Europe, for instance, is said to have enabled meaningful competition between handset manufacturers, driving down prices and spurring innovation in features that were crucial to creating consumer demand; see Koski, "Factors for Success in Mobile Telephony" (2006). See also David and Greenstein, "Economics of Compatibility Standards" (1990); Link, "Market Structure and Voluntary Product Standards" (1983); Robb, "Significance of Company and National Standards to Industrial Management" (1956); Skinner, "The Present Status of Standards" (1928), as well as from a political science perspective: Carpenter, *Reputation and Power* (2010).

[59] Blind and Jungmittag, "The Impact of Standards on Productivity in Manufacturing" (2005); Jungmittag, et al., "Innovation, Standardisation, and the Long-Term Production Function" (1999); Temple, ed. *The Empirical Economics of Standards* (2005).

[60] Leuz and Wysocki, "Economic Consequences of Financial Reporting and Disclosure Regulation" (2007), esp. 21ff. See also Schneider, *The Road to International Financial Stability* (2003).

The international harmonization of standards promises significant further benefits—already substantially realized by some—including increases in the quality and comparability of published accounts and declines in the cost of capital in the case of financial reporting standards, or increased exports after switching to international product standards.[61] And the potential for gains from inter- or transnational regulatory harmonization is far from exhausted. A recent study by the Congressional Research Service reports that transatlantic differences in standards and regulations for product and financial markets, which could be overcome through international or transatlantic harmonization, cost the U.S. alone at least 1 percent and up to 3 percent of GDP per year.[62]

The promise of such gains has provided a major impetus for the internationalization and privatization of rule-making analyzed in this book and is part of what drew us to this research topic. Unlike most of the studies noted above, however, we explicitly recognize that standardization does not just benefit everyone equally. Indeed, even if all stakeholders gain, the benefits are likely to be unevenly distributed—international standardization thus may resemble a coordination game with distributional conflict.[63] This prompted us to raise the questions introduced in chapter 1, which have motivated our analysis throughout, most importantly: Who writes the rules in transnational focal institutions? Who wins, who loses, and why?

Our answers to these question have important implications for several literatures in economics and business studies. We first discuss three concerns often noted in the economic literature on standards, then turn to the broader issue of information asymmetries.

Two prominent concerns arise specifically in the literature on product standards. First, although these standards are generally recognized by economic historians as fostering innovation,[64] they also can stifle innovation if standardization takes place too early, cutting short the development

---

[61] E.g., Barth et al., "International Accounting Standards and Accounting Quality" (2007), though cf. Ball, "International Financial Reporting Standards" (2006). Blind, *The Economics of Standards* (2004), 292ff; Moenius, "Do National Standards Hinder or Promote Trade in Electrical Products?" (2006), 58.

[62] Ahearn, *Transatlantic Regulatory Cooperation* (2008), 5. See also Council, *Conclusions on Standardisation and Innovation* (2008); Wilber and Eichbrecht, "Transatlantic Trade, the Automotive Sector" (2010); and WTO, *World Trade Report 2005* (2005).

[63] In addition, it can of course be outright detrimental for some stakeholders, most clearly for firms that cannot withstand the intensified competition from foreign producers.

[64] E.g., Kindleberger, "Standards as Public, Collective and Private Goods" (1983); Lecraw, "Some Economic Effects of Standards" (1984); Russell, "Industrial Legislatures" (2007).

of alternative, possibly superior technologies[65]—or when it occurs too late and thus deprives other innovators of an essential building block for further technological development.[66] While both concerns are valid, economists and scholars of business administration have tended to focus on the former, not least since companies have commercial incentives to establish their proprietary technology as a standard in order to collect monopolistic rents.[67] Second and relatedly, economic analyses have examined the risk that switching costs, possibly exacerbated by network effects, "lock" the customer into a relationship with a particular producer after the initial technological choice. Such lock-in has distributional consequences at the micro level (redistributing resources from the consumer to the rent-collecting producer) and efficiency losses at the macro level due to reduced competition.[68]

When private standard-setting is purely market-based—as most of the economics literature has until recently assumed[69]—then both of the above problems should only arise when switching costs are high or there are strong network effects. When a technical specification is declared "the standard" by a focal institution, however, the problem of monopoly rents for intellectual property rights holders can arise even in the absence of network effects. To some extent, economists have recognized the resulting need for a separate analysis of innovation and lock-in under what we call nonmarket private rule-making; several have developed theoretical models of and some have begun to examine empirically, the intellectual property rights regimes in various private-sector standard-setting organizations, including major private standard-setters such as DIN or the IEEE.[70] They

[65] David, "Clio and the Economics of QWERTY" (1985).

[66] These issues are discussed in some detail in Swann, "Do Standards Enable or Constrain Innovation?" (2005). See also Sykes, *Product Standards for Internationally Integrated Goods Markets* (1995).

[67] E.g., Ordover, et al., "Non-Price Anticompetitive Practices" (1985); Heilman, "The Products of Our Times" (2007).

[68] While it is possible to write a model in which intensified ex ante competition among the producers (in anticipation of the ex post rents) nullifies the ill effects of lock-in, the assumptions required for such a model are heroic, and Joseph Farrell and Paul Klemperer find virtually no empirical support for such self-correcting markets when switching costs and/or network effects are substantial.

[69] See the critique of the economics literature on industrial standards by Funk and Methe, "Market- and Committee-Based Mechanisms in the Creation and Diffusion of Global Industry Standards: The Case of Mobile Communication" (2001).

[70] Blind, "Driving Forces for Standardization" (2002); Farrell and Simcoe, "Choosing the Rules for Formal Standardization" (2009); Lerner and Tirole, "A Model of Forum Shopping" (2006).

show, for instance, that intellectual property rights disclosure rules reduce the likelihood that participants write patented technology into a standard. These theoretical models, however, leave out the ever more important international dimension, and their exclusive focus on the property rights regimes betrays a very thin notion of institutions, which cannot explain why rule-making in a transnational focal institution can lead to the adoption of a standard that enshrines and privileges one stakeholder's intellectual property rights even when those rights have been disclosed, as occurred in ISO adoption of Microsoft's open office standard. Our theory complements these models with a richer understanding of institutions, promising greater analytical leverage, as explained below.

A related third but analytically distinct concern is that international standardization itself can be used strategically for private gain, both in product and financial markets. Even though international trade law may generally and quite effectively constrain governments' use of distinctive national standards for protectionist purposes,[71] both governments and private actors are free to deny market access to any foreign producer who fails to meet international standards. Moreover, with integrated global product markets, success in international standardization that minimizes one's own switching costs tends to impose higher costs on foreign competitors. As discussed in chapter 7, for instance, when U.S. firms in ISO TC 172 sought to align the requirements for technical drawings under ISO 10110 with U.S. domestic requirements in order to reduce their own costs, their proposals would have imposed "billions" of new costs on their European competitors.[72] And when the small Dutch medical devices manufacturer Wassenburg intensified its participation in international standardization, it did so not just to pry open foreign markets—Wassenburg increased its turnover by 40 percent from new sales to the UK alone—but also to push for an ISO/CEN standard that would be so stringent that many of its international competitors could not meet it.[73]

Institutional complementarity theory provides an explanation of seemingly aberrant cases, such as ISO-open source (where the multinational

---

[71] Staiger and Sykes, "International Trade and Domestic Regulation" (2009).

[72] The corresponding case in international financial markets standard-setting consists of U.S. firms' success in international harmonization, which not only means higher adjustment costs for any foreign firms not previously using U.S. GAAP, but also may raise the relative cost of capital for foreign competitors if the changes in valuation resulting from the switch are perceived as earnings volatility.

[73] de Vries, "Standards for Business" (2006), 134; Schaap and de Vries, *Wat levert normalisatie u op?* (2005), 84–86.

giant Microsoft packed the delegations of several P-members of the pertinent committee), and unexplained variation, such as why the U.S. firms failed with their ISO10110 proposal but Wassenburg largely succeeded in its attempt. More broadly, our work complements the newer scholarship on private nonmarket rule-making in economics and business administration by offering a more comprehensive understanding of that rule-making as a political process. This richer notion of institutions has important theoretical and practical payoffs. It allows us to see, for instance, that the focal position of an organization such as ISO or IASB can greatly facilitate overcoming lock-in based on network effects through coordinated switching. Assessing the likelihood of such an outcome, however, requires an understanding of the nonmarket process through which standards are developed, changed, or withdrawn in such an organizations, for which we provide the analytical framework. Our theoretical account of the institutional context in which the explicit collaboration among market competitors takes place (at the national *and international level*) may in turn lead to better models of the economic consequences of standard-setting.

Finally, our analytical framework allows us to speak to a long-standing concern of the theoretical literature in economics: information asymmetries which, as George Akerlof famously showed, can substantially depress markets.[74] Information asymmetry is an important concern both in product markets, where buyers often are concerned whether sellers are disclosing private information about the safety, longevity, or compatibility of a product, and in financial markets, where stock owners or potential investors often worry whether managers are disclosing their private information about a company's financial health including information about the likely success of R&D investments. This suggests conceptualizing standards as a means for overcoming information asymmetries, especially since both product and financial standardization entails specifying how to measure the characteristics of interest, such as asset valuation, the product longevity under conditions of "normal" use, or other components of performance. Measurement and disclosure standards can diminish the particular concerns noted above and more generally increase the efficiency of gathering and providing information. Such standards also make information about competing products or alternative investments comparable, thus allowing a more efficient allocation of resources.

---

[74] Akerlof, "The Market for Lemons: Quality Uncertainty and the Market Mechanism" (1970).

There is no guarantee, however, that standards will have such benefi-
cial effects; the extent to which they will, is a function of the specific
provisions of the standard, which again calls for an analytical framework
for understanding the process through which international standards are
developed. Specifically, institutional complementarity theory implies that
we should be more cautious than optimistic when looking to standards
as a way to overcome asymmetries. Information asymmetries, while socially suboptimal, usually benefit at least *some* individual stakeholders,
and those who would be expected to benefit the most are least likely to
be present during the rule-making due to resource constraints.[75] Unless
proponents of good standards succeed in shaping the—national yet nongovernmental—positions of their respective countries, international standards may not yield major improvements for overcoming information
asymmetries.

[75] We will return in the conclusion to the issue of resources, including expertise, as a con-
straint on participatory global governance.

CHAPTER NINE

Conclusions and Implications for Global Governance

W E HAVE, in this book, explored a hitherto little studied or understood type of regulation in the world economy: global rule-making by private-sector focal institutions. The prominence and economic significance of this type of regulation has risen sharply over the last decade or two. We have sought to shed light on the global regulatory organizations by asking: Who exactly gets to write the rules in these private bodies? What is the process of rule-writing? Who are the winners and losers in this process, and why?

To answer these questions and gain a better understanding of the nonmarket type of global private governance, we have advanced the following argument. In rapidly growing areas of global private regulation, where central state institutions are not directly involved, the representation of domestic regulatory preferences is to a large extent mediated by, or channeled through, domestic governance structures that are also private. Some such domestic systems are characterized by organizational hierarchy, with a single standard-setting body at the apex of an institutional structure that resembles a pyramid, while others are characterized by institutional fragmentation and competition among multiple standard-setters contesting each other's authority to represent the country's stakeholders at the international level. We have argued that, given the structure of rule-making at the international level—which privileges timely involvement and speaking with a single voice—firms operating in a hierarchical and coordinated domestic system are likely to be in a more favorable position when seeking to influence rule-making in global private standard-setting bodies than firms in fragmented domestic systems. In sum, we have argued that greater institutional complementarity between domestic and international bodies gives stakeholders with hierarchical domestic institutions a significant advantage vis-à-vis stakeholders from countries with fragmented domestic institutions.

In the second part of the book, we have put this argument to the test and shown its usefulness for specific cases of global private governance. Domestic institutions differ, often reflecting the legacies of political and economic conditions at the times they were established. A given country may therefore have very different institutional arrangements in some parts of its political economy than in others. Specifically, the United States has hierarchical institutions in the realm of private financial standard-setting but extremely fragmented institutions in the realm of product standardization. In Europe, by contrast, we find highly fragmented institutions in the realm of financial standard-setting but hierarchical domestic institutions in the realm of product standard-setting. These differences in domestic institutions, combined with very similar international institutions across the two issue areas, enable us to conduct a rigorous test of the explanatory power of our argument. We examine a number of implications of our argument, using data that we collected through two major international multi-industry business surveys on regulatory processes in product and financial markets.

The findings, presented mostly in chapters 5 and 7, strongly support our propositions. Statistical analyses that control for a wealth of factors show that U.S. firms tend to do much better than their European counterparts in getting their preferences for international financial standards taken into account by the International Accounting Standards Board (IASB), but European firms do much better than American firms in getting their preferences for international product standards taken into account by ISO and IEC. A large amount of additional information from our business surveys—supplemented by information from interviews, internal documents, and published materials—shows that the institutional differences, emphasized by our argument, are in fact key reasons for the U.S. success in the financial realm and the European success in product standards.

IMPLICATIONS FOR PUBLIC POLICY AND GLOBAL GOVERNANCE

Our analysis has important implications for public policy and more broadly for normative debates over global governance. We conclude our discussion of global private governance by highlighting two key issues: institutional reform to improve the fit between domestic and international institutions and the questions of legitimacy raised by private rule-making of the type analyzed in this book.

Improving the Fit between Domestic and International Institutions

One of the strongest findings—from our statistical and our qualitative analyses alike—is that firms pay a real cost for a poor fit between domestic and international institutions. Firms and policymakers who want to increase their country's influence in global private governance through greater institutional complementarity can try to achieve this objective in any one of three ways: change the existing international organization; establish a new, competing international organization with decision-making procedures that are more advantageous to firms (and possibly other interests) from countries with fragmented domestic institutions; or change domestic institutions to make them more complementary with the existing international organization. We discuss these options in turn. We find that change at the international level is highly unlikely, leaving domestic institutional change as the only viable avenue, but even this will require policymakers to actively champion change against entrenched interests.

Every few years, some national member bodies of the ISO and IEC submit a proposal to change the voting rules in these nongovernmental bodies from the current 1-country-1-vote system to a system of weighted votes, giving larger countries more weight. Such proposals do not stand a chance since they would require a large number of current members to vote in favor of a proposal to reduce their own power (i.e., to eliminate one of their sources of influence within the organization). Consequently, such proposals are usually not even taken up for formal debate in the ISO or IEC Council anymore. In the IASB, demands for institutional change from the losers (Europe) have been a bit more successful, but the changes the IASB has made have proven ultimately extremely marginal. In sum, attempting to change the existing international institutions is not a promising way to improve institutional complementarity.

Similarly, setting up alternative, competing standard-setting organizations is largely futile. Such competing organizations would become credible alternatives to the existing ones only if their standards achieved uptake by users on a global scale. In rare cases, it may be possible to establish such an alternative source of global standards, namely when stakeholders from institutionally disadvantaged countries have such substantial market power that their threat of de facto standardization (through informal collaboration among a small group of them) is credible. But generally, it is hard to see why countries that do well under the current international regime would abandon it for a less favorable one—especially since creating institutions is usually costly.[1]

Equally doomed seems the recently fashionable strategy among U.S. product standard-setters, with some support from the U.S. government, to "promote the principles of our standard-setting system globally"[2] by pushing developing countries to adopt domestic standardization systems akin to the American one for product standards.[3] Our analysis of international rule-making suggests that developing countries adopting a fragmented national standard-setting infrastructure (modeled on the American one for products or the European one for financial rule-making) will only be further marginalized given the low complementarity between such domestic institutions and the structure of IASB, IEC, and ISO. In fact, the strategy does not even hold a meaningful promise of boosting the influence of countries with such systems at the international level, since countries that lack institutions for aggregating domestic preferences into a single national position will make poor allies.

Increasing complementarity by changing domestic institutions therefore emerges as the only realistic option for improving a country's position in international rule-making. In the issue areas analyzed in this book, this would entail changing the American domestic institutions for product standardization and the European domestic institutions for financial standardization. Domestic institutional change, however, is also extremely difficult to achieve. As discussed briefly at the end of chapter 3 and in the empirical chapters, institutional adaptation, that is, a shift from a fragmented toward a more hierarchical, coordinated domestic system of standardization, does not occur spontaneously on the promise of the gains it would bring. Domestic institutional standard-setting structures tend to have become entrenched in path-dependent, self-reinforcing ways during the many decades preceding globalization. This creates powerful organizational and social interests that vehemently oppose any radical

---

[1] On the costliness of establishing international institutions, see Keohane, *After Hegemony* (1984). On the specific difficulties of establishing a new technical standard-setter to credibly compete with an existing focal institution, see Büthe, "Engineering Uncontestedness?" (2010).

[2] U.S. Patent and Trademark Office, Statement before the WIPO Standing Committee on the Law of Patents, 25 March 2009.

[3] See, e.g., Delaney, *Choosing Standards Based on Merit* (2010), and Purcell, ed. *A National Survey of United States Standardization Policies* (2009).

overhaul of the domestic institutional system bound to undermine their power.[4]

The difficulty of reforming domestic institutions is illustrated by the U.S. attempts to change the domestic system for setting product standards. In March 1998, Raymond Kammer, director of the Commerce Department's National Institute of Standards and Technology (NIST), issued a clarion call for the United States to reform its standard-setting system for product markets: "Our current domestic standards system is not succeeding at the international level. . . . The United States needs an effective national standards strategy if we are to compete effectively in the global market." He went on to strongly urge domestic standards bodies to work together "to resolve [the] differences with one another to achieve a unified U.S. approach in international fora."[5]

Heeding his call, more than three hundred representatives from the U.S. standards community convened in Washington at a summit sponsored by NIST and ANSI in late 1998. The purpose of the summit was to begin a process of developing strategies that would help to improve U.S. involvement in international standardization. The summit resulted two years later in a publication titled a "National Standards Strategy for the United States." This report opened by noting that the "European Union is aggressively and successfully promoting its technology and practices . . . through its national representation in the international standards

---

[4]The sociological argument, developed to explain isomorphism, may unintentionally supplement this political-economic argument to provide a more complete explanation of the persistence of the fragmented domestic structure of standard-setting (for financial markets in Europe, for product markets in the United States) even after the international market integration rendered such domestic institutions inefficient and even after it became apparent that a different institutional structure provides competitive advantages. Each country's domestic standard-setting body exists at the intersection of two organizational fields: the country's domestic political economy, in which they are deeply embedded, and the global system of international standard-setting. The former creates strong incentives for maintaining an inefficient status quo, not just in the form of material stakes but also because the status quo is protected by "normative and cultural-cognitive" elements, even while the latter creates incentives for institutional change (see Scott, *Institutions and Organizations* (2008), 153). Accordingly, institutional change may end up being easier for the Europeans in the realm of financial standards than for Americans in the realm of product standards, since fragmentation and contestation among numerous rule-makers carries a strongly positive normative connotation in the United States as the embodiment of "market competition," whereas fragmentation and contestation has few such normative overtones in Europe.

[5]Kammer, "Prepared Remarks at ANSI Board Meeting" (1998).

activities of the ISO [and] IEC," and warned that "the U.S. will lose market share as competitors work hard to shape standards to support their own technologies and methods."[6] It then went on to emphasize the need for much greater coordination and information-sharing among domestic standard-setters to succeed at the international level.

A year after the publication of the "National Standards Strategy," we interviewed a prominent figure in the domestic standards community, the president of one of the largest U.S. standard-setting bodies, and specifically asked about the impact of the report. His response was striking: "Nothing has changed. We know we have a problem, but it is not easy to change our ways. We do not trust our domestic competitors enough to pool resources and coordinate our standards activities; it's not the way we have run our business in the past."[7]

In 2005, ANSI published a revised version of the 2000 report and titled it "United States Standards Strategy." The report stresses that the "global economy has raised the stakes in standards development. Competition for the advantages that accompany a widespread adoption of technology has reached a new level."[8] The report is a reminder to the national standard-setting community of the urgent need to improve national coordination and of the high cost of failing to do so. Consistent with our argument about the stickiness of institutional arrangements, little has changed in the U.S. standard-setting system since the publication of the 2005 report. Similarly in Europe, attempts to reform the domestic and regional institutions for aggregating European preferences as inputs into international financial reporting standard-setting have so far yielded little progress. Germany's GASB, for instance, remains weak and is frequently criticized for its ineffectiveness at the international level—to the point where its financial viability has been called into question.[9] Nonetheless, domestic institutional change remains the only viable option for improving the fit between domestic and international institutions, since such a change can be achieved unilaterally by a country whose current institutions exhibit poor complementarity with the international ones.[10]

---

[6] ANSI, *National Standards Strategy for the United States* (2000).

[7] Not-for-attribution interview, May 2001 (West Conshohocken, Pennsylvania).

[8] ANSI, *United States Standards Strategy* (2005).

[9] Hütten et al., "Die deutsche Stimme erhalten" (2010).

[10] See also Büthe and Witte, *Product Standards in Transatlantic Trade and Investment* (2004), 52ff.

Private Rules and Public Interest

Global private-sector regulation has considerable distributional implications. In this book, we have focused on the distributional battles involving firms and industries from the United States and Europe. Private-sector regulation, however, may have other distributional consequences: it may promote industry interests at the expense of public interests. As Braithwaite and Drahos note: "Industry can utterly dominate [rule-making in standards-developing organizations] because no one else has the energy to do so,"[11] and private rule-making and public policy goals do not always go hand in hand.

The problem is not new. When the European Union introduced the so-called New Approach some twenty-five years ago—an attempt to speed up EU rule-making by delegating regulatory authority to private-sector European standard-setters—many observers questioned the legitimacy and even legality of the New Approach. They argued that private standards bodies, dominated by business interests, would be blind to broader social issues, and that the delegation of powers to these private actors would render legislative control over their decisions impossible.[12] The following quote by the leader of a major European consumer group is typical of the kind of concerns expressed by non-industry groups:

> It must be recalled that in placing . . . reliance on the use of standardization, the European and national public authorities have delegated enormous responsibility. Whereas governments and elected parliaments would have had the final say on consumer safety issues, considerable power has been delegated to what are effectively powerful national and European [standards] monopolies to interpret the broad requirements for safety contained in the European legislative framework. Consumer participation in this process then is no luxury but a necessity to counterbalance the enormous influence of industry . . . [and] ensure that the results of the European standardization process help meet legitimate public policy objectives.[13]

[11] Braithwaite and Drahos, *Global Business Regulation* (2000), 624.

[12] Joerges et al., "The Law's Problems with the Involvement of Nongovernmental Actors in Europe's Legislative Processes" (1999).

[13] Anne-Lore Köhne, president of BEUC (Bureau Européen des Unions des Consommateurs), address at an international conference entitled "Standardization for the 21st Century." In *Conference Reports* (Brussels: Commission–DG Enterprise 1999).

In response to such concerns, the EU member states sought to improve the accountability and transparency of private-sector standard-setters and increase participation by nonindustry groups in European standardization.[14] For example, in April 1992, they issued a declaration emphasizing that the involvement of "social partners . . . at every stage of the standardization process and at every level of [European] Standardization Bod[ies] . . . —from Working Group to General Assembly—is a political precondition for the acceptability and further development of European standardization."[15] At the end of the same year, yielding to considerable political pressure, the main European standard-setting organization CEN introduced a new category of membership,[16] so-called "Associate Members," to integrate into the CEN structure "social partners" such as the European Association for the Coordination of Consumer Representation in Standardization (ANEC)[17] and the European Trade Union Technical Bureau for Health and Safety (TUTB).[18]

Further, the EU member states have been changing the structure of their financial support to European standardizers, gradually cutting back on general lump-sum subsidies and switching to project-based financing. They also have increased the practice of employing independent experts to monitor regional standardization.[19]

Last but not least, the member states have adopted a series of EU directives that provide for continuous supervision of the process of implementing standards. The Directive on General Product Safety,[20] for example, gives national governments or regulatory agencies considerable discretion to impose restrictions on the circulation of products that they find to be harmful to consumers notwithstanding conformity with

---

[14] For details, see Mattli, "Public and Private Governance in Setting International Standards" (2003), esp. 212–21.

[15] *OJ* C 96 of 15 April 1992, 23. See also Council Resolution of 28 October 1999 on the Role of Standardization in Europe, *OJC* 141, 19 May 2000.

[16] CEN stands for Comité Européen de Normalisation (European Committee for Standardization).

[17] ANEC stands for Association de Normalisation Européenne pour les Consommateurs.

[18] TUTB was established in 1989 by the European Trade Union Confederation (ETUC) to monitor the drafting, transposition, and application of European legislation regulating the working environment.

[19] Joerges et al., "The Law's Problems with the Involvement of Nongovernmental Actors in Europe's Legislative Processes" (1999), 23 and Egan, "Regulatory Strategies, Delegation and European Market Integration" (1998), 500.

[20] Directive 92/59/EEC, 1992 OJ L 228/24.

European standards. Similarly, the Product Liability Directive[21] offers national courts leeway to determine whether a product meets "legitimate consumer expectations" (and whether standards reflect the latest scientific and technical knowledge).

In sum, "European standardization [today] . . . does not operate in a legal vacuum but is in varying intensity embedded into legal frameworks and constantly fed and controlled through networks of non-governmental and governmental actors."[22] This interplay between private and public governance elements has conferred upon European standardization a high degree of legitimacy, which it lacked in the 1980s. European standardization has thereby come to replicate the governance arrangement that is distinctive of most national private-sector standard-setters in Europe. As discussed in chapter 6, such national standard-setting processes are regulated and must involve the broadest-possible range of societal interests, facilitated by financial assistance to weaker groups—most notably consumer groups.

In the last few years, a growing chorus of scholars and observers has been raising concerns about global regulation that are very similar to those expressed twenty years ago about trends in European regulation. Eyal Benvenisti and George Downs, for instance, lament that the move toward new global regulation, in which private-sector actors play an increasingly central role, lacks democratic accountability and legitimacy: it "circumvent[s] domestic democratic and supervisory processes that had developed over the years through the efforts of civil society, legislatures and courts. By doing so it threatens to effectively disenfranchise both voters and legislators in a host of areas."[23]

A case in point is consumer participation in international product standardization.[24] Such participation is strikingly weak. Indeed, a 2004

---

[21] Directive 85/374/EEC, 1985 OJ L 210/29.

[22] Joerges et al., "The Law's Problems with the Involvement of Nongovernmental Actors" (1999), 49–50, 59–61.

[23] Benvenisti and Downs, "Toward Global Checks and Balances" (2009), 367. See also Quack, "Law, Expertise, and Legitimacy in Transnational Economic Governance" (2010); Black, "Constructing and Contesting Legitimacy and Accountability in Polycentric Regulatory Regimes" (2008); Graz and Nölke, eds., *Transnational Private Governance and Its Limits* (2008); Zürn, "Global Governance and Legitimacy Problems" (2004); and especially Sabel, "Design, Deliberation, and Democracy" (1995), who emphasizes that transnationally instutionalized global governance need not entail the abdication of governance to the private sector and the market.

[24] Other nonindustry or noncommercial groups such as trade unions are similarly limited or effectively excluded from effective participation in international standardization.

survey undertaken by the EU Commission into consumer participation in standardization found that the "participation of consumer organisations in *international* standardisation . . . seems to be out of reach for them at present."[25] There are at least three reasons for the weak role consumer groups play in global product regulation. First, direct access to ISO/IEC technical committees is difficult. The only group allowed to represent consumer interests within such committees—independently of national member body representatives—is Consumers International (CI), an umbrella organization representing more than two hundred independent consumer organizations from almost one hundred countries.[26] CI must apply for liaison status, separately for each ISO/IEC technical committee in which it wants to participate. Such status is not given as a right but only at the discretion of the committee chairperson, and it merely offers the possibility to participate as a nonvoting member.[27] Second, international standards bodies to provide almost no financial support for the participation of consumer representatives, hampering CI's ability to send observers to all important committees. In the words of a European Commission survey participant: "The lack of resources . . . forces consumer associations to make a strict selection of what they consider to be the most important [standards issues] for consumers."[28] The absence of significant financial assistance offered at the international level reflects, in part, the practice of some key ISO/IEC members. As discussed in chapter 6, American private-sector standard-setting bodies have always staunchly opposed any government interference and contend that willingness to pay is the best measure of interest in standardization. Unsurprisingly, those who see no need for financial assistance domestically oppose

[25] European Commission, Health and Consumer Protection Directorate-General, *Evaluation Report: Questionnaire on Consumer Representation in Standardisation Activities at National, European and International Level* (2005), 4.

[26] CI's status as sole representative of consumers at the international level is a consequence of its observer status on the United Nations Economic and Social Committee.

[27] Farquhar, "Consumer Representation in International Standards" (2006), 27; see also Dawar, "Global Governance and Its Implications for Consumers" (2006). The ISO established in 1978 the Committee on Consumer Policy (COPOLCO) to encourage consumer participation in standards work. However, inclusion of consumer representatives on national delegations to the annual COPOLCO meetings depends on ISO member bodies—the national standards organizations. Attendance lists of COPOLCO meetings show that at times less than half of national delegations included consumer representatives, see Farquhar (2006), 28.

[28] European Commission, Health and Consumer Protection Directorate-General, *Evaluation Report: Questionnaire on Consumer Representation in Standardisation Activities at National, European and International Level*, 10.

the idea internationally. And third, consumer representatives are frequently viewed as "outsiders" in private-sector rule-making bodies. Heavily outnumbered by industry representatives, they often are no more than tolerated. Or as put by CI:

> Many consumers [believe] . . . when they are invited to join [a technical committee] that their views are being sought and will be valued. The reality can be different; the invitation may have come simply because the meeting host was required to demonstrate that all major stakeholders were involved in the process. Once the goal of having a consumer representative attend the meeting ha[s] been achieved there [i]s no further need of the consumer representative and substantive input from [consumers] would not be encouraged.[29]

The ISO and IEC are not the only major global private rule-making bodies singled out for lacking proper representation of noncommercial stakeholders. The IASB, similarly, has been a target of criticism. In 2008, the European Parliament issued a report highly critical of the IASB governance structure, observing: "[The] IASB lack[s] transparency, legitimacy, [and] accountability."[30] The report went on to make a series of proposals to remedy perceived institutional deficiencies. The proposals include strengthening the due process of IASB to enable previously rarely represented groups, such as investors, to play a prominent role in rule-making; the creation of a public oversight body involving domestic legislators and financial market supervisors; transparent appointment procedures of Board members and trustees drawn from all main groups with an interest in international financial reporting; and a new funding structure that avoids conflicts of interests.[31]

These proposals heed calls by politicians and scholars alike to apply lessons from domestic administrative law to debates on how to improve global public and private governance. Laura Dickinson, for example, writes: "Privatization is now as significant a phenomenon internationally as it is domestically . . . I [thus] suggest [that] the domestic U.S.

---

[29] Evans and Farquhar, *First Steps in Standards Representation* (2005), 10.

[30] European Parliament, Committee on Economic and Monetary Affairs, *Report on International Financial Reporting Standards and the Governance of International Accounting Standards Board* (2008).

[31] One possible arrangement would be for securities regulators in countries subscribing to IASB rules to add a levy to their listing fees; another is for the IASB to be funded via contributions from central banks, financial services regulators, and governments.

administrative law literature may provide a useful set of responses to privatization that has been overlooked by international law scholars, policymakers, and activists."[32] Administrative law offers a system of institutionalized procedural and substantive norms intended to assure that all those affected by regulation will be heard during the rule-making process; that decisions will be taken in a transparent manner on the basis of disclosed reasons and in compliance with norms of proportionality and means-end rationality; and that regulations are subject to review by a judicial or another independent body upon request.

In a wide-ranging study on trends in global institutional reform, Benedict Kingsbury, Nico Krisch, and Richard Stewart are sanguine about the potential for growth of administrative law principles and mechanisms in global governance. They conclude that a *global* administrative law is not only possible but in the process of being created.[33]

Greater transparency, more provisions for participation, and related reforms may indeed be necessary first steps to ensure that global regulation will come to reflect a wide range of interests. But, as we have argued elsewhere, such steps are far from sufficient—especially in global private governance.[34] Recent research shows, for instance, that investors and other users of corporate financial accounts play virtually no role in IASB's due process, which is ostensibly designed to ensure above all that IFRS-based accounts serve investor interests.[35] Lack of effective participation and accountability in highly technical domains may be caused not just by exclusion or nontransparent procedures but also by ignorance, information deficits, erroneous beliefs, or collective action dilemmas. The creation of more robust notice-and-comment procedures, for example, will achieve little when the problem is ignorance or lack of technical expertise by the subjects of a particular governance arrangement. Greater procedural transparency and formal rules guaranteeing procedural inclusion of all affected parties may be in vain if those parties' participation is in fact prevented by a lack of financial resources or collective action problems.[36]

In short, the debate on how to render global private governance more accountable and legitimate has only just begun. Early reform suggestions

---

[32] Dickinson, "Public Law Values in a Privatized World" (2006), 383.

[33] Kingsbury et al., "The Emergence of Global Administrative Law" (2005).

[34] Mattli and Büthe, "Global Private Governance" (2005).

[35] E.g., Königsgruber, "Lobbying bei der Rechnungslegungsstandardsetzung" (2009).

[36] Mattli and Büthe, "Global Private Governance" (2005).

are helpful, and administrative law undoubtedly has many more lessons to offer. However, real change and improvement will necessitate considerably more far-reaching and radical measures than the present discourse suggests. Reforming private regulatory governance in Europe under the New Approach took some twenty years of struggles between industry and nonindustry groups. Reforms at the global level are bound to be considerably more contentious and protracted.

Financial Reporting Standards Survey

ADDITIONAL SURVEY RESULTS

WHILE OUR MULTI-INDUSTRY survey (described in greater detail in chapter 5) was primarily designed to examine the insights derived from our global private regulation framework for the analysis of international financial reporting standard-setting, we also gathered data on several other key issues in current debates about international financial market regulation. These findings do not directly speak to the theoretical framework or the key analytical questions that have motivated this book but are likely to be of great interest to many readers. We therefore provide the most interesting additional findings in this appendix.

FAIR VALUE (MARK-TO-MARKET) ACCOUNTING

A prominent and often controversial issue, particularly since the onset of the financial crisis of 2007–9, has been the use of "fair value" accounting, which requires firms—and banks—to value and revalue their assets and liabilities based on the price that could be obtained in the current market if they were sold, even if the firm has no intent of selling them.[1]

This principle has been strongly supported by accounting experts in the major accounting and auditing firms and academia in the U.S., where most preparers and analysts have many years' experience with fair value accounting, since it has been an element of FASB's U.S. GAAP for some time. IASB's endorsement of the fair value principle (with limited exceptions) may therefore be seen as a further indication of U.S. influence in international standard-setting, consistent with our argument. The level

---

[1] See, e.g., André et al., "Fair Value Accounting and the Banking Crisis" (2009); Véron, "Fair Value Accounting Is the Wrong Scapegoat for this Crisis" (2008).

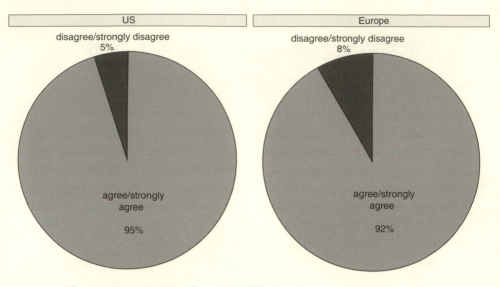

US	Europe
disagree/strongly disagree 5%	disagree/strongly disagree 8%
agree/strongly agree 95%	agree/strongly agree 92%

Figure A.1.1 "IASB will move to full fair value accounting." *N* = 522.

of support for fair value accounting among publicly listed companies, however, is less clear. Various claims have been made about support and opposition, but no large-scale systematic cross-national analysis has been conducted.

To examine this issue, we asked survey respondents to indicate whether and to what extent they agreed or disagreed with two statements about the move to fair value accounting. We inquired about respondents' expectations with the statement: "IASB will increasingly move to full fair value accounting (i.e., move away from historic cost [accounting])," and about their normative assessment of the move to fair value via the statement: "IASB *should* move to full fair value accounting" (emphasis in the original). Their response options were: strongly disagree, disagree, neither agree nor disagree, agree, or strongly agree.[2]

As figure A.1.1 shows, large majorities of survey respondents on both sides of the Atlantic expect the move toward fair value accounting to

[2] Of the *N* = 681 total responses regarding the first statement, 33 percent of the American and 20 percent of the European responses were "neither agree nor disagree," indicating respondent uncertainty or lack of a clear expectations about the IASB's plans. Those responses were omitted in figure A.1.1.

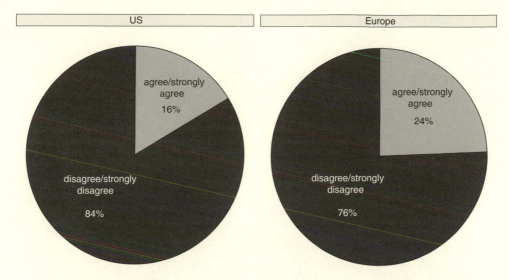

Figure A.1.2 "IASB *should* move to full fair value accounting." *N* = 526.

continue. But as figure A.1.2 shows, the majority considers this shift not desirable. In fact, U.S. and European publicly listed firms are strikingly similarly in their normative assessments, with more than three out of every four European and four out of every five American firms disagreeing with the statement that IASB *should* move to full fair value accounting.[3]

Global Convergence of Standards and Practices

While our analysis focuses on the United States and Europe, the IASB aims to set truly global rules for financial reporting. And as shown by figure 1.1 in the introduction of the book, it has succeeded in convincing almost a hundred countries to adopt requirements for some or all domestic companies with publicly traded financial instruments (stocks or bonds) to use IFRS. The global ambition of the project has prompted some to caution that global harmonization may lead to increasing divergence between financial reporting rules and practices, since compliance

---

[3] Of the *N* = 678 total responses regarding this statement, 27 percent of the American and 21 percent of the European responses were "neither agree nor disagree." Those responses were omitted in Figure A.1.2.

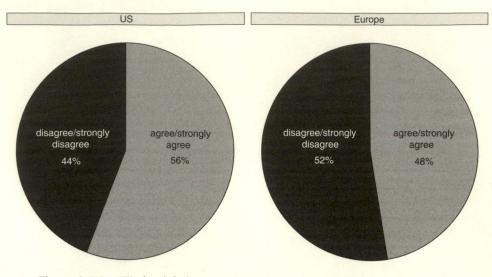

Figure A.1.3 "Truly global accounting rules and practices are unlikely to be achieved, because legal environments and business cultures differ too much across countries and regions." $N = 548$.

with technical norms is not automatic.[4] "Substantial differences among countries in implementation of IFRS [would then] risk being concealed by a veneer of uniformity."[5]

There are, in fact, several possible reasons why global convergence in accounting rules, might not result in a true convergence in accounting practices. Cultural differences may lead to different interpretations of the same principles.[6] Differences in enforcement and in incentives for implementation might lead to differences in implementation.[7] And differences in corporate governance and ownership structure may make the same information less informative or less useful in different contexts.[8]

[4] The range of incentives for compliance, which creates the first-mover advantage analyzed in chapters 4–7, do not apply to all of those targeted by the technical norms, especially in developing countries.

[5] Ball, "IFRS: Pros and Cons for Investors" (2006), 5.

[6] See, e.g., Ding et al., "Why Do National GAAP Differ from IAS? The Role of Culture" (2005) or Jeanjean and Stolowy, "Do Accounting Standards Matter?" (2008). See also Hopwood, "The Archaeology of Accounting Systems" (1987).

[7] E.g., Walter, *Governing Finance: East Asia's Adoption of International Standards* (2008).

[8] See Roberts et al, *International Financial Reporting: A Comparative Approach* (2005), 108ff as well as Hermann and Hague, "Convergence" (2006) and Rezaee et al., "Convergence in Accounting Standards" (2010), 144.

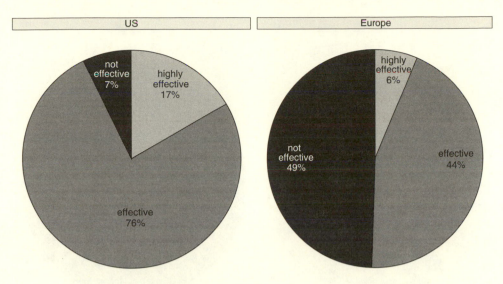

Figure A.1.4 Effectiveness of Writing Comment Letters. $N = 258$.

What are U.S. and European financial executives' views of the chances for *global* convergence of not just standards but also practices? To find out, we asked survey respondents to indicate the extent to which they agreed or disagreed with the statement indicated in figure A.1.3. Clearly, many remain skeptical about the possibility of achieving truly global accounting rules and practices, as almost half of the European respondents and more than half of American respondents agreed with the statement.[9]

EFFECTIVENESS OF PARTICIPATION IN IASB DUE PROCESS VIA COMMENT LETTERS AND PARTICIPATION IN FIELD TESTS

As discussed in chapter 5, we asked survey respondents who had sought to influence the specific content of forthcoming international financial reporting standards during the drafting stage what means their firms had for exerting such influence. We then also asked them to indicate how

[9] Of the $N = 687$ respondents who answered this question, 24 percent of Americans and 19 percent of Europeans indicated no real opinion on this issue by selecting "neither agree nor disagree" as their answer. Those responses were omitted in figure A.1.3.

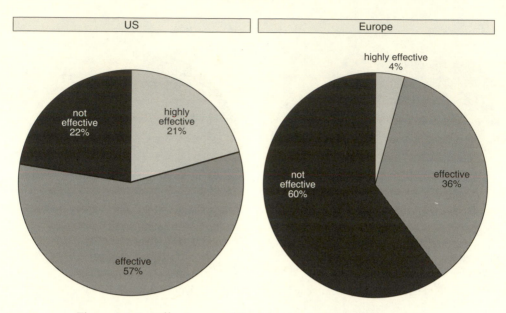

Figure A.1.5 Effectiveness of Participating in Field Tests. N = 131.

effective the various methods were to influence the content of those standards.[10]

The responses regarding two possible methods of providing input into the IASB standard-setting process are particularly noteworthy. As described in chapter 4, the IASB invites comment letters from stakeholders during the Exposure Draft stage.[11] On most exposure drafts, it receives several hundred comment letters.[12] The IASB may also invite companies to participate in "field tests" during which a proposed new accounting rule is "tried out" on the company's accounts (in collaboration with IASB

[10] The question wording was: "In your experience, how effective is each of the following methods for affecting the specific provisions of a proposed standard before it is finalized?" The three response options were "highly effective," "effective," and "not effective." In addition, a "don't know" option was offered for each influence method.

[11] Most comment letters come from publicly traded companies, whose financial reports are the target of IASB rule-making, and from accounting/audit service firms; comment letters from investors and other "users" of financial reports are comparatively rare but not insignificant, see Georgiou, "The IASB Standard-Setting Process: Participation and Perceptions of Financial Statement Users" (2010).

[12] See, e.g., Jorissen et al., "Formal Participation in IASB's Due Process" (2010); Zeff, "Political Lobbying on Accounting Standards" (2008). Comment letters also were an important means of influencing the IASB's predecessor, the IASC, see Larson and Kenny, "Research Note" (1998); Larson, "An Examination of Comment Letters to the IASC" (2008).

staff) to gain experience with the consequences and possible difficulties of implementation in various contexts, should the rule be adopted as an International Financial Reporting Standard.[13] As figures A.1.4 and A.1.5 show, U.S. and European firms differ greatly in their ability to influence international standards using these means.[14]

A far greater share of U.S. firms than European firms experience submitting comment letters and participating in field tests as effective (or even "highly effective"). This striking finding is consistent with our theoretical argument,[15] though a systematic, unbiased analysis of comment letters as a lobbying tool is currently not possible since IASB only makes a selection of such letters publicly available.[16]

[13] See IASCF, *Due Process Handbook for the IASB* (2006), 24–25. See also Sutton, "Lobbying of Accounting Standard-Setting Bodies" (1984), 89ff.

[14] To ensure that the differences are based on reporting firms' experiences, we show in figures A.1.4 and A.1.5 only the responses for those who had at least "rarely" used the method in question. We exclude "don't know" responses.

[15] Comment letters and field tests also have a long tradition in the U.S. domestic process of setting standards for financial reporting, and the long-standing centrality of FASB—in contrast to the fragmented institutions in Europe—creates incentives for U.S. firms to have invested in learning how to exert influence through these means. To the extent that IASB remains central to global rule-making, it may create similar incentives for European firms, though there is no reason to expect that it would allow them to overcome the disadvantages of domestic institutional fragmentation.

[16] Comment letters may also be invited during the Discussion Paper stage, and stakeholders may, under the Rules of Procedure, submit them at any time. The IASB has made publicly available only letters received at the Exposure Draft stage for select projects. Based on a nuanced analysis of published comment letters on five exposure drafts and subsequent changes to the provisions of IASB standards, Thomas Bowe Hansen also finds U.S. firms to be generally more successful than European firms when lobbying the IASB through comment letters, see Hansen, "Lobbying of the International Accounting Standards Board" (2009).

Product Standards Survey

ADDITIONAL SURVEY RESULTS

THIS APPENDIX offers two further findings of general interest drawn from our product standards survey. These revealing findings concern a common distinction among two kinds of product standards and the desirability of the shift of rule-making to international standards bodies ISO and IEC.

DESIGN VERSUS PERFORMANCE STANDARDS

The first finding addresses the relative desirability of *design* and *performance* standards. A *design standard* stipulates precisely how, for instance, a machine must be built or a product designed, specifying dimensions, shapes, or placement of particular elements of the product. For example, a product standard for head rests of car seats may state the exact height or width, the thickness of the cushion, and particular materials to be used on such a head restraint. A *performance standard*, by contrast, only stipulates the objective to be achieved and the level of performance. In our head restraint case, a performance standard may only require that the head restraint keep a crash test dummy's head upright under the influence of force up to a specified magnitude. Manufacturers would then be free to achieve that objective in whatever way they deem most effective or efficient.[1]

Design and performance standards each have advantages and disadvantages. One of the most important benefits of design standards is that implementation tends to be easier to monitor and enforce: an inspector can determine compliance simply by checking whether a product is composed

---

[1] See Breyer, *Regulation and Its Reform* (1982), 105f. See also Hemenway, *Performance vs. Design Standards* (1980).

of the specified parts. Establishing compliance with performance standards may be harder or more costly, especially if measurement is difficult.[2] Moreover, representatives of developing countries have repeatedly expressed a preference for international standard-setters such as ISO to develop design standards, because the greater specificity of these standards may provide more opportunities for developing country engineers to learn from participation in technical committees about specific technological solutions to the problem that a standard is intended to address.[3]

Performance standards, by contrast, offer greater flexibility, allowing manufacturers to find new ways to achieve the stipulated performance through product innovation, as the example of the head rest safety standards illustrate. Design standards are inherently less flexible, with important implications for a global economy integrated through international trade, as aptly described by Samuel Krislov: "Design standards have a socially undesirable effect that is of great hidden advantage to those regulated [by these technical rules]. . . . By fixing technology (or at least retarding innovation) design standards help underwrite existing capital investment and discourage entry of new participants and new advances."[4] Where potential "new participants" are foreign producers, design standards easily become a technical barrier for imports. The TBT-Agreement of the WTO therefore clearly states a preference for performance standards: "Whenever appropriate, the standardizing body shall specify standards based on product requirements in terms of performance rather than design or descriptive characteristics."[5]

Against this backdrop, we asked our respondents whether they prefer design or performance standards. Interestingly and as shown in figure A.2.1, among those who expressed a preference, we find that large majorities on both sides of the Atlantic prefer performance standards.[6]

---

[2] See, e.g., Mitchell, "Regime Design Matters" (1994).

[3] Not-for-attribution interviews, Geneva, February 2009.

[4] Krislov, *How Nations Choose Product Standards* (1997), 19.

[5] WTO, "TBT-Agreement" (1994) Annex 3 (titled Code on Good Practice for the Preparation, Adoption and Application of Standards), esp. Substantive Provision I. Breyer (1982, 105), however, cautions not to overdraw the difference: "In practice . . . it is not difficult to write performance standards that could be met only by a machine of a certain design. . . . Alternatively, [a standards developing organization may] pick that design which best meets certain performance criteria, and if that [SDO] changes the standard readily as technology changes, the use of design standards may not differ significantly from the use of performance standards."

[6] Figure based only on the 803 respondents who expressed a preference. Among the total respondents ($N = 1359$), 39 percent of U.S. firms and 46 percent of European firms said that they are indifferent between the two types.

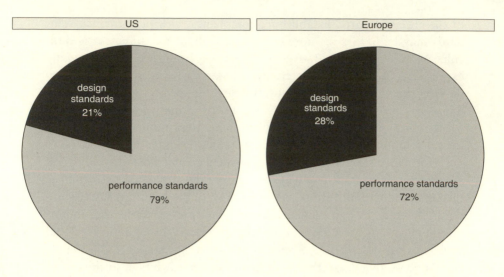

Figure A.2.1 Design versus Performance Standards: Respondent's Company Prefers . . . N = 803.

This suggests that the debate over design versus performance standards is not one that divides European and American firms.

SHIFT TO GLOBAL PRIVATE GOVERNANCE

Our second finding of general interest complements the information provided in table 7.2. and is particularly revealing. The table reported a striking similarity in American and European perceptions regarding the growing importance of ISO and IEC in the world economy. Overwhelming majorities of European and American respondents believe that standards will increasingly be developed at the international level. In our survey, we also asked the participating firms whether they considered this shift of rule-making to the global level desirable. Specifically, we asked them to indicate whether and to what extent they agreed or disagreed with the statement: "Standards *should* be developed first and foremost at the international level."

Based on our argument about institutional complementarity, we would expect to see a markedly different normative assessment of this proposition between Americans and Europeans. Americans, handicapped by their domestic institutional structure, are likely to view increasing levels of

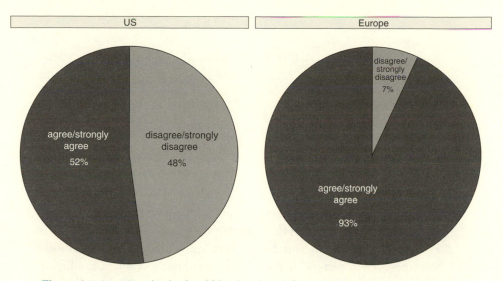

Figure A.2.2 "Standards *should* be developed first and foremost at the international level." *N* = 1116.

ISO/IEC standardization less favorably than the Europeans, who do well in international product standardization. Our findings, summarized in figure A.2.2, strongly support this expectation: an overwhelming majority of European respondents agree or strongly agree with the statement, whereas American firms are almost evenly divided about the shift to global private governance.[7]

[7] Here again, the figure is based on the *N* = 1116 respondents who expressed an opinion. Of the *N* = 1344 total respondents who answered the question, 20 percent of U.S. respondents but only 10 percent of European respondent indicated that they were uncertain (selected "neither agree nor disagree").

Survey Methods

THIS BOOK draws on a large number of sources and a variety of research methods, but the core empirical analysis is based on two multi-country, multi-industry business surveys. The infamous 3 November 1948 picture of the triumphant Harry Truman, holding a copy of the day's Chicago Tribune with the headline "Dewey Defeats Truman," serves as a pointed reminder that any inferences drawn from survey research are only as good as the survey methods. We have briefly discussed how we conducted our surveys in chapters 5 and 7, respectively. This appendix provides a more detailed, technical discussion for social scientists and others interested in our survey methods.

Claims about large groups—groups such as British consumers, French CFOs, or American manufacturers—based on surveys among some fraction of the individuals or businesses that constitute these groups, are part of everyday life. Opinion polls, including polls ostensibly aimed at business firms or businessmen, pop up regularly on the internet, including on the pages of search engines, newspapers, TV stations, and e-commerce websites. And a constant stream of "findings" from business surveys is published in newspapers, magazines, and specialist trade publications. Media-reported business surveys, in particular, are notorious for using "convenience samples": they are often conducted among local firms, business friends and acquaintances of the editor, or among the advertisers of a given TV station or publication. Online surveys, moreover, often allow any participant to self-select for inclusion in the survey. As Poduri Rao points out, surveys using such sampling methods *may* elicit from these "readily available" respondents accurate information about the experiences and opinions of the survey "population," that is, the larger group about which we want to draw inferences based on the survey responses.[1] But there is no method for estimating the likelihood of drawing accurate inferences from surveys using convenience sampling and similar methods—all bets are off, and the opinions expressed may be as representative as those on call-in radio shows.[2]

To avoid these pitfalls, social-scientific surveys usually rely on some variant of probability sampling, where the probability that any individual member or any subset of the population will be in the sample can be exactly calculated. The simplest form of such probability sampling involves random selection of the survey respondents, in which every member of the population has an equal chance of being selected. It automatically yields—on average—a sample that is representative of the population from which it is drawn, but also allows the researcher to estimate the likelihood of a highly unrepresentative sample. When identifiable subpopulations differ considerably, an alternative form of probability sampling, stratified random sampling, is preferable over simple random sampling.[3] We implement stratified sampling through employee-sampling, a variant of "dollar-sampling." Selection here is random, conditional on a prior probability of selection proportional to the firm's size, where size is measured by the number of employees. This method has several benefits. First, in any typical industry, there are a few large firms and many small firms. Employee-sampling safeguards against the risk that simple random selection might leave us with an unrepresentative sample consisting only of small firms.[4] Second, this method achieves the main objectives of stratified sampling without superimposing ultimately arbitrary stratum

---

[1] For our product standards survey, the particular population consisted of manufacturing firms in the five specified industries; for the financial reporting standards survey, all stock market-listed companies (in the countries for which they were selected).

[2] See Rao, *Sampling Methodologies with Applications* (2000), 8; Lohr, "Coverage and Sampling" (2008). See also King et al., *Designing Social Inquiry* (1994), 135f.

[3] Standard stratified sampling generally involves dividing the population of interest into several "subpopulations," each of which is more homogeneous than the population as a whole. Each stratum is then assigned a probability, followed by random sampling within each stratum separately. In size-based stratified sampling, a stratum is thus a group of firms of similar size.

[4] For more detailed discussion of multiple variants of stratified sampling and related issues, see the chapter on "Sampling Procedures" from Weisberg et al., *An Introduction to Survey Research and Data Analysis* (1996), 38–76, especially the discussion of "probability proportionate to size" (PPS) sampling (47f). "Dollar sampling" is one of the best-known ways to implement PPS in when sampling economic units such as firms, widely used by auditors, see e.g. Leslie et al., *Dollar-Unit Sampling* (1980); Wilburn, *Practical Statistical Sampling for Auditors* (1984), 174ff.

boundaries. The method effectively makes each firm its own stratum and assigns each of them a probability of selection equal to the firm's contribution to total employment in the industry.[5]

A simple, hypothetical case illustrates the method: assume that we want to draw a sample of three firms from among ten firms in a given industry. These firms differ vastly in size, measured here by the number of employees. From a comprehensive list of the firms in that industry, we now compile a table with three columns (table A.3.1), including one column that records each firm's number of employees and one column with the cumulative total.

To select the first firm, we have a random number generator select a number between 1 and 2000, inclusive. Let us say the selected number is 1291. The 1291st employee works in Company E. We thus have selected firm E, which therefore gets removed from the list (reducing the total number of employees in firms available for selection to 1630).[6] We next have the random number generator select a number between 1 and 1630: 1118 selects Company D. If 571 is then selected as the third random number (from between 1 and 1620 now), Company A becomes the third company in our sample.

Scientific surveys with probability sampling tend not to achieve or even approach a response rate of 100 percent; some will inevitably not answer the questions. Surveys that seek answers to numerous questions from business managers who are trained to think that "time is money"—typically too much money for researchers to pay them—have a particularly hard time getting high response rates. Business surveys that do not work

---

[5] The same logic can be applied to sets of firms broader or narrower than a particular industry; in our financial reporting survey, for instance, we sampled from among all firms listed on a country's stock market. Sales or other measures of a firm's economic size could be used instead of employment. In preliminary research, we found that the number of employees is the most reliably reported measure, whereas sales or measures of profitability/performance are often treated as sensitive and proprietary. Another way to think about employee sampling is that we are random-sampling employees in the given industry (or in the specified portion of the economy), but we are thus selecting as survey participants the firms in which the randomly sampled employees happen to work. Note also that research on sampling for work about business firms has found that the variance (on almost any quantity of interest) tends to be higher among larger firms than smaller ones, so that the larger, high-variability units should be sampled at a higher rate, e.g. Lohr, *Sampling: Design and Analysis* (2010), 87f.

[6] To ensure independence of the observations, we allowed only one response per firm and therefore sampled without replacement; see Lohr, *Sampling: Design and Analysis* (2010), 549ff.

TABLE A.3.1
Firms in Industry X (Hypothetical)

	Number of employees	Cumulative # of employees
Company A	1000	1000
Company B	73	1073
Company C	40	1113
Company D	10	1123
Company E	370	1493
Company F	50	1543
Company G	7	1550
Company H	400	1950
Company I	20	1970
Company J	30	2000

with a well-established panel[7] typically get response rates of no more than 15 percent; response rates are even much lower the higher up the sought-after respondents are in the corporate hierarchy: CEO and CFO surveys typically have response rates between 2 percent and 3 percent.[8] Thanks to various steps that we took to boost response rates (discussed below), we did much better: we had more than twice the response rate of a typical business survey in our product standards survey, and ten times the response rate of a typical CFO survey in our financial standards

---

[7] Some regular business surveys, such as the monthly business confidence survey of the German *ifo* Institute for Economic Research, work with groups of firms or business executives that are representative of a national economy as a whole and who participate regularly, allowing comparisons of individual responses over time. Such regular participants are collectively known as a panel. Due to long-established relationships between the research institutes and these participants, panel-based business surveys tend to achieve higher response rates; see Büthe, "The Political Sources of Business Confidence" (2002).

[8] Not-for-attribution interview with the editor of a major business and finance magazine, Durham, NC, 3 January 2006.

survey.[9] Nonetheless, any nonresponse raises the possibility of bias due to self-selection. Good survey researchers therefore seek to establish ex post whether the actual respondents and the larger population, from which the sample was drawn, are "alike" on various dimensions that might affect their responses.[10]

To assess the representativeness of our actual survey respondents, we compare their responses on some basic "demographic" questions to what is known about the larger population of firms, about which we seek to draw inferences (see first sections of chapters 5 and 7). From what we are able to observe, we see no evidence of any systematic (i.e., nonrandom) nonresponse. Note, however, that such "balance tests," which can be easily implemented in general public opinion surveys when the characteristics of the population are well known from a census, are much more difficult to conduct in business surveys: we ask firms, for instance, about their current reliance on foreign financial markets for capital or access to foreign markets for sales—an important determinant of their stakes in international accounting or product standards, respectively—precisely because it is not generally known what share of firms relies on foreign markets and to what extent. We therefore have to rely primarily on good survey and sampling methods to provide us with samples that allow valid inferences.[11] Hence, we turn next to the steps we took to guard against self-selection and other sources of bias and the methods we used to boost response rates; then, we describe separately for each survey how we selected the countries and industries included in our survey and how we conducted the sampling.

[9] We conservatively calculated response rates of 32% for the product standard survey and 25% for the accounting standards survey. These response rates were calculated by adding all responses received where the respondent had at least answered two screens of questions and dividing by the total number of invitations sent (= total number of firms sampled for the survey in question). The number of explicit refusals to participate was very small. Whenever an e-mail was returned as undeliverable for any reason, we searched for another email for the intended recipient or called. Most nonparticipants, however, simply did not respond to our e-mail(s). There is a high likelihood that many of those intended participants never received our e-mails due to spam filters or other technical impediments, so the actual response rate among those who actually received our emails was probably far higher.

[10] See, for instance, Tomz, "Domestic Audience Costs in International Relations" (2007), 826, 837f. See also Lohr, *Sampling* (2010), 329–64.

[11] The concern here is with external validity. In addition, to ensure internal validity, we control in our statistical analyses for a variety of possibly confounding factors that differ across individual participants by including them in our statistical models.

GENERAL ONLINE SURVEY METHODS ISSUES

Safeguarding against Selection Bias in Online Business Surveys

Both of our surveys were conducted online, accessed via a website with an easily recognizable URL (www.standards-survey.com). Conducting the survey online had several advantages, as discussed below, but carried the risk of technology-induced bias.[12] To safeguard against such bias, we also formatted the questionnaire for printing on paper and always offered to send the questionnaire to potential survey respondents by fax, mail, or email attachment.[13]

Another key concern about online surveys is the validity of responses. To safeguard against self-selected respondents and duplicate submissions, we assigned each firm in our sample a unique user ID, which included several random numbers and letters, as well as a password. Access to the survey questionnaire was then controlled by an application that checked the user IDs and passwords against a database and only allowed the submission of one completed questionnaire per user ID.[14]

Strategies for Boosting Response Rates

We sought to maximize our response rates by several means. First, in both surveys, after selecting firms and respondents, we obtained e-mail addresses for virtually all intended respondents (one for each firm that we had selected through our sampling procedures), as discussed in more detail below. We then issued our invitations for participation in the survey via e-mail. In the few cases where we could not obtain an e-mail

---

[12] Bias would result from excluding firms that are less attuned to the internet if these firms' lesser exposure resulted in a different experience with international standardization.

[13] The primary questionnaire web pages were encoded in HTML with JavaScript. To further safeguard against technology-induced selection bias, the survey access page checked browser compatibility and provided users with instructions for activating JavaScript if it was turned off in the user's browser. The welcome page also offered the option of using a graphically simpler version of the survey questionnaire, which was encoded solely in HTML and thus compatible with all security measures (such as firewalls) on corporate computer networks. We also provided multiple ways to alert us to any technical problems encountered in accessing or answering the survey questionnaire.

[14] In the product standards survey this was implemented via Unix-based access restrictions on Columbia University's server, where the actual questionnaire was hosted. In the financial reporting standards survey, this restriction was implemented via the Viewsflash survey software, administered by Duke University OIT.

address, the invitation to participate and the reminders were sent by phone, fax, or regular mail. Issuing invitations by e-mail allowed us not only to include the URL for the survey as a link, along with the individual user ID and password, but also allowed us at minimal cost to send reminder e-mails to all those in our sample who had not yet completed the survey. We generally sent three reminders, allowing in each case at least two weeks between e-mails.[15] The first reminder e-mail almost doubled the initial number of responses; the second reminder resulted in a substantial further boost in the response rate. A final reminder, sent shortly before closing the survey and alerting recipients of the impending end of the survey period, resulted in a small number of additional responses.[16]

Second, conducting the survey online may as such have helped boost our response rate. Based on preliminary research and interviews, we knew that the standards experts for product and financial standards, respectively, were regularly using internet-based tools during the workday and that many of them preferred online communications to phone calls or the exchange of paperwork. Our system of user IDs and passwords allowed participants to respond to any number of the survey questions at one time and return to the survey at another time. In addition, the safeguards against technological bias, described above, may also have helped as, in each of the two surveys, a few respondents per country made use of the option to receive (and submit back to us) paper copies of the survey by mail or fax.[17]

Third, we made every effort to convey to the intended survey participants not just the general importance of the topic but why our research results would be *of interest to them*. Here, we emphasized that our work would help them better understand the nature and consequences of an important aspect of economic globalization, and specifically the process of establishing transnational rules that directly affect their business' operation and profitability. Parts of these initial "invitations" to participate

---

[15] We sent an equal number of follow-up letters or faxes, or made phone calls to those for whom we could not obtain an e-mail address.

[16] The system also allowed us to differentiate between those who had started but not yet completed the survey and those who had never even looked at the questionnaire, allowing us to send a differently worded reminder message to the former group.

[17] Their responses exhibited no notable differences vis-à-vis other respondents, suggesting that the method of administering the survey (hard copy versus online) made no difference, so that the availability of both formats simply increased our response rate.

in the survey were tailored to the targeted business managers: the initial communications all took place in the respondents' native language,[18] for instance, and included a statement from a senior business figure—widely respected in the recipient's country—endorsing our research project as important and urging participation in the survey.[19] Last but not least, to create an incentive, we promised to provide actual survey respondents (only) advance access to a report summarizing key findings from our research. Beyond this report, survey participants did not receive any compensation.

Key Choices and Sampling Implementation: Product Standards Survey

The product standards survey was conducted in the United States and four European countries: Germany, Spain, Sweden, and the United Kingdom. These four countries were selected to have both Northern and Southern European countries and to have some variation in country size. In each country, the survey was conducted among firms in five industries: chemicals, rubber and plastics products, medical instruments and medical devices, petroleum products, and iron and steel.[20] As noted in chapter 7, these five industries were selected above all to ensure comparable stakes in international standardization, and preliminary research had shown that the importance of trade was generally high in these industries

---

[18] The questionnaires themselves were also presented to respondents in the national language in France, Germany and Spain. In Sweden, initial phone calls or e-mails were conducted or sent in Swedish, but preliminary interviews suggested that survey questionnaire could and should be presented in English.

[19] The surveys were funded primarily by research grants from Columbia University, Duke University, Oxford University, and the British Academy. To ensure the independence of the research, we neither sought nor accepted any material support from firms, business associations, or other third parties.

[20] We defined these industries starting from the Standard Industry Classification (SIC) codes of the U.S. government. Specifically, rubber and plastics were defined as all enterprises with SIC group code 30, including all subgroups; iron and steel products: 331 and 332, including subgroups (but not 333 nor 339); medical instruments/devices: 384 including all subgroups; petroleum products: 29 including all subgroups; chemicals: 28 including all subgroups. We then used various concordances to identify the corresponding codes under newer US-Canada(-Mexico) NAICS and the EU's NACE system.

and relatively comparable in the United States and Europe. We also sought to include some very traditional industries, such as iron and steel or petroleum products, as well as fast-changing, high-tech industries such as medical instruments and medical devices.[21]

Potential survey participants were selected by compiling comprehensive lists of all firms in each of the industries with the aid of business directories, trade and professional associations, and standards organizations. These lists, complemented by information about each firm's number of employees from databases such as Orbis and Hoovers, constituted the sampling frame from which we drew our stratified random sample, using the employee sampling method discussed above. For each of the firms thus selected to be in our sample, we searched business directories, websites, and other sources to identify the most suitable respondent—usually the firm's "standards manager" or someone with similarly broad responsibility for standards and standardization issues in the firm's research & development, engineering, or production departments. We then searched for the email addresses of these standards experts and contacted them (one per company) to invite them to participate in our survey.[22] Most of these initial contacts took place via e-mail, though we turned to telephone, fax or even postal mail if we could not obtain a functioning email address for the identified standards expert.

Note, finally, that only a few companies explicitly declined participation in the survey. Those firms in our sample from which we do not have survey data, usually never responded at all. We have no way of knowing whether our e-mails ever reached the intended recipient in those cases. This implies that our reported response rates reported in chapters 5 and 7 are conservative estimates; the actual response rate may have been significantly higher.

---

[21] We found only minor differences across industries (and across countries within Europe); we conclude from this that our findings are not a function of the experience of any particular industry, only.

[22] In some cases, this required calling the company and occasionally directly talking with the intended recipient. In this case, the initial pitch for participation in the survey coincided with identification of the individual within the firm who had the requisite technical knowledge to answer our questions while also having enough seniority to speak on behalf of the firm.

Key Choices and Sampling Implementation: Financial Reporting Standards Survey

The financial reporting standards survey was conducted in the United States and the three European countries with the largest capital markets, though with considerable variation in the historical importance of capital markets: Germany, France, and the United Kingdom. We only considered companies with publicly traded financial securities for inclusion in our accounting standards survey, since these firms must file regular financial statements and thus have an immediate stake in the specific provisions of financial reporting standards and the shift from domestic to international standards.

To identify such companies (across all industries), we started with lists of all the companies listed on the major stock exchanges of the United States, the United Kingdom, France, and Germany. These lists constituted our sampling frame, from which we drew a stratified random sample of six hundred to eight hundred firms per country, with probability of selection proportional to firm size, using the employee-sampling method described above. To ensure the specific applicability of our theoretical framework, which emphasizes the complementarity between a stakeholder's domestic institutions and the institutional structure at the international level, we restricted our sample (as a matter of ex ante choice) to companies that have actual business operations, with separate financial reporting, in the country for which they might be sampled. To qualify as a U.S. company, for example, it was not sufficient to export to the United States or have U.S. sales, or to have only a U.S. postal address or a nominal legal representative for purposes of a U.S. stock market listing. We thus excluded, for instance, an Indian and a Hong Kong company listed on the London Stock Exchange, a Mexican and a Canadian company listed on the NYSE, as well as a Dutch and an Israeli company listed on the *Frankfurter Wertpapierbörse*, because these companies are not domestic companies of the United Kingdom, United States, and Germany, respectively, in the sense of having access to, and involvement in, their domestic institutions, which are at the heart of our argument.

We then searched for e-mail addresses of the chief financial officers (CFOs), chief accounting officers (CAOs), or functionally equivalent financial executives and invited them (one person per firm) to participate in the survey on behalf of their firms. If CFO or CAO contact information was not obtainable or where the positions were open, we contacted the CEOs. Where e-mail addresses were unobtainable, we contacted the CFO by phone, mail, or fax. As in the case of the product standards survey, we do not know how many of these invitations in fact reached their intended recipients, so that the reported response rate of 25 percent is again conservative.

VIGNETTES AND ANCHOR POINTS

One small methodological innovation should be noted. Gary King and Jonathan Wand have in recent years pioneered the use of vignettes (brief scenarios given to survey participants as part of a survey) to improve cross-cultural and interpersonal comparability of survey responses, especially when the response options are ordinal.[23] Vignettes allow the researcher to establish a common point of reference against which survey respondents can be compared even if they assign a different meaning to a "scale from 1 to 10" for like or dislike, intensity of pain, or other assessments of the world around them. Vignettes can significantly improve the accuracy of the interpretation of survey results, but they come at a substantial cost, especially in business surveys, where respondents' patience and willingness to answer additional questions about hypothetical scenarios is very limited. To achieve similar benefits without the cost of increased survey or item nonresponse, we have in our surveys included among the response options what may be called an anchor point—an objective common referent point in the otherwise ordinal scale. For a 5-point ordinal frequency scale, for instance, we specified "half of the time" as the middle option between rarely, sometimes, often, and very often. The use of such anchoring response options may warrant more general use.

[23] King et al., "Enhancing the Validity and Cross-Cultural Comparability of Measurement in Survey Research" (2004); King and Wand, "Evaluating and Selecting Anchoring Vignettes" (2007); Wand et al., "Anchors: Software for Anchoring Vignette Data" (2011). See also Collier et al., "Critiques, Responses, and Trade-Offs: Drawing Together the Debate" (2004), esp. 205f.

▪▪▪ References ▪▪▪

Abbott, Kenneth W., and Duncan Snidal. 2000. "Hard and Soft Law in International Governance." *International Organization* vol. 54 no. 3 (summer): 421–456.

———. 2001. "International 'Standards' and International Governance." *Journal of European Public Policy* vol. 8 no. 3 (June): 345–370.

———. 2009. "The Governance Triangle: Regulatory Standards Institutions and the Shadow of the State." In *The Politics of Global Regulation*, edited by Walter Mattli and Ngaire Woods. Princeton: Princeton University Press, 44–88.

ACCA (Association of Chartered Certified Accountants). 2005. "ACCA Urges ASB to Get On with IFRS Convergence." *ACCA News*, 13 September 2005. Online at http://www.accaglobal.com/archive/news/general/2472809 (last accessed 20 July 2010).

Ahearn, Raymond J. 2008. *Transatlantic Regulatory Cooperation: Background and Analysis (CRS Report for Congress)*. Washington, DC: Congressional Research Service.

Ahmed, Shamima, and David M. Potter. 2006. *NGOs in International Politics*. Bloomfield, CT: Kumarian Press.

Aikens, Dave. 2009. "ANS OP1.110 Draft Specifications." *Photonics NY Industry Newsletter* vol. 5 no. 3 (April).

Akerlof, George A. 1970. "The Market for Lemons: Quality Uncertainty and the Market Mechanism." *Quarterly Journal of Economics* vol. 84 no. 3 (August): 488–500.

Albrecht, Albert B. 2010. *The American Machine Tool Industry: Its History, Growth and Decline*. Richmond, IN: Albert Albrecht.

Alexander, David. 1993. "A European True and Fair View?" *European Accounting Review* vol. 2 no. 1 (May): 59–80.

Alexander, David, and Simon Archer. 2000. "On the Myth of 'Anglo-Saxon' Financial Accounting." *International Journal of Accounting* vol. 35 no. 4 (October): 539–557.

———. 2003. "On the Myth of 'Anglo-Saxon' Financial Accounting: A Response to Nobes." *International Journal of Accounting* vol. 38 no. 4 (winter): 503–504.

Alvarez, Manuel. 2009. "IFRS 8—Operating Segments." In *IFRS Änderungskommentar 2009*, edited by Hendrik Vater et al. Weinheim: Wiley-VCH, 55–82.

Amable, Bruno, Ekkehard Ernst, and Stefano Palombarini. 2005. "How Do Financial Markets Affect Industrial Relations? An Institutional Complementarities Approach." *Socioeconomic Review* vol. 3: 311–330.

American Forest & Paper Association. 2009. "Why is the standard paper size in the U.S. 8 ½" x 11"?" Online at http://www.afandpa.org/paper.aspx?id=511 (last accessed 12 July 2009).

ANSI (American National Standards Institute). 1996. *American Access to the European Standardization Process*. New York: ANSI.

———. 2000. *National Standards Strategy for the United States*. Washington, DC: ANSI.

———. 2002. *Guide for U.S. Delegates to Meetings of the IEC and ISO*. Washington, DC: ANSI.

———. 2005. *United States Standards Strategy*. Washington, DC: ANSI.

———. 2010. *Overview of the U.S. Standardization System: Voluntary Consensus Standards and Conformity Assessment Activities*. 3rd ed. Washington, DC: ANSI.

André, Paul, et al. 2009. "Fair Value Accounting and the Banking Crisis in 2008: Shooting the Messenger." *Accounting in Europe* vol. 6 no. 1 (June): 3–24.

Anonymous. 1987. "Europe Sets Out Its Stall." *Financial Times*, 13 August.

———. 1997. "Bilanzen aus der Provinz." *Börsen Zeitung*, 2 October.

———. 1998. "G4+1 Gets a Rival." *Accountancy*, 8 January.

———. 2000. "Reform in Germany." *The Accountant*, 21 July.

———. 2006. "Accounting: New Commission Expert Group to Ensure Balanced Advice on Accounting Standards" (Brussels, 17 July 2006 [IP/06/1001]). Online at: http://www.iasplus.com/europe/0607sarg.pdf (last accessed 17 December 2009).

———. 2009. "Product Positioning: Beyond WTO Access." Information Backgrounder prepared for the Regional Briefing of National Consultation Facilitators. Online http://www.scribd.com/doc/13559115/Non-Bindging-Standards (last accessed 21 December 2009).

Aoki, Masahiko. 1994. "The Contingent Governance of Teams: Analysis of Institutional Complementarity." *International Economic Review* vol. 35 no. 3 (August): 657–676.

Arthur, W. Brian. 1989. "Competing Technologies, Increasing Returns, and Lock-in by Historical Events." *The Economic Journal* vol. 99 no. 394 (March): 116–131.

Auer, Marietta. 2008. "Relations: The Anti-Network. A Comment on Annelise Riles." *American Journal of Comparative Law* vol. 56 no. 3 (summer): 631–638.

Austin, Marc, and Helen Milner. 2001. "Strategies of European Standardization." *Journal of European Public Policy* vol. 8 no. 3 (special issue: Governance and International Standards Setting, edited by Walter Mattli): 411–431.

Avant, Deborah D., Martha Finnemore, and Susan K. Sell, eds. 2010. *Who Governs the Globe?* New York: Cambridge University Press.

Bach, David, and Abraham L. Newman. 2007. "The European Regulatory State and Global Public Policy: Micro-Institutions, Macro-Influence." *Journal of European Public Policy* vol. 14 no. 6 (September): 827–846.

———. 2010. "Governing Lipitor and Lipstick: Capacity, Sequencing, and

Power in International Pharmaceutical and Cosmetics Regulation." *Review of International Political Economy* vol. 17 no. 4 (October): 665–695.

Baker, H. Kent, John R. Nofsinger, and Daniel G. Weaver. 2002. "International Cross-Listing and Visibility." *Journal of Financial and Quantitative Analysis* vol. 37 no. 3 (September): 495–521.

Baldwin, Robert E. 1971. *Nontariff Distortions of International Trade*. Washington, DC: Brookings Institution.

Ball, Ray. 2006. "International Financial Reporting Standards (IFRS): Pros and Cons for Investors." *Accounting and Business Research* vol. 36 International Accounting Policy Forum (2006): 5–27.

Barnett, Michael N., and Martha Finnemore. 1999. "The Politics, Power, and Pathologies of International Organizations." *International Organization* vol. 53 no. 4 (autumn): 699–732.

———. 2004. *Rules for the World: International Organizations in Global Politics*. Ithaca, NY: Cornell University Press.

Baron, David P. 2001. "Private Politics, Corporate Social Responsibility, and Integrated Strategy." *Journal of Economics and Management Strategy* vol. 10 no. 1 (spring): 7–45.

Barrows, Samuel. 2009. "Racing to the Top . . . at Last: The Regulation of Safety in Shipping." In *The Politics of Global Regulation*, edited by Walter Mattli and Ngaire Woods. Princeton: Princeton University Press, 189–210.

Barth, Mary E., Wayne R. Landsman, and Mark H. Lang. 2007. "International Accounting Standards and Accounting Quality." *Stanford University Graduate School of Business Research Paper* no. 1976 (September).

Bartley, Tim. 2003. "Certifying Forests and Factories: States, Social Movements, and the Rise of Private Regulation in the Apparel and Forest Products Field." *Politics and Society* vol. 31 no. 3 (September): 433–464.

———. 2005. "Corporate Accountability and the Privatization of Labor Standards: Struggles over Codes of Conduct in the Apparel Industry." *Research in Political Sociology* vol. 14: 211–244.

———. 2007. "Institutional Emergence in an Era of Globalization: The Rise of Transnational Private Regulation of Labor and Environmental Conditions." *American Journal of Sociology* vol. 113 no. 2 (September): 297–351.

Basedow, Jürgen. 2008. "The State's Private Law and the Economy: Commercial Law as an Amalgam of Public and Private Rule-Making." *American Journal of Comparative Law* vol. 56 no. 3 (summer): 703–721.

Basel Committee on Banking Supervision. 2000. *Report to G-7 Finance Ministers and Central Bank Governors on International Accounting Standards*.

Bensel, Richard Franklin. 2000. *The Political Economy of American Industrialization, 1877–1900*. New York: Cambridge University Press.

Benson, Henry. 1976. "The Story of International Accounting Standards." *Accountancy: The Journal of the Institute of Chartered Accountants of England and Wales* vol. 87 no. 995 (July): 34–39.

Benvenisti, Eyal, and George Downs. 2009. "Toward Global Checks and Balances." *Constitutional Political Economy* vol. 20 no. 3/4 (September): 366–387.

Berger, Suzanne, and Ronald Dore, eds. 1996. *National Diversity and Global Capitalism*. Ithaca, NY: Cornell University Press.

Bernhard, William, and David Leblang. 1999. "Democratic Institutions and Exchange Rate Commitments." *International Organization* vol. 53 no. 1 (winter): 71–97.

Bernstein, Lisa. 1992. "Opting Out of the Legal System: Extralegal Contractual Relations in the Diamond Industry." *Journal of Legal Studies* vol. 21 no. 1 (January): 115–157.

Besen, Stanley, and Joseph Farrell. 1994. "Choosing How to Compete: Strategies and Tactics in Standardization." *Journal of Economic Perspectives* vol. 8 no. 2 (spring): 117–131.

Bhagwati, Jagdish. 1988. *Protectionism*. Cambridge, MA: MIT Press.

Bhagwati, Jagdish, and Robert E. Hudec, eds. 1996. *Fair Trade and Harmonization*. 2 vols. Cambridge, MA: MIT Press.

Bhatia, S. Joe. 2009. "Comments on 74 FR 5977 'Executive Order on Federal Regulatory Review.'" Online at http://www.reginfo.gov/public/jsp/EO/fedRegReview/ansi_comments.pdf (last accessed 10 June 2010).

Bignami, Francesca E. 2005. "Transgovernmental Networks vs. Democracy: The Case of the European Information Privacy Network." *Michigan Journal of International Law* vol. 26 no. 3 (spring): 807–868.

Black, Julia. 2008. "Constructing and Contesting Legitimacy and Accountability in Polycentric Regulatory Regimes." *Regulation and Governance* vol. 2 no. 2 (June): 137–164.

Blind, Knut. 2002. "Driving Forces for Standardization at Standardization Development Organizations." *Applied Economics* vol. 34 no. 16 (10 Nov): 1985–1998.

———. 2004. *The Economics of Standards: Theory, Evidence, Policy*. Cheltenham, UK: Edward Elgar.

Blind, Knut, and Andre Jungmittag. 2005. "The Impact of Standards on Productivity in Manufacturing: A Panel Approach Covering Four Countries and Twelve Sectors." In *The Empirical Economics of Standards*, edited by Paul Temple. London: Department of Trade and Industry, Economics Paper no. 12, 61–75.

Bolton, Lesley. 2003. "IAS: Best Chance in a Generation?" *Accountancy* vol. 132 no. 1323 (November): 16.

———. 2006. "Recipe for Dissent." *Accountancy* vol. 137 no. 1351 (March): 90–91.

———. 2008. "Tweedie's Best of Breed." *Accountancy* vol. 141 no. 1373 (January): 26–28.

Boxenbaum, Eva, and Stefan Jonsson. 2008. "Isomorphism, Diffusion and Decoupling." In *Organizational Institutionalism*, edited by Justin Greenwood et al. Los Angeles: Sage, 78–98.

Bradley, Curtis A., and Judith Kelley, eds. 2008. "Special Issue: The Law and Politics of International Delegation." *Law and Contemporary Problems* vol. 71 no. 1 (winter).

Braithwaite, John, and Peter Drahos. 2000. *Global Business Regulation.* New York: Cambridge University Press.

Breyer, Stephen. 1982. *Regulation and Its Reform.* Cambridge, MA: Harvard University Press.

Brown, Richard. 1905. *A History of Accounting and Accountants.* Edinburgh: T.C. & E.C. Jack.

Bruce, Robert. 2009. "Asian-Oceanian Standards Setters Group Created." *Insight* (London, IASB) 10 June. Online at http://www.ifrs.org/Archive/ INSIGHT+journal/Asian-Oceanian+Standards+Setters+Group+created.htm (last accessed 30 October 2010).

Brüggemann, Ulf, et al. 2009. "How Do Individual Investors React to Global IFRS Adoption?" Manuscript, Lancaster University, July 2009.

BSI (British Standards Institution). 2010. *Annual Report 2009.* London: BSI.

———. 2010. *Enabling Lighter Touch Regulation: The Role of Standards.* London: BSI.

Buckley, John, and Marlene Buckley. 1974. *The Accounting Profession.* Los Angeles: Melville.

Büthe, Tim. 2002. "Taking Temporality Seriously: Modeling History and the Use of Narratives as Evidence." *American Political Science Review* vol. 96 no. 3 (September): 481–494.

———. 2002. "The Political Sources of Business Confidence: The Impact of Partisan Politics, Globalization, and Institutional Variation on the Economic Expectations of Firms in Advanced Capitalist Democracies." Ph.D. diss., Columbia University, New York.

———. 2004. "Governance through Private Authority? Non-State Actors in World Politics." *Journal of International Affairs* vol. 58 no. 1 (fall): 281–290.

———. 2007. "Review of Hawkins et al., Delegation and Agency in International Organizations." *Perspectives on Politics* vol. 5 no. 4 (December): 861–862.

———. 2007. "The Politics of Competition and Institutional Change in the European Union: The First Fifty Years." In *Making History: European Integration and Institutional Change at Fifty*, vol. 8, *State of the European Union,* edited by Sophie Meunier and Kathleen McNamara. Oxford: Oxford University Press, 175–193.

———. 2008. "Institutional Change in the European Union: Two Narratives of European Commission Merger Control Authority, 1955–2004." Manuscript, Duke University.

———. 2008. "The Globalization of Health and Safety Standards: Delegation of Regulatory Authority in the SPS-Agreement of 1994 Agreement Establishing the World Trade Organization." *Law and Contemporary Problems* vol. 71 no. 1 (winter): 219–255.

———. 2009. "Private and Public Politics in International Market Regulation." Manuscript, Duke University and UC Berkeley, January.

———. 2009. "Technical Standards as Public and Club Goods: Who Is Financing the International Accounting Standards Board (IASB) and Why?" In *Voluntary Programs: A Club Theory Approach*, edited by Matthew Potoski and Aseem Prakash. Cambridge, MA: MIT Press, 2009: 157–179.

———. 2009. "The Politics of Food Safety in the Age of Global Trade: The Codex Alimentarius Commission in the SPS-Agreement of the WTO." In *Import Safety: Regulatory Governance in the Global Economy*, edited by Cary Coglianese, Adam Finkel and David Zaring. Philadelphia: University of Pennsylvania Press, 88–109.

———. 2010. "The Dynamics of Principals and Agents: Institutional Persistence and Change in U.S. Financial Regulation, 1934–2003." Manuscript, Duke University, March.

———. 2010. "Engineering Uncontestedness? The Origin and Institutional Development of the International Electrotechnical Commission (IEC)." *Business and Politics* vol. 12 no. 3 (October, special issue: Private Regulation in the Global Economy, edited by Tim Büthe).

———. 2010. "The Power of Norms; the Norms of Power: Who Governs International Electrical and Electronic Technology?" In *Who Governs the Globe?*, edited by Deborah D. Avant, Martha Finnemore and Susan K. Sell. New York: Cambridge University Press, 292–332.

Büthe, Tim, and Walter Mattli. 2010. "International Standards and Standard-Setting Bodies." In *Oxford Handbook of Business and Government*, edited by David Coen, Graham Wilson and Wyn Grant. New York: Oxford University Press, 440–471.

Büthe, Tim, and Jan Martin Witte. 2004. *Product Standards in Transatlantic Trade and Investment: Domestic and International Practices and Institutions*. Washington, DC: American Institute for Contemporary German Studies.

Cafaggi, Fabrizio. 2009. "Private Regulation in European Private Law." *EUI Law Working Papers* no. 2009/31.

Cairns, David. 1990. "Aid for the Developing World." *Acountancy* vol. 105 no. 1159 (March): 82–85.

———, ed. 1999. *The IASC: Evolution, Achievements, and Prospects*. London: IASC.

———. 2001. *International Accounting Standards Survey 2000: An Assessment of the Use of IAS in the Financial Statements of Listed Companies*. Henley-on-Thames: David Cairns International Financial Reporting.

Camfferman, Kees, and Stephen A. Zeff. 2007. *Financial Reporting and Global Capital Markets: A History of the International Accounting Standards Committee, 1973–2000*. Oxford: Oxford University Press.

Campbell, John L. 2004. *Institutional Change and Globalization*. Princeton: Princeton University Press.

Cargill, Carl F. 1989. *Information Technology Standardization: Theory, Process, and Organization.* Boston: Digital Press.

Carlsson, Bo. 1989. "Small-Scale Industry at a Crossroads: U.S. Machine Tools in Global Perspective." *Small Business Economics* vol. 1 no. 4 (December): 245–261.

Carpenter, Daniel P. 2010. *Reputation and Power: Organizational Image and Pharmaceutical Regulation at the FDA.* Princeton: Princeton University Press.

Cashore, Benjamin. 2002. "Legitimacy and the Privatization of Environmental Governance: How Non-State Market-Driven (NSMD) Governance Systems Gain Rule-Making Authority." *Governance* vol. 15 no. 4 (October): 503–529.

Cashore, Benjamin, Graeme Auld, and Deanna Newsom. 2004. *Governing through Markets: Forest Certification and the Emergence of Non-State Authority.* New Haven: Yale University Press.

CEN. 2009. "CEN–European Committee for Standardization: Statistics." Brussels: CEN. Online at http://www.cen.eu/cenorm/aboutus/statistics/index.asp# (last accessed 21 December 2009).

Chandler, Alfred Dupont. 1962. *Strategy and Structure: Chapters in the History of the Industrial Enterprise.* Cambridge, MA: MIT Press.

———. 1965. *The Railroads: The Nation's First Big Business.* New York: Harcourt, Brace and World.

———. 1977. *The Visible Hand: The Managerial Revolution in American Business.* Cambridge, MA: Belknap Press.

Chasan, Emily. 2009. "Investor Group Says FASB's Independence Has Eroded." Reuters online 22 June 2009. http://www.reuters.com/article/idUSN2252330420090623 (last accessed 17 July 2010).

Cheit, Ross E. 1990. *Setting Safety Standards: Regulation in the Public and Private Sectors.* Berkeley: University of California Press.

Chen, Maggie Xiaoyang, Tsunehiro Otsuki, and John S. Wilson. 2006. "Do Standards Matter for Export Success?" *World Bank Policy Research Paper* no. 3809 (January).

Chiapello, Eve, and Karim Medjad. 2009. "An Unprecedented Privatisation of Mandatory Standard-Setting: The Case of European Accounting Policy." *Critical Perspectives on Accounting* vol. 20 no. 4 (May): 448–468.

Choi, Frederick, and Gerhard Mueller. 1992. *International Accounting.* 2nd edition. Englewood Cliffs, NJ: Prentice-Hall.

Chopping, David, and Moore Stephens, eds. 2010. *Accounting Standards 2010–11.* London: Wolters Kluwer.

CIMA (Chartered Institute of Management Consultants). 2009. "Consolidation of Accountancy Bodies: Discussion Board Document." Published on CIMAsphere (http://community.cimaglobal.com) on 4 June 2009 (last accessed 20 July 2010)

Clapp, Jennifer. 1998. "The Privatization of Global Environmental Governance: ISO 14000 and the Developing World." *Global Governance* vol. 4 no. 3 (July–September): 295–316.

Codding, George A. 1964. *The Universal Postal Union: Coordinator of the International Mails.* New York: New York University Press.

Codding, George A., and Anthony M. Rutkowski. 1982. *The International Telecommunications Union in a Changing World.* Dedham, MA: Artech House.

Coglianese, Cary, Adam Finkel, and David Zaring, eds. 2009. *Import Safety: Regulatory Governance in the Global Economy.* Philadelphia: University of Pennsylvania Press.

Collier, David, Henry E. Brady, and Jason Seawright. 2004. "Critiques, Responses, and Trade-Offs: Drawing Together the Debate." In *Rethinking Social Inquiry: Diverse Tools, Shared Standards*, edited by Henry E. Brady and David Collier. Lanham, MD: Roman and Littlefield, 195–227.

Conard, Alfred F. 1976. *Corporations in Perspective.* Mineola, NY: Foundation Press.

Conybeare, John A. C. 1980. "International Organization and the Theory of Property Rights." *International Organization* vol. 34 (1980): 307–334.

Cooke, Colin A. 1950. *Corporation, Trust, and Company: A Legal History.* Manchester: Manchester University Press.

Cooley, Alexander, and James Ron. 2002. "The NGO Scramble: Organizational Insecurity and the Political Economy of Transnational Action." *International Security* vol. 27 no. 1 (summer): 5–39.

Cooper, Richard N. 1989. "International Cooperation in Public Health as a Prologue to Macroeconomic Cooperation." In *Can Nations Agree? Issues in International Economic Cooperation*, edited by Richard N. Cooper. Washington, DC: Brookings Institution, 183–190.

Cornish, Steven. 2005. "ISO, CEN, and the Vienna Agreement." *ANSI Background Papers.* Washington, DC: American National Standards Institute, August. Online at http://publicaa.ansi.org/sites/apdl/Documents / Standards%20Activities/Background%20Papers/ISO-CEN-Vienna.doc (last accessed 21 December 2009).

Council of the European Union. 2008. *Council Conclusions on Standardisation and Innovation* 2891st Competitiveness (Market, Industry and Research) Council Meeting, Brussels, 25 September 2008. Online at http://ec.europa.eu/ enterprise/policies/european-standards/files/standards_policy/standardisation_ innovation/doc/councilconclusions_20080925_en.pdf (last accessed 30 October 2010).

Cowhey, Peter F. 1990. "The International Telecommunications Regime: The Political Roots of Regimes for High Technology." *International Organization* vol. 44 no. 2 (spring): 169–199.

Cox, Robert W. 1983. "Gramsci, Hegemony and International Relations: An Essay in Method." *Millennium: Journal of International Studies* vol. 12 no. 2 (summer): 162–175.

Cox, Robert W. and Harold K. Jacobson. 1974. *The Anatomy of Influence:*

Decision-Making in International Organizations. New Haven: Yale University Press.

Cunningham, Lawrence A. 2008. "The SEC's Global Accounting Vision: A Realistic Appraisal of a Quixotic Quest." *North Carolina Law Review* vol. 87 no. 1 (December): 1–81.

Cutler, A. Claire, Virginia Haufler, and Tony Porter, eds. 1999. *Private Authority and International Affairs.* Albany, NY: State University of New York Press.

Dahl, Robert A. 1985. *A Preface to Economic Democracy.* Berkeley: University of California Press.

Dai, Xinyuan. 2005. "Why Comply? The Domestic Constituency Mechanism." *International Organization* vol. 59 no. 2 (spring): 363–398.

Dalton, Russell J., Paul Allen Beck, and Scott C. Flanagan. 1984. "Electoral Change in Advanced Industrial Democracies." In *Electoral Change in Advanced Industrial Democracies: Realignment or Dealignment*, edited by Russell J. Dalton, Scott Flanagan and Paul Allen Beck. Princeton: Princeton University Press, 3–21.

Damro, Chad. 2006. "Transatlantic Competition Policy: Domestic and International Sources of EU-US Cooperation." *European Journal of International Relations* vol. 12 no. 2 (June): 171–196.

David, Paul A. 1985. "Clio and the Economics of QWERTY." *American Economic Review* vol. 75 no. 2 (Papers and Proceedings of the 97th Annual Meeting of the American Economics Association, May): 332–337.

David, Paul A., and Shane Greenstein. 1990. "Economics of Compatibility Standards: An Introduction to Recent Research." *Economics of Innovation and New Technology* vol. 1 no. 1/2: 3–41.

David, Paul A., and Edward Steinmueller. 1994. "Economics of Compatibility Standards and Competition in Telecommunication Networks." *Information Economics and Policy* vol. 6 no. 3–4 (December, special issue: The Economics of Standards, edited by Cristiano Antonelli): 217–241.

Dawar, Kamala. 2006. "Global Governance and Its Implications for Consumers." *Consumer Policy Review* vol. 16 no. 1 (Jan/Feb): 2–4.

Delaney, Helen. 2010. *Choosing Standards Based on Merit: Liberalizing Regulation, Trade and Development.* West Conshohocken, PA: ASTM International.

Deloitte Audit Ireland. 2010. "Segment Reporting: Why the Controversy?" Online at http://www.deloitte.com/view/en_IE/ie/services/audit/183b3b0be12fb110VgnVCM100000ba42f00aRCRD.htm (last accessed 2 June 2010).

Deloitte Touche Tohmatsu. 2001–2; 2004. *IAS in Your Pocket.* London: Deloitte, various years.

———. 2002. "Use of IAS for Reporting by Domestic Companies, by Country." (http://www.iasplus.com/country/useias.htm from 4/9/2002 at web.archive.org).

————. 2003; 2005–10. *IFRS in Your Pocket*. London: Deloitte, various years.

————. 2004. "Use of IFRS for Reporting by Domestic Listed Companies, by Country." (http://www.iasplus.com/country/useias.htm from 4/7/2004 at web .archive.org).

————. 2008. *IFRSs and US GAAP: A Pocket Comparison (IASPlus Guide)*. London: Deloitte, July 2008.

————. 2010. "Use of IFRS by Jurisdiction." Online at http://www.iasplus.com/country/useias.htm (6/3/2010).

————. 2010. "Accounting Standards Updates by Jurisdictions." Online at http://www.iasplus.com/country/country.htm (6/3/2010).

DeSombre, Elizabeth. 2000. *Domestic Sources of International Environmental Policy: Industry, Environmentalists, and U.S. Power*. Cambridge, MA: MIT Press.

————. 2006. *Flagging Standards: Globalization and Environmental, Safety, and Labor Regulation at Sea*. Cambridge, MA: MIT Press.

Deutsches Aktieninstitut. 2010. *DAI Factbook 2009*. Frankfurt am Main: Deutsches Aktieninstitut.

Deutsche Börse AG. 2009. *Factbook 2009*. Frankfurt am Main: Deutsche Börse Group. Online at http://deutsche-boerse.com/INTERNET/IP/ip_stats .nsf/maincontent/Factbook+Kassamarkt?Opendocument& (last accessed 7 September 2010).

de Vries, Henk J. 1999. *Standards for the Nation: Analysis of National Standardization Organizations*. Dordrecht: Kluwer Academic Publishers.

————. 2006. "Standards for Business: How Companies Benefit from Participation in International Standards Setting." In *International Standardization as a Strategic Tool*. Geneva: International Electrotechnical Commission, 131–141.

Dickie, Mure. 2008. "China's Phone Standard Fails to Win Gold." *Financial Times*, 11 August.

Dickinson, Laura. 2006. "Public Law Values in a Privatized World." *Yale Journal of International Law* vol. 31 no. 2 (summer): 383–426.

DiMaggio, Paul J. 1988. "Interest and Agency in Institutional Theory." In *Institutional Patterns and Organizations: Culture and Environment*, edited by Lynne G. Zucker. Cambridge, MA: Ballinger, 3–22.

DiMaggio, Paul J., and Walter W. Powell. 1983. "The Iron Cage Revisited: Institutional Isomorphism and Collective Rationality in Organizational Fields." *American Sociological Review* vol. 48 no. 2 (April): 147–160.

DIN. 2009. *Geschäftsbericht 2008: Zugang im Focus*. Berlin: Beuth Verlag, April.

Ding, Yuan, Thomas Jeanjean, and Hervé Stolowy. 2005. "Why Do National GAAP Differ from IAS? The Role of Culture." *International Journal of Accounting* vol. 40 no. 4 (December): 325–350.

Drezner, Daniel W. 2004. "The Global Governance of the Internet: Bringing the State Back In." *Political Science Quarterly* vol. 119 no. 3 (fall): 477–498.

———. 2005. "Globalization, Harmonization, and Competition: The Different Pathways to Policy Convergence." *Journal of European Public Policy* vol. 12 no. 5 (Special Issue: Mutual Recognition as a New Mode of Governance): 841–859.

———. 2007. *All Politics Is Global: Explaining International Regulatory Regimes*. Princeton: Princeton University Press.

Dzinkowski, Ramona. 2008. "Convergence or Conversion?" *Accountancy* vol. 141 no. 1373 (January): 114–115.

Eberlein, Burkard, and Edgar Grande. 2005. "Beyond Delegation: Transnational Regulatory Regimes and the EU Regulatory State." *Journal of European Public Policy* vol. 12 no. 1 (February): 89–112.

Economist Editorial Staff. 1945. "Standard Production." *The Economist* vol. 148 no. 5298 (10 March): 318–19.

———. 1945. "UNSCC" *The Economist* vol. 148 no. 5297 (3 March): 286–287.

Edwards, John R. 1989. *A History of Financial Accounting*. London: Routledge.

EFRAG. 2004. *Annual Review 2004*. Brussels: EFRAG.

———. 2006. *Annual Review 2006*. Brussels: EFRAG.

EFRAG and EC. 2006. "Working Arrangement between the European Commission and EFRAG." Brussels: EFRAG and European Commission. Online at: http://www.efrag.org/images/Efrag/EFRAG-EC%20Working%20Arrangement .pdf (last accessed 17 December 2009).

Egan, Michelle. 1998. "Regulatory Strategies, Delegation, and European Market Integration." *Journal of European Public Policy* vol. 5 no. 3 (September): 487–508.

———. 2001. *Constructing a European Market: Standards, Regulation, and Governance*. New York: Oxford University Press.

Egyedi, Tineke M. 2000. "The Standardised Container: Gateway Technologies in Cargo Transport." *Homo Oeconomicus* vol. 17 no. 3 (Euras Yearbook of Standardization vol. 3): 231–262.

Ehrlich, Sean D. 2007. "Access to Protection: Domestic Institutions and Trade Policy in Democracies." *International Organization* vol. 61 no. 3 (summer): 571–605.

Eichengreen, Barry. 1999. *Toward a New International Financial Architecture: A Practical Post-Asia Agenda*. Washington, DC: Institute for International Economics.

Emenyou, Emmanuel N., and Sidney J. Gray. 1992. "EC Accounting Harmonization: An Empirical Study of Measurement Practices in France, Germany and the UK." *Accounting and Business Research* vol. 23 no. 89 (winter): 49–58.

EOS. 2009. "Harmonization of Egyptian Standards" Cairo: Egyptian Organization for Standardization and Quality. Online at http://www.eos.org.eg/ Public/en-us/Egyptian+Standards/Harmonization+of+Egyptian +Standards .htm (last accessed 21 December 2009).

Erdmann, Jeanne. 2009. "The Appointment of a Representative Commission." Online at http://www.iec.ch/about/history/articles/appointment_commission .htm (last accessed 5 May 2009).

European Commission, Directorate General for Health and Consumer Protection. 2005. *Evaluation Report: Questionnaire on Consumer Representation in Standardisation Activities at National, European and International Level* (January). Online at http://ec.europe.eu/consumers/cons_org/eval_report_ en.pdf (last accessed on 14 Dec 2009).

European Communities. 2002. "Regulation (EC) No. 1606/2002 of the European Parliament and of the Council, of 19 July 2002, on the Application of International Accounting Standards," *Official Journal of the European Communities* (11 September): L243.

Evans, Chris, and Bruce J. Farquhar. 2005. *First Steps in Standards Representation: A Guide for Consumer Organizations*. London: Consumers International. Online at http://www.consumersinternational.org/media/308752/ first%20steps%20in%20standards%20representation-%20a%20guide% 20for%20consumer%20organisations%20(english).pdf (last accessed 30 October 2010).

Evans, Peter B., Harold K. Jacobson, and Robert D. Putnam, eds. 1993. *Double-Edged Diplomacy: International Bargaining and Domestic Politics*. Berkeley: University of California Press.

FAF (Financial Accounting Foundation). 2008. "The Financial Accounting Foundation Board of Trustees Approves Changes to Oversight, Structure and Operations of FAF, FASB and GASB." Press Release. Norwalk, CT: FAF, 26 February.

———. 2010. "By-Laws of the Financial Accounting Foundation." Norwalk, CT: FAF, February.

Falke, Josef, and Harm Schepel, eds. 2000. *Legal Aspects of Standardisation in the Member States of the EC and of EFTA*. Luxembourg: Office for Official Publications of the European Communities.

Farquhar, Bruce. 2006. "Consumer Representation in International Standards." *Consumer Policy Review* vol. 16 no. 1 (January/February): 26–30.

Farrell, Henry. 2003. "Constructing the International Foundations of E-Commerce: The EU-US Safe Harbor Arrangement." *International Organization* vol. 57 no. 2 (spring): 277–306.

———. 2006. "Regulating Information Flows: States, Private Actors, and E-Commerce." *Annual Review of Political Science* vol. 9 (2006): 353–374.

Farrell, Joseph, and Paul Klemperer. 2007. "Coordination and Lock-In: Competition with Switching Costs and Network Effects." In *Handbook of Industrial Organization*, edited by Mark Armstrong and Robert M. Porter. Amsterdam: Elsevier, 1967–2072.

Farrell, Joseph and Garth Saloner. 1985. "Standardization, Compatibility, and Innovation." *Rand Journal of Economics* vol. 16 no. 1 (spring): 70–83.

———. 1986. "Installed Base and Compatibility: Innovation, Product Preannouncements, and Predation." *American Economic Review* vol. 76 no. 5 (December): 940–955.

Farrell, Joseph, and Timothy S. Simcoe. 2009. "Choosing the Rules for Formal Standardization." Manuscript, UC Berkeley and University of Toronto, March.

FASB (Financial Accounting Standards Board). 2005. *Emerging Issues Task Force Operating Procedures.* Norwalk, CT: FASB

———. 2010. *Rules of Procedure, Amended and Restated through May 1, 2010.* Norwalk, CT: FASB.

———. 2010. "FASAC Members as of January 2010." Online at http://www .fasb.org/fasac/fasacmem.shtml (last accessed 17 July 2010).

FASB and IASB. 2004. *Memorandum of Understanding: The Norwalk Agreement.* Online at: http://www.fasb.org/news/memorandum.pdf (last accessed 17 December 2009).

Fearon, James D. 1998. "Bargaining, Enforcement, and International Cooperation." *International Organization* vol. 52 no. 2 (spring): 269–305.

Feder, Norman Menachem. 2002. "Deconstructing Over-the-Counter Derivatives." *Columbia Business Law Review* vol. 17 no. 3 (2002): 677–748.

Financial Stability Forum. 2000. *Issues Paper of the Task Force on Implementation of Standards.* Online at http://www.financialstabilityboard.org/publications/ r_0003.pdf (last accessed 30 October 2010).

Financial Times (Editorial Board). 2008. "Software Wars." *Financial Times,* 3 April.

Financial Times (Lex). 2008. "Sony and Blu-ray." *Financial Times,* 8 January: 14.

Finegold, David, et al. 1994. *The Decline of the U.S. Machine-Tool Industry and Prospects for Its Sustainable Recovery.* Washington, DC: RAND Corporation.

Finnemore, Martha. 1996. "Norms, Culture, and World Politics: Insights from Sociology's Institutionalism." *International Organization* vol. 50 no. 2 (spring): 325–347.

Fioretos, Orfeo. 2011. "Historical Institutionalism in International Relations." *International Organization,* forthcoming.

Flagg, Cedric R., and Robert P. Ware. 1954. "Standards and Specifications: Paper Presented before the Divisions of Chemical Literature of the American Chemical Society at the 122nd Meeting of the ACS, 1952." *Advances in Chemistry* vol. 10 (June): 449–454.

Flynn, Finbarr and Takako Taniguchi. 2010. "Japan Urges to Form Third Force on Accounting Standards." *Bloomberg/Businessweek* 9 February 2010. Online at http://www.bloomberg.com/apps/news?pid=20601208&sid=aS30CW6gc4fM (last accessed 16 May 2010).

Frankel, Christian, and Erik Højbjerg. 2011. "The Political Standardizer." *Business and Society* vol. 50, forthcoming.

Frary, Mark, with Paul Tunbridge. 2006. "The World of Electricity: 1820–1904." Geneva: IEC. Online at http://www.iec.ch/about/history/articles/world_of_ electricity.htm (last accessed 5 May 2009).

Frontard, Raymond. 1997. "Standards-Related Activities: The Global View." In *Friendship Among Equals: Recollections from ISO's First Fifty Years*, edited by Jack Latimer. Geneva: ISO Central Secretariat, 43–56.

Funk, Jeffrey L., and David T. Methe. 2001. "Market- and Committee-Based Mechanisms in the Creation and Diffusion of Global Industry Standards: The Case of Mobile Communication." *Research Policy* vol. 30 no. 4 (April): 589–601.

G-7. 1997. *Final Report to the G-7 Heads of State and Government on Promoting Financial Stability.*

———. 1998. *Declaration of G-7 Finance Ministers and Central Bank Governors.*

———. 1998. *Strengthening the Architecture of the Global Financial System: Report of the G-7 Finance Ministers to the G-7 Heads of State or Government for their Meeting in Birmingham.*

G-20. 2009. Final communiqués signed by the leaders of the world's largest economies: "The Global Plan for Recovery and Reform" and "Declaration on Strengthening the Financial System," 2 April 2009. Online at http://www.londonsummit.gov.uk/en/summit-aims/summit-communique/ (last accessed 31 August 2010).

———. 2009. *Leaders Statement: The Pittsburgh Summit, September 24–25.* Online at http://www.g20.org/Documents/pittsburgh_summit_leaders_statement_250909.pdf (last accessed 31 August 2010).

Gabel, H. Landis, ed. 1991. *Competitive Strategies for Product Standards: The Strategic Use of Compatibility Standards for Competitive Advantage.* London: McGraw-Hill.

Garcia, D. Linda. 1993. "Standard Setting in the United States: Public and Private Sector Roles." *IEEE Micro* vol. 13 no. 6 (November/December): 28–35.

Gauch, Stephan. 2008. "+ vs. –: Dynamics and Effects of Competing Standards of Recordable DVD-Media." In *The Dynamics of Standards*, edited by Tineke M. Egyedi and Knut Blind. Cheltenham, UK: Edward Elgar, 47–67.

Gazal-Ayal, Oren. 2007. "Economic Analysis of Standard Form Contracts: The Monopoly Case." *European Journal of Law and Economics* vol. 24 no. 2 (October): 119–136.

Genschel, Philipp. 1997. "How Fragmentation Can Improve Co-ordination: Setting Standards in International Telecommunications." *Organization Studies* vol. 18 no. 4 (June): 603–622.

Genschel, Philipp, and Raymund Werle. 1993. "From National Hierarchies to International Standardization: Modal Change in the Governance of Telecommunications." *Journal of Public Policy* vol. 13 no. 3 (July–September): 203–225.

Georgiou, George. 2010. "The IASB Standard-Setting Process: Participation and Perceptions of Financial Statement Users." *British Accounting Review* vol. 42 no. 2 (June): 103–118.

Gereffi, Gary, Ronie Garcia-Johnson, and Erika Sasser. 2001. "The NGO-Industrial Complex." *Foreign Policy* no. 125 (July–August): 56–65.

Gesmer and Updegrove, LLP. 2009. "Standard Setting Organizations and Standards List." http://www.consortiuminfo.org/links (last visited 1/2/2009).

Geuther, Albrecht, ed. 1992. *Festschrift 75 Jahre DIN, 1917 bis 1992: Ein Haus mit Geschichte und Zukunft*. Berlin: Beuth Verlag.

Giersberg, Georg. 2007. "Internationale Bilanzvorschriften etabliert: Endgültiger Durchbruch mit der Akzeptanz durch die amerikanische Börsenaufsicht." *Frankfurter Allgemeine Zeitung*, 31 December: 19.

Glinski, Carola. 2007. "Corporate Codes of Conduct: Moral or Legal Obligation?" In *The New Corporate Accountability: Corporate Social Responsibility and the Law*, edited by Doreen McBarnet, Aurora Voiculescu, and Tom Campbell. New York: Cambridge University Press, 119–147.

Gordon, Paul D., and Sidney J. Gray. 1994. *European Financial Reporting: United Kingdom*. London: Routledge.

Gormann, Maryann. 2009. "Conformity Assessment, Standards, and Trade: An Interview with Ann Weeks of Underwriters Laboratories." *ASTM Standardization News* vol. 37 no. 2 (March/April).

Gourevitch, Peter A. 1977. "International Trade, Domestic Coalitions, and Liberty: Comparative Responses to the Crisis of 1873–1896." *Journal of Interdisciplinary History* vol. 8 no. 2 (autumn): 281–313.

———. 2003. "Corporate Governance: Global Markets, National Politics." In *Governance in a Global Economy: Political Authority in Transition*, edited by Miles Kahler and David A. Lake. Princeton: Princeton University Press, 305–331.

Grant, Ruth W., and Robert O. Keohane. 2005. "Accountability and Abuses of Power in World Politics." *American Political Science Review* vol. 99 no. 1 (February): 29–43.

Graz, Jean-Christophe, and Andreas Nölke, eds. 2008. *Transnational Private Governance and Its Limits*. London: Routledge.

Green, Jessica F. 2010. "Private Standards in the Climate Regime: The Greenhouse Gas Protocol." *Business and Politics* vol. 12 no. 3 (October 2010, special issue: Private Regulation in the Global Economy, edited by Tim Büthe).

Green, Wilmer. 1930. "Brief Resume of the Life of Luca Pacioli and His Book Entitled 'Summa de Arithmetica, Geometria, Proportioni et Proportionalita.'" In *History and Survey of Accountancy*. Brooklyn, NY: Standard Text Press, 88–105.

Greene, A. M. 1955. *History of the ASME Boiler Code*. New York: American Society of Mechanical Engineers.

Grewal, David Singh. 2008. *Network Power: The Social Dynamics of Globalization*. New Haven: Yale University Press.

Grey, Vince. 1997. "Setting Standards: A Phenomenal Success Story." In *Friendship Among Equals: Recollections from ISO's First Fifty Years*, edited by Jack Latimer. Geneva: ISO Central Secretariat, 33–42.

Grieco, Joseph M. 1990. *Cooperation Among Nations: Europe, America, and Non-Tariff Barriers to Trade*. Ithaca, NY: Cornell University Press.

Grindley, Peter. 1995. *Standards, Strategy, and Policy: Cases and Stories*. Oxford: Oxford University Press.

Groetzinger, Jon. 1975. "The New GATT Code and the International Harmonization of Product Standards." *Cornell International Law Journal* vol. 8 no. 2 (May): 168–188.

Guler, Isin, Mauro F. Guillén, and John Muir MacPherson. 2002. "Global Competition, Institutions and the Diffusion of Organization Practices: The International Spread of ISO 9000 Quality Certificates." *Administrative Science Quarterly* vol. 47 no. 2 (June): 207–232.

Hadfield, Gillian K. 2001. "Privatizing Commercial Law." *Regulation* vol. 24 no. 1 (spring): 40–45.

———. 2004. "Delivering Legality on the Internet: Developing Principles for the Private Provision of Commercial Law." *American Law and Economics Review* vol. 6 no. 1 (spring): 154–184.

———. 2009. "The Public and the Private in the Provision of Law for Global Transactions." In *Contractual Certainty in International Trade: Empirical Studies and Theoretical Debates on Institutional Support for Global Economic Exchanges*, edited by Volkmar Gessner. Oxford: Hart, 239–256.

Hall, Peter A. 1992. "The Movement from Keynesianism to Monetarism: Institutional Analysis and British Economic Policy in the 1970s." In *Structuring Politics: Historical Institutionalism in Comparative Analysis*, edited by Sven Steinmo, Kathleen Thelen, and Frank Longstreth. New York: Cambridge University Press, 90–113.

Hall, Peter A., and Daniel W. Gingerich. 2002. "Varieties of Capitalism and Institutional Complementarities in the Macroeconomy: An Empirical Analysis." Manuscript, Harvard University.

Hall, Peter A., and David Soskice. 2001. "An Introduction to Varieties of Capitalism." In *Varieties of Capitalism: The Institutional Foundations of Comparative Advantage*, edited by Peter A. Hall and David Soskice. New York: Oxford University Press, 1–68.

Hall, Peter A., and Rosemary C. R. Taylor. 1996. "Political Science and the Three New Institutionalisms." *Political Studies* vol. 44 no. 5 (December): 936–957.

Hall, Rodney Bruce, and Thomas J. Biersteker, eds. 2002. *The Emergence of Private Authority in Global Governance*. Cambridge: Cambridge University Press.

Hambly, Graham. 2010. "Editor's Note: 'We Have a Complaint!' " *PQ Magazine* (London) May: 3.

Hamilton, Robert W. 1978. "The Role of Nongovernmental Standards in the Development of Mandatory Federal Standards Affecting Safety or Health." *Texas Law Review* vol. 56 no. 8 (November): 1329–1484.

Hannan, Michael T., and John Freeman. 1977. "The Population Ecology of Organizations." *American Journal of Sociology* vol. 82 no. 5 (March): 929–964.

Hanney, Brian. 2007. "MPs Attack IFRS 8: Standard Will Give Multinationals 'Carte Blanche.'" *Accountancy Magazine Online* (4 May).

Hansen, Thomas Bowe. 2009. "Lobbying of the International Accounting Standards Board: An Empirical Investigation." Available at SSRN: http://ssrn.com/abstract=1081413 (last accessed 30 October 2010).

Hanson, David. 2005. *CE Marking, Product Standards and World Trade*. Cheltenham, UK: Edward Elgar.

Harris, Trevor S. 1995. *International Accounting Standards versus US-GAAP Reporting: Empirical Evidence based on Case Studies*. Cincinnati: South-Western College Publishing.

Haskins, Mark, Kenneth Ferris, and Thomas Selling. 2000. *International Reporting and Analysis: A Contextual Emphasis*. 2nd edition. Boston: Irwin McGraw-Hill.

Haufler, Virginia. 2001. *The Public Role of the Private Sector: Industry Self-Regulation in a Global Economy*. Washington, DC: Carnegie Endowment for International Peace.

———. 2003. "Globalization and Industry Self-Regulation." In *Governance in a Global Economy: Political Authority in Transition*, edited by Miles Kahler and David A. Lake. Princeton: Princeton University Press, 226–252.

———. 2009. "The Kimberley Process, Club Goods, and Public Enforcement of a Private Regime." In *Voluntary Programs: A Club Theory Perspective*, edited by Matthew Potoski and Aseem Prakash. Cambridge, MA: MIT Press, 89–105.

Hawkins, Darren G., et al., eds. 2006. *Delegation and Agency in International Organizations*. New York: Cambridge University Press.

Heffes, Ellen M. 2008. "FAF Proposed Changes Spur Former FASB Member Comments." *Financial Executive* vol. 24 no. 2 (March): 14–15.

Hegarty, John. 1993. "Accounting Integration in Europe: Still on Track." *Journal of Accountancy* vol. 175 no. 5 (May): 92–95.

Heilman, Jeff. 2007. "The Products of Our Times: How to Make Standards-Setting Work for You." *IP Business* vol. 5 no. 1 (spring/summer): 6–9.

Heires, Marcel. 2008. "The International Organization for Standardization (ISO)." *New Political Economy* vol. 13 no. 3 (September): 357–367.

Heisenberg, Dorothee, and Marie-Helene Fandel. 2003. "Exporting EU Regimes Abroad: The EU Privacy Directive as a Global Standard." In *The Emergent Global Information Policy Regime*, edited by Sandra Braman. New York: Palgrave, 109–129.

Helleiner, Eric. 1994. *States and the Reemergence of Global Finance: From Bretton Woods to the 1990s*. Ithaca, NY: Cornell University Press.

Hemenway, David. 1979. *Standards Systems in Canada, the U.K., West Germany and Denmark: An Overview*. Washington, DC: Office of Standards

Information, Analysis, and Development, Office of Engineering Standards, NIST.

———. 1980. *Performance vs. Design Standards*. Washington, DC: Department of Commerce, National Bureau of Standards.

Hermann, Don, and Ian P. N. Hague. 2006. "Convergence: In Search of the Best." *Journal of Accountancy* vol. 201 no. 1 (January): 69–73.

Heyvaert, Veerle. 2009. "Globalizing Regulation: Reaching Beyond the Borders of Chemical Safety." *Journal of Law and Society* vol. 36 no. 1 (March): 110–128.

Hill, Andrew, and Andrew Parker. 2002. "Standard-Setters Are Targeting Stock Options Again." *Financial Times*, 11 November: 21.

Hille, Kathrin. 2009. "4G Focus Behind China Mobile Deal." *Financial Times*, 30 April.

Hilpert, Georg, and Anja Vomberg. 2006. "Die Wiener und Dresdner Vereinbarung." *KAN (Kommission Arbeitsschutz und Normung) Brief* (Sankt Augustin: Verein für Arbeitssicherheit in Europa) vol. 9 no. 1 (spring): 12–14.

Hinsley, F. H. 1966. *Sovereignty*. New York: Basic Books.

Hirschman, Albert O. 1970. *Exit, Voice, And Loyalty: Responses to Decline in Firms, Organizations, and States*. Cambridge, MA: Harvard University Press.

Hoarau, Christian. 2009. "The Reform of the French Standard-Setting System: Its Peculiarities, Limits, and Political Context." *Accounting in Europe* vol. 6 no. 2 (December): 127–148.

Höpner, Martin. 2005. "What Connects Industrial Relations with Corporate Governance? Explaining Institutional Complementarity." *Socioeconomic Review* vol. 3 no. 2 (May): 331–358.

Hopwood, Anthony. 1987. " The Archaeology of Accounting Systems." *Accounting Organizations and Society* vol. 12 no. 3: 207–234.

———. 1994. "Some Reflections on 'The Harmonization of Accounting Within the EU.' " *European Accounting Review* vol. 3 no. 2 (July): 241–252.

House, John. 2005. "Global Standards Here to Stay." *Accountancy* vol. 136 no. 1344 (August): 72–73.

Hughes, Jennifer. 2008. "US Set to Adopt IFRS Rule." *Financial Times*, 28 August.

Hughes, Stephen G., and Nigel Haworth. 2010. *The International Labour Organisation: Coming in from the Cold*. London: Routledge.

Hunt, Bishop. 1936. *The Development of the Business Corporation in England 1800–1867*. Cambridge, MA: Harvard University Press.

Hütten, Christoph, et al. 2010. "Die deutsche Stimme erhalten." *Frankfurter Allgemeine Zeitung* 26 July: 12.

IASC (International Accounting Standards Committee). 1988. *Survey of the Use and Application of International Accounting Standards*. London: IASC.

IASCF (International Accounting Standards Committee Foundation). 2006. *Due Process Handbook for the IASB*. London: IASCF Publications Department.

————.2009. *Revised Constitution*. London: IASC Foundation Publications. Online at http://www.iasb.org/NR/rdonlyres/A3010B6C-3F80-401F-BE81-359E1E015E22/0/Constitution final.pdf (last accessed 20 July 2009).

————. 2009. *The IASB and the IASCF: Who We Are and What We Do*. London: IASCF.

IEC. 2009. *Annual Report 2008*. Geneva: International Electrotechnical Commission.

————. 2009. "About the IEC: Mission and Objectives." Geneva: IEC. Online at http://www.iec.ch/about/mission-e.htm (last accessed 20 December 2009).

————. 2010. "IEC in Figures". Online at http://www.iec.ch/news_centre/iec_figures/ (last accessed 31 August 2010).

————. 2010. "Members of the IEC". Online at http://www.iec.ch/dyn/www/f?p=102:5:0 (last accessed 31 August 2010).

IEC-CENELEC. 1996. "IEC - CENELEC (Dresden) Agreement." Geneva–Brussels: IEC and CENELEC. Online at http://www.iec.ch/about/partners/agreements/cenelec-e.htm (last accessed 21 December 2009).

IFRS Foundation. 2010. "Constitution." IASC Foundation Publications, (last accessed 30 May 2010).

IMF (International Monetary Fund). 1999. *Report of the Management Director to the Interim Committee on Progress in Strengthening the Architecture of the International Financial System*. Washington, DC.: IMF Publications.

Immergut, Ellen M. 2006. "Historical-Institutionalism in Political Science and the Problem of Change." In *Understanding Change: Models, Methodologies, and Metaphors*, edited by Andreas Wimmer and Reinhart Kössler. Houndmills, UK: Palgrave Macmillan, 237–259.

International Bank for Reconstruction and Development. 1995. *Financial Accounting, Reporting and Auditing Handbook*. Washington, DC: World Bank Publications.

International Labour Office. 1998. *International Labour Standards: A Worker's Education Manual*. Geneva: International Labour Office.

ISO. 2007. "The ISO Timeline." Online at http://www.iso.org/iso/about/the_iso_story/iso_story_timeline.htm (last accessed 20 December 2009).

————. 2009. "Discover ISO: The ISO Brand." Online at http://www.iso.org/iso/about/discover-iso_the-iso-brand.htm (last accessed 12 July 2009).

————. 2009. "Discover ISO: What's Different about ISO 9001 and ISO 14001." Online at http://www.iso.org/iso/about/discover-iso_whats-different-about-iso-9001-and-iso-14001.htm (last accessed 24 October 2009).

————. 2010. *ISO in Figures for the Year 2009 (at 31 December)*. Geneva: International Organization for Standardization. Online at http://www.iso.org/iso/about/iso_in_figures.htm (last accessed 31 August 2010).

————. 2010. "ISO Members." Online at http://www.iso.org/iso/about/iso_members.htm (last accessed 31 August 2010).

ISO-CEN. 1991. "Agreement on Technical Cooperation between ISO and

CEN (Vienna Agreement)." Geneva–Brussels: ISO and CEN. Text and associated documents at http://www.iso.org/va (last accessed 21 December 2009).

ISO/IEC. 2007. *Using and Referencing ISO and IEC Standards for Technical Regulations*. Geneva: ISO and IEC Central Secretariats, September.

———. 2009. *Directives*, part 1. 7th ed. Geneva: International Organization for Standardization and International Electrotechnical Commission.

ITC (UNCTAD/WTO International Trade Centre) with the Commonwealth Secretariat (CS). 2003. *Influencing and Meeting International Standards: Challenges for Developing Countries*. Geneva: ITC/CS, 2003.

Jacobsson, Bengt. 2000. "Standardization and Expert Knowledge." In *A World of Standards*, edited by Nils Brunsson and Bengt Jacobsson. New York: Oxford University Press, 40–49.

Jaffee, Daniel. 2007. *Brewing Justice: Fair Trade Coffee, Sustainability, and Survival*. Berkeley: University of California Press.

Jansen, Nils, and Ralf Michaels. 2008. "Beyond the State? Rethinking Private Law: Introduction to the Issue." *American Journal of Comparative Law* vol. 56 no. 3 (summer): 527–540.

Jeanjean, Thomas, and Hervé Stolowy. 2008. "Do Accounting Standards Matter? An Exploratory Analysis of Earnings Management Before and After IFRS Adoption." *Journal of Accounting and Public Policy* vol. 27 no. 6 (November–December): 480–494.

Jensen, Nathan M. 2003. "Democratic Governance and Multinational Corporations: Political Regimes and Inflows of Foreign Direct Investment." *International Organization* vol. 57 no. 3 (summer): 587–616.

Jo, Hyeran. 2009. "Diffusion of International Accounting Standards: Domestic-International Linkages." Paper presented at the Annual Meeting of the American Political Science Association, Toronto, September.

Joerges, Christian, Harm Schepel, and Ellen Vos. 1999. "The Law's Problems with the Involvement of Non-Governmental Actors in Europe's Legislative Processes: The Case of Standardization Under the 'New Approach.'" *EUI Working Paper, Law no. 99/9*.

Jones, Ruth, and Joe Lubenow. 2008. "Universal Postal Union (UPU) International Postal Addressing Standards." Paper delivered at the ISO (TC211) Workshop on Address Standards, Copenhagen, 25 May.

Jopson, Barney. 2007. "UK Investors in Plea to Brussels over IFRS 8." *Financial Times,* 21 March.

Jopson, Barney, and David Pilling. 2005. "Accounting Rivals Face a Struggle to Stay in Tune." *Financial Times,* 9 March.

Jordana, Jacint, and David Levi-Faur, eds. 2004. *The Politics of Regulation: Institutions and Regulatory Reforms of the Age of Governance*. Northampton, MA: Edward Elgar.

Jorissen, Ann, et al. 2010. "Formal Participation in IASB's Due Process of

Standard-Setting: A Multi-Issue/Multi-Period Analysis." *European Accounting Review* vol. 19, forthcoming.

Josselin, Daphné, and William Wallace, eds. 2001. *Non-State Actors in World Politics*. New York: Palgrave.

Jungmittag, Andre, Knut Blind, and Hariolf Grupp. 1999. "Innovation, Standard-isation, and the Long-Term Production Function: A Cointegration Analysis for Germany 1960–1996." *Schmollers Jahrbuch: Zeitschrift für Wirtschafts-und Sozialwissenschaften* vol. 119: 205–222.

Jupille, Joseph, Walter Mattli, and Duncan Snidal. 2008. *International Institutional Choice for Global Commerce*. Manuscript, University of Colorado, Boulder.

Kaiser, Karl. 1969. "Das internationale System der Gegenwart als Faktor der Beeinträchtigung demokratischer Außenpolitik." *Politische Vierteljahresschrift* vol. 10 no. 1 (March, Sonderheft "Die anachronistische Souveränität," edited by E.-O. Czempiel): 340–358.

Kalafsky, Ronald V., and Alan D. MacPherson. 2002. "The Competitive Characteristics of U.S. Manufacturers in the Machine Tool Industry." *Small Business Economics* vol. 19 no. 4 (December): 355–369.

Kammer, Raymond. 1998. "Prepared Remarks by NIST Director Ray Kammer at the American National Standards Institute Board Meeting, West Conshohocken, PA, 18 March." Online at http://www.nist.gov/director/speeches/ansitalk.cfm (last accessed 7 September 2010).

Karolyi, G. Andrew. 1998. "Why Do Companies List Shares Abroad? A Survey of the Evidence and Its Managerial Implications." *Financial Markets, Institutions, and Instruments* vol. 7 no. 1 (February): 1–60.

Katz, Michael L., and Carl Shapiro. 1985. "Network Externalities, Competition, and Compatibility." *American Economic Review* vol. 75 no. 3 (June): 424–440.

Katznelson, Ira, and Martin Shefter, eds. 2002. *Shaped by War and Trade: International Influences on American Political Development*. Princeton: Princeton University Press.

Katzenstein, Peter J., ed. 1978. *Between Power and Plenty: Foreign Economic Policies of Advanced Industrial States*. Madison, WI: University of Wisconsin Press.

Kawamoto, Akira, et al. 1997. "Product Standards, Conformity Assessment, and Regulatory Reform." In *OECD Report on Regulatory Reform*, edited by the Organization for Economic Coopertion and Development. Paris: OECD, 275–328.

Kawasaki, Dawn. 2009. *Industry Assessment: Machine Tools and Metalworking Equipment*. Washington, DC: Department of Commerce: International Trade Association.

Keating, Barry P. 1981. "Standards: Implicit, Explicit and Mandatory." *Economic Inquiry* vol. 19 no. 3 (July): 449–458.

Keck, Margaret, and Kathryn Sikkink. 1998. *Activists Beyond Borders: Advocacy Networks in International Politics*. Ithaca, NY: Cornell University Press.

Keister, Oriville. 1965. "The Mechanics of Mesopotamian Record-keeping." *National Association of Accountants Bulletin* (February): 18–24.

Kennedy, Scott, Richard P. Suttmeier, and Jun Su. 2008. *Standards, Stakeholders, and Innovation*. Seattle: National Bureau of Asian Research.

Keohane, Robert O. 1971. "Big Influence of Small Allies." *Foreign Policy* no. 2 (spring): 161–182.

———. 1984. *After Hegemony: Cooperation and Discord in the World Political Economy*. Princeton: Princeton University Press.

———. 1989. "International Institutions: Two Approaches." In *International Institutions and State Power: Essays in International Relations Theory*. Boulder, CO: Westview Press, 158–179.

Keohane, Robert O., and Joseph S. Nye. (1977) 1989. *Power and Interdependence*. 2nd edition. New York: Harper Collins Publishers.

Kindleberger, Charles P. 1983. "Standards as Public, Collective and Private Goods." *Kyklos* vol. 36 no. 3 (September): 377–396.

King, Gary, et al. 2004. "Enhancing the Validity and Cross-Cultural Comparability of Measurement in Survey Research." *American Political Science Review* vol. 97 no. 4 (February): 567–583.

King, Gary, Robert O. Keohane, and Sidney Verba. 1994. *Designing Social Inquiry: Scientific Inference in Qualitative Research*. Princeton: Princeton University Press.

King, Gary, Michael Tomz, and Jason Wittenberg. 2000. "Making the Most of Statistical Analyses: Improving Interpretation and Presentation." *American Journal of Political Science* vol. 44 no. 2 (April): 341–355.

King, Gary, and Jonathan Wand. 2007. "Comparing Incomparable Survey Responses: Evaluating and Selecting Anchoring Vignettes." *Political Analysis* vol. 15 no. 1 (winter): 46–66.

Kingsbury, Benedict, Nico Krisch, and Richard B. Stewart. 2005. "The Emergence of Global Administrative Law." *Law and Contemporary Problems* vol. 68 no. 3/4 (summer/autumn): 15–61.

Kirchgaessner, Stephanie. 2008. "AIG under Fire." *Financial Times,* 8 October: 3.

Kirkland, Edward C. 1961. *Industry Comes of Age: Business, Labor, and Public Policy, 1860–1897*. New York: Holt, Rinehart and Winston.

Kirton, John J., and Michael E. Trebilcock, eds. 2004. *Hard Choices, Soft Law: Voluntary Standards in Global Trade, Environment and Social Governance*. Burlington, VT: Ashgate.

Knight, Jack. 1992. *Institutions and Social Conflict*. New York: Cambridge University Press.

Kollman, Kelly, and Aseem Prakash. 2001. "Green By Choice? Cross-National Variations in Firms' Responses to EMS-Based Environmental Regimes." *World Politics* vol. 53 no. 3 (April): 399–430.

Königsgruber, Roland. 2009. "Lobbying bei der Rechnungslegungsstandardset-zung: Ein Literaturüberblick." *Zeitschrift für Betriebswirtschaft* vol. 79 no. 11 (November): 1309–1329.

Kono, Daniel Y. 2006. "Optimal Obfuscation: Democracy and Trade Policy Transparency." *American Political Science Review* vol. 100 no. 3 (August): 369–384.

Koski, Heli. 2006. "Factors for Success in Mobile Telephony: Why Diffusion in the United States and Europe Differs." In *How Revolutionary Was the Digital Revolution?* edited by John Zysman and Abraham L. Newman. Palo Alto: Stanford University Press, 324–336.

Krasner, Stephen D. 1991. "Global Communications and National Power: Life on the Pareto Frontier." *World Politics* vol. 43 no. 3 (April): 336–366.

———, ed. 2001. *Problematic Sovereignty: Contested Rules and Political Possibilities*. New York: Columbia University Press.

Kretschmer, Tobias, and Katrin Muehlfeld. 2004. "Co-opetition in Standard-Setting: The Case of the Compact Disc." *NET Institute (New York) Working Paper* no. 04-14 (October).

Krislov, Samuel. 1997. *How Nations Choose Product Standards and Standards Change Nations*. Pittsburgh: University of Pittsburgh Press.

Kuert, Willy. 1997. "The Founding of the ISO: 'Things are Going the Right Way.'" In *Friendship Among Equals: Recollections from ISO's First Fifty Years*, edited by Jack Latimer. Geneva: ISO Central Secretariat, 13–21.

Kuhn, Markus. 2006. "International Standard Paper Sizes." Online manuscript, Cambridge University, May 2006 (http://www.cl.cam.ac.uk/~mgk25/iso-paper.html, last accessed 30 October 2010).

Lake, David A. 1988. "The State and American Trade Strategy in the Pre-Hegemonic Era." In *The State and American Foreign Economic Policy*, edited by G. John Ikenberry et al., 33–58.

———. 2007. "Delegating Divisible Sovereignty: Sweeping a Conceptual Mine-field." *Review of International Organizations* vol. 2 no. 3 (September): 219–237.

Larson, Robert K. 2008. "An Examination of Comment Letters to the IASC: Special Purpose Entities." *Research in Accounting Regulation* vol. 20: 27–46.

Larson, Robert K., and Sara York Kenny. 1998. "Research Note: Developing Countries' Involvement in the IASC's Standard-Setting Process." *Advances in International Accounting* vol. 11, supplement 1: 17–41.

Latimer, Jack, ed. 1997. *Friendship Among Equals: Recollections from ISO's First Fifty Years*. Geneva: International Organization for Standardization (ISO) Central Secretariat.

Lauterbach, Claire. 2007. "The Costs of Cooperation: Civilian Casualty Counts in Iraq." *International Studies Perspectives* vol. 8 no. 4 (November): 429–445.

Lauterslager, Hans. 2008. "An Interview with Kees A. S. Immink, Optical Disc Engineer, Phillips N.V., May 15, 2001." New York: Audio Engineering Society Oral History Project (DVD).

Lecraw, Donald J. 1984. "Some Economic Effects of Standards." *Applied Economics* vol. 16 no. 4 (August): 507–522.

———. 1987. "Japanese Standards: A Barrier to Trade?" In *Product Standardization and Competitive Strategy*, edited by H. Landis Gabel: Elsevier Science Publishers, 29–46.

Lee, Thomas, Ashton Bishop, and Robert Parker, eds. 1996. *Accounting History from the Renaissance to the Present*. New York: Garland.

Leight, Walter G., and Krista J. Johnsen Leuteritz. 1998. *Toward a National Standards Strategy: Conference Summary Report*. Gaithersburg, MD: U.S. Department of Commerce, NIST.

Leive, David M. 1976. *International Regulatory Regimes: Case Studies in Health, Meteorology, and Food*. 2 vols. Lexington, MA: Lexington Books.

Leone, Marie. 2008. "FASB Parent: Five Is More than Seven." CFO.com, 26 February 2008. Online at http://www.cfo.com/article.cfm/10756502 (last accessed 17 July 2010).

Lerner, Josh, and Jean Tirole. 2006. "A Model of Forum Shopping." *American Economic Review* vol. 96 no. 4 (September): 1091–1113.

Leslie, Donald A., Albert D. Teitlebaum, and Rodney J. Anderson. 1980. *Dollar-Unit Sampling: A Practical Guide for Auditors*. London: Pittman.

Leuz, Christian, and Peter Wysocki. 2007. "Economic Consequences of Financial Reporting and Disclosure Regulation: What Have We Learned?" Manuscript, University of Chicago and MIT, June.

Levi, Margaret, and April Linton. 2003. "Fair Trade: A Cup at a Time?" *Politics and Society* vol. 31 no. 3 (September): 407–432.

Levinson, Mark. 2006. *The Box: How the Shipping Container Made the World Smaller and the World Economy Bigger*. Princeton: Princeton University Press.

Levit, Janet K. 2005. "A Bottom-Up Approach to International Lawmaking: The Tale of Three Trade Finance Instruments." *Yale Journal of International Law* vol. 30 no. 1 (winter): 125–210.

———. 2008. "Bottom-Up Lawmaking Through a Pluralist Lens: The ICC Banking Commission and the Transnational Regulation of Letters." *Emory Law Journal* vol. 57 no. 5 (2008): 1147–1226.

Liebowitz, Stan J., and Stephen E. Margolis. 1999. *Winners, Losers and Microsoft: Competition and Antitrust in High Technology*. Oakland: The Independent Institute.

Lijphart, Arend. 1968. "Typologies of Democratic Systems." *Comparative Political Studies* vol. 1 no. 1 (April): 3–44.

Ling, June. 2000. "The Evolution of the ASME Boiler and Pressure Vessel Code." *Journal of Pressure Vessel Technology* vol. 122 no. 3 (August 2000): 242–246.

Link, Albert N. 1983. "Market Structure and Voluntary Product Standards." *Applied Economics* vol. 16 no. 3 (June): 393–401.

Locke, L. Leland. 1923. *The Ancient Quipu: A Peruvian Knot Record*. New York: American Museum of Natural History.

Lohr, Sharon L. 2008. "Coverage and Sampling." In *International Handbook of Survey Methodology*, edited by Edith D. de Leeuw, Joop J. Hox and Don A. Dillman. New York: Lawrence Erlbaum, 97–112.

———. 2010. *Sampling: Design and Analysis*. 2nd edition. Boston, MA: Brooks/Cole.

Lohr, Steve. 2006. "OpenDocument Format Fights Back." *New York Times* 3 March.

Loya, Thomas, and John Boli. 1999. "Standardization in the World Polity: Technical Rationality over Power." In *Constructing World Culture: International Non-Governmental Organizations since 1875*, edited by John Boli and George Thomas. Stanford, CA: Stanford University Press, 169–197.

Lukes, Rudolf. 1979. *Überbetriebliche technische Normung in den Rechtsordnungen ausgewählter EWG- und EFTA-Staaten: Frankreich, Großbritannien, Italien, Österreich, Schweden: Organisation der Normung, Einfluß des Staates, Beziehungen zum Verbraucherschutz*. Köln: Carl Heymanns Verlag.

Lukes, Steven. 2004. *Power: A Radical View*. 2nd edition. New York: Palgrave.

Macaulay, Stewart. 1986. "Private Government." In *Law and the Social Sciences*, edited by Leon Lipson and Stanton Wheeler. New York: Russell Sage Foundation, 445–518.

Mahoney, James, and Kathleen Thelen. 2010. "A Theory of Gradual Institutional Change." In *Explaining Institutional Change: Ambiguity, Agency, and Power*, edited by James Mahoney and Kathleen Thelen. New York: Cambridge University Press, 1–37.

Maiello, Michael. 2002. "Tower of Babel." *Forbes* vol. 170 no. 2 (22 July 2002): 166.

Mallett, Robert L. 1998–99. "Why Standards Matter." *Issues in Science and Technology* vol. 15 no. 2 (winter): 63–66.

Mansfield, Edward D., and Marc L. Busch. 1995. "The Political Economy of Nontariff Barriers: A Cross-National Analysis." *International Organization* vol. 49 no. 4 (autumn): 723–749.

Manuele, Fred A. 2005. "Global Harmonization of Safety Standards." *Professional Safety* vol. 50 no. 1 (November).

Marceau, Gabrielle, and Joel P. Trachtman. 2002. "TBT, SPS, and GATT: A Map of the WTO Law of Domestic Regulation." *Journal of World Trade* vol. 36 no. 5 (October): 811–881.

Martin, Lisa. 2000. *Democratic Commitments: Legislatures and International Cooperation*. Princeton: Princeton University Press.

Martin, Lisa, and Beth Simmons. 1998. "Theories and Empirical Studies of International Institutions." *International Organization* vol. 52 no. 4 (autumn): 729–757.

Martinez-Diaz, Leonardo. 2001. "Private Expertise and Global Economic Governance: The Case of International Accounting Standards (1972–2001)." M.Phil. thesis, Oxford University.

Mattessich, Richard 2000. *The Beginning of Accounting and Accounting Thought*. New York: Garland.

Mattli, Walter. 2001. "The Politics and Economics of International Institutionalized Standards Setting: An Introduction." *Journal of European Public Policy* vol. 8 no. 3 (special issue: Governance and International Standards Setting): 328–345.

———. 2003. "Public and Private Governance in Setting International Standards." In *Governance in a Global Economy: Political Authority in Transition*, edited by Miles Kahler and David A. Lake. Princeton: Princeton University Press, 197–229.

Mattli, Walter, and Tim Büthe. 2003. "Setting International Standards: Technological Rationality or Primacy of Power?" *World Politics* vol. 56 no. 1 (October): 1–42.

———. 2005. "Accountability in Accounting? The Politics of Private Rule-Making in the Public Interest." *Governance* vol. 18 no. 3 (July): 399–429.

———. 2005. "Global Private Governance: Lessons From a National Model of Setting Standards in Accounting." *Law and Contemporary Problems* vol. 68 no. 3/4 (summer/autumn): 225–262.

Mattli, Walter, and Ngaire Woods, eds. 2009. *The Politics of Global Regulation*. Princeton: Princeton University Press.

Matutes, Carmen, and Pierre Regibeau. 1996. "A Selective Review of the Economics of Standardization: Entry Deterrence, Technolgical Progress and International Competition." *European Journal of Political Economy* vol. 12 no. 2 (September, special issue: The Economics of Standardization, edited by Manfred J. Holler and Jacques-François Thisse): 183–209.

McClure, E. Ray, et al. 1983. *The Competitive Status of the U.S. Machine Tool Industry: A Study of the Influences of Technology in Determining International Industrial Competitive Advantage. Report Prepared by the Machine Tool Panel, Committee on Technology and International Economic and Trade Issues of the Office of the Foreign Secretary, National Academy of Engineering and the Commission on Engineering and Technical Systems, National Research Council*. Washington, DC: National Academy Press for the National Research Council and the National Academy of Engineering.

McCormack, Richard A. 2009. "U.S. Machine Tool Industry Is On the Brink: How Does an Industry Survive Without Any Orders?" *Manufacturing and Technology News* vol. 16 no. 5 (March).

McDermott, Constance L., Emily Noah, and Benjamin Cashore. 2008. "Differences That 'Matter'? A Framework for Comparing Environmental Certification Standards and Government Policies." *Journal of Environmental Policy & Planning* vol. 10 no. 1 (March 2008): 47–70.

McWilliam, Robert C. 2000. "Business Standards and Government: The Roles Taken by the British Government in the Formation of British Standards." *Homo Oeconomicus* vol. 17 no. 3 (Euras Yearbook of Standardization vol. 3): 323–344.

———. 2001. *BSI: The First Hundred Years.* London: Thanet Press.

Meidinger, Errol. 2006. "The Administrative Law of Global Public-Private Regulation: The Case of Forestry." *European Journal of International Law* vol. 17 no. 1 (February): 47–87.

Meyer, John W. 1980. "The World Polity and the Authority of the Nation-State." In *Studies of the Modern World-System*, edited by Albert Bergesen. New York: Academic Press, 109–137.

Meyer, John W., et al. 1997. "World Society and the Nation State." *American Journal of Sociology* vol. 103 no. 1 (July): 144–181.

Meyer, John W., and Brian Rowan. 1977. "Institutionalized Organizations: Formal Structure as Myth and Ceremony." *American Journal of Sociology* vol. 83 no. 2 (September): 340–363.

Michaels, Ralf, and Nils Jansen. 2006. "Private Law Beyond the State: Europeanization, Globalization, Privatization." *American Journal of Comparative Law* vol. 54 no. 4 (winter): 843–890.

Middleton, R. W. 1980. "The GATT Standards Code." *Journal of World Trade Law* vol. 14 no. 3 (May/June): 201–219.

Mikol, Alain. 1995. "The History of Financial Reporting in France." In *European Financial Reporting: A History*, edited by Peter J. Walton. London: Academic Press, 91–121.

Milek, John T. 1972. "The Role of Management in Company Standardization." In *Speaking of Standards*, edited by Rowen Glie. Boston: Cahner Books, 129–144.

Milgrom, Paul R., and John Roberts. 1995. "Complementarities and Fit: Strategy, Structure, and Organizational Change in Manufacturing." *Journal of Accounting and Economics* vol. 19 no. 2–3 (March–May): 179–208.

Miller, Paul B. W., Rodney J. Redding, and Paul R. Bahnson. 1998. *The FASB: The People, the Process, and the Politics.* 4th edition. Boston: Irwin, McGraw-Hill.

Mills, Geoffrey. 1994. "Early Accounting in Northern Italy: The Role of Commercial Development and the Printing Press in the Expansion of Double-Entry from Genoa, Florence and Venice." *The Accounting Historians Journal* vol. 21 no. 1 (June): 81–96.

Milner, Helen V. 1988. *Resisting Protectionism: Global Industries and the Politics of International Trade.* Princeton: Princeton University Press.

———. 1992. "International Theories of Cooperation Among Nations: Strengths and Weaknesses." *World Politics* vol. 44 no. 3 (April): 466–496.

———. 1997. *Interests, Institutions, and Information: Domestic Politics and International Relations.* Princeton: Princeton University Press.

Mitchell, Ronald B. 1994. "Regime Design Matters: Intentional Oil Pollution and Treaty Compliance." *International Organization* vol. 48 no. 3 (summer): 425–458.

Moe, Terry M. 2005. "Power and Political Institutions." *Perspectives on Politics* vol. 3 no. 2 (June): 215–233.

Moenius, Johannes. 2004. "Information versus Product Adaptation: The Role of Standards in Trade." Manuscript, Northwestern University, February.

———. 2006. "Do National Standards Hinder or Promote Trade in Electrical Products?" In *International Standardization as a Strategic Tool*. Geneva: International Electrotechnical Commission, 53–68.

Moody, Nicholas. 2008. "Institutes Present a Combined Front: French Audit Industry." *The Accountant* no. 6050 (January).

Moran, Michael. 2003. *The British Regulatory State: High Modernism and Hyper-Innovation*. Oxford: Oxford University Press.

Morrow, James D. 1994. "Modeling the Forms of International Cooperation: Distribution versus Information." *International Organization* vol. 48 no. 3 (summer): 387–423.

Mosley, Layna. 2006. "Constraints, Opportunities and Information: Financial Market-Government Relations around the World." In *Globalization and Egalitarian Redistribution*, edited by Pranab Bardhan, Samuel Bowles and Michael Wallerstein. Princeton: Princeton University Press, 87–112.

———. 2011. *Working Globally? Multinational Production and Labor Rights*. New York: Cambridge University Press.

Motaal, Doaa Abdel. 2002. "The Agreement on Technical Barriers to Trade, The Committee on Trade and the Environment, and Eco-Labeling." In *Trade, Environment and the Millennium*, edited by Gary P. Sampson and W. Bradnee Chambers. New York: United Nations University Press, 267–285.

Murphy, Craig N. 1994. *International Organization and Industrial Change: Global Governance since 1850*. New York: Oxford University Press.

Murphy, Craig N., and JoAnne Yates. 2008. *The International Organization for Standardization (ISO): Global Governance through Voluntary Consensus*. London: Routledge.

Murphy, Dale D. 2004. *The Structure of Regulatory Competition: Corporations and Public Policies in a Global Economy*. New York: Oxford University Press.

Myers, Charles T. 1999. "The Development of International Accounting Standards: The Public/Private Nexus." Paper presented at the Annual Meeting of the American Political Science Association.

Naoi, Megumi. 2009. "Shopping for Protection: The Politics of Choosing Trade Instruments in a Partially Legalized World." *International Studies Quarterly* vol. 53 no. 2 (June): 421–444.

Neveling, Nicholas. 2007. "EU Delays IFRS 8 Ratification in Shock Move: European Parliament Tables Resolution Forcing European Commission to Reappraise Divisive IFRS 8." *Accountancy Age* (25 April).

Newman, Abraham L. 2008. *Protectors of Privacy: Regulating Personal Data in the Global Economy*. Ithaca, NY: Cornell University Press.

Nobes, Christopher, ed. 2001. *Gaap 2000: Survey of National Accounting Rules*. London: International Forum on Accountancy Development (IFAD).

———. 2003. "On the Myth of 'Anglo-Saxon' Financial Accounting: A Comment." *International Journal of Accounting* vol. 38 no. 1 (spring): 95–104.

Nobes, Christopher, and Robert Parker, eds. 2004. *Comparative International Accounting*. 8th edition. Essex: Prentice Hall.

———, eds. 2008. *Comparative International Accounting*. 10th edition. Harlow, England: Financial Times/Prentice Hall.

North, Douglass C. 1990. *Institutions, Institutional Change, and Economic Performance*. Cambridge: Cambridge University Press.

NRC (National Research Council). 1995. *Standards, Conformity Assessment, and Trade into the 21st Century*. Washington, DC: National Academy Press.

Oatley, Thomas, and Robert Nabors. 1998. "Redistributive Cooperation: Market Failure, Wealth Transfers, and the Basle Accord." *International Organization* vol. 52 no. 1 (winter): 35–54.

Oberthür, Sebastian, and Herrmann E. Ott. 1999. *The Kyoto Protocol: International Climate Policy for the 21st Century*. Berlin: Springer Verlag.

OECD (Organization for Economic Coopertion and Development). 2000. *An Assessment of the Costs for International Trade in Meeting Regulatory Requirements*. Paris: OECD Working Party of the Trade Committee.

OEOSC Newsletter Editor. 2010. "U.S. Optics Industry to Adopt ISO 10110 Drawing Standards." *OEOSC Optical Standards News* online (June). Online at http://www.optstd.org/news.htm (last accessed 6 June 2010).

Olshan, Marc A. 1993. "Standards Making Organizations and the Rationalization of American Life." *Sociological Quarterly* vol. 34 no. 2 (May): 319–335.

Ord, Lewis C. 1945. *Secrets of Industry*. New York: Emerson Books.

Ordelheide, Dieter. 1993. "True and Fair View: A European and a German Perspective." *European Accounting Review* vol. 2 no. 1 (May): 81–90.

Ordover, Janusz A., Alan O. Sykes, and Robert D. Willig. 1985. "Nonprice Anticompetitive Practices By Dominant Firms Toward the Producers of Complementary Products." In *Antitrust and Regulation: Essays in Memory of John J. McGowan*, edited by Franklin M. Fisher. Cambridge, MA: MIT Press, 115–130.

OTA (Office of Technology Assessment of the Congress of the United States). 1992. *Global Standards: Building Blocks for the Future*. Washington DC: Government Printing Office.

Pagano, Marco, Ailsa A. Röell, and Josef Zechner. 2002. "The Geography of Equity Listing: Why Do Companies List Abroad?" *Journal of Finance* vol. 57 no. 6 (December): 2651–2694.

Palmer, Maija. 2008. "Microsoft Wins Key ISO Certification." *Financial Times,* 1 April.

Parks, Robert. 1993. "Optical Drawing Standards Focus on 'How,' Not 'What.'" *Optics and Photonics News* vol. 4 no. 8 (August): 46.

Partnoy, Frank. 2001. "The Shifting Contours of Global Derivatives Regulation." *University of Pennsylvania Journal of International Economic Law* vol. 22 no. 3 (fall): 421–496.

———. 2007. "Second-Order Benefits from Standards." *Boston College Law Review* vol. 48 no. 1 (January): 169–191.

Percy, Sally. 2005. "ICAEW Grows Slower than Rivals." *Accountancy* vol. 140 no. 1369 (September): 7.

Perry, James, and Andreas Nölke. 2006. "The Political Economy of International Accounting Standards." *Review of International Political Economy* vol. 13 no. 4 (October): 559–586.

Perry, Michelle. 2010. "Competition or Merger?" *Accounting and Business* (ACCA, London) 14 July 2005.

Philips. 2007. "Optical Recording: Beethoven's Ninth Symphony of Greater Importance than Technology." Historical website at http://web.archive.org/web/20080129201342/www.research.philips.com/newscenter/dossier/optrec/beethoven.html

Pierson, Paul. 2000. "Increasing Returns, Path Dependence, and the Study of Politics." *American Political Science Review* vol. 94 no. 2 (June): 251–267.

———. 2000. "The Limits of Design: Explaining Institutional Origins and Change." *Governance* vol. 13 no. 4 (October): 475–499.

———. 2004. *Politics in Time: History, Institutions, and Social Analysis.* Princeton: Princeton University Press.

Pollack, Mark A., and Gregory C. Shaffer. 2009. *When Cooperation Fails: The Law and Politics of Genetically Modified Foods.* New York: Oxford University Press.

Porter, Tony. 2005. "Private Authority, Technical Authority, and the Globalization of Accounting Standards." *Business and Politics* vol. 7 no. 3 (December).

Posner, Elliot. 2009. "Making Rules for Global Finance: Transatlantic Regulatory Cooperation at the Turn of the Millennium." *International Organization* vol. 63 no. 4 (fall): 665–699.

———. 2010. "Sequence as Explanation: The International Politics of Accounting Standards." *Review of International Political Economy* vol. 17 no. 4 (October) 639–664.

Power, Michael. 1997. *The Audit Society: Rituals of Verification.* Oxford: Oxford University Press.

Prakash, Aseem, and Matthew Potoski. 2006. *The Voluntary Environmentalists: Green Clubs, ISO 14001, and Voluntary Environmental Regulations.* New York: Cambridge University Press.

———. 2010. "The International Organization for Standardization as a Global

Governor: A Club Theory Perspective." In *Who Governs the Globe?* edited by Deborah D. Avant, Martha Finnemore and Susan K. Sell. New York: Cambridge University Press, 72–101.

Price, Leslie D. 1972. "The Benefit of Standardization to Industry." In *Speaking of Standards*, edited by Rowen Glie. Boston: Cahner Books, 1972: 169–178.

Purcell, Donald E., ed. 2009. *A National Survey of United States Standardization Policies*. Washington, DC: Center for Global Standards Analysis.

Putnam, Robert D. 1988. "Diplomacy and Domestic Politics: The Logic of Two-Level Games." *International Organization* vol. 42 no. 3 (summer): 427–460.

Quack, Sigrid. 2010. "Law, Expertise, and Legitimacy in Transnational Economic Governance." *Socio-Economic Review* vol. 8 no. 1 (January): 3–16.

Radebaugh, Lee H., Gunther Gebhardt, and Sidney J. Gray. 1995. "Foreign Exchange Listings: A Case Study of Daimler-Benz." *Journal of International Financial Management and Accounting* vol. 6 no. 2 (summer): 158–192.

Raeburn, Anthony. 2006. "IEC Technical Committee Creation: The First Half-Century (1906–1949)." Online at http://www.iec.ch/about/history/overview/overview_1906-1949.htm (last accessed August 10, 2008).

———. 2006. "Development and Growth of IEC Technical Committees: 1950 to 2006." Online at http://www.iec.ch/about/history/overview/overview_1950-2006.htm (last accessed August 10, 2008).

Rao, Poduri S. R. S. 2000. *Sampling Methodologies with Applications*. Boca Raton, FL: Chapman and Hall.

Rappoport, Carla. 1986. "Japanese Ski Makers Freeze out the Opposition." *Financial Times,* 4 September: 1.

———. 1986. "Skiing Dispute Goes to GATT." *Financial Times,* 14 September: 8.

Ray, Edward John, and Howard P. Marvel. 1984. "The Pattern of Protection in the Industrial World." *Review of Economics and Statistics* vol. 66 no. 3 (August): 452–458.

Raybaud-Turillo, Brigitte, and Robert Teller. 2009. "Droit et Comptabilite." In *Encyclopédie de Comptabilité, Contrôle de Gestion et Audit*, edited by Bernard Colasse. Paris: Economica, 705–717.

Raynolds, Laura T., Douglas L. Murray, and John Wilkinson, eds. 2007. *Fair Trade: The Challenges of Transforming Globalization*. London: Routledge.

Reason, Tim, and Marie Leone. 2007. "Downsizing FASB." CFO.com, 18 December 2007. Online at http://www.cfo.com/article.cfm/10327925 (last accessed 17 July 2010).

Reinalda, Bob, and Bertjan Verbeek, eds. 2004. *Decision Making Within International Organizations*. London: Routledge.

Renard, Marie-Christine. 2003. "Fair Trade: Quality, Market and Conventions." *Journal of Rural Studies* vol. 19 no. 1 (January): 87–96.

Rezaee, Zabihollah, L. Murphy Smith, and Joseph Z. Szendi. 2010. "Convergence in Accounting Standards: Insights from Academicians and Practitioners." *Advances in Accounting* vol. 26 no. 1 (June): 142–154.

Richard, Jacques. 1992. "De l'histoire du plan comptable français et de sa réforme éventuelle." In *Annales de Management*, edited by Robert Le Duff and José Allouche. Paris: Economica, 69–82.

Richardson, Alan J., and Burkard Eberlein. 2010. "Legitimating Transnational Standard-Setting: The Case of the International Accounting Standards Board." *Journal of Business Ethics* (forthcoming).

Riles, Annelise. 2008. "The Anti-Network: Private Global Governance, Legal Knowledge, and the Legitimacy of the State." *American Journal of Comparative Law* vol. 56 no. 3 (summer): 605–630.

Ripley, William Z. 1927. *Main Street and Wall Street*. Boston: Little and Brown.

Risse-Kappen, Thomas. 1995. *Cooperation among Democracies: The European Influence on U.S. Foreign Policy*. Princeton: Princeton University Press.

Robb, H. W. 1956. "Significance of Company and National Standards to Industrial Management." In *National Standards in a Modern Economy*, edited by Dickson Reck. New York: Harper & Brothers, 295–302.

Roberts, Clare, Pauline Weetman, and Paul Gordon. 2005. *International Financial Reporting: A Comparative Approach*. 3rd edition. Harlow, UK: Pearson Education.

Rodger, Ian. 1986. "Japanese in Flurry over Ski Standards Protest." *Financial Times*, 23 September: 6

Roht-Arriaza, Naomi. 1995. "Shifting the Point of Regulation: The International Organization for Standardization and Global Lawmaking on Trade and the Environment." *Ecology Law Quarterly* vol. 22 no. 3: 479–539.

Ronit, Karsten, and Volker Schneider. 2000. *Private Organizations in Global Politics*. London: Routledge.

Rosenau, James N., and Ernst-Otto Czempiel, eds. 1992. *Governance without Government: Order and Change in World Politics*. Cambridge: Cambridge University Press.

Rudder, Catherine E. 2008. "Private Governance as Public Governance: A Paradigmatic Shift." *Journal of Politics* vol. 70 no. 4 (October): 899–913.

Rupert, Oliver. 2004. *Forest Certification Matrix: Finding Your Way through Forest Certification Schemes*. Brussels: Confederation of European Paper Industries.

Ruppert, Louis. 1956. *Brief History of the International Electrotechnical Commission*. Geneva: Bureau Central de la Commission Electrotechnique Internationale (IEC).

Russell, Andrew L. 2007. "Industrial Legislatures: Consensus Standardization in the Second and Third Industrial Revolutions." Ph.D. diss., Johns Hopkins University, Baltimore.

Sabel, Charles F. 1995. "Design, Deliberation, and Democracy: On the New Pragmatism of Firms and Public Institutions." In *Liberal Institutions, Economic Constitutional Rights, and the Role of Organizations*, edited by Karl-Heinz Ladeur. Baden-Baden: Nomos Verlag, 1995: 101–49.

Salter, Liora. 1988. *Mandated Science: Science and Scientists in the Making of Standards*. Dordrecht: Kluwer Academic.

——. 1999. "The Standards Regime for Communication and Information Technologies." In *Private Authority and International Affairs*, edited by A. Claire Cutler, Virginia Haufler and Tony Porter. Albany, NY: State University of New York Press, 97–127.

Salustro, Edouard. 2003. "France: Two Overlapping Paths of Progress." *The Accountant* (London) no. 6001 (December): 10.

Sanchanta, Mariko. 2008. "Sony Wins Next-Generation DVD Battle." *Financial Times* 20 February: 20.

Sarkissian, Sergei, and Michael J. Schill. 2004. "The Overseas Listing Decision: New Evidence of Proximity Preference." *Review of Financial Studies* vol. 17 no. 3 (autumn): 769–809.

SASI Editorial Staff. 2007. "Conflicting Standards under Fire: A Common International Standard for Fire-Fighters' Clothing is Still Some Years Away." *Safety at Sea International* no. 11: 42–44.

Schaap, Arjan, and Henk de Vries. 2005. *Wat levert normalisatie u op?* Delft: NEN.

Scheid, Jean-Claude, and Peter Walton. 1992. *European Financial Reporting: France*. London: Routledge.

Schepel, Harm. 2005. *The Constitution of Private Governance: Product Standards in the Regulation of Integrating Markets*. Portland: Hart Publishers.

Schmidt, Susanne K., and Raymund Werle. 1993. "Technical Controversy in International Standardisation." *MPIfG Discussion Papers* no. 93/5 (March).

Schneider, Benu. 2003. *The Road to International Financial Stability: Are Key Financial Standards the Answer?* New York: Palgrave Macmillan.

Schneider, Dieter. 1995. "The History of Financial Reporting in Germany." In *European Financial Reporting: A History*, edited by Peter Walton. London: Academic Press, 123–155.

Schofer, Evan. 1999. "Science Associations in the International Sphere, 1875–1990: The Rationalization of Science and the Scientization of Society." In *Constructing World Culture: International Non-Governmental Organizations since 1875*, edited by John Boli and George Thomas. Stanford, CA: Stanford University Press, 249–266.

Schouhamer Immink, Kees A. 1998. "The Compact Disc Story." *Journal of the Audio Engineering Society* vol. 46 no. 5 (May): 458–465.

——. 2007. "Shannon, Beethoven, and the Compact Disc." *IEEE Information Theory Society Newsletter* vol. 57 no. 4 (December): 42–46.

Schruff, Wienand. 2006. "Die Rolle des Hauptfachausschusses (HFA) des IdW." *Die Wirtschaftsprüfung* vol. 59: 1–8.

Schulz, Klaus-Peter. 2005. *Einflußmöglichkeiten des Arbeitsschutzes auf die ISO-Normung*, Kan Bericht Nr.34. Sankt Augustin: Kommission Arbeitsschutz und Normung.

Schwartz, Alan, and Louis L. Wilde. 1979. "Intervening in Markets on the Basis of Imperfect Information: A Legal and Economic Analysis." *University of Pennsylvania Law Review* vol. 127 no. 3 (January): 630–682.

Scott, W. Richard. 2008. *Institutions and Organizations: Ideas and Interets.* 3rd edition. Los Angeles: Sage.

Scott, W. Richard, and John W. Meyer. 1991. "The Organization of Societal Sectors: Propositions and Early Evidence." In *The New Institutionalism in Organizational Analysis*, edited by Walter W. Powell and Paul J. DiMaggio. Chicago: University of Chicago Press, 108–140.

SEC (Securities and Exchange Commission). 2008. "Roadmap to IFRS Adoption"/"Proposed Rule # 33-8982/34-58960 (File #S7-27-08)." *Federal Register,* 14 November.

———. 2010. "Commission Statement in Support of Convergence and Global Accounting Standards." SEC Release Nos. 33-9109; 34-61578, 24 February. Washington, DC: SEC.

———. Office of the Chief Accountant. 2010. *Work Plan for the Consideration of Incorporating International Financial Reporting Standards into the Financial Reporting System for U.S. Issuers.* Washington, DC: SEC.

Shaffer, Gregory C. 2000. "Globalization and Social Protection: The Impact of EU and International Rules in the Ratcheting up of U.S. Data Privacy Standards." *Yale Journal of International Law* vol. 25 no. 1 (winter): 1–88.

———. 2009. "How Business Shapes Law: A Socio-Legal Framework." *Connecticut Law Review* vol. 42 no. 1 (November): 147–184.

Simmons, Beth A. 2001. "The International Politics of Harmonization: The Case of Capital Market Regulation." *International Organization* vol. 55 no. 3 (summer): 589–620.

Sikka, Prem, and Hugh Willmott. 1995. "The Power of 'Independence': Defending and Extending the Jurisdiction of Accounting in the UK." *Accounting, Organizations and Society* vol. 20 no. 6 (August): 547–581.

Singer, David Andrew. 2007. *Regulating Capital: Setting Standards for the International Financial System.* Ithaca, NY: Cornell University Press.

Skinner, C. E. 1928. "The Present Status of Standards in the Electrical Industry." *Annals of the American Academy of Political and Social Science* vol. 137 (May): 151–156.

Slaughter, Anne-Marie. 2004. *A New World Order.* Princeton: Princeton University Press.

Smith, David Eugene. 1958. *History of Mathematics.* 2 Vols. New York: Courier Dover Publications.

Smith, Philip. 2007. "Convergence Is 'Some Way Off.'" *Accountancy* vol. 139 no. 1365 (May): 8.

Snidal, Duncan. 1985. "Coordination versus Prisoners' Dilemma: Implications for International Cooperation and Regimes." *American Political Science Review* vol. 79 no. 4 (December): 923–945.

Snyder, David V. 2003. "Private Lawmaking." *Ohio State Law Journal* vol. 64 no. 2: 371–448.

Soble, Jonathan. 2008. "Toshiba Counts Cost of HD Defeat." *Financial Times,* 20 March: 20.

Spindler, Gerald. 1998. "Market Processes, Standardisation, and Tort Law." *European Law Journal* vol. 4 no. 3 (September): 316–336.

SPRING Singapore Staff. 2005. "Standardization for Market Access and Competitiveness." *Enterprise Today: A Publication of SPRING Singapore* (September/October).

Spruyt, Hendrik. 2001. "The Supply and Demand of Governance in Standard-Setting: Insights from the Past." *Journal of European Public Policy* vol. 8 no. 3 (June, special issues: Governance and International Standards Setting; edited by Walter Mattli): 371–391.

SRI. 1971. *Industrial Standards.* Menlo Park, CA: SRI, The Long Range Planning Service.

Staiger, Robert W., and Alan O. Sykes. 2009. "International Trade and Domestic Regulation." *NBER Working Paper Series* no. 15541 (November 2009).

Standish, Peter E. M. 1990. "Origins of the Plan Comptable Général: A Study in Cultural Intrusion and Reaction." *Accounting and Business Research* vol. 20 no. 80 (autumn): 337–351.

Stein, Arthur A. 1982. "Coordination and Collaboration: Regimes in an Anarchic World." *International Organization* vol. 36 no. 2 (spring): 294–324.

Sterk, Werner, ed. 2009. *Beteiligung des Arbeitsschutzes an der Normung: Kolloquium anlässlich des 15-jährigen Bestehens der KAN, 1994–2009.* Sankt Augustin: Komission Arbeitsschutz und Normung.

Stokdyk, John. 2010. "FRRP Unhappy with IFRS 8 Dodgers," AccountingWeb (14 January 2010). London: SiftMedia. Online at http://www.accountingweb .co.uk/topic/financial-reporting/frrp-unhappy-ifrs-8-dodgers/397976 (last accessed 2 June 2010).

Stone, Randall W. 2008. "The Scope of IMF Conditionality." *International Organization* vol. 62 no. 4 (October 2008): 589–620.

Stover, John F. 1997. *American Railroads.* 2nd edition. Chicago: University of Chicago Press.

Streeck, Wolfgang, and Kathleen Thelen, eds. 2005. *Beyond Continuity: Institutional Change in Advanced Political Economies.* New York: Oxford University Press.

Sturen, Olle. 1997. "The Expansion of ISO: Decade by Decade." In *Friendship Among Equals: Recollections from ISO's First Fifty Years,* edited by Jack Latimer. Geneva: ISO Central Secretariat, 57–67.

Surowiecki, James. 2002. "Turn of the Century." *Wired* vol. 10 no. 1 (January): 84–89.

Sutton, Francis Xavier, et al. 1956. *The American Business Creed.* Cambridge, MA: Harvard University Press.

Sutton, Timothy G. 1984. "Lobbying of Accounting Standard-Setting Bodies in the U.K. and the U.S.A.: A Downsian Analysis." *Accounting, Organizations, and Society* vol. 9 no. 1: 81–95.

Swann, G. M. Peter. 2000. *The Economics of Standardization: Final Report for Standards and Technical Regulations Directorate, Department of Trade and Industry.* Manchester: Manchester Business School Report.

———. 2005. "Do Standards Enable or Constrain Innovation?" In *The Empirical Economics of Standards*, edited by Paul Temple. London: Department of Trade and Industry (Economics Paper no. 12), 2005: 76–120.

Sykes, Alan. 1995. *Product Standards for Internationally Integrated Goods Markets.* Washington, DC: Brookings Institution.

Tamm Hallström, Kristina. 2000. "Organizing the Process of Standardization." In *A World of Standards*, edited by Nils Brunsson and Bengt Jacobsson. New York: Oxford University Press, 85–99.

———. 2004. *Organizing International Standardization: ISO and the IASC in Quest of Authority.* New York: Oxford University Press.

———. 2005. "International Standardization Backstage: Legitimacy and Competition in the Social Responsibility Field." Paper presented at the SCORE conference, Stockholm, Sweden, October.

Tate, Jay. 2001. "National Varieties of Standardization." In *Varieties of Capitalism: The Institutional Foundations of Comparative Advantage*, edited by Peter A. Hall and David Soskice. New York: Oxford University Press, 442–473.

Taylor, George Rogers, and Irene D. Neu. 1956. *The American Railroad Network, 1861–1890.* Cambridge, MA: Harvard University Press.

Taylor, Peter L. 2005. "In the Market but Not of It: Fair Trade Coffee and Forest Stewartship Council Certification as Market-Based Social Change." *World Development* vol. 33 no. 1 (January): 129–147.

Temple, Paul, ed. 2005. *The Empirical Economics of Standards.* London: Department of Trade and Industry (Economics Paper no. 12).

Thelen, Kathleen. 1999. "Historical Institutionalism in Comparative Politics." *Annual Review of Political Science* vol. 2: 369–404.

———. 2003. "How Institutions Evolve: Insights from Comparative Historical Analysis." In *Comparative-Historical Analysis: Innovations in Theory and Methods*, edited by James Mahoney and Dietrich Rueschemeyer. Cambridge: Cambridge University Press, 208–240.

Thelen, Kathleen, and Sven Steinmo. 1992. "Historical Institutionalism in Comparative Politics." In *Structuring Politics: Historical Institutionalism in Comparative Analysis*, edited by Sven Steinmo, Kathleen Thelen and Frank Longstreth. New York: Cambridge University Press, 1–32.

Thorell, Per, and Geoffrey Whittington. 1994. "The Harmonization of Accounting Within the European Union." *European Accounting Review* vol. 3 no. 2 (July): 215–239.

Tomz, Michael. 2007. "Domestic Audience Costs in International Relations:

An Experimental Approach." *International Organization* vol. 61 no. 4 (fall): 821–840.

Töpfer, Armin, et al. 2000. "Unternehmerischer Nutzen." In *Gesamtwirtschaftlicher Nutzen der Normung, Zusammenfassung der Ergebnisse: Wissenschaftlicher Endbericht mit Praktischen Beispielen*, edited by DIN (Deutsches Institut für Normung) et al. Berlin: Beuth Verlag, 23–34.

Toth, Robert B., ed. 1996. *Standards Activities of Organizations in the United States*. Washington, DC: US Government Printing Office for the U.S. Dept. of Commerce, Technology Administration, National Institute of Standards and Technology.

Trachtman, Joel. 2003. "Addressing Regulatory Divergence Through International Standards: Financial Services." In *Domestic Regulation and Service Trade Liberalization*, edited by Aaditya Mattoo and Pierre Sauvé. Washington, DC: World Bank, 27–41.

Trebilcock, Michael J., and Donald N. Dewees. 1981. "Judicial Control of Standard Form Contracts." In *The Economic Approach to Law*, edited by Paul Burrows and Cento G. Veljanovski. London: Butterworth, 93–119.

Trebilcock, Michael J., and Robert Howse. 2005. *The Regulation of International Trade*. 3rd edition. New York: Routledge.

UK Government and BSI. 2002. "Memorandum of Understanding between the United Kingdom Government and the British Standards Institution in Respect of Its Activities as the United Kingdom's National Standards Body." (First signed in 1981) London, 2002. Online at http://www.dius.gov.uk/~/media/publications/F/file11950 (last accessed 21 December 2009).

Universal Postal Union (UPU). 2007. *General Information on UPU Standards*. Berne: UPU International Bureau.

U.S. Department of Commerce. 2004. *Standards and Competitiveness—Coordinating for Results: Removing Standards-Related Trade Barriers Through Effective Collaboration*. Washington, DC: Department of Commerce.

U.S. House of Representatives, Committee on Science. 2000. *The Role of Standards in Today's Society and in the Future: Hearing before the Subcommittee on Technology, 13 September 2000*. Washington, DC: U.S. Government Printing Office.

———. 2001. *Standards-Setting and United States Competitiveness: Hearing Before the Subcommittee on Environment, Technology and Standards, 28 June*. Washington DC: U.S. Government Printing Office.

———. 2005. *China, Europe, and Use of Standards as Trade Barriers: How Should the U.S. Respond? Hearing before the Subcommittee on Environment, Technology, and Standards, 11 May*. Washington, DC: Government Printing Office.

Vad, Torben Bundgaard Petersen. 1998. *The Europeanization of Standardization: Technical Standards and Multi Level Governance in Europe*. Copenhagen: Copenhagen University.

Van Hulle, Karel. 1993. "Harmonization of Accounting Standards in the EC: Is It the Beginning or Is It the End?" *European Accounting Review* vol. 2 no. 2 (September): 387–396.

Van Riper, Robert. 1994. *Setting Standards for Financial Reporting: FASB and the Struggle for Control of a Critical Process.* Westport, CT: Quorum Books.

Véron, Nicolas. 2007. *The Global Accounting Experiment.* Brussels: Bruegel.

———. 2008. "Fair Value Accounting is the Wrong Scapegoat for this Crisis." *Accounting in Europe* vol. 5 no. 2 (December): 63–69.

Victor, David G., and Lesley A. Coben. 2005. "A Herd Mentality in the Design of International Environmental Agreements?" *Global Environmental Politics* vol. 5 no. 1 (February): 24–57.

Vitols, Sigurt. 1998. "Are German Banks Different?" *Small Business Economics* vol. 10 no. 2 (June): 79–91.

———. 2004. "Changes in Germany's Bank-Based Financial System: A Varieties of Capitalism Perspective." *WZB Discussion Paper SP II* no. 2004/03 (March).

Vogel, David. 1995. *Trading Up: Consumer and Environmental Regulation in a Global Economy.* Cambridge, MA: Harvard University Press.

———. 1996. *Kindred Strangers: The Uneasy Relationship Between Politics and Business in America.* Princeton: Princeton University Press.

———. 2003. "The Hare and the Tortoise Revisited: The New Politics of Consumer and Environmental Regulation in Europe." *British Journal of Political Science* vol. 33 no. 4 (October): 557–580.

———. 2005. *The Market for Virtue: The Potential and Limits of Corporate Social Responsibility.* Washington, DC: Brookings Institution Press.

———. 2008. "Private Global Business Regulation." *Annual Review of Political Science* vol. 11: 261–282.

———. 2011. *The Politics of Precaution.* Princeton: Princeton University Press (forthcoming).

Vosko, Leah F. 2004. "Standard Setting at the International Labour Organization: The Case of Precarious Employment." In *Hard Choices, Soft Law: Voluntary Standards in Global Trade, Environment and Social Governance,* edited by John J. Kirton and Michael J. Trebilcock. Aldershot, UK: Ashgate, 134–152.

Vreeland, James. 2007. *The International Monetary Fund: Politics of Conditional Lending.* London: Routledge.

Wallenstein, Gerd D. 1990. *Setting Global Telecommunications Standards: The Stakes, the Players, and the Process.* Norwood: Artech House Publishers.

Walter, Andrew. 2008. *Governing Finance: East Asia's Adoption of International Standards.* Ithaca, NY: Cornell University Press.

Walton, Peter. 1992. "Harmonization of Accounting in France and Britain: Some Evidence." *Abacus* vol. 28 no. 2 (September): 186–199.

Walton, Peter, Axel Haller, and Bernard Raffournier. 2003. *International Accounting.* 2nd edition. London: Thomson.

Wand, Jonathan, Gary King, and Olivia Lau. 2011. "Anchors: Software for Anchoring Vignette Data." *Journal of Statistical Software*, forthcoming.

Weber, Max. 1972 (1921/22). *Wirtschaft und Gesellschaft: Grundriß der verstehenden Soziologie*. 5th rev. and extended edition. Johannes Winckelmann, ed. Tübingen: J.C.B. Mohr.

Weisberg, Herbert F., Jon A. Krosnick, and Bruce D. Bowen. 1996. *An Introduction to Survey Research and Data Analysis*. 3rd edition. Glenview, IL: Scott, Foresman.

Weiss, Martin B. H., and Marvin Sirbu. 1990. "Technological Choice in Voluntary Standards Committees: An Empirical Analysis." *Economics of Innovation and New Technology* vol. 1 no. 1/2: 111–133.

West, Brian. 2000. "The Professionalisation of Accounting." In *The History of Accounting* edited by John R. Edwards. London: Routledge, 11–35.

Wilber, Vann H., and Paul T. Eichbrecht. 2010. "Transatlantic Trade, the Automotive Sector: The Role of Regulation in a Global Industry, Where We Have Been and Where We Need to Go, How Far Can EU-US Cooperation Go Toward Achieving Regulatory Harmonization?" In *Systemic Implications of Transatlantic Regulatory Cooperation and Competition*, edited by Simon J. Evenett and Robert M. Stern. Singapore: World Scientific.

Wilburn, Arthur J. 1984. *Practical Statistical Sampling for Auditors*. New York: M. Dekker

Wilson, Allistor. 1994. "Harmonisation: Is It Now or Never for Europe?" *Accountancy* vol. 114 no. 1215 (November): 98.

Wimmer, Andreas, and Reinhart Kössler, eds. 2006. *Understanding Change: Models, Methodologies, and Metaphors*. Houndmills, UK: Palgrave Macmillan.

Wines, Michael. 1981. "Should Groups that Set Standards Be Subject to Federal Standards?" *National Journal* vol. 13 no. 39 (26 September): 1717–1719.

Woerter, Everett. 1972. "Value of Properly Planned Standardization." In *Speaking of Standards*, edited by Rowen Glie. Boston: Cahner Books, 120–128.

Wolfensohn, James D. 1997. "Accounting and Society: Serving the Public Interest." Remarks to the World Congress of Accountants, Paris, 26 October.

Woodward, C. Douglas. 1972. *BSI: The Story of Standards*. London: British Standards Institution.

WTO (World Trade Organization). 1994. "Agreement on Technical Barriers to Trade." (TBT-Agreement). Marakesh Agreement Establishing the World Trade Organization of 15 April 1994, Annex 1A (Legal Instruments Resulting from the Uruguay Round), 1867 U.N.T.S. 493.

———. 1996. *Singapore Ministerial Declaration Adopted on 13 December 1996*.

———. 2005. *World Trade Report 2005: Exploring the Links Between Trade, Standards, and the WTO*. Geneva: World Trade Organization.

———. 2009. *World Trade Report 2009: Trade Policy Commitments and Contingency Measures*. Geneva: World Trade Organization.

———. 2009. Committee on Technical Barriers to Trade. *Fourteenth Annual Review of the Implementation and Operation of the TBT Agreement*. Geneva: World Trade Organization (G/TBT/25).

Yates, JoAnne, and Craig N. Murphy. 2006. "Coordinating International Standards: The Formation of the ISO." Manuscript, MIT.

———. 2008. "Charles Le Maistre: Entrepreneur in International Standardization." *Entreprises et Histoire* no. 51 (June): 10–27.

Zacher, Mark W., and Tania J. Keefe. 2008. *The Politics of Global Health Governance: United by Contagion*. New York: Palgrave Macmillan.

Zeff, Stephen A. 1972. *Forging Accounting Principles in Five Countries: A History and an Analysis of Trends*. Champaign, IL: Stipes Publishing.

———. 2002. "'Political' Lobbying on Proposed Standards: A Challenge to the IASB." *Accounting Horizons* vol. 16 no. 1 (March): 43–54.

———. 2008. "Political Lobbying on Accounting Standards: US, UK and International Experience." In *Comparative International Accounting*, edited by Christopher Nobes and Robert Parker. Harlow, UK: Financial Times/Prentice Hall, 206–234.

Zeghal, Daniel, and Karim Mhedhbi. 2006. "The Analysis of Factors Affecting the Adoption of International Accounting Standards by Developing Countries." *International Journal of Accounting* vol. 41 no. 4 (December): 373–386.

Zimmermann, Jochen, Jörg R. Werner, and Philipp B. Volmer. 2008. *Global Governance in Accounting: Rebalancing Public Power and Private Commitment*. Houndmills, UK: Palgrave Macmillan.

Zürn, Michael. 2004. "Global Governance and Legitimacy Problems." *Government and Opposition* vol. 39 no. 2 (spring): 260–287.

Zysman, John. 1983. *Governments, Markets, and Growth: Financial Systems and the Politics of Industrial Change*. Ithaca, NY: Cornell University Press.

Zysman, John, and Abraham L. Newman, eds. 2006. *How Revolutionary Was the Digital Revolution? National Responses, Market Transitions, and Global Technology*. Palo Alto: Stanford University Press.

3 5282 00715 8523